PART ONE: ENGLAND

A
Random
Walk
Down
Wall Street

THE TIME-TESTED STRATEGY FOR SUCCESSFUL INVESTING

Burton G. Malkiel

W. W. Norton & Company
NEW YORK · LONDON

Copyright © 2003, 1999, 1996, 1990, 1985, 1981, 1975, 1973 by
W. W. Norton & Company, Inc.

Manufacturing by The Haddon Craftsmen, Inc.

LIBRARY OF CONGRESS CATALOGING-IN-PUBLICATION DATA

Malkiel, Burton Gordon.
A random walk down Wall Street : the time tested strategy
for successful investing completely revised and updated /
Burton G. Malkiel.

p. cm.
Includes index.
ISBN 0-393-05782-8
1. Investments. 2. Stocks. 3. Random walks (Mathematics) I. Title.
HG4521 .M284 2003
332.6—dc21

2002153052

W. W. Norton & Company, Inc., 500 Fifth Avenue, New York, N.Y. 10110
www.wwnorton.com

W. W. Norton & Company Ltd., Castle House, 75/76 Wells Street,
London W1T 3QT

1 2 3 4 5 6 7 8 9 0

To Nancy and Skipper

Contents

Preface

It has now been over thirty years since I began writing the first edition of *A Random Walk Down Wall Street*. The message of the original edition was a very simple one: Investors would be far better off buying and holding an index fund than attempting to buy and sell individual securities or actively managed mutual funds. I boldly stated that buying and holding all the stocks in a broad stock-market average—as index funds do—was likely to outperform professionally managed funds whose high expense charges and large trading costs detract substantially from investment returns.

Now, over thirty years later, I believe even more strongly in that original thesis, and there's more than a six-figure gain to prove it. I can make the case with great simplicity. An investor with $10,000 at the start of 1969 who invested in a Standard & Poor's 500-Stock Index Fund would have had a portfolio worth $327,000 by 2002, assuming that all dividends were reinvested. A second investor who instead purchased shares in the average actively managed fund would have seen his investment grow to $213,000. The difference is dramatic. Through June 30, 2002, the index investor was ahead by $114,000, an amount 50 percent greater than the final stake of the average investor in a managed fund. And the index returns were calculated after deducting the typical expenses ($\frac{2}{10}$ of 1 percent) charged for running an index fund.

Why then an eighth edition of this book? If the basic message hasn't changed, what has? The answer is that there have been enormous changes in the financial instruments available to the public. A book meant to provide a comprehensive investment guide for individual investors needs to be updated to cover the full range of investment products available. In addition, investors can benefit from a critical analysis of the wealth of new information provided by academic researchers and market professionals—made comprehensible in prose accessible to everyone with an interest in investing. There have been so many bewildering claims about the stock market that it's important to have a book that sets the record straight.

Over the past thirty years, we have become accustomed to accepting the rapid pace of technological change in our physical environment. Innovations such as cellular and video telephones, cable television, compact discs, DVDs, microwave ovens, laptop computers, the Internet, e-mail, and new medical advances from organ transplants and laser surgery to nonsurgical methods of treating kidney stones and unclogging arteries have materially affected the way we live. Financial innovation over the same period has been equally rapid. In 1973, when the first edition of this book appeared, we did not have money market funds, NOW accounts, ATMs, index mutual funds, ETFs, tax-exempt funds, emerging market funds, floating-rate notes, inflation protection securities, equity REITs, Roth IRAs, 529 college savings plans, zero-coupon bonds, S&P index futures and options, and new trading techniques such as "portfolio insurance" and "program trading," just to mention a few of the changes that have occurred in the financial environment. Much of the new material in this book has been included to explain these financial innovations and to show how you as a consumer can benefit from them. Moreover, an entire new chapter (chapter 4) has been added to analyze the extraordinary Internet bubble of the turn of the century and to underscore the important lessons investors should learn from that experience.

This edition takes a hard look at the basic thesis of earlier editions of *Random Walk*—that the market prices stocks so efficiently that a blindfolded chimpanzee throwing darts at the *Wall Street Journal* can select a portfolio that performs as well as those managed by the experts. Through the past thirty years that thesis has held up remarkably well. More than two-thirds of professional portfolio managers have been outperformed by the unmanaged S&P 500 Index. Nevertheless, a number of studies by academics and practitioners, completed during the 1980s and 1990s, and a new field of economics called behavioral finance, have cast doubts on the validity of the theory. And the stock-market crash of October 1987, as well as the crashette of July 2002, raised further questions concerning the vaunted efficiency of the market. This edition explains the recent controversy and reexamines the claim that it's possible to "beat the market." I conclude in chapter 11 that reports of the death of the efficient-market theory are vastly exaggerated. I will, however, review the evidence on a number of techniques of stock selection that are believed to tilt the odds of success in favor of the individual investor.

The book remains fundamentally a readable investment guide for individual investors. As I have counseled individuals and families about financial strategy, it has become increasingly clear to me that one's capacity for risk-bearing depends importantly upon one's age and ability to earn income from noninvestment sources. It is also the case that the risk involved in most investments decreases with the length of time the investment can be held. For these reasons, optimal investment strategies must be age-related. Chapter 14, entitled "A Life-Cycle Guide to Investing," should prove very helpful to people of all ages. This chapter alone is worth the cost of a high-priced appointment with a personal financial adviser.

Finally, the facts and figures in the book have been completely revised and updated. I survey the stock and bond markets during the early 2000s and present a set of strategies that should successfully carry investors into the new millennium.

My debts of gratitude to those mentioned in earlier editions continue. In addition, I must mention the names of a number of people who were particularly helpful in making special contributions to the eighth edition. These include John Bogle, John

Brennen, Markus Brunnermeier, James Litvack, Jonathan Malkiel, Whitney Malkiel, Jianping Mei, Gail Paster, and Emily Paster. Special thanks go to Lynne Brady, Ker Moua, and Crystal Shannon of the Vanguard Group of Investment Companies and to Kevin Laughlin of the Bogle Research Institute for assembling much of the financial data used in updating this edition. Costin Bontas, Matthew Moore, and Basak Yeltekin provided superb research assistance. Diana Prout made an extraordinary contribution by transforming my illegible drafts and dictation tapes into readable text. Eve Lazovitz and Drake McFeely and Ann Adelman of W. W. Norton provided indispensable assistance in bringing this edition to publication. Patricia Taylor continued her association with the project and made extemely valuable editorial contributions to the eighth edition.

My wife, Nancy Weiss Malkiel, made by far the most important contributions to the successful completion of the past four editions. In addition to providing the most loving encouragement and support, she read carefully through various drafts of the manuscript and made innumerable suggestions that clarified and vastly improved the writing. She even corrected several errors that had eluded me and a variety of proofreaders and editors over the first four editions. Most important, she has brought incredible joy to my life. No one more deserved the dedication of a book than she and her second-best friend.

Burton G. Malkiel
Princeton University
September 2002

Acknowledgments
from
Earlier Editions

My debts of gratitude to practitioners, financial institutions, and academic colleagues who have helped me with the earlier editions of this book are enormous in both number and degree. Here, I acknowledge the many individuals who offered extremely valuable suggestions and criticisms.

Many research assistants have labored long in compiling information for this book. Especially useful contributions were made by Shane Antos, Jonathan Curran, Barry Feldman, Ethan Hugo, Paul Messaris, Barry Schwartz, Greg Smolarek, Ray Soldavin, Elizabeth Woods, and Yaxiao Xu. Helen Talar, Phyllis Fafalios, and Lugene Whitley not only faithfully and accurately typed several drafts of the manuscript, but also offered extremely valuable research assistance as well. Elvira Giaimo provided most helpful computer programming. Many of the supporting studies for this book were conducted at Princeton's Bendheim Center for Finance. I am also grateful to Arthur Lipper Corporation for permission to use their mutual-fund rankings.

A vital contribution was made by Patricia Taylor, a professional writer and editor. She read through complete drafts of the book and made innumerable contributions to the style, organization, and content of the manuscript. She deserves much of the credit for whatever lucid writing can be found in these pages.

My association with W. W. Norton & Company has been an extremely pleasant one, and I am particularly grateful to Donald Lamm, Robert Kehoe, Ed Parsons, and Deborah Makay, as well as my editor, Starling Lawrence, for his invaluable help.

The contribution of Judith Malkiel was of inestimable importance. She painstakingly edited every page of the manuscript and was helpful in every phase of this undertaking. This acknowledgment of my debt to her is the largest understatement of all.

Finally, I would like to acknowledge with deep gratitude the assistance of those following individuals who made important contributions to earlier editions. They include: Peter Asch, Leo Bailey, Howard Baker, Jeffrey Balash, David Banyard, William Baumol, Clair Bein, G. Gordon Biggar, Jr., John Bogle, John Brennen, Claire Cabellus, Lester Chandler, Andrew Clarke, Abby Joseph Cohen, Douglas Daniels, Pia Ellen, Andrew Engel, Steve Feinstein, Barry Feldman, Roger Ford, Stephen Goldfeld, William Grant, Leila Heckman, William Helman, Roger Ibbotson, Deborah Jenkins, Barbara Johnson, George S. Johnston, Kay Kerr, Walter Lenhard, James Litvack, Ian MacKinnon, Barbara Mains, Jonathan Malkiel, Sol Malkiel, Edward Mathias, Jianping Mei, Melissa McGinnis, Will McIntosh, Kelley Mingone, William Minicozzi, Keith Mullins, Gabrielle Napolitano, James Norris, H. Bradlee Perry, George Putnam, Donald Peters, Michelle Peterson, Richard Quandt, James Riepe, Michael Rothschild, Joan Ryan, Robert Salomon, Jr., George Sauter, George Smith, Willy Spat, Shang Song, James Stetler, James Stoeffel, H. Barton Thomas, Mark Thompson, Jim Troyer, David Twardock, Linda Wheeler, Frank Wisneski, and Robert Zenowich.

PART ONE

Stocks
and
Their
Value

1
Firm Foundations and Castles in the Air

What is a cynic? A man who knows the price of everything, and the value of nothing.

—Oscar Wilde, *Lady Windermere's Fan*

In this book I will take you on a random walk down Wall Street, providing a guided tour of the complex world of finance and practical advice on investment opportunities and strategies. Many people say that the individual investor has scarcely a chance today against Wall Street's professionals. They point to techniques the pros use such as "program trading," "portfolio insurance," and investment strategies using complex derivative instruments, and they read news reports of accounting fraud, corporate scams, mammoth takeovers, and the highly profitable activities of well-financed arbitrageurs. This complexity suggests that there is no longer any room for the individual investor in today's institutionalized markets. Nothing could be further from the truth. You can do as well as the experts—perhaps even better. As I'll point out later, it was the steady investors who kept their heads when the stock market tanked in October 1987, and then saw the value of their holdings eventually recover and continue to produce attractive returns. And many of the pros lost their shirts during the 1990s using derivative strategies they failed to understand as well as during the early 2000s when they overloaded their portfolios with overpriced tech stocks.

This book is a succinct guide for the individual investor. It covers everything from insurance to income taxes. It gives advice on shopping for the best mortgage and planning an Individual Retirement Account. It tells you how to buy life insurance and how to avoid getting ripped off by banks and brokers. It will even tell you what to do about gold and diamonds. But primarily it is a book about common stocks—an investment medium that not only has provided generous long-run returns in the past but also appears to represent good possibilities for the years ahead. The life-cycle investment guide described in Part Four gives individuals of all age groups specific portfolio recommendations for meeting their financial goals.

What Is a Random Walk?

A random walk is one in which future steps or directions cannot be predicted on the basis of past actions. When the term is applied to the stock market, it means that short-run changes in stock prices cannot be predicted. Investment advisory services, earnings predictions, and complicated chart patterns are useless. On Wall Street, the term "random walk" is an obscenity. It is an epithet coined by the academic world and hurled insultingly at the professional soothsayers. Taken to its logical extreme, it means that a blindfolded monkey throwing darts at a newspaper's financial pages could select a portfolio that would do just as well as one carefully selected by the experts.

Now, financial analysts in pin-striped suits do not like being compared with bare-assed apes. They retort that academics are so immersed in equations and Greek symbols (to say nothing of stuffy prose) that they couldn't tell a bull from a bear, even in a china shop. Market professionals arm themselves against the academic onslaught with one of two techniques, called fundamental analysis and technical analysis, which we will examine in Part Two. Academics parry these tactics by obfuscating the random-walk theory with three versions (the "weak," the "semi-strong," and the "strong") and by creating their own theory, called the new investment technology. This last includes a concept called beta, and I intend to trample on that a bit. By the early 2000s, even some academics joined the professionals in

arguing that the stock market was at least somewhat predictable
after all. Still, as you can see, there's a tremendous battle going
on, and it's fought with deadly intent because the stakes are
tenure for the academics and bonuses for the professionals.
That's why I think you'll enjoy this random walk down Wall
Street. It has all the ingredients of high drama—including fortunes made and lost and classic arguments about their cause.

But before we begin, perhaps I should introduce myself and
state my qualifications as guide. I have drawn on three aspects
of my background in writing this book; each provides a different perspective on the stock market.

First is my employment at the start of my career as a market
professional with one of Wall Street's leading investment firms.
It takes one, after all, to know one. In a sense, I remain a market
professional in that I currently chair the investment committee
of an insurance company that invests more than $500 billion in
assets and sit on the board of one of the largest investment companies in the nation, which controls a total of $500 billion in
assets. This perspective has been indispensable to me. Some
things in life can never fully be appreciated or understood by a
virgin. The same might be said of the stock market.

Second is my current position as an economist. Specializing
in securities markets and investment behavior, I have acquired
detailed knowledge of academic research and findings on
investment opportunities. I have relied on many new research
findings in framing recommendations for you.

Last, and certainly not least, I have been a lifelong investor
and successful participant in the market. How successful I will
not say, for it is a peculiarity of the academic world that a professor is not supposed to make money. A professor may inherit
lots of money, marry lots of money, and spend lots of money,
but he or she is never, never supposed to earn lots of money; it's
unacademic. Anyway, teachers are supposed to be "dedicated,"
or so politicians and administrators often say—especially when
trying to justify the low academic pay scales. Academics are
supposed to be seekers of knowledge, not of financial reward. It
is in the former sense, therefore, that I shall tell you of my vic-
tories on Wall Street.

This book has a lot of facts and figures. Don't let that worry
you. It is specifically intended for the financial layperson and

offers practical, tested investment advice. You need no prior knowledge to follow it. All you need is the interest and the desire to have your investments work for you.

Investing as a Way of Life Today

At this point, it's probably a good idea to explain what I mean by "investing" and how I distinguish this activity from "speculating." I view investing as a method of purchasing assets to gain profit in the form of reasonably predictable income (dividends, interest, or rentals) and/or appreciation over the long term. It is the definition of the time period for the investment return and the predictability of the returns that often distinguish an investment from a speculation. An excellent analogy from the first classic *Superman* movie comes to mind. When the evil Luthor bought land in Arizona with the idea that California would soon slide into the ocean, thereby quickly producing far more valuable beach-front property, he was speculating. Had he bought such land as a long-term holding after examining migration patterns, housing construction trends, and the availability of water supplies, he would probably be regarded as investing— particularly if he viewed the purchase as likely to produce a dependable future stream of cash returns.

Let me make it quite clear that this is not a book for speculators: I am not going to promise you overnight riches. I am not promising you stock-market miracles as one best-selling book of the 1990s claimed. Indeed, a subtitle for this book might well have been *The Get Rich Slowly but Surely Book*. Remember, just to stay even, your investments have to produce a rate of return equal to inflation.

Inflation in the United States and throughout most of the developed world fell to the 2 percent level in the early 2000s, and some analysts believe that relative price stability will continue indefinitely. They suggest that inflation is the exception rather than the rule and that historical periods of rapid technological progress and peacetime economies were periods of stable or even falling prices. It may well be that little or no inflation will occur during the first decades of the twenty-first century, but I believe investors should not dismiss the possibility that inflation will accelerate again at some time in the future. While productivity growth accelerated in the 1990s, history tells us that the pace of improvement has always been uneven. Moreover, as our economies become increasingly service-oriented, productivity improvements will be harder to come by. It still will take four musicians to play a string quartet and one surgeon to perform an appendectomy throughout the twenty-first century, and if musicians' and surgeons' salaries rise over time, so will the cost of concert tickets and appendectomies. Thus, it would be a mistake to think that upward pressure on prices is no longer a worry.

If inflation were to proceed at a 3 to 4 percent rate—a rate much lower than we had in the 1970s and early 1980s—the effect on our purchasing power would still be devastating. The following table shows what an average inflation rate of approximately 4 percent has done over the 1962–2002 period. My morning newspaper has risen 1,400 percent. My afternoon Hershey bar has risen tenfold, and it's actually smaller than it was in 1962, when I was in graduate school. If inflation continued at the same rate, today's morning paper would cost more than a dollar by the year 2010. It is clear that if we are to cope with even a mild inflation, we must undertake investment strategies that maintain our real purchasing power; otherwise, we are doomed to an ever-decreasing standard of living.

The Bite of Inflation

	Average 1962	Average 2002	Percentage Increase	Compound Annual Rate of Inflation
Consumer Price Index	30.20	179.80	495.4%	4.1%
Hershey bar	$.05	$.55	1,000.0	5.9
New York Times	.05	.75	1,400.0	6.8
First-class postage	.04	.37	825.0	5.4
Gasoline (gallon)	.31	1.39	348.4	3.4
Hamburger (McDonald's double)	.28*	3.19	1039.3	5.9
Chevrolet	2,529.00	23,725.00	838.1	5.5
Refrigerator freezer	470.00	850.00	80.9	1.5

Source: For 1962 prices, *Forbes*, Nov. 1, 1977, and various government and private sources for 2002 prices.

*1963 data.

Investing requires work, make no mistake about it. Romantic novels are replete with tales of great family fortunes lost through neglect or lack of knowledge on how to care for money. Who can forget the sounds of the cherry orchard being cut down in Chekhov's great play? Free enterprise, not the Marxist system, caused the downfall of the Ranevsky family: They had not worked to keep their money. Even if you trust all your funds to an investment adviser or to a mutual fund, you still have to know which adviser or which fund is most suitable to handle your money. Armed with the information contained in this book, you should find it a bit easier to make your investment decisions.

Most important of all, however, is the fact that investing is fun. It's fun to pit your intellect against that of the vast investment community and to find yourself rewarded with an increase in assets. It's exciting to review your investment returns and to see how they are accumulating at a faster rate than your salary. And it's also stimulating to learn about new ideas for products and services, and innovations in the forms of financial investments. A successful investor is generally a well-rounded individual who puts a natural curiosity and an intellectual interest to work to earn more money.

Investing in Theory

All investment returns—whether from common stocks or exceptional diamonds—are dependent, to varying degrees, on future events. That's what makes the fascination of investing: It's a gamble whose success depends on an ability to predict the future. Traditionally, the pros in the investment community have used one of two approaches to asset valuation: the firm-foundation theory or the castle-in-the-air theory. Millions of dollars have been gained and lost on these theories. To add to the drama, they appear to be mutually exclusive. An understanding of these two approaches is essential if you are to make sensible investment decisions. It is also a prerequisite for keeping you safe from serious blunders. Toward the end of the twentieth century, a third theory, born in academia and named the new investment technology, became popular on "the Street." Later in the book, I will describe that theory and its application to investment analysis.

The Firm-Foundation Theory

The firm-foundation theory argues that each investment instrument, be it a common stock or a piece of real estate, has a firm anchor of something called intrinsic value, which can be determined by careful analysis of present conditions and future prospects. When market prices fall below (rise above) this firm foundation of intrinsic value, a buying (selling) opportunity arises, because this fluctuation will eventually be corrected—or so the theory goes. Investing then becomes a dull but straightforward matter of comparing something's actual price with its firm foundation of value.

It is difficult to ascribe to any one individual the credit for originating the firm-foundation theory. S. Eliot Guild is often given this distinction, but the classic development of the technique and particularly of the nuances associated with it was worked out by John B. Williams.

In *The Theory of Investment Value*, Williams presented an actual formula for determining the intrinsic value of stock. Williams based his approach on dividend income. In a fiendishly clever attempt to keep things from being simple, he introduced the concept of "discounting" into the process. Discounting basically involves looking at income backwards. Rather than seeing how much money you will have next year (say $1.05 if you put $1 in a savings certificate at 5 percent interest), you look at money expected in the future and see how much less it is currently worth (thus, next year's $1 is worth today only about 95¢, which could be invested at 5 percent to produce approximately $1 at that time).

Williams actually was serious about this. He went on to argue that the intrinsic value of a stock was equal to the present (or discounted) value of all its future dividends. Investors were advised to "discount" the value of moneys received later. Because so few people understood it, the term caught on and "discounting" now enjoys popular usage among investment people. It received a further boost under the aegis of Professor Irving Fisher of Yale, a distinguished economist and investor.

The logic of the firm-foundation theory is quite respectable and can be illustrated best with common stocks. The theory stresses that a stock's value ought to be based on the stream of earnings a firm will be able to distribute in the future in the

form of dividends. It stands to reason that the greater the present dividends and their rate of increase, the greater the value of
the stock; thus, differences in growth rates are a major factor in
stock valuation. Now the slippery little factor of future expectations sneaks in. Security analysts must estimate not only long-
term growth rates but also how long an extraordinary growth
can be maintained. When the market gets overly enthusiastic
about how far in the future growth can continue, it is popularly
held on Wall Street that stocks are discounting not only the
future but perhaps even the hereafter. The point is that the firm-
foundation theory relies on some tricky forecasts of the extent
and duration of future growth. The foundation of intrinsic
value may thus be less dependable than is claimed.

The firm-foundation theory is not confined to economists
alone. Thanks to a very influential book, Benjamin Graham and
David Dodd's *Security Analysis*, a whole generation of Wall
Street security analysts was converted to the fold. Sound
investment management, the practicing analysts learned, simply consisted of buying securities whose prices were temporarily below intrinsic value and selling ones whose prices were
temporarily too high. It was that easy. Of course, instructions
for determining intrinsic value were furnished, and any analyst
worth his or her salt could calculate it with just a few taps of the
personal computer. Perhaps the most successful disciple of the
Graham and Dodd approach was a canny midwesterner named
Warren Buffett, who is often called "the sage of Omaha." Buffett
compiled a legendary investment record, allegedly following
the approach of the firm-foundation theory.

The Castle-in-the-Air Theory

The castle-in-the-air theory of investing concentrates on
psychic values. John Maynard Keynes, a famous economist and
successful investor, enunciated the theory most lucidly in 1936.
It was his opinion that professional investors prefer to devote
their energies not to estimating intrinsic values, but rather to
analyzing how the crowd of investors is likely to behave in the
future and how during periods of optimism they tend to build
their hopes into castles in the air. The successful investor tries

to beat the gun by estimating what investment situations are most susceptible to public castle-building and then buying before the crowd.

According to Keynes, the firm-foundation theory involves too much work and is of doubtful value. Keynes practiced what he preached. While London's financial men toiled many weary hours in crowded offices, he played the market from his bed for half an hour each morning. This leisurely method of investing earned him several million pounds for his account and a ten-fold increase in the market value of the endowment of his college, King's College, Cambridge.

In the depression years in which Keynes gained his fame, most people concentrated on his ideas for stimulating the economy. It was hard for anyone to build castles in the air or to dream that others would. Nevertheless, in his book *The General Theory of Employment, Interest and Money*, he devoted an entire chapter to the stock market and to the importance of investor expectations.

With regard to stocks, Keynes noted that no one knows for sure what will influence future earnings prospects and dividend payments. As a result, Keynes said, most persons are "largely concerned, not with making superior long-term forecasts of the probable yield of an investment over its whole life, but with foreseeing changes in the conventional basis of valuation a short time ahead of the general public." Keynes, in other words, applied psychological principles rather than financial evaluation to the study of the stock market. He wrote, "It is not sensible to pay 25 for an investment of which you believe the prospective yield to justify a value of 30, if you also believe that the market will value it at 20 three months hence."

Keynes described the playing of the stock market in terms readily understandable by his fellow Englishmen: It is analogous to entering a newspaper beauty-judging contest in which one must select the six prettiest faces out of a hundred photographs, with the prize going to the person whose selections most nearly conform to those of the group as a whole.

The smart player recognizes that personal criteria of beauty are irrelevant in determining the contest winner. A better strategy is to select those faces the other players are likely to fancy. This logic tends to snowball. After all, the other participants are likely to play the game with at least as keen a perception. Thus, the optimal strategy is not to pick those faces the player thinks are prettiest, or those the other players are likely to fancy, but rather to predict what the average opinion is likely to be about what the average opinion will be, or to proceed even further along this sequence. So much for British beauty contests.

The newspaper-contest analogy represents the ultimate form of the castle-in-the-air theory of price determination. An investment is worth a certain price to a buyer because she expects to sell it to someone else at a higher price. The investment, in other words, holds itself up by its own bootstraps. The new buyer in turn anticipates that future buyers will assign a still higher value.

In this kind of world, there is a sucker born every minute— and he exists to buy your investments at a higher price than you paid for them. Any price will do as long as others may be willing to pay more. There is no reason, only mass psychology. All the smart investor has to do is to beat the gun—get in at the very beginning. This theory might less charitably be called the "greater fool" theory. It's perfectly all right to pay three times what something is worth as long as later on you can find some innocent to pay five times what it's worth.

The castle-in-the-air theory has many advocates, in both the financial and the academic communities. Robert Shiller, in his best-selling book *Irrational Exuberance*, argues that the mania in Internet and high-tech stocks during the late 1990s can only be explained in terms of mass psychology. At universities, so-called behavioral theories of the stock market, stressing crowd psychology, gained favor during the early 2000s at leading economics departments and business schools across the developed world. The psychologist Daniel Kahneman won the Nobel Prize in Economics in 2002 for his seminal contributions to the field of "behavioral finance." Earlier, Oskar Morgenstern was a leading champion. The views he expressed in *Theory of Games and Economic Behavior*, of which he was co-author, have had a significant impact not only on economic theory but also on national security decisions and strategic corporate planning. In 1970 he co-authored another book, *Predictability of Stock Market Prices*, in which he and his colleague, Clive Granger, argued that the search for intrinsic value in stocks is a search for the will-o'-

the-wisp. In an exchange economy the value of any asset depends on an actual or prospective transaction. Morgenstern believed that every investor should post the following Latin maxim above his desk:

Res tantum valet quantum vendi potest.
(A thing is worth only what someone else will pay for it.)

How the Random Walk Is to Be Conducted

With this introduction out of the way, come join me for a random walk through the investment woods, with an ultimate stroll down Wall Street. My first task will be to acquaint you with the historical patterns of pricing and how they bear on the two theories of pricing investments. It was Santayana who warned that if we did not learn the lessons of the past we would be doomed to repeat the same errors. Therefore, in the pages to come I will describe some spectacular crazes—both long past and recently past. Some readers may pooh-pooh the mad public rush to buy tulip bulbs in seventeenth-century Holland and the eighteenth-century South Sea Bubble in England. But no one can disregard the new-issue mania of the early 1960s, the "Nifty Fifty" craze of the 1970s, or the biotechnology bubble of the 1980s. The incredible boom in Japanese land and stock prices and the equally spectacular crash of those prices in the early 1990s, as well as the "Internet craze" of the late 1990s, provide continual warnings that we are not immune from the errors of the past.

These more recent speculative "bubbles" all involved the savvy institutions and investment pros. All too many investors are lazy and careless—a terrifying combination when greed gets control of the market and everyone wants to cash in on the latest craze or fad.

Then I throw in my own two cents' worth of experience. Even in the midst of a period of speculation, I believe, it is possible to find a logical basis for security prices. At the end of Part One I present some rules that should be helpful in giving investors a sense of value and in protecting you from the horrible blunders made by many professional investment managers.

2

The Madness of Crowds

October. This is one of the peculiarly dangerous months to speculate in stocks in. The others are July, January, September, April, November, May, March, June, December, August and February.

—Mark Twain, *Pudd'nhead Wilson*

Greed run amok has been an essential feature of every spectacular boom in history. In their frenzy for money, market participants throw over firm foundations of value for the dubious but thrilling assumption that they too can make a killing by building castles in the air. Such thinking can, and has, enveloped entire nations.

The psychology of speculation is a veritable theater of the absurd. Several of its plays are presented in this chapter. The castles that were built during the performances were based on Dutch tulip bulbs, English "bubbles," and good old American blue-chip stocks. In each case, some of the people made some money some of the time, but only a very few emerged unscathed.

History, in this instance, does teach a lesson: Although the castle-in-the-air theory can well explain such speculative binges, outguessing the reactions of a fickle crowd is a most dangerous game. "In crowds it is stupidity and not mother-wit that is accumulated," Gustave Le Bon noted in his 1895 classic on crowd psychology. It would appear that not many have read the book. Skyrocketing markets that depend on purely psychic support have invariably succumbed to the financial law of gravitation. Unsustainable prices may persist for years, but eventually they reverse themselves. Such reversals come with the suddenness of an earthquake; and the bigger the binge, the greater the resulting hangover. Few of the reckless builders of castles in the air have been nimble enough to anticipate these reversals perfectly and escape without losing a great deal of money when everything came tumbling down.

The Tulip-Bulb Craze

The tulip-bulb craze was one of the most spectacular get-rich-quick binges in history. Its excesses become even more vivid when one realizes that it happened in staid old Holland in the early seventeenth century. The events leading to this speculative frenzy were set in motion in 1593 when a newly appointed botany professor from Vienna brought to Leyden a collection of unusual plants that had originated in Turkey. The Dutch were fascinated with this new addition to the garden— but not with the professor's asking price (he had hoped to sell the bulbs and make a handsome profit). One night a thief broke into the professor's house and stole the bulbs, which were subsequently sold at a lower price but at greater profit.

Over the next decade or so the tulip became a popular but expensive item in Dutch gardens. Many of these flowers succumbed to a nonfatal virus known as mosaic. It was this mosaic that helped to trigger the wild speculation in tulip bulbs. The virus caused the tulip petals to develop contrasting colored stripes or "flames." The Dutch valued highly these infected bulbs, called bizarres. In a short time, popular taste dictated that the more bizarre a bulb, the greater the cost of owning it.

Slowly, tulipmania set in. At first, bulb merchants simply tried to predict the most popular variegated style for the coming year, much as clothing manufacturers do in gauging the public's taste in fabric, color, and hemlines. Then they would buy an extra large stockpile to anticipate a rise in price. Tulip-bulb prices began to rise wildly. The more expensive the bulbs became, the more people viewed them as smart investments. Charles Mackay, who chronicled these events in his book *Extra-*

ordinary Popular Delusions and the Madness of Crowds, noted that the ordinary industry of the country was dropped in favor of speculation in tulip bulbs: "Nobles, citizens, farmers, mechanics, seamen, footmen, maid-servants, even chimney sweeps and old clotheswomen dabbled in tulips." Everyone imagined that the passion for tulips would last forever and buyers from all over the world would come to Holland and pay whatever prices were asked for them.

People who said the prices could not possibly go higher watched with chagrin as their friends and relatives made enormous profits. The temptation to join them was hard to resist; few Dutchmen did. In the last years of the tulip spree, which lasted approximately from 1634 to early 1637, people started to barter their personal belongings, such as land, jewels, and furniture, to obtain the bulbs that would make them even wealthier. Bulb prices reached astronomical levels.

Part of the genius of financial markets is that when there is a real demand for a method to enhance speculative opportunities, the market will surely provide it. The instruments that enabled tulip speculators to get the most action for their money were "call options" similar to those popular today in the stock market.

A call option conferred on the holder the right to buy tulip bulbs (call for their delivery) at a fixed price (usually approximating the current market price) during a specified period. He was charged an amount called the option premium, which might run 15 to 20 percent of the current market price. An option on a tulip bulb currently worth 100 guilders, for example, would cost the buyer only about 20 guilders. If the price moved up to 200 guilders, the option holder would exercise his right; he would buy at 100 and simultaneously sell at the then current price of 200. He then had a profit of 80 guilders (the 100 guilders' appreciation less the 20 guilders he paid for the option). Thus he enjoyed a fourfold increase in his money, whereas an outright purchase would only have doubled his money. By using the call option it was possible to play the market with a much smaller stake as well as get more action out of any money invested. The call is one way to leverage one's investment. Leveraging is any technique that increases the potential rewards (and risks) of an investment. Such devices helped to ensure broad participation in the market. The same is true today.

The history of the period was filled with tragicomic episodes. One such incident concerned a returning sailor who brought news to a wealthy merchant of the arrival of a shipment of new goods. The merchant rewarded him with a breakfast of fine red herring. Seeing what he thought was an onion on the merchant's counter, and no doubt thinking it very much out of place amid silks and velvets, he proceeded to take it as a relish for his herring. Little did he dream that the "onion" would have fed a whole ship's crew for a year. It was a costly Semper Augustus tulip bulb. The sailor paid dearly for his relish—his no longer grateful host had him imprisoned for several months on a felony charge.

The current glut of historians generate work for themselves by reinterpreting the past. Some financial historians have reexamined the evidence about various financial bubbles and have argued that considerable rationality in pricing may have existed after all. One of these revisionist historians, Peter Garber, has suggested that tulip-bulb pricing in seventeenth-century Holland was far more rational than is commonly believed.

Garber makes some good points and I do not mean to imply that no rationality at all existed to the structure of bulb prices during the period. The Semper Augustus, for example, was a particularly rare and beautiful bulb and, as Garber reveals, it was valued greatly even in the years before the tulipmania. Moreover, Garber's research indicates that rare individual bulbs commanded high prices even after the general collapse of bulb prices, albeit at levels that were only a fraction of their peak prices. But Garber can find no rational explanation for such phenomena as a twenty-fold increase in tulip-bulb prices during January of 1637 followed by an even larger decline in prices in February. Apparently, as happens in all speculative crazes, prices eventually got so high that some people decided they would be prudent and sell their bulbs. Soon others followed suit. Like a snowball rolling downhill, bulb deflation grew at an increasingly rapid pace, and in no time at all panic reigned.

Government ministers stated officially that there was no reason for tulip bulbs to fall in price—but no one listened. Dealers went bankrupt and refused to honor their commitments to buy tulip bulbs. A government plan to settle all contracts at 10 percent of their face value was frustrated when bulbs fell even below this mark. And prices continued to decline. Down and down they went until most bulbs became almost worthless— selling for no more than the price of a common onion.

The South Sea Bubble

Suppose your broker has called you and recommended that you invest in a new company with no sales or earnings—just great prospects. "What business?" you say. "I'm sorry," your broker explains, "no one must know what the business is, but I can promise you enormous riches." A con game, you say. Right you are, but 300 years ago in England this was one of the hottest new issues of the period. And, just as you guessed, investors got very badly burned. The story illustrates how fraud can make greedy people even more eager to part with their money.

At the time of the South Sea Bubble, the British were ripe for throwing away money. A long period of English prosperity had resulted in fat savings and thin investment outlets. In those days, owning stock was considered something of a privilege. As late as 1693, for example, only 499 souls benefited from owner- ship of East India stock. They reaped rewards in several ways, not least of which was that their dividends were untaxed. Also, their number included women, for stock represented one of the few forms of property that British women could possess in their own right. The South Sea Company, which obligingly filled the need for investment vehicles, had been formed in 1711 to restore faith in the government's ability to meet its obligations. The company took on a government IOU of almost £10 million. As a reward, it was given a monopoly over all trade to the South Seas. The public believed immense riches were to be made in such trade, and regarded the stock with distinct favor.

From the very beginning, the South Sea Company reaped profits at the expense of others. Holders of the government securities to be assumed by the company simply exchanged their securities for those of the South Sea Company. Those with prior knowledge of the plan quietly bought up government securities selling as low as £55 and then turned them in at par for £100 worth of South Sea stock when the company was incorporated. Not a single director of the company had the slightest experience in South American trade. This did not stop them from quickly outfitting African slave ships (the sale of slaves being one of the most lucrative features of South American trade). But even this venture did not prove profitable, because the mortality rate on the ships was so high.

The directors were, however, wise in the art of public appearance. An impressive house in London was rented, and the boardroom was furnished with thirty black Spanish upholstered chairs whose beechwood frames and gilt nails made them handsome to look at but uncomfortable to sit in. In the meantime, a shipload of company wool that was desperately needed in Vera Cruz was sent instead to Cartagena, where it rotted on the wharf from lack of buyers. Still, the stock of the company held its own and even rose modestly over the next few years despite the dilutive effect of "bonus" stock dividends and a war with Spain which led to a temporary collapse in trading opportunities. John Carswell, the author of an excellent history, *The South Sea Bubble*, wrote of John Blunt, a director and one of the prime promoters of the securities of the South Sea Company, that "he continued to live his life with a prayer-book in his right hand and a prospectus in his left, never letting his right hand know what his left hand was doing."

Across the Channel, another stock company was formed by an exiled Englishman named John Law. Law's great goal in life was to replace metal as money and create more liquidity through a national paper currency backed by the state and controlled through a network of local agencies. To further his purpose, Law acquired a derelict concern called the Mississippi Company and proceeded to build a conglomerate that became one of the largest capital enterprises ever to exist.

The Mississippi Company attracted speculators and their money from throughout the Continent. The word "millionaire" was invented at this time, and no wonder: The price of Mississippi stock rose from 100 to 2,000 in just two years, even though there was no logical reason for such an increase. At one time the inflated total market value of the stock of the Mississippi Company in France was more than eighty times that of all the gold and silver in the country.

Meanwhile, back on the English side of the Channel, a bit of jingoism now began to appear in some of the great English houses. Why should all the money be going to the French Mississippi Company? What did England have to counter this? The answer was the South Sea Company, whose prospects were beginning to look a bit better, especially with the December 1719 news that there would be peace with Spain and hence the way to the South American trade would at last be clear. Mexicans supposedly were waiting for the opportunity to empty their gold mines in return for England's abundant supply of cotton and woolen goods. This was free enterprise at its finest.

In 1720, the directors, an avaricious lot, decided to capitalize on their reputation by offering to fund the entire national debt, amounting to £31 million. This was boldness indeed, and the public loved it. When a bill to that effect was introduced in Parliament, the stock promptly rose from £130 to £300.

Various friends and backers who had shown interest in getting the bill passed received as their reward an option with a twist: The individual was granted a certain amount of stock without having to pay for it; it was simply "sold" back to the company when the price went up, and the individual only collected the profit. Among those rewarded were George I's mistress and her "nieces," all of whom bore a startling resemblance to the king.

On April 12, 1720, five days after the bill became law, the South Sea Company sold a new issue of stock at £300. The issue could be bought on the installment plan—£60 down and the rest in eight easy payments. Even the king could not resist; he subscribed for stock totaling £100,000. Fights broke out among other investors surging to buy. The price had to go up—and the eager buyers were right. It advanced to £340 within a few days. To ease the public appetite, the South Sea directors announced another new issue—this one at £400. But the public was ravenous. Within a month the stock was £550, and it was still rising. On June 15 yet another issue was put forth, and this time the payment plan was even easier—10 percent down and not another payment for a year. The stock hit £800. Half the House of Lords and more than half the House of Commons signed on. Eventually, the price rose to £1,000. The speculative craze was in full bloom.

Not even the South Sea Company was capable of handling the demands of all the fools who wanted to be parted from their money. Investors looked for other new ventures where they could get in on the ground floor. Just as speculators today search for the next Intel and the next Microsoft, so in England in the early 1700s they looked for the next South Sea Company. Promoters obliged by organizing and bringing to the market a flood of new issues to meet the insatiable craving for investment.

As the days passed, new financing proposals ranged from ingenious to absurd—from importing a large number of jackasses from Spain (even though there was an abundant supply in England) to making salt water fresh. Increasingly the promotions involved some element of fraud, such as making boards out of sawdust. There were nearly one hundred different projects, each more extravagant and deceptive than the other, but each offering the hope of immense gain. They soon received the name of "bubbles," as appropriate a name as could be devised. Like bubbles, they popped quickly—usually within a week or so.

The public, it seemed, would buy anything. New companies seeking financing during this period were organized for such purposes as: the building of ships against pirates; encouraging the breeding of horses in England (there were two issues for this purpose); trading in human hair; building of hospitals for bastard children; extracting of silver from lead; extracting sunlight from cucumbers; and even for producing a wheel of perpetual motion.

The prize, however, must surely go to the unknown soul who started "A Company for carrying on an undertaking of great advantage, but nobody to know what it is." The prospectus promised unheard-of rewards. At nine o'clock in the morning, when the subscription books opened, crowds of people from all walks of life practically beat down the door in an effort to subscribe. Within five hours 1,000 investors handed over their money for shares in the company. Not being greedy himself, the promoter promptly closed up shop and set off for the Continent. He was never heard from again.

Not all investors in the bubble companies believed in the feasibility of the schemes to which they subscribed. People were "too sensible" for that. They did believe, however, in the "greater fool" theory—that prices would rise, that buyers would be found, and that they would make money. Thus, most investors considered their actions the height of rationality as, at least for a while, they could sell their shares at a premium in the "after market," that is, the trading market in the shares after their initial issue.

Whom the gods would destroy, they first ridicule. Signs that the end was near were demonstrated with the issuance of a pack of South Sea playing cards. Each card contained a caricature of a bubble company, with an appropriate verse inscribed underneath. One of these, the Puckle Machine Company, was supposed to produce machines discharging both round and square cannonballs and bullets. Puckle claimed that his machine would revolutionize the art of war. The eight of spades, shown on the following page, described it as follows:

> A rare invention to destroy the crowd,
> Of fools at home instead of foes abroad:
> Fear not my friends, this terrible machine,
> They're only wounded who have shares therein.

Many individual bubbles had been pricked without dampening the speculative enthusiasm, but the deluge came in August with an irreparable puncture to the South Sea Company. This was self-administered by its directors and officers. Realizing that the price of the shares in the market bore no relationship to the real prospects of the company, they sold out in the summer.

The news leaked and the stock fell. Soon the price of the shares collapsed and panic reigned. The chart on page 44 shows the spectacular rise and fall of the stock of the South Sea Company. Government officials tried in vain to restore confidence, and a complete collapse of the public credit was barely averted. Similarly, the price of Mississippi Company shares fell to a pittance as the public realized that an excess of paper currency creates no real wealth, only inflation. Big losers in the South Sea Bubble included Isaac Newton, who exclaimed, "I can calculate the motions of heavenly bodies, but not the madness of people." So much for castles in the air.

To protect the public from further abuses, Parliament passed the Bubble Act, which forbade the issuing of stock certificates

Puckle's Machine

A rare invention to Destroy the Crowd,
Of Fools at Home instead of Foes Abroad:
Fear not my Friends, this terrible Machine,
They're only Wounded that have Shares therein.

British South Sea Company Stock Price, 1717–1722

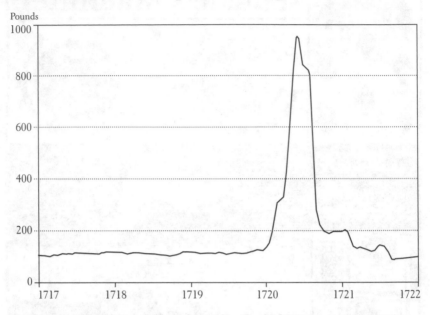

Source: Larry Neal, *The Rise of Financial Capitalism* (Cambridge University Press, 1990).

by companies. For more than a century, until the act was repealed in 1825, there were relatively few share certificates in the British market.

Wall Street Lays an Egg

The bulbs and bubbles are, admittedly, ancient history. Could the same sort of thing happen in sophisticated modern times? Let's turn to more recent and familiar events from our own past and see. America, the land of opportunity, had its turn in the 1920s. And given our emphasis on freedom and growth, we produced one of the most spectacular booms and loudest crashes civilization has ever known.

Conditions could not have been more favorable for a speculative craze. The country had been experiencing unrivaled prosperity. One could not but have faith in American business, and as Calvin Coolidge said, "The business of America is business." Businessmen were likened to religious missionaries and almost deified. Such analogies even were made in the opposite direction. Bruce Barton, of the New York advertising agency Batten, Barton, Durstine & Osborn, wrote in *The Man Nobody Knows* that Jesus was "the first businessman," and his parables were "the most powerful advertisements of all time."

Beginning in 1928, stock-market speculation became a national pastime. From early March 1928 through early September 1929, the market's percentage increase equaled that of the entire period from 1923 through early 1928. The price rises for the major industrial corporations sometimes reached 10 or 15 points per day. The extent of these rises is illustrated in the table below.

Security	Opening Price March 3, 1928	High Price September 3, 1929*	Percentage Gain in 18 Months
American Telephone & Telegraph	179^1/$_2$	335^5/$_8$	87.0
Bethlehem Steel	56^7/$_8$	140^3/$_8$	146.8
General Electric	128^3/$_4$	396^1/$_4$	207.8
Montgomery Ward	132^3/$_4$	466^1/$_2$	251.4
National Cash Register	50^3/$_4$	127^1/$_2$	151.2
Radio Corporation of America	94^1/$_2$	505	434.5

*Adjusted for stock splits and the value of rights received subsequent to March 3, 1928.

Not "everybody" was speculating in the market, as was commonly assumed. Borrowing to buy stocks (buying on margin) did increase from only $1 billion in 1921 to almost $9 billion in 1929. Nevertheless, only about 1 million persons owned stocks on margin in 1929. Still, the speculative spirit was at least as widespread as in the previous crazes and was certainly unrivaled in its intensity. More important, stock-market speculation was central to the culture. John Brooks, in *Once in Golconda*,* recounted the remarks of a British correspondent newly arrived in New York: "You could talk about Prohibition, or Hemingway, or air conditioning, or music, or horses, but in the end you had to talk about the stock market, and that was when the conversation became serious."

*Golconda, now in ruins, was a city in India. According to legend, everyone who passed through it became rich.

Unfortunately, there were hundreds of smiling operators only too glad to help the public construct castles in the air. Manipulation on the stock exchange set new records for unscrupulousness. No better example can be found than the operation of investment pools. One such undertaking raised the price of RCA stock 61 points in four days. Let me explain how the pools could manipulate the price of a stock.

An investment pool required close cooperation on the one hand and complete disdain for the public on the other. Generally such operations began when a number of traders banded together to manipulate a particular stock. They appointed a pool manager (who justifiably was considered something of an artist) and promised not to double-cross each other through private operations.

The pool manager accumulated a large block of stock through inconspicuous buying over a period of weeks. If possible, he obtained an option to buy a substantial block of stock at the current market price within a stated period of, say, three or six months. Next he tried to enlist the stock's specialist on the exchange floor as an ally.

Pool members were in the swim with the specialist on their side. A stock-exchange specialist functions as a broker's broker. If a stock was trading at $50 a share and you gave your broker an order to buy at $45, the broker typically left that order with the specialist. If and when the stock fell to $45, the specialist then executed the order. All such orders to buy below the market price or sell above it were kept in the specialist's supposedly private "book." Now you see why the specialist could be so valuable to the pool manager. The book gave information about the extent of existing orders to buy and sell at prices below and above the current market. It was always helpful to know as many of the cards of the public players as possible. Now the real fun was ready to begin.

Generally, at this point the pool manager had members of the pool trade among themselves. For example, Haskell sells 200 shares to Sidney at 40, and Sidney sells them back at 40⅛. The process is repeated with 400 shares at prices of 40¼ and 40½. Next comes the sale of a 1,000-share block at 40⅝, followed by another at 40¾. These sales were recorded on ticker tapes across the country and the illusion of activity was conveyed to the thousands of tape watchers who crowded into the brokerage offices of the country. Such activity, generated by so-called wash sales, created the impression that something big was afoot.

Now, tipsheet writers and market commentators under the control of the pool manager would tell of exciting developments in the offing. The pool manager also tried to ensure that the flow of news from the company's management was increasingly favorable—assuming the company management was involved in the operation. If all went well, and in the speculative atmosphere of the 1928–29 period it could hardly miss, the combination of tape activity and managed news would bring the public in.

Once the public came in, the free-for-all started and it was time discreetly to "pull the plug." Because the public was doing the buying, the pool did the selling. The pool manager began feeding stock into the market, first slowly and then in larger and larger blocks before the public could collect its senses. At the end of the roller-coaster ride the pool members had netted large profits and the public was left holding the suddenly deflated stock.

But people didn't have to band together to defraud the public. Many individuals, particularly corporate officers and directors, did quite well on their own. Take Albert Wiggin, the head of Chase, the nation's second-largest bank at the time. In July 1929 Mr. Wiggin became apprehensive about the dizzy heights to which stocks had climbed and no longer felt comfortable speculating on the bull side of the market. (He was rumored to have made millions in a pool boosting the price of his own bank.) Believing that the prospects for his own bank's stock were particularly dim (perhaps because of his previous speculation), he sold short more than 42,000 shares of Chase stock. Selling short is a way to make money if stock prices fall. It involves selling stock you do not presently own in the expectation of buying it back later at a lower price. It's like hoping to buy low and sell high, but in reverse order.

Wiggin's timing was perfect. Immediately after the short sale the price of Chase stock began to fall, and when the crash came in the fall the stock dropped precipitously. When the account was closed in November, he had netted a multimillion-dollar profit from the operation. Conflicts of interest apparently did not trouble Mr. Wiggin. In fairness to Mr. Wiggin, it should be pointed out that he did retain a net ownership position in Chase stock during this period. Nevertheless, the rules in existence today would not allow an insider to make short-swing profits from trading his own stock.

On September 3, 1929, the market averages reached a peak that was not to be surpassed for a quarter of a century. The "endless chain of prosperity" was soon to break; general business activity had already turned down months before. Prices drifted for the next day, and on the following day, September 5, the market suffered a sharp decline known as the "Babson Break."

This was named in honor of Roger Babson, a frail, goateed, pixyish-looking financial adviser from Wellesley, Massachusetts. At a financial luncheon that day he had said, "I repeat what I said at this time last year and the year before, that sooner or later a crash is coming." Wall Street professionals greeted the new pronouncements from the "sage of Wellesley," as he was known, with their usual derision.

As Babson implied in his statement, he had been predicting the crash for several years and he had yet to be proven right. Nevertheless, at two o'clock in the afternoon, when Babson's words were quoted on the "broad" tape (the Dow Jones financial news tape, which was an essential part of the furniture in every brokerage house across the country), the market went into a nosedive. In the last frantic hour of trading, 2 million shares changed hands—American Telephone and Telegraph went down 6 points, Westinghouse 7, and U.S. Steel 9 points. It was a prophetic episode, and after the Babson Break the possibility of a crash, which was entirely unthinkable a month before, suddenly became a common subject for discussion.

Confidence faltered. September had many more bad than good days. At times the market fell sharply. Bankers and government officials assured the country that there was no cause for concern. Professor Irving Fisher of Yale, one of the progenitors of the intrinsic-value theory, offered his soon-to-be-immortal opinion that stocks had reached what looked like a "permanently high plateau."

By Monday, October 21, the stage was set for a classic stock-market break. The declines in stock prices had led to calls for more collateral from margin customers. Unable or unwilling to meet the calls, these customers were forced to sell their holdings. This depressed prices and led to more margin calls and finally to a self-sustaining selling wave.

The volume of sales on October 21 zoomed to more than 6 million shares. The ticker fell way behind, to the dismay of the tens of thousands of individuals watching the tape from brokerage houses around the country. Nearly an hour and forty minutes had elapsed after the close of the market before the last transaction was actually recorded on the stock ticker.

The indomitable Fisher dismissed the decline as a "shaking out of the lunatic fringe that attempts to speculate on margin." He went on to say that prices of stocks during the boom had not caught up with their real value and would go higher. Among other things, the professor believed that the market had not yet reflected the beneficent effects of Prohibition, which had made the American worker "more productive and dependable."

On October 24, later called "Black Thursday," the market volume reached almost 13 million shares. Prices sometimes fell $5 and $10 on each trade. Many issues dropped 40 and 50 points during a couple of hours. On the next day, Herbert Hoover offered his famous diagnosis, "The fundamental business of the country . . . is on a sound and prosperous basis."

Tuesday, October 29, 1929, was among the most catastrophic days in the history of the New York Stock Exchange. Only October 19 and 20, 1987, rivaled in intensity the panic on the exchange. More than 16.4 million shares were traded on that day in 1929. (A 16-million-share day in 1929 would be equivalent to more than a 2-billion-share day in 2002 because of the greater number of shares now listed on the New York Stock Exchange.) Prices fell almost perpendicularly, and kept on falling, as is illustrated by the following table, which shows the extent of the decline during the autumn of 1929 and over the next three years. With the exception of "safe" AT&T, which lost only three-quarters of its value, most blue-chip stocks had fallen 95 percent or more by the time the lows were reached in 1932.

Security	High Price September 3 1929*	Low Price November 13 1929	Low Price for Year 1932
American Telephone & Telegraph	304	197$^{1}/_{4}$	70$^{1}/_{4}$
Bethlehem Steel	140$^{3}/_{8}$	78$^{1}/_{4}$	7$^{1}/_{4}$
General Electric	396$^{1}/_{4}$	168$^{1}/_{8}$	8$^{1}/_{2}$
Montgomery Ward	137$^{7}/_{8}$	49$^{1}/_{4}$	3$^{1}/_{2}$
National Cash Register	127$^{1}/_{2}$	59	6$^{1}/_{4}$
Radio Corporation of America	101	28	2$^{1}/_{2}$

*Adjusted for stock splits and the value of rights received subsequent to September 3, 1929.

Perhaps the best summary of the debacle was given by *Variety*, the show-business weekly, which headlined the story: "Wall Street Lays an Egg." The speculative boom was dead and billions of dollars of share values—as well as the dreams of millions— were wiped out. The crash in the stock market was followed by the most devastating depression in the history of the country.

Again, there are revisionist historians who say there was a method to the madness of the stock-market boom of the late 1920s. Harold Bierman, Jr., for example, in his book *The Great Myths of 1929*, has suggested that, without perfect foresight, stocks were not obviously overpriced in 1929 because it appeared that the economy would continue to prosper. After all, very intelligent people, such as Irving Fisher and John Maynard Keynes, believed that stocks were reasonably priced.* Bierman goes on to argue that the extreme optimism undergirding the stock market might even have been justified were it not for inappropriate monetary policies. The crash itself, in his view, was precipitated by the Federal Reserve Board's policy of raising interest rates to punish speculators. There are at least grains of truth in Bierman's arguments, and economists today often blame the severity of the 1930s' depression on the Federal Reserve for allowing the money supply to decline sharply. Nevertheless, history teaches us that very sharp increases in stock prices (as well as in the general level of the prices of goods and services) are seldom followed by a gradual return to relative price stability. Even if prosperity had continued into the 1930s,

---

*By December 1929, however, even Irving Fisher admitted that the previous high prices were explainable "partly because of unreasoning and unintelligent mania for buying."

stock prices could never have sustained their advance of the late 1920s.

In addition, the anomalous behavior of closed-end investment company shares (which I will cover in detail in chapter 15) provides clinching evidence of wide-scale stock-market irrationality during the 1920s. The "fundamental" value of these closed-end funds consists of the market value of the securities they hold. In most periods since 1930, these funds have sold at discounts of about 20 percent from their asset values. From January to August 1929, however, the typical closed-end fund sold at a premium of 50 percent. Moreover, the premiums for some of the best known funds were astronomical. Goldman, Sachs Trading Corporation sold at twice its net asset value. Tri-Continental Corporation sold at 256 percent of its asset value. This meant that you could go to your broker and buy, say, AT&T at whatever its market price was, or you would purchase it through the fund at 2½ times the market value. The decimals in these examples are not misplaced. Market prices were two or three times the (inflated) value of their underlying assets. Clearly, it was irrational speculative enthusiasm that drove the prices of these funds far above the value at which their individual security holdings could be purchased.

An Afterword

Why are memories so short? Why do such speculative crazes seem so isolated from the lessons of history? I have no apt answer to offer, but I am convinced that Bernard Baruch was correct in suggesting that a study of these events can help equip investors for survival. The consistent losers in the market, from my personal experience, are those who are unable to resist being swept up in some kind of tulip-bulb craze. It is not hard, really, to make money in the market. As we shall see later, investors who select a portfolio of stocks by throwing darts at the stock listings in the *Wall Street Journal* can make fairly handsome long-run returns. What is hard to avoid is the alluring temptation to throw your money away on short, get-rich-quick speculative binges. It is an obvious lesson, but one frequently ignored.

3

Stock Valuation from the Sixties through the Nineties

Everything's got a moral if only you can find it.

—Lewis Carroll, *Alice's Adventures in Wonderland*

The madness of the crowd can be truly spectacular. The examples I have just cited, plus a host of others, have convinced more and more people to put their money under the care of a professional—someone who knows what makes the market tick and who can be trusted to act prudently. Thus most of us find that at least a part (and often all) of our investable funds are in the hands of institutional portfolio managers—those who run the large pension and retirement funds, mutual funds, investment counseling organizations, and the like. Although the crowd may be mad, the institution is above all that. The institution is, to borrow a phrase from Tennyson, "of loyal nature and of noble mind." Very well, let us then take a look at the sanity of institutions.

The Sanity of Institutions

By the 1990s, institutions accounted for more than 90 percent of the trading volume on the New York Stock Exchange. Surely, in a market where professional investors dominate trading, the game must have changed. The hardheaded, sharp-penciled reasoning of the pros ought to be a guarantee that the extravagant excesses of the past will be avoided.

And yet professional investors participated in several distinct speculative movements from the 1960s through the 1990s. In each case, professional institutions bid actively for stocks not because they felt such stocks were undervalued under the firm-foundation principle, but because they anticipated that some greater fools would take the shares off their hands at even more inflated prices. Because these speculative movements relate to present-day markets, I think you'll find this institutional tour especially useful.

The Soaring Sixties

The New "New Era":
The Growth-Stock/New-Issue Craze

We start our journey when I did—in 1959, when I had just gone to Wall Street. Growth was the magic word in those days, taking on an almost mystical significance. Growth companies such as IBM and Texas Instruments sold at price-earnings multiples of more than 80. (A year later they sold at multiples in the 20s and 30s.)

Questioning the propriety of such valuations became almost heretical. These prices could not be justified on firm-foundation principles. But investors firmly believed that buyers would come forward eagerly to pay even higher prices. Lord Keynes must have smiled quietly from wherever it is that economists go when they die.

I recall vividly one of the senior partners of my firm shaking his head and admitting that he knew of no one over forty with any recollection of the 1929–32 crash who would buy and hold the high-priced growth stocks. But the young Turks held sway. *Newsweek* quoted one broker as saying that speculators have the idea that anything they buy "will double overnight. The horrible thing is, it has happened."

More was to come. Promoters, eager to satisfy the insatiable thirst of investors for the space-age stocks of the Soaring Sixties, created new offerings by the dozens. More new issues were offered in the 1959–62 period than at any previous time in history. The new-issue mania rivaled the South Sea Bubble in its intensity and also, regrettably, in the fraudulent practices that were revealed.

It was called the tronics boom, because the stock offerings often included some garbled version of the word "electronics" in their title, even if the companies had nothing to do with the electronics industry. Buyers of these issues didn't really care what the companies made—so long as it sounded electronic, with a suggestion of the esoteric. For example, American Music Guild, whose business consisted entirely of the door-to-door sale of phonograph records and players, changed its name to Space-Tone before "going public." The shares were sold to the public at 2 and, within a few weeks, rose to 14.

The name was the game. There were a host of "trons" such as Astron, Dutron, Vulcatron, and Transitron, and a number of "onics" such as Circuitronics, Supronics, Videotronics, and several Electrosonics companies. Leaving nothing to chance, one group put together the winning combination—Powertron Ultrasonics.

Jack Dreyfus, of Dreyfus and Company, commented on the mania as follows:

> Take a nice little company that's been making shoelaces for 40 years and sells at a respectable six times earnings ratio. Change the name from Shoelaces, Inc. to Electronics and Silicon Furth-Burners. In today's market, the words "electronics" and "silicon" are worth 15 times earnings. However, the real play comes from the word "furth-burners," which no one understands. A word that no one understands entitles you to double your entire score. Therefore, we have six times earnings for the shoelace business and 15 times earnings for electronic and silicon, or a total of 21 times earnings. Multiply this by two for furth-burners and we now have a score of 42 times earnings for the new company.

In a later investigation of the new-issue phenomenon, the Securities and Exchange Commission (SEC) uncovered considerable evidence of fraudulence and market manipulation. For example, some investment bankers, especially those who underwrote the smaller new issues, would often hold a substantial volume of securities off the market. This made the market so "thin" at the start that the price would rise quickly in the after market. In one "hot issue" that almost doubled in price on the first day of trading, the SEC found that a considerable portion of the entire offering was sold to broker-dealers, many of whom held on to their allotments for a period until the shares could be sold at much higher prices. The SEC also found that many underwriters allocated large portions of hot issues to insiders of the firms such as partners, relatives, officers, and other securities dealers to whom a favor was owed. In one instance, 87 percent of a new issue was allocated to "insiders" rather than to the general public, as was proper.

The following table shows some representative new issues of this period and records their price movements after the shares were issued. At least for a while, the new-issue buyers did very well indeed. Large advances over their already inflated initial offering prices were scored for such companies as Boonton Electronics and Geophysics Corporation of America. The speculative fever was so great that even Mother's Cookie could count on a sizable gain. Think of the glory they could have achieved if they had called themselves Mothertron's Cookitronics. Ten years later, the shares of most of these companies were almost worthless.

Security	Offering Date	Offering Price	Bid Price First Day of Trading	High Bid Price 1961	Low Bid Price 1962
Boonton Electronics Corp.	March 6, 1961	$5^{1}/_{2}$*	$12^{1}/_{4}$*	$24^{1}/_{2}$*	$1^{5}/_{8}$*
Geophysics Corp. of America	December 8, 1960	14	27	58	9
Hydro-Space Technology	July 19, 1960	3	7	7	1
Mother's Cookie Corp.	March 8, 1961	15	23	25	7

*Per unit of 1 share and 1 warrant.

Where was the SEC all this time? Hadn't it changed the rule from "Let the buyer beware" to "Let the seller beware"? Aren't new issuers required to register their offering with the SEC? Can't they (and their underwriters) be punished for false and misleading statements?

Yes to all these questions and yes, the SEC was there, but by law it had to stand by quietly. As long as a company has prepared (and distributed to investors) an adequate prospectus, the SEC can do nothing to save buyers from themselves. For example, many of the prospectuses of the period contained the following type of warning in bold letters on the cover.

WARNING: THIS COMPANY HAS NO ASSETS OR EARNINGS AND WILL BE UNABLE TO PAY DIVIDENDS IN THE FORSEEABLE FUTURE. THE SHARES ARE HIGHLY RISKY.

But just as the warnings on packs of cigarettes do not prevent many people from smoking, so the warning that this investment may be dangerous to your wealth cannot block a speculator from forking over his money if he is hell-bent on doing so. The SEC can warn a fool but it cannot prevent him from parting with his money. And the buyers of new issues were so convinced the stocks would rise in price (no matter what the company's assets or past record) that the underwriter's problem was not how he could sell the shares but how to allocate them among the frenzied purchasers.

Fraudulence and market manipulation are different matters. Here the SEC can take and has taken strong action. Indeed, many of the little known brokerage houses on the fringes of respectability, which were responsible for most of the new issues and for manipulation of their prices, were suspended for a variety of peculations.

The staff of the SEC is limited, however; the major problem is the attitude of the general public. When investors are infused with a get-rich-quick attitude and are willing to snap up any piece of bait, anything can happen—and usually does. Without public greed, the manipulators would not stand a chance.

The tronics boom came back to earth in 1962. Yesterday's hot issue became today's cold turkey. Many professionals refused to accept the fact that they had speculated recklessly. They blamed the decline on President Kennedy's tough stand with the steel industry, which led to a rollback of announced price hikes.

Others did recognize the speculative mania and said simply that growth stocks were "too high" in 1961. Very few pointed out that it is always easy to look back and say when prices were too high or too low. Fewer still said that no one seems to know the proper price for a stock at any given time.

Synergy Generates Energy: The Conglomerate Boom

I've said before that part of the genius of the financial market is that if a product is demanded, it is produced. The product that all investors desired was expected growth in earnings per share. And if growth wasn't to be found in a name, it was only to be expected that someone would find another way to produce it. By the mid-1960s, creative entrepreneurs had discovered that growth meant *synergism*.

Synergism is the quality of having 2 plus 2 equal 5. Thus it seemed quite plausible that two separate companies with an earning power of $2 million each might produce combined earnings of $5 million if the businesses were consolidated. This magical, mystical, surefire profitable new creation was called a conglomerate.

Although antitrust laws at that time kept large companies from purchasing firms in the same industry, it was possible for a while to purchase firms in other industries without interference from the Justice Department. The consolidations were carried out in the name of synergism. Ostensibly, mergers would allow the conglomerate to achieve greater financial strength (and thus greater borrowing capabilities at lower rates); to enhance marketing capabilities through the distribution of complementary product lines; to give greater scope to superior managerial talents; and to consolidate, and thus make more efficient, operating services such as personnel and accounting departments. All this led to synergism—a stimulation of sales and earnings for the combined operation that would have been impossible for the independent entities alone.

In fact, the major impetus for the conglomerate wave of the 1960s was that the acquisition process itself could be made to produce growth in earnings per share. Indeed, the managers of conglomerates tended to possess financial expertise rather than the operating skills required to improve the profitability of the acquired companies. By an easy bit of legerdemain, they could put together a group of companies with no basic potential at all and produce steadily rising per-share earnings. The following example shows how this monkey business was performed.

Suppose we have two companies—the Able Circuit Smasher Company, an electronics firm, and Baker Candy Company, which makes chocolate bars. Each has 200,000 shares outstanding. It's 1965 and both companies have earnings of $1 million a year, or $5 per share. Let's assume neither business is growing and that, with or without merger activity, earnings would just continue along at the same level.

The two firms sell at different prices, however. Because Able Circuit Smasher Company is in the electronics business, the market awards it a price-earnings multiple of 20 which, multiplied by its $5 earnings per share, gives it a market price of $100. Baker Candy Company, in a less glamorous business, has its earnings multiplied at only 10 times and, consequently, its $5 per-share earnings command a market price of only $50.

The management of Able Circuit would like to become a conglomerate. It offers to absorb Baker by swapping stock at the rate of two for three. The holders of Baker shares would get two shares of Able stock—which have a market value of $200—for every three shares of Baker stock—with a total market value of $150. Clearly this is a tempting proposal, and the stockholders of Baker are likely to accept cheerfully. The merger is approved.

We have a budding conglomerate, newly named Synergon, Inc., which now has 333,333 shares* outstanding and total earnings of $2 million to put against them, or $6 per share. Thus by 1966, when the merger has been completed, we find that earnings have risen by 20 percent, from $5 to $6, and this growth seems to justify Able's former price-earnings multiple of 20. Consequently, the shares of Synergon (née Able) rise from $100 to $120, everybody's judgment is confirmed, and all go home rich and happy. In addition, the shareholders of Baker who were bought out need not pay any taxes on their profits until they sell their shares of the combined company. The top three lines of the table below illustrate the transaction thus far.

A year later, Synergon finds Charlie Company, which earns $10 per share or $1 million with 100,000 shares outstanding.

---

*The 200,000 original shares of Able plus an extra 133,333, which get printed up to exchange for Baker's 200,000 shares according to the terms of the merger.

Charlie Company is in the relatively risky military-hardware business so its shares command a multiple of only 10 and sell at $100. Synergon offers to absorb Charlie Company on a share-for-share exchange basis. Charlie's shareholders are delighted to exchange their $100 shares for the conglomerate's $120 shares. By the end of 1967, the combined company has earnings of $3 million, shares outstanding of 433,333, and earnings per share of $6.92.

	Company	Earnings Level	Number of Shares Outstanding	Earnings per Share	Price-Earnings Multiple	Price
Before merger 1965	Able	$1,000,000	200,000	$ 5.00	20	$100
	Baker	1,000,000	200,000	5.00	10	50
After first merger 1966	Synergon (Able and Baker combined)	2,000,000	333,333*	6.00	20	120
	Charlie	1,000,000	100,000	10.00	10	100
After second merger 1967	Synergon (Able, Baker, and Charlie combined)	3,000,000	433,333	6.92	20	138³/₈

*The 200,000 original shares of Able plus an extra 133,333, which get printed up to exchange for Baker's 200,000 shares according to the terms of the merger.

Here we have a case where the conglomerate has literally manufactured growth. None of the three companies was growing at all; yet simply by virtue of the fact of their merger, the unwary investor who may finger his *Stock Guide* to see the past record of our conglomerate will find the following figures:

Earnings per Share

	1965	1966	1967
Synergon, Inc.	$5.00	$6.00	$6.92

Clearly, Synergon is a growth stock and its record of extraordinary performance appears to have earned it a high and possibly even an increasing multiple of earnings.

The trick that makes the game work is the ability of the electronics company to swap its high-multiple stock for the stock of another company with a lower multiple. The candy company can only "sell" its earnings at a multiple of 10. But when these earnings are packaged with the electronics company, the total earnings (including those from selling chocolate bars) could be sold at a multiple of 20. And the more acquisitions Synergon could make, the faster earnings per share would grow and thus the more attractive the stock would look to justify its high multiple.

The whole thing is like a chain letter—no one would get hurt as long as the growth of acquisitions proceeded exponentially. Of course, the process could not continue for long, but the possibilities were mind-boggling for those who got in at the start. It seems difficult to believe that Wall Street professionals could be so myopic as to fall for the conglomerate con game, but accept it they did for a period of several years. Or perhaps as subscribers to the castle-in-the-air theory, they only believed that other people would fall for it.

The story of Synergon describes the standard conglomerate earnings "growth" gambit. A lot of other monkeyshines also were practiced. Convertible bonds (or convertible preferred stocks) often were used as a substitute for shares in paying for acquisitions. A convertible bond is an IOU of the company, paying a fixed interest rate, that is convertible at the option of the holder into shares of the firm's common stock. As long as the earnings of the newly acquired subsidiary were greater than the relatively low interest rate that was placed on the convertible bond, it was possible to show even more sharply rising earnings per share than those in the previous illustration. This is because no new common stocks at all had to be issued to consummate the merger, and thus the combined earnings could be divided by a smaller number of shares.

One company was truly creative in financing its acquisition program. It used a convertible preferred stock that paid no cash dividend at all.* Instead, the conversion rate of the security was to be adjusted annually to provide that the preferred stock be convertible into more common shares each year. The older

---

*Convertible preferred stock is similar to a convertible bond in that the preferred dividend is a fixed obligation of the company. But neither the principal nor the preferred dividend is considered a debt, so the company can usually skip a payment with greater freedom. Of course, in the example above, the stock paid no cash dividend at all.

pros in Wall Street shook their heads in disbelief over these shenanigans.

It is hard to believe that investors did not count the dilution potential of the new common stock that would be issued if the bondholders or preferred stockholders were to convert their securities into common stock. Indeed, as a result of such manipulations, corporations are now required to report their earnings on a "fully diluted" basis, to account for the new common shares that must be set aside for potential conversions. But most investors in the mid-1960s ignored such niceties and were satisfied only to see steadily and rapidly rising earnings.

Automatic Sprinkler Corporation (later called A-T-O, Inc., and later still, at the urging of its modest chief executive officer Mr. Figgie, Figgie International) is a good example of how the game of manufacturing growth was actually played during the 1960s. Between 1963 and 1968, the company's sales volume rose by more than 1,400 percent. This phenomenal record was due solely to acquisitions. In the middle of 1967, four mergers were completed in a twenty-five-day period. These newly acquired companies were all selling at relatively low price-earnings multiples and thus helped to produce a sharp growth in earnings per share. The market responded to this "growth" by bidding up the price-earnings multiple to more than 50 times earnings in 1967. This boosted the price of the company's stock from about $8 per share in 1963 to $73⅝ in 1967.

Mr. Figgie, the president of Automatic Sprinkler, performed the public relations job necessary to help Wall Street build its castle in the air. He automatically sprinkled his conversations with talismanic phrases about the energy of the free-form company and its interface with change and technology. He was careful to point out that he looked at twenty to thirty deals for each one he bought. Wall Street loved every word of it.

Mr. Figgie was not alone in conning Wall Street. Managers of other conglomerates almost invented a new language in the process of dazzling the investment community. They talked about market matrices, core technology fulcrums, modular building blocks, and the nucleus theory of growth. No one from Wall Street really knew what the words meant, but they all got the nice, warm feeling of being in the technological mainstream.

Conglomerate managers also found a new way of describing

the businesses they had bought. Their shipbuilding businesses became "marine systems." Zinc mining became the "space minerals division." Steel fabrication plants became the "materials technology division." A lighting fixture or lock company became part of the "protective services division." And if one of the "ungentlemanly" security analysts (somebody from City College of New York rather than Harvard Business School) had the nerve to ask how you can get 15 to 20 percent growth from a foundry or a meatpacker, the typical conglomerate manager suggested that his efficiency experts had isolated millions of dollars of excess costs; that his marketing research staff had found several fresh, uninhabited markets; and that the target of tripling profit margins could be easily realized within two years. To this add talk of breakfast and Sunday meetings with your staff, and the image of the hardworking, competent, go-go atmosphere is complete.

Instead of going down with merger activity, the price-earnings multiples of conglomerate stocks rose higher and higher. Prices and multiples for a selection of conglomerates in 1967 are shown in the following table.

	1967		1969	
Security	High Price	Price-Earnings Multiple	Low Price	Price Earnings Multiple
Automatic Sprinkler (A-T-O, Inc.)	$73^5/_8$	51.0	$10^7/_8$	13.4
Litton Industries	$120^1/_2$	44.1	55	14.4
Teledyne, Inc.	$71^1/_2$*	55.8	$28^1/_4$	14.2

*Adjusted for subsequent split.

The music slowed drastically for the conglomerates on January 19, 1968. On that day, the granddaddy of the conglomerates, Litton Industries, announced that earnings for the second quarter of that year would be substantially less than had been forecast. It had recorded 20 percent yearly increases for almost a decade. The market had so thoroughly come to believe in alchemy that the announcement was greeted with disbelief and shock. In the selling wave that followed, conglomerate stocks declined by roughly 40 percent before a feeble recovery set in.

Worse was to come. In July, the Federal Trade Commission announced that it would make an in-depth investigation of the conglomerate merger movement. Again the stocks went tumbling down. The SEC and the accounting profession finally made their move and began to make attempts to clarify the reporting techniques for mergers and acquisitions. The sell orders came flooding in. These were closely followed by new announcements from the SEC and the U.S. Assistant Attorney General in charge of antitrust, indicating a strong concern about the accelerating pace of the merger movement.

The aftermath of this speculative phase revealed two disturbing factors. First, conglomerates were mortal and were not always able to control their far-flung empires. Indeed, investors became disenchanted with the conglomerate's new math; 2 plus 2 certainly did not equal 5 and some investors wondered if it even equaled 4. Second, the government and the accounting profession expressed real concern about the pace of mergers and about possible abuses. These two worries on the part of investors reduced—and in many cases eliminated—the premium multiples that had been paid in anticipation of earnings from the acquisition process alone. This result in itself makes the alchemy game almost impossible, for the acquiring company has to have an earnings multiple larger than the acquired company if the ploy is to work at all.

The combination of lower earnings and flattened price-earnings multiples led to a drastic decline in the prices of conglomerates, as the preceding table indicates. The professional investors were hurt the most in the wild scramble for chairs. Few mutual or pension funds were without large holdings of conglomerate stocks. Castles in the air are not reserved as the sole prerogative of individuals; institutional investors can build them, too. An interesting footnote to this episode is that during the 1980s and 1990s deconglomeration came into fashion. Many of the old conglomerates began to shed their unrelated, poor-performing acquisitions to boost their earnings.

Many of these sales were financed through a popular innovation of the 1980s, the leveraged buyout (LBO). Under an LBO the purchaser, often the management of the division assisted by professional deal makers, puts up a very thin margin of equity, borrowing 90 percent or more of the funds needed to complete the transaction. The tax collector helps out by allowing the bought-out entity to increase the value of its depreciable asset base. The combination of high interest payments and larger depreciation charges ensures that taxes for the new entity will remain low or nonexistent for some time. If things go well, the owners can reap windfall profits. William Simon, a former secretary of the Treasury, made a multimillion-dollar killing on one of the earliest LBOs of the 1980s, Gibson Greeting Cards. A number of the early LBOs of the 1980s proved to be quite successful. Later in the decade, however, as the LBO wave accelerated and the prices paid for the companies tended to increase as did their associated debt levels, fewer of these transactions fulfilled expectations. As the economy turned less robust in the late 1980s and early 1990s, the high fixed-interest costs of companies in debt up to their eyeballs placed these entities in considerable financial jeopardy. The financial fallout in the early 1990s from the explosion of some of the most poorly considered LBOs injured not only many individual investors but many banks and life insurance companies as well.

Performance Comes to the Market: The Bubble in Concept Stocks

With conglomerates shattering about them, the managers of investment funds found another magic word: performance. Obviously, it would be easier to sell a mutual fund with stocks in its portfolio that went up in value faster than the stocks in its competitors' portfolios.

And perform some funds did—at least over short periods of time. Fred Carr's highly publicized Enterprise Fund racked up a 117 percent total return (including both dividends and capital gains) in 1967 and followed this with a 44 percent return in 1968. The corresponding figures for the Standard & Poor's 500-Stock Index were 25 percent and 11 percent, respectively. This performance brought large amounts of new money into the fund. The public found it fashionable to bet on the jockey rather than the horse.

How did these jockeys do it? They concentrated the portfolio in dynamic stocks, which had a good story to tell, and at the first sign of an even better story, they would quickly switch. For a while the strategy worked well and led to many imitators. The camp followers were quickly given the accolade "go-go funds," and the fund managers often were called "youthful gunslingers." The public's investment dollars flowed into the riskiest of the performance funds.

The performance game spread to all kinds of investing institutions. Just as some government policymakers in the early 2000s were touting common stock investing as a way to shore up the Social Security system, so in the late 1960s, business managers asked whether they might be able to reduce their current retirement expenses by switching more of their pension funds from bonds into common stocks with exciting growth possibilities. Even university endowment–fund managers were pressured to strive for performance. McGeorge Bundy of the Ford Foundation chided the portfolio managers of universities:

> It is far from clear that trustees have reason to be proud of their performance in making money for their colleges. We recognize the risks of unconventional investing, but the true test of performance in the handling of money is the record of achievement, not the opinion of the respectable. We have the preliminary impression that over the long run caution has cost our colleges and universities much more than imprudence or excessive risk-taking.

And so performance investing took hold of Wall Street in the late 1960s. The commandments for fund managers were simple: Concentrate your holdings in a relatively few stocks and don't hesitate to switch the portfolio around if a more desirable investment appears. And because near-term performance was especially important (investment services began to publish monthly records of mutual-fund performance) it would be best to buy stocks with an exciting concept and a compelling and believable story. You had to be sure the market would recognize the beauty of your stock now—not far into the future. Hence, the birth of the so-called concept stock.

But even if the story was not totally believable, as long as the investment manager was convinced that the average opinion would think that the average opinion would believe the story, that's all that was needed. The author Martin Mayer quoted one fund manager as saying, "Since we hear stories early, we can figure enough people will be hearing it in the next few days to give the stock a bounce, even if the story doesn't prove out." Many Wall Streeters looked on this as a radical new investment strategy, but John Maynard Keynes had it all spotted in 1936.

Eventually, it reached a point where any concept would do. Enter Cortess W. Randell. His concept was a youth company for the youth market. He became founder, president, and major stockholder of National Student Marketing (NSM). First, he sold an image—one of affluence and success. He owned a personal white Learjet named Snoopy, an apartment in New York's Waldorf Towers, a castle with a mock dungeon in Virginia, and a yacht that slept twelve. Adding to his image was an expensive set of golf clubs propped up by his office door. Apparently the only time the clubs were used was at night when the office cleanup crew drove wads of paper along the carpet.

He spent most of his time visiting the financial community or calling them on the sky phone from his Lear, and sold the concept of NSM in the tradition of a South Sea Bubble promoter. Randell's real métier was evangelism. The concept that Wall Street bought from Randell was that a single company could specialize in servicing the needs of young people. NSM built its early growth via the merger route, just as the ordinary conglomerates of the 1960s had done. The difference was that each of the constituent companies had something to do with the college-age youth market from posters and records to sweatshirts and summer job directories. What could be more appealing to a youthful gunslinger than a youth-oriented concept stock—a full-service company to exploit the youth subculture? Glowing press releases and Randell's earnings projections for the company became increasingly optimistic.

Although some thistles were found among such roses (the earnings growth was produced by the old conglomerate gambit, with the generous support of some creative accounting), the "concept" investors bought heavily in the company and blithely ignored all questions. When Gerry Tsai's Manhattan Fund bought 120,000 shares for $5 million, it became clear that Randell had obtained the imprimatur of Wall Street's performance investors. Even some of the most august and conservative banks on pension funds bought stock. University endowment–fund managers, heeding the words of McGeorge Bundy, also bought in the mad scramble for performance. Blocks of NSM were bought by Harvard, Cornell, and the University of Chicago. Bundy himself practiced what he preached, and the previously conservatively managed Ford Foundation Fund also bought a large block.

The following table clearly shows that institutional investors are at least as adept as the general public at building castles in the air.

Security	High Price 1968–69	Price-Earnings Multiple at High	Number of Institutional Holders Year-End 1969	Low Price 1970	Per-centage Decline
Four Seasons Nursing Centers of America	90³/₄	113.4	24	0.20	99
National Student Marketing	35¹/₄*	111.7	21	⁷/₈	98
Performance Systems	23	∞	13	¹/₈	99

*Adjusted for subsequent stock split.

There were other concepts. Health care, for example, attracted quite a few adherents. Given the increasing numbers of older people and the spread of federal and private health insurance plans, someone was bound to make lots of money. Four Seasons Nursing Centers of America looked just like that someone. The biggest and most aggressive mutual funds bought in.

The company expanded at a feverish pace, financing itself largely through the issuance of debt. These borrowings were sweetened, however, with so-called equity kickers. This meant that attached to each bond were warrants to buy common stock of Four Seasons at fixed prices. Thus, if the stock price contin-ued to go up, the bondholders could exercise their warrants and make additional profits. As the debt mounted no one seemed to worry much about the old ideas of prudent debt ratios, for this was a new concept and the rules of the game had changed. On June 26, 1970, the company filed a petition for reorganization under Chapter Ten of the Bankruptcy Act.

Minnie Pearl's concept is our last example of the period. Minnie Pearl was a fast-food franchising firm that was as accommodating as all get-out. To please the financial community, Minnie Pearl's chickens became Performance Systems. After all, what better name could be chosen for performance-oriented investors? On Wall Street a rose by any other name does not smell as sweet. The ∞ shown in the table under "price-earnings multiple" indicates that the multiple was infinity. Performance Systems had no earnings at all to divide into the stock's price at the time it reached its high in 1968. As the table indicates, Minnie Pearl laid an egg—and a bad one at that. The subsequent performance for this and the other stocks listed was indeed truly remarkable—although not quite what their buyers had anticipated.

Why did the stocks perform so badly? One general answer was that their price-earnings multiples were inflated beyond reason. If a multiple of 100 drops to a more normal multiple of 20, you have lost 80 percent of your investment right there. In addition, most of the concept companies of the time ran into severe operating difficulties. The reasons were varied: too rapid expansion, too much debt, loss of management control, and so on. These companies were run by executives who were primarily promoters, not sharp-penciled operating managers. Fraudulent practices also were common. For example, NSM's Cortess Randell pleaded guilty to accounting fraud and served eight months in prison.

The Sour Seventies

The Nifty Fifty

In the 1970s, Wall Street's pros vowed to return to "sound principles." Concepts were out and investing in blue-chip companies was in. These were companies, so the thinking went, that would never come crashing down like the speculative favorites of the 1960s. Nothing could be more prudent than to buy their shares and then relax on the golf course while the long-term rewards materialized.

There were only four dozen or so of these premier growth stocks that so fascinated the institutional investors. Their names were familiar—IBM, Xerox, Avon Products, Kodak,

McDonald's, Polaroid, and Disney—and they were called the "Nifty Fifty." They were "big capitalization" stocks, which meant that an institution could buy a good-sized position without disturbing the market. And because most pros realized that picking the exact correct time to buy is difficult if not impossible, these stocks seemed to make a great deal of sense. So what if you paid a price that was temporarily too high? These stocks were proven growers, and sooner or later the price you paid would be justified. In addition, these were stocks that—like the family heirlooms—you would never sell. Hence they also were called "one decision" stocks. You made a decision to buy them, once, and your portfolio-management problems were over.

These stocks provided security blankets for institutional investors in another way, too. They were so respectable. Your colleagues could never question your prudence in investing in IBM. True, you could lose money if IBM went down, but that was not considered a sign of imprudence (as it would be to lose money in a Performance Systems or a National Student Marketing). Like greyhounds in chase of the mechanical rabbit, big pension funds, insurance companies, and bank trust funds loaded up on the Nifty Fifty one-decision growth stocks. Hard as it is to believe, the institutions had started to speculate in blue chips. In the table below, I have listed the price-earnings multiples achieved by a handful of these stocks in 1972 as well as their multiples at the start of the 1980s. Institutional managers blithely ignored the fact that no sizable company could ever grow fast enough to justify an earnings multiple of 80 or 90. They once again proved the maxim that stupidity well packaged can sound like wisdom.

Security	Price-Earnings Multiple 1972	Price-Earnings Multiple 1980
Sony	92	17
Polaroid	90	16
McDonald's	83	9
Intl. Flavors	81	12
Walt Disney	76	11
Hewlett-Packard	65	18

Perhaps one might argue that the craze was simply a manifestation of the return of confidence in late 1972. Richard Nixon had been reelected by a landslide, peace was "at hand" in Vietnam, price controls were due to come off, inflation was apparently "under control," and no one knew what OPEC was.

But, in fact, the market had already started to decline in early 1972 and, when it did, the Nifty Fifty mania became even more pathological. For as the market in general collapsed, the Nifty Fifty continued to command record earnings multiples and, on a relative basis, the overpricing greatly increased. There appeared to be a "two-tier" market. *Forbes* magazine commented as follows:

> [The Nifty Fifty appeared to rise up] from the ocean; it was as though all of the U.S. but Nebraska had sunk into the sea. The two tier market really consisted of one tier and a lot of rubble down below.
>
> What held the Nifty Fifty up? The same thing that held up tulip-bulb prices in long-ago Holland—popular delusions and the madness of crowds. The delusion was that these companies were so good that it didn't matter what you paid for them; their inexorable growth would bail you out.

The end was inevitable. The Nifty Fifty craze ended like all other speculative manias. The Nifty Fifty were—in the words of *Forbes* columnist Martin Sosnoff—taken out and shot one by one. The oil embargo and the difficulty of obtaining gasoline hit Disney and its large stake in Disneyland and Disney World. Production problems with new cameras hit Polaroid. The stocks sank like stones into the ocean. A critical cover story in *Forbes* magazine sent Avon Products down almost 50 percent in six months. The real problem was never the particular needle that pricked each individual bubble. The problem was simply that the stocks were overpriced. Sooner or later the same money managers who had worshiped the Nifty Fifty decided to make a second decision and sell. In the debacle that followed, the premier growth stocks fell completely from favor. To be fair, however, I should point out that the problem was not usually with the companies themselves. Investors who bought those same stocks in 1980 generally made handsome returns (well above the market average) through the end of the century.

The Roaring Eighties

The Roaring Eighties had its fair share of speculative excesses, and again unwary investors paid the price for building castles in the air. The decade started with another spectacular new-issue boom.

The Triumphant Return of New Issues

The high-technology, new-issue boom of the first half of 1983 was an almost perfect replica of the 1960s episodes, with the names altered slightly to include the new fields of biotechnology and microelectronics. The 1983 craze made the promoters of the 1960s look like pikers. The total value of new issues during 1983 was greater than the cumulative total of new issues for the entire preceding decade. For investors, initial public offerings were the hottest game in town.

Typical of the period was a "promising" new company in the personal robot business. Was the robot ready for the task? Well, not quite. The company, called Androbot, planned to manufacture a line of personal robots. The company's major product, B.O.B. (an acronym for Brains on Board), was nearly ready for manufacture; just a few small problems remained. Apparently, product development was not yet complete, and it was not clear that the "significant technological obstacles" mentioned in the prospectus could be overcome. Moreover, software applications had not been developed, and the prospectus suggested that early prototype models were not yet, in the computer vernacular, user friendly. Finally, it was not clear that any of Androbot's products could be mass-produced or that a market for the products existed at the prices that would have to be charged. But the proposed market capitalization of Androbot was less than $100 million (for a company with no sales, earnings, or net assets), and that didn't buy much in the heady new-issue market of 1983.

As was true in the earlier new-issue booms, even companies in more mundane businesses were favored in the market. A chain of three restaurants in New Jersey called "Stuff Your Face, Inc." was registered with the SEC. Indeed, the enthusiasm extended to "quality" issues such as Fine Art Acquisitions Ltd. This was not some philistine outfit peddling discount clothing or making computer hardware. This was a truly aesthetic enterprise. Fine Art Acquisitions, the prospectus tells us, was in the business of acquiring and distributing fine prints and Art Deco sculpture replicas. One of the company's major assets consisted of a group of nude photographs of Brooke Shields taken about midway between her time in the stroller and her entrance to Princeton. Apparently, there were some potential legal problems, such as a suit by Mom Shields, who had some objection to the exploitation of these pictures of the prepubescent eleven-year-old Brooke. But, after all, this was for "artistic" purposes and obviously this was a class company.

Probably the offering of Muhammad Ali Arcades International burst the bubble. This offering was not particularly remarkable considering all the other garbage coming out at the time. It was unique, however, in that it showed that a penny could still buy a lot. The company proposed to offer units of one share and two warrants for the modest price of 1¢. Of course, this was 333 times what insiders had recently paid for their own shares, which wasn't unusual either, but when it was discovered that the champ himself had resisted the temptation to buy any stock in his namesake company, investors began to take a good look at where they were. Most did not like what they saw. The result was a dramatic decline in small company stocks in general and in the market prices of initial public offerings in particular. In the course of a year, many investors lost as much as 90 percent of their money.

The prospectus cover of Muhammad Ali Arcades International featured a picture of the former champ standing over a fallen opponent. In his salad days, Ali used to claim that he could "float like a butterfly and sting like a bee." It turned out that the Ali Arcades offering (as well as the Androbot offering that was scheduled for July 1983) never did get floated. But many others did, particularly stocks of those companies on the bleeding edge of technology. As has been true time and time again, it was the investors who got stung.

Concepts Conquer Again: The Biotechnology Bubble

What electronics was to the 1960s, biotechnology became to the 1980s. In its cover story "Biotech Comes of Age" in January 1984, *BusinessWeek* put its imprimatur on the boom. "The fun-

damental question—'Is the technology real?'—has been settled," the magazine reported. The biotech revolution was
likened to that of the computer. The magazine reported that
gene-splicing progress "has out-distanced the most optimistic
forecasts" and projected dramatic increases in the sales of
biotechnology products.

Such optimism was also reflected in the prices of biotech
company stocks. Genentech, the most substantial company in
the industry, came to market in 1980. During the first twenty
minutes of trading, the stock almost tripled in value, as
investors anticipated that they were purchasing the next IBM at
its initial public offering. Other new issues of biotech companies were eagerly gobbled up by hungry investors who saw a
chance to get into a multibillion-dollar new industry on the
ground floor. The key product that drove the first wave of the
biotech frenzy was Interferon, a cancer-fighting drug. Analysts
predicted that sales of Interferon would exceed $1 billion by
1982. (In reality, sales of this successful product were barely
$200 million in 1989, but there was no holding back the dreams
of castles in the air.) Analysts continually predicted an explosion of earnings two years out for the biotech companies. Analysts were continually disappointed. But the technological
revolution was real and hope springs eternal. Even weak companies benefited under the umbrella of the technology potential.

Valuation levels of biotechnology stocks reached levels previously unknown to investors. In the 1960s, speculative growth
stocks might have sold at 50 times earnings in the 1960s. In the
1980s, some biotech stocks sold at 50 times sales. As a student
of valuation techniques, I was fascinated to read how security
analysts rationalized these prices. Because biotech companies
typically had no current earnings (and realistically no positive
earnings expected for several years) and little sales, new valuation methods had to be devised. My favorite was the "product
asset valuation" method recommended by one of Wall Street's
leading securities houses. Basically, the method involved the
estimation of the value of all the products in the "pipeline" of
each biotech company. Even if the planned product involved
nothing more than the drawings of a genetic engineer, a potential sales volume and a profit margin were estimated for each
product that was merely a glint in some scientist's eye. Sales

could be estimated by taking the "expected clinical indications" for the future drug, predicting the potential number of patient users, and assuming a generous price tag. The total value of the "product pipeline" would then give the analyst a fair idea of the price at which the company's stock should sell.

None of the potential problems seemed real to the optimists. Perhaps U.S. Food and Drug Administration approval would be delayed. (Interferon was delayed for several years.) Would the market bear the fancy drug price tags that were projected? Would patent protection be possible as virtually every product in the biotechnology pipeline was being developed simultaneously by several companies, or were patent clashes inevitable? Would much of the potential profit from a successful drug be siphoned off by the marketing partner of the biotech company, usually one of the major drug companies? In the mid-1980s, none of these potential problems seemed real. Indeed, the biotech stocks were regarded by one analyst as less risky than standard drug companies because there were "no old products which need to be offset because of their declining revenues." We had come full circle—having positive sales and earnings was actually considered a drawback because those profits might decline in the future.

From the mid-1980s to the late 1980s, most biotechnology stocks lost three-quarters of their market value. They plunged in the crash of 1987 and continued heading south even as the market recovered in 1988. Market sentiment had changed from acceptance of an exciting story and multiples in the stratosphere to a desire to stay closer to earth with low-multiple stocks that actually pay dividends. Nor did the fate of the biotechnology industry improve in the early 1990s. By the mid-1990s, the industry was losing money at a rate of $4 billion per year.

ZZZZ Best Bubble of All

My favorite boom and bust of the late 1980s is the story of ZZZZ Best. Here was an incredible Horatio Alger story that captivated investors. In the fast-paced world of entrepreneurs who strike it rich before they can shave, Barry Minkow was a genuine legend of the 1980s. Minkow's career began at age nine. His family could not afford a baby-sitter so Barry often went to work at the carpet-cleaning shop managed by his mother. There he began soliciting jobs by phone. By age ten he was actually clean-ing carpets. Working evenings and summers, he saved $6,000 within the next four years and by the age of fifteen he bought some steam-cleaning equipment and started his own carpet-cleaning business in the garage of the family home. The com-pany was called ZZZZ Best (pronounced "zeee best"). Still in high school and too young to drive, Minkow hired a crew to pick up and clean carpets while he sat in class fretting over each week's payroll. With Minkow working a punishing schedule (and having friends drive him to appointments), the business flourished. He was proud of the fact that he hired his father and mother to work for the business. By age eighteen, Minkow was a millionaire.

Minkow's insatiable appetite for work extended to self-pro-motion. He took on all the tangible trappings of success. He drove a red Ferrari and lived in a $700,000 home with a large pool in which a big black Z was painted on the bottom. He also publicly extolled good old-fashioned American virtues. He wrote a book entitled *Making It in America* in which he claimed that teenagers didn't work hard enough. He gave generously to charities and appeared on antidrug commercials with the slo-gan, "My act is clean, how's yours?" By this time, ZZZZ Best had 1,300 employees and locations throughout California as well as in Arizona and Nevada.

Was more than 100 times earnings too much to pay for a mundane carpet-cleaning company? Of course not, when the company was run by a genius and a spectacularly successful businessman, who could also show his toughness. Minkow's favorite line to his employees was "My way or the highway." And he once boasted that he would fire his own mother if she stepped out of line. When Minkow told Wall Street that his com-pany was better run than IBM and that it was destined to become "the General Motors of carpet cleaning," investors lis-tened with rapt attention. As one security analyst told me at the time, "This one can't miss."

In 1987, Minkow's bubble burst with shocking suddenness. It turned out that ZZZZ Best was cleaning more than carpets— it was also laundering money for the mob. ZZZZ Best was accused of acting as a front for organized crime figures who would buy equipment for the company with "dirty" money and replace their investment with "clean" cash skimmed from the proceeds of ZZZZ Best's legitimate carpet-cleaning business. But in fact, the spectacular growth of the company was itself mainly an elaborate fiction produced with fictitious contracts, phony credit card charges, and the like. The whole operation was a giant Ponzi scheme in which money was recycled from one set of investors to pay off another. In addition, Minkow was charged with skimming millions from the company treasury for his own personal use. Minkow, as well as all the investors in ZZZZ Best, were in wall-to-wall trouble.

The next chapter of the story (after Chapter Eleven) occurred in 1989 when Minkow, then twenty-three, was convicted of fifty-seven counts of fraud, sentenced to twenty-five years in prison, and required to make restitution of $26 million he was accused of stealing from the company. The U.S. district judge, in rejecting pleas for leniency, told Minkow, "You are dangerous because you have this gift of gab, this ability to communicate." The judge added, "You don't have a conscience."

But the story does not end there. Minkow spent fifty-four months in Lampoc Federal Prison, where he became a born-again Christian, earning a bachelor's and master's correspondence school degree from Liberty University, founded by Jerry Falwell. After his release in December 1994, he became senior pastor at Community Bible Church in California, where he held his congregation in rapt attention with his evangelical style. He also has become a one-man media conglomerate, using his unique skills as a communicator to speak out on how he got away with committing fraud. He has written two books, *Clean Sweep* and *Fraud from A to Z Best*, has conducted a daily nationally syndicated radio program, and uses his charismatic skills as a much-in-demand lecturer. In July 2002, following the Enron and WorldCom scandals, he was hired as a special adviser for the FBI on how to spot fraud.

What Does It All Mean?

The lessons of market history are clear. Styles and fashions in investors' evaluations of securities can and often do play a critical role in the pricing of securities. The stock market at times conforms well to the castle-in-the-air theory. For this reason, the game of investing can be extremely dangerous.

Another lesson that cries out for attention is that investors should be very wary of purchasing today's hot "new issue." Most initial public offerings underperform the stock market as a whole. And if you buy the new issue after it begins trading, usually at a higher price, you are even more certain to lose. Investors would be well advised to treat new issues with a healthy dose of skepticism.

Certainly investors in the past have built many castles in the air with IPOs. Remember that the major sellers of the stock of IPOs are the managers of the companies themselves. They try to time their sales to coincide with a peak in the prosperity of their companies or with the height of investor enthusiasm for some current fad. In such cases, the urge to get on the bandwagon—even in high-growth industries—produced a profitless prosperity for investors.

The Nervy Nineties

The Japanese Yen for Land and Stocks

One of the largest booms and busts of the late twentieth century involved the Japanese real estate and stock markets. From 1955 to 1990, the value of Japanese real estate increased more than 75 times. By 1990, the total value of all Japanese property was estimated at nearly $20 trillion—equal to more than 20 percent of the entire world's wealth and about double the total value of the world's stock markets. America is twenty-five times bigger than Japan in terms of physical acreage, and yet Japan's property in 1990 was appraised to be worth five times as much as all American property. Theoretically, the Japanese could have bought all the property in America by selling off metropolitan Tokyo. Just selling the Imperial Palace and its grounds at their appraised value would have raised the cash to buy all of California.

The stock market countered by rising like a helium balloon on a windless day. Stock prices increased 100-fold from 1955 to 1990. At their peak in December 1989, Japanese stocks had a total market value of about $4 trillion, almost 1.5 times the value of all U.S. equities and close to 45 percent of the world's equity market capitalization. Firm-foundation investors were aghast at such figures. They read with dismay that Japanese stocks sold at more than 60 times earnings, almost 5 times book value, and more than 200 times dividends. In contrast, U.S. stocks sold at about 15 times earnings, and London equities sold at 12 times earnings. The high prices of Japanese stocks were even more dramatic on a company-by-company comparison. The value of NTT Corporation, Japan's telephone giant, which was privatized during the boom, exceeded the value of AT&T, IBM, Exxon, General Electric, and General Motors put together. Dai Ichi Kangyo Bank sold at 56 times earnings, whereas an equivalent U.S. bank, Citicorp, sold at 5.6 times earnings. Nomura Securities, Japan's largest stockbroker, sold at a market value exceeding the total value of all U.S. brokerage firms combined.

Two myths propelled the real estate and stock markets. The first was that land prices could never go down in Japan, and the second was that stock prices could only go up. These myths were fueled by large amounts of cash from the Japanese tradition of almost compulsive saving and by extremely low returns from regular savings accounts, which yielded less than 1 percent. Playing the stock market became a national preoccupation. Almost overnight, Japanese male commuters switched from their usual pornographic comic books to lurid tales of vivid conquests of the stock market. It is said that in Britain there is a betting shop (or turf accountant) on every corner. In Japan, there was a stockbroker on every corner. Nomura Securities reached intellectual customers through its ad featuring Copernicus and Ptolemy. This ad compared Nomura's perpetually bullish stock outlook with the enlightened Copernican view that the earth and planets revolved around the sun. The naysaying view that stock and real estate markets were dangerously high was compared with Ptolemy's conviction that the sun revolved around the earth. Another sales brochure, put out by a Japanese stockbroker, featured a housewife with a cloud draping her hand and an arrow about to fly ever upward. This was clearly a time for building castles in the air.

Japanese corporations also played a major role in the market frenzy. Businesses were allowed to set up tax-advantaged speculative trading accounts (called *toklein* accounts) to play the market. During the boom, firms often made more money from trading stock than from producing goods.

Supporters of the stock market had answers to all the logical objections that could be raised. Were price-earnings ratios in the stratosphere? "No" said the salespeople at Kabuto-cho (Japan's Wall Street). "Japanese earnings are understated relative to U.S. earnings because depreciation charges are overstated and earnings do not include the earnings of partially owned affiliated firms." Price-earnings multiples adjusted for these effects would be much lower. Were yields, at well under ½ of 1 percent, unconscionably low? The answer was that this simply reflected the low interest rates at the time in Japan. Was it dangerous that stock prices were 5 times the value of assets? Not at all. The book values did not reflect the dramatic appreciation of the land owned by Japanese companies. And the high value of Japanese land was "explained" by both the density of Japanese population and the various regulations and tax laws restricting the use of habitable land.

In fact, none of the "explanations" for the soaring heights of the real estate and stock markets could hold water. Even when earnings and dividends were adjusted, the multiples were still far higher than in other countries and extraordinarily inflated relative to Japan's own history. Moreover, Japanese profitability had been declining and the strong yen was bound to make it more difficult for Japan to export its products. Although land was scarce in Japan, its manufacturers, such as its auto makers, were finding abundant land for new plants at attractive prices in foreign lands. And rental income had been rising far more slowly than land values, indicating a falling rate of return on real estate unless prices continued to skyrocket. Finally, the low interest rates that had been underpinning the market had already begun to rise in 1989.

Perhaps the cleverest "explanation" for the runaway Japanese real estate and stock markets was that "Japan was different." Every professional with whom I talked in the late 1980s was convinced that the powerful Ministry of Finance (MoF) would somehow find a way to avoid any unpleasantness. It could restrict land available for development if prices started to fall. It could change a rule here or there, or institute a new regulation

The Japanese Stock-Market Bubble
Japanese Stock Prices Relative to Book Values, 1980–2000

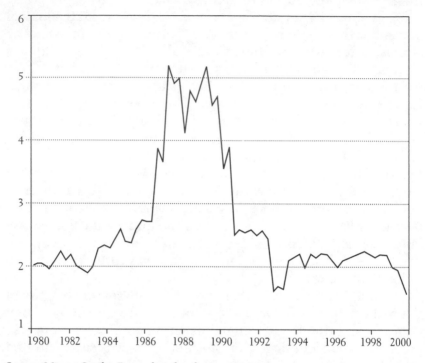

Source: Morgan Stanley Research and author's estimates.

to cure any ills in the stock market. The view was widespread in world financial markets that the Japanese market was "rigged" and would continue to be so as part of a government policy to promote lofty stock prices and cheap capital for economic growth. How often we make egregious errors by ignoring history and economic fundamentals and conclude that "this time it's different."

Much to the distress of those speculators who had concluded that the fundamental laws of financial gravity were not applicable to Japan, Isaac Newton arrived there in 1990. Interestingly, it was the government itself which dropped the apple. The Bank of Japan (Japan's Federal Reserve) saw the ugly spectre of a general inflation stirring among the borrowing frenzy and the liquidity boom underwriting the rise in land and stock prices. And so the central bank restricted credit and engineered a rise in interest rates. The hope was that further rises in property prices would be choked off and the stock market might be eased downward.

Interest rates, which had already been going up during 1989, rose sharply in 1990. The stock market was not eased down; instead, it collapsed. The fall was almost as extreme as the U.S. stock-market crash from the end of 1929 to mid-1932. The Japanese (Nikkei) stock-market index reached a high of almost 40,000 on the last trading day of the decade of the 1980s. By mid-August 1992, the index had declined to 14,309, a drop of about 63 percent. In contrast, the Dow Jones Industrial Average fell 66 percent from December 1929 to its low in the summer of 1932 (although the decline was over 80 percent from the September 1929 level). The Japanese stock market remained at low levels throughout the 1990s despite a fall in interest rates, and its powerful economy suffered a sharp recession during the late 1990s. The chart on page 80 shows quite dramatically that the rise in stock prices during the mid- and late 1980s represented a change in valuation relationships. The fall in stock prices from 1990 on simply reflected a return to the price-book value relationships that were typical in the early 1980s.

It is more difficult to date and measure the collapse in the real estate market because property rarely changes hands. Nevertheless, the air also rushed out of the real estate balloon during the early 1990s. Various measures of land prices and property values indicate a decline roughly as severe as that of the stock market. The bursting of the bubble destroyed the myth that Japan was different and its asset prices would always rise. The financial laws of gravity know no geographic boundaries.

The collapse of the bubble in Japan had profound effects on the financial system and on the Japanese economy. Unlike the case in the United States, commercial banks, life insurance companies, and even nonfinancial corporations themselves hold large amounts of stocks and real estate. The bursting of the bubble weakened the entire financial system and was followed by a severe recession that lasted into the next century.

4
The Biggest Bubble
of All:
Surfing on the Internet

If you can keep your head when all about you are losing theirs . . .
Yours is the Earth and everything that's in it . . .
—Rudyard Kipling, *If—*

W e save for last what was undoubtedly the
biggest bubble of the twentieth century—if not of all time.
Indeed, comparing the Internet bubble to the tulip-bulb craze
is undoubtedly unfair to the flowers. Most bubbles have been
associated with some new technology (as in the tronics or
biotech booms) or with some new business opportunity (as
when the opening of profitable new trade opportunities
spawned the South Sea Bubble). The Internet was associated
with both: it represented a new technology, and it offered new
business opportunities that promised to revolutionize the way
we obtain information and purchase goods and services. The
promise of the Internet spawned the largest creation and largest
destruction of wealth of all time. When the bubble popped,
over $8 trillion of market value evaporated. It was as if a year's
output of the economies of Germany, France, England, Italy,
Spain, Holland, and Russia had completely disappeared.

How Bubbles Arise

Robert Shiller, in *Irrational Exuberance*, describes bubbles
in terms of "positive feedback loops." A bubble starts when any

group of stocks, in this case those associated with the excitement of the Internet, begin to rise. The updraft encourages more people to buy the stocks, which causes more TV and print coverage, which causes even more people to buy, which creates big profits for early Internet stockholders. The successful investors tell you at cocktail parties how easy it is to get rich, which causes the stocks to rise further, which pulls in larger and larger groups of investors. But the whole mechanism is a kind of Ponzi scheme where more and more credulous investors must be found to buy the stock from the earlier investors. Eventually, one runs out of greater fools.

What electronics was for the 1960s, and biotechnology was to the 1980s, the Internet was for investors in the late 1990s and early 2000. Internet companies, unimpeded by earnings and with only minuscule revenues, floated on the hot air created by their adeptness at burning cash raised from credulous investors. The higher they got, the prettier the scenery. The venerable investment firm Goldman Sachs argued in mid-2000 that the cash burned by the dot-com companies was primarily an "investor sentiment" issue and not a "long-term risk" for the sector or "space" as it was often called. Goldman stated this august opinion just as the market was drastically deflating. A few months later, hundreds of Internet companies were bankrupt, proving that the Goldman report was inadvertently correct. The cash-burn rate was not a long-term risk—it was a short-term risk.

The Internet promised an era of technological change as important as the industrial revolution at the end of the nineteenth century. The information revolution was going to transform the way we communicated, the way consumers and businesses made purchases and sales, and the way we received information and learned. Use of the Net was doubling every few months, and it was claimed that the process was only in its infancy. Unprecedented growth was not only possible but also inevitable. Moreover, the mass-market interactive communications network that was needed to power the Internet presented seemingly unlimited profit potential. Anyone scoffing at the potential for the "New Economy" was a hopeless Luddite doomed to seething envy of all those profiting from it. As the chart on page 84 indicates, the NASDAQ Index, an index essentially representing high-tech New Economy companies, more than tripled from late 1998 to March 2000. The price-earnings multiples of the stocks in the index that had earnings soared to over 100.

NASDAQ Composite Stock Index
July 1999–July 2002

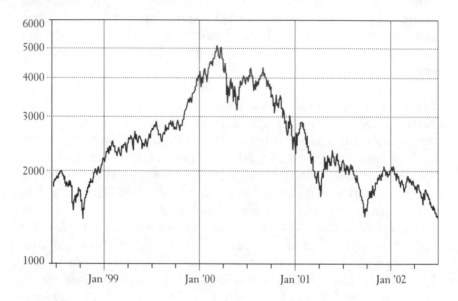

A Broad-Scale High-Tech Bubble

At the bubble's height, scoffers were as hard to find as the Maytag repairman. Surveys of investors in early 2000 revealed that expectations of future stock returns ranged from 15 percent per year to 25 percent or higher. After all, since 1982, the stock market had produced greater than 18 percent returns. And for companies such as Cisco and JDS Uniphase, widely known as producing "the backbone of the Internet," 15 percent returns per year were considered a slam dunk. But Cisco was selling at a triple-digit multiple of earnings and had a market capitalization of almost $600 billion. If Cisco grew its earnings at 15 percent per year, it would still be selling at a well above average multiple ten years later.

And if Cisco returned 15 percent per year for the next twenty-five years and the national economy continued to grow at 6 percent over the same period, Cisco would have been bigger than the entire economy. Obviously, there was a complete disconnect between stock-market valuations and any reasonable expectations of future growth. And even blue-chip Cisco lost over 90 percent of its market value when the bubble burst. As for JDS Uniphase, the following chart plots its prices from mid-1997 through mid-2002 against the NASDAQ Index. By comparison, the bubble in the overall index is hardly noticeable.

Comparison of JDS Uniphase Stock with the NASDAQ Composite Index July 1997–July 2002

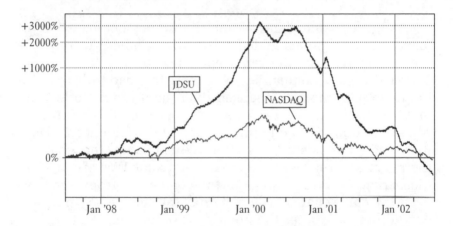

Stocks of companies such as Amazon.com and Priceline.com —the drum majors of the Internet parade—rose to dizzying heights. Amazon, with relatively modest revenues from book sales and with large losses, sold at prices that made its total market capitalization (the price of its stock multiplied by the number of shares) larger than the total market values of all the publicly owned booksellers such as Barnes & Noble. Jeff Bezos, Amazon's CEO, was *Time* magazine's 1999 "Person of the Year." Priceline, an auction company whose site sold empty airline seats while losing buckets of money, sold at a total market cap-

italization that exceeded the capitalization of the major carriers
United, Delta, and American Airlines combined. The mania for
Internet-related stocks seemed to know no bounds. The disastrous results for investors, even in the leading New Economy
stocks, is shown in the table that follows.

How Even the Leading New Economy Stocks Ruined Investors

Stock	High 2000	Low 2001–2002	Percentage Decline
Amazon.com	75.25	5.51	92.7
Cisco Systems	82.00	8.12	90.1
Corning	113.33	1.10	99.0
JDS Uniphase	297.34	1.58	99.5
Lucent Technologies	74.93	.55	99.3
Nortel Networks	143.62	.43	99.7
Priceline.com	165	1.05	99.4
Yahoo.com	238	8.45	96.4

As in the name game during the tronics boom, when all
manner of companies added the suffix "tronics" to increase
their attractiveness, the same happened during the Internet
mania. Dozens of companies, even those that had little or nothing to do with the Net, changed their names to include Web-
oriented designations such as dot-com, dotnet, or Internet.
Three researchers from Purdue University, M. Cooper, D. Dim-
itrov, and P. R. Rau studied sixty-three companies that changed
their names in 1998 and 1999 to include some Web orientation.
Measuring the price change of the companies from five days
prior to a name change (when word of the change began to leak
out) to five days after the change was announced, they confirmed a remarkable effect. Companies that changed their
names enjoyed a 125 percent greater increase in price during
that ten-day period than that of their peers. This more than
doubling of the stock price occurred even when the company's
core business had nothing whatsoever to do with the Net.
Titling their paper "A Rose by Any Other Name," the authors
concluded that investors were willing to throw their money at
almost anything that claimed an Internet link. In a later paper
examining the post-bubble period, they found that stock prices
benefited when dot-com was deleted from the firm's name.
    An example of the complete insanity that gripped the mar-

ket—an insanity that went well beyond irrational exuberance—is the case of PalmPilot, the maker of Personal Digital Assistants (PDAs). Palm was owned by a company called 3Com, which decided to spin it off to its shareholders. Since PDAs were touted as a *sine qua non* of the digital revolution, it was assumed that PalmPilot would be a particularly exciting stock and that the combined value of PalmPilot and the rest of 3Com's business would be larger than if the two businesses remained together. Little did 3Com know how strongly the market would react.

In early 2000, 3Com sold 5 percent of its shares in Palm in an initial public offering and announced its intention to spin off all the remaining shares to the 3Com shareholders. Palm took off so fast that its market capitalization became twice as large as that of 3Com. But remember that 3Com still owned 95 percent of Palm. It turned out that the value of 95 percent of Palm was almost $25 billion greater than the total market capitalization of 3Com. It was as if all of 3Com's other assets were worth a negative $25 billion. If you wanted to buy PalmPilot you could have bought 3Com and owned the rest of 3Com's business for minus $61 per share. In its mindless search for riches, the market created anomalies that were even stranger than the fraudulent accounting practices that were soon to be revealed.

An Unprecedented New-Issue Craze

In the first quarter of 2000, 916 venture capital firms invested $15.7 billion in 1009 startup Internet companies. Many were playing catch-up: an astonishing 159 initial public offerings (IPOs) had been successfully completed in the previous quarter. It was as if the stock market was on steroids. As was the case during the South Sea Bubble, many companies that received financing were absurd. Almost all turned out to be dot-com catastrophes. Consider the following example of Internet startups.

- Digiscents offered a peripheral you could plug into your computer that would make Web sites and computer games smell. The company ran through millions from venture capitalists trying to develop such a product.

- Flooz offered an alternative currency—Flooz that could be e-mailed to friends and family. It was not quite money because there were only a few places you could use it, but it sure made a unique gift. In order to jump-start the company, Flooz.com turned to an old business school maxim that "any idiot can sell a one-dollar bill for eighty cents." Flooz.com launched a special offer to American Express platinum card holders allowing them to buy $1,000 of Flooz currency for just $800. Shortly before declaring bankruptcy, Flooz itself was Floozed when Filipino and Russian gangs bought $300,000 of its currency using stolen credit card numbers.

- IAM.COM offered a data base of pictures of aspiring actors built with $50 million of venture capital. Casting directors certainly did not want to pay for such a site. They had quite enough candidates as is.

- How about Zing.com? It looked like a real winner, gaining 1.7 million visitors to its Web site. The business was to let you download some free software. How were they going to make money? By making you look at advertising from other dot-com-bombs (unable to pay their bills) while you were waiting for your software to download.

- Consider Pets.com, a real dog if there ever was one. The company had a sock-puppet mascot that starred in its TV commercials and even made an appearance at a Macy's Thanksgiving Day Parade. Unfortunately, the popularity of its mascot did not compensate for the fact that it's hard to make a profit individually shipping low-margin 25-pound bags of kibble.

The names alone of many of the Internet ventures stretch credulity: Bunions.com, Crayfish, Zap.com, Gadzooks, Fogdog, FatBrain, Jungle.com, Scoot.com, mylackey.com, and, moreover, Moreover.com. And then there was ezboard.com which produced Internet pages called toilet paper, to help you "get the poop" on the online community. These were not business models. They were models for business failure.

The Internet bubble and its effervescent new issues floated into the leading business schools. Students from Stanford and

Harvard had typically spent the summer between their first and second year interning with various firms. In 1999, large numbers of students working in the Internet and high-tech sectors did not come back to school. Making millions from stock options was easy—why waste another year getting your MBA. Those who did return flocked to courses such as "Entrepreneurial Finance." In one course taught at the Harvard Business School, student groups entered a competition to produce a coherent business plan for a new venture. The plans would be critiqued by professors and fellow students. One student plan was panned by everyone as ill conceived and poorly executed. While the students presenting the plan had difficulty passing the course, they had no trouble raising $10 million from venture capitalists to start a new company.

Philip J. Kaplan proved to be a brilliant chronicler of the stupidity of the new dot-com financings. Deciding to kill some time during a Memorial Day weekend just after the bubble deflated, he set up a Web site F**kedcompany.com that offered the latest gossip about sinking dot-com companies as well as a betting pool on when the companies would go under. (The Web site could be accessed by filling in the expurgated characters censored above.) The Web site attracted 4 million viewers. Kaplan then published a book named after the site where he ridiculed 100 of the most ludicrous of the dot-com business ideas. Here is how Kaplan described the flameout of SwapIt.com.

SO LET ME GET THIS STRAIGHT:

1) I send them a CD.

2) They give me useless "SwapIt Bucks."

3) They go out of business.

4) I get nothing.

Great, sign me up!

SwapIt.com was a fiercely stupid idea. The premise was that people could trade used CDs and video games with one another by physically mailing their crap to SwapIt.com. Users would then be issued "SwapIt Bucks" that they could use to buy other people's crap that had also been sent to the company.

The genius of the eBay business model was that eBay carried no inventory. But SwapIt, by dealing with both inventory and fulfillment, had all the costs and none of the benefits.

Whatever the new issue, investors greeted it with hurrahs and fistfuls of cash, especially if the company was part of the New Economy. In previous bubbles, new issues would rise what was now seen as a paltry 25 or 50 percent. In the New Economy era, some IPOs soared 500 percent or more. VA Linux rose over 730 percent in its first day of trading to almost $200 per share. In 2002, the company clung to life at less than a dollar a share. During 1999, the *average* IPO increased in price by over 70 percent during the first day of trading.

There were Wall Street pros who warned of the excesses. But when Bill Hambrecht, founder of the investment banking firm Hambrecht & Quist, one of the most successful bankers bringing new companies to market, warned his fellow pros, "Hey, guys, this isn't going to turn out well," no one listened. The reaction was, "What can be better than this? I sell stock at ten and it goes to one hundred and everyone gets rich." Hambrecht reflected, "I felt like the designated driver at a New Year's Eve party."

TheGlobe.com

My most vivid memory of the IPO boom dates back to an early morning in November 1998, when I was being interviewed on a TV show. As I waited in the "green room," I thought how out of place it was to be sitting next to two young men dressed in jeans who, while in their early twenties, looked like teenagers. Little did I realize that they were the first superstars of the Internet boom and the featured attractions on the show. Stephen Paternot and Todd Krizelman had formed a company called TheGlobe.com in Todd's dorm room at Cornell. Their company was an online message board system that hoped to generate large revenues from selling banner advertising. In earlier times, one needed actual revenues and profits to come to market with an IPO, but TheGlobe.com had neither. Nevertheless, this was a new era, and their bankers, Credit Suisse First

Doonesbury

Boston, brought them to market at a price of $9 per share. The price immediately soared to $97, at that time the largest first day gain in history, giving the company a market value of nearly $1 billion and making the two founders multimillionaires. That was the day we learned that investors would throw money at businesses that only five years before would not have passed normal due diligence hurdles.

The initial public offering of TheGlobe.Com was the catalyst that launched the pathological phase of the Internet bubble. The relationship between profits and share price had been severed, and a wave of money-losing ventures rushed to the market with IPOs. As for Paternot, a CNN segment in 1999 caught him at a trendy New York nightclub dancing on a table, in shiny plastic black pants, with his trophy model girlfriend. On camera Paternot was heard to say, "Got the girl, got the money. Now I'm ready to live a disgusting, frivolous life." Well, life may be disgusting now that Paternot and Krizelman are known as the "global poster boys of Internet excess." As for TheGlobe.com, the company closed its Web site in 2001. In Paternot's tell-all book *A Very Public Offering*, he admits how little he knew about how to run a company. "My principal experience as a businessman," he writes, "was the constant sense of being on the verge of death: always pushing as hard as possible and in constant denial of the inevitable."

While the party was still going strong in early 2000, John Doerr, a leading venture capitalist with the preeminent firm of Kleiner Perkins, called the rise in Internet-related stocks "the greatest legal creation of wealth in the history of the planet." In 2002, he neglected to write that it was also the greatest legal destruction of wealth on the planet.

Security Analysts $peak Up

Wall Street's high-profile securities analysts provided much of the hot air floating the Internet bubble. Analysts such as Mary Meeker of Morgan Stanley, Henry Blodgett of Merrill Lynch, and Jack Grubman of Salomon Smith Barney became household names and were accorded the status of sports heroes or rock stars. Meeker was dubbed by *Barron's* magazine the "Queen of the 'Net." Blodgett was known as "King Henry," while Grubman acquired the sobriquet "Telecom Guru" and in the words of one worshipful CEO was almost a "demigod."

Like sports heroes, each of them was earning a multimillion-dollar salary. Their incomes, however, were based not on the quality of their analysis but rather on their ability to steer lucrative investment banking business to their firms by implicitly promising that their ongoing favorable research coverage would provide continuing support for the initial public offerings in the after market.

Traditionally, a "Chinese Wall" was supposed to separate the research function of Wall Street firms, which is supposed to work for the benefit of investors, from the very profitable investment banking function, which works for the benefit of corporate clients. But during the bubble, that wall became more like Swiss cheese.

Analysts were the very public cheerleaders for the boom. Blodgett flatly stated that traditional valuation metrics were not relevant in "the big-bang stage of an industry." Meeker suggested, in a flattering *New Yorker* profile in 1999, that "this is a time to be rationally reckless." Their public comments on individual stocks made prices soar. And why not? Stock selections were described in terms of powerful baseball hits: A stock that would be expected to quadruple was a "Four Bagger." More exciting stocks might be "Ten Baggers." And as *The Industry Standard* remarked, "When Mary Meeker Talks, Net Stocks Go Bananas."

Securities analysts always find reasons to be bullish. They seldom utter the four-letter "sell" word because they do not want to endanger current or future investment banking relationships or to offend corporate chief financial officers on whom they rely for information. Traditionally, ten stocks are rated "buys" for each one that is rated "sell." But during the bubble, the ratio of buys to sells reached close to 100 to 1. And as stocks climbed more and more, Americans became convinced that investing was easy. They watched CNBC to listen to interviews with their favorite investment gurus, and they could not get enough of the fluff the analysts were peddling. When the bubble burst, the celebrity analysts faced death threats and lawsuits and their firms faced investigations and fines by the SEC and the New York State attorney general. Blodgett was renamed the "clown prince" of the Internet bubble by the *New York Post*. Grubman was ridiculed before a congressional committee for his continuous touting of WorldCom stock and investigated by the New York State Attorney General for changing his stock ratings to help obtain investment banking business. Both Blodgett and Grubman left their firms. *Fortune* magazine summed it all up with a picture of Mary Meeker on the cover and the caption: "Can We Ever Trust Wall Street Again?"

New Valuation Metrics

In order to justify ever higher prices for Internet-related companies, security analysts began to use a variety of "new metrics" that could be used to value the stocks. After all, the New Economy stocks were a breed apart—they should certainly not be held to the fuddy-duddy old-fashioned standards that had been used to value traditional old economy companies. And so valuation criteria such as price to earnings, price to book value, or even price to sales were abandoned in favor of a whole new set of valuation metrics. Unconventional methods of valuation seemed appropriate to the cutting-edge, New Economy companies that were promising to revolutionize the way we communicated, went to school, shopped, invested, and received our news and entertainment.

Somehow, in the brave new Internet world, sales, revenues, and profits were irrelevant. In order to value Internet companies, analysts looked instead at "eyeballs"—the number of people viewing a Web page or "visiting" a Web site. In addition, measurements were made of "page views per user per month." Particularly important were numbers of "engaged shoppers"—those who spent at least three minutes on a Web site. Mary Meeker gushed enthusiastically about Drugstore.com because 48 percent of the eyeballs viewing the site were "engaged shoppers." No one seemed to care whether the engaged shopper forked over greenbacks and bought anything from the company. Sales were so old-fashioned. Drugstore.com reached a price of $67.50 during the height of the bubble of 2000. By the fall of the next year—when eyeballs started looking at profits—it was a "penny" stock.

"Mind share" was another popular nonfinancial metric that convinced me that investors had lost their collective minds. For example, online home seller Homestore.com was highly recommended in October 2000 by Morgan Stanley because 72 percent of all the time spent by Internet users on real estate Web sites was spent on properties listed by Homestore.com. But "mind share" did not lead to Internet users making up their minds to buy the properties listed and did not prevent Homestore.com from falling 99 percent from its high during 2001.

Special metrics were established for telecom companies.

According to one TV commercial for the Janus Fund, its security analysts clambered into tunnels to count the miles of fiber-optic cable in the ground rather than examining the tiny fraction that was actually lit up with voice, picture, or data traffic. Similarly, the "infrastructure build" was taken as a sign of strength, and telecom overcapacity and brutal pricing pressures were, for a time, ignored. The philosophy was "If we build it, they will come." Each telecom company borrowed money with abandon and enough fiber was laid to circle the earth 1,500 times. As a sign of the times, global telecom company and Internet service provider PSI Net (now bankrupt) put its name on the Baltimore Ravens' football field. As the prices of telecom stocks continued to skyrocket well past any normal valuation standards, security analysts did what they often do—they just lowered their standards.

The ease with which telecoms could raise money from Wall Street led to massive oversupply—too much long-distance fiber-optic cable, too many computers, and too many telecom companies. The industry literally choked to death. By 2000, dozens of upstart telecom carriers hawking high-speed Internet service went bankrupt. In 2002, even mighty WorldCom declared bankruptcy. And the big equipment companies such as Lucent and Nortel, which had engaged in risky vendor financing deals, suffered staggering losses and laid off tens of thousands of workers. About a trillion dollars was thrown into telecom investments during the bubble. Most of it has simply vaporized. One of the jokes making the rounds of the Internet in 2001 went as follows:

> Tip of the Week
>
> If you bought $1,000 worth of Nortel stock one year ago, it would now be worth $49.
>
> If you bought $1,000 worth of Budweiser (the beer, not the stock) one year ago, drank all the beer, and traded in the cans for the nickel deposit, you would have $79.
>
> My advice to you . . . start drinking heavily.

By the fall of 2002, the $1,000 put into Nortel stock was worth only $3.

The Writes of the Media

The bubble was aided and abetted by the media—which turned us into a nation of traders.

Like the stock market, journalism is subject to the laws of supply and demand. Since investors wanted more information about Internet investing opportunities, the supply of magazines increased to fill the need. And since readers were not interested in downbeat skeptical analyses, they flocked to those publications that promised an easy road to riches. Investment magazines featured stories of "the ten best stocks for the quarter ahead" or "the best mutual funds for the next six months" or "stocks likely to double in the months ahead." In particular, the red-hot Internet stocks were fascinating to journalists, who fanned the speculative flames and seduced investors into the market with promises of enormous riches ahead. As Jane Bryant Quinn remarked, it was "investment pornography"—soft core rather than hard core, "but pornography all the same."

A number of business and technology magazines devoted to the Internet sprang up to satisfy what seemed to be an insatiable public desire for more information. *Wired* described itself as the vanguard of the digital revolution. *The Industry Standard* was the new weekly of the Internet economy, and its IPO tracker was the most widely followed index in Silicon Valley. *Business 2.0* prided itself as the "oracle of the New Economy." The proliferation of publications was a classic sign of a speculative bubble. The historian Edward Chancellor pointed out that during the 1840s, fourteen weeklies and two dailies were introduced to cover the new railroad industry. During the financial crises of 1847, many of the rail publications perished. When *The Industry Standard* failed in 2001, the *New York Times* editorialized, "it may well go down as the day the buzz died."

The Internet itself became the media. No longer did the individual investor need to consult the *Wall Street Journal* or call a broker to get a stock's price quote. All the information needed was available online in real time. The Web provided stock summaries, analyst ratings, past stock charts, forecasts of next quarter's earnings and long-term growth, and instant access to any news items about most any stock, including changes in the advice dispensed by Wall Street security analysts. What previously had been available only to professionals was now available to individuals. The Internet had democratized the investment process. And if you wanted to check a fact with an engineer at one of the computer-chip companies, or if you sought reassurance from other investors, a variety of Internet chat rooms were only a mouse click away. The amount of gossip concerning every Internet company was staggering. Investors learned about Net stocks on the Internet and used the Internet to place their trades. The technology of the Internet played an important enabling role in perpetuating the bubble.

Online brokers were also a critical factor in fueling the Internet boom. Trading was cheap, at least in terms of the small dollar amount of commissions charged. (Actually, the costs of trading were larger than most online brokers advertised since much of the cost is buried in the spread between a dealer's "bid" price, the price at which a customer could sell, and the "asked" price, the price at which a customer could buy. Moreover, customer orders were not always routed to the market where the best price could be obtained but rather to the market that paid the online broker the most for routing the order flow.) The discount brokerage firms advertised heavily and made it seem that it was easy to beat the market. In one commercial, the customer boasted that she did not simply want to beat the market but to "throttle its scrawny little body to the ground and make it beg for mercy." After all, the online brokers offered instant research, real-time quotes, and charting tools that supposedly made any rank amateur able to trade with the pros. In another popular TV commercial, Stuart, the cybergeek from the mailroom, was encouraging his old-fashioned boss to make his first online stock purchase with the exhortation, "Let's light this candle." When the boss protested that he knew nothing about the stock, Stuart said, "Let's research it." After one click on the keyboard, the boss, thinking himself much wiser, bought his first 100 shares.

Television supplied continuous air for floating the Internet bubble. Cable networks such as CNBC, CNNfn, and Bloomberg became cultural phenomena. They filled each day with programming about the stock market and amplified the boom. Across the world, health clubs, airports, bars, and restaurants were permanently tuned in to CNBC. The stock market was treated like a sports event with a pre-game show (what to expect before the market opened), a play-by-play during trading hours, and a post-game show to review the day's action and to prepare investors for the next. CNBC implied that listening would put you "ahead of the curve." Most guests interviewed during the day were bullish. CNBC's commentators like Maria (the money honey) Bartiromo particularly favored scheduling interviews with analysts who could say with confidence that some $50 dot-com stock would soon go to $500. There was no need to remind a CNBC anchor that, just as the family dog that bites the baby is likely to have a short tenure, sourpuss skeptics did not encourage high ratings.

The market was a hotter story than sex. Even Howard Stern would interrupt more usual discussions about porn queens and body parts to muse about the stock market and then to tout some particular Internet stocks.

The result was that turnover reached an all-time high. The average holding period for a typical stock was not measured in years or even months but rather in days and hours. Redemption ratios of mutual funds (the percentage of the funds' assets redeemed) soared and the volatility of individual stock prices exploded. The twenty most volatile stocks in each trading day used to rise or fall by 5 percent. By early 2000, the biggest percentage changes in price were all 50 percent or more. And there were 10 million Internet "day traders," many of whom had quit their jobs to go down the easy path to riches. For them, the long term meant later in the morning. Day traders showed a special affinity for Internet stocks. It was lunacy. People who would spend hours researching the pros and cons of buying a $50 kitchen appliance would risk tens of thousands on a chat-room tip. Terrance Odean, a finance professor who studies investor behavior, found with his colleagues that most Internet traders actually lost money even during the bubble, systematically buying and selling the wrong stocks, and that they performed worse the more they traded. The average survival time for day traders was about six months.

Fraud Slithers In and Strangles the Market

Speculative manias, such as the Internet bubble, bring out the worst aspects of our system. The South Sea Bubble of the eighteenth century led to a vast number of fraudulent new issues designed to meet the public's insatiable appetite for speculative vehicles. The speculative frenzy of the 1920s led to a degree of manipulation of the stock exchanges that set new records for unscrupulousness. Let there be no mistake: it was the extraordinary New Economy mania that encouraged a string of business scandals that shook the capitalist system to its roots.

Many businesses were managed not for the creation of long-run value but for the immediate gratification of speculators. When Wall Street's conflicted sell-side analysts looked for high short-term forecasted earnings to justify outlandishly high stock prices, many corporate managers willingly obliged. And if aggressive earnings targets proved hard to meet, "creative accounting" could be used so that not only the published street estimates but even the "whisper numbers" could be surpassed. One spectacular example was the rise and subsequent bankruptcy of Enron—at one time the seventh largest corporation in America. The collapse of Enron, where over $65 million of market value was wiped out, can only be understood in the context of the enormous bubble in the New Economy part of the stock market. Enron was seen as the perfect New Economy stock that could dominate the market not only for energy but also for broadband communications, widespread electronic trading, and commerce.

Enron was a clear favorite of Wall Street analysts. Even after it began to unravel during the fall of 2001, sixteen out of seventeen security analysts covering Enron had "buy" or "strong buy" ratings on the stock. Old utility and energy companies were likened by *Fortune* magazine to "a bunch of old fogies and their wives shuffling around to the sounds of Guy Lombardo." Enron was likened to a young Elvis Presley "crashing through the skylight" in his skintight gold-lamé suit. The writer left out the part where Elvis ate himself to death. Enron set the standard for thinking outside the box—the quintessential killer app, paradigm-shifting company. Unfortunately, it also set new standards for obfuscation and deception.

One of the scams perpetrated by Enron management was the establishment of a myriad of complex partnerships that obfuscated the true financial position of the firm and led to an overstatement of Enron's earnings. Here is how one of the simpler ones worked. Enron formed a joint venture with Blockbuster to rent out movies online. The deal failed several months later. But after the venture was formed, Enron secretly set up a partnership with a Canadian bank which essentially lent Enron $115 million in exchange for future profits from the Blockbuster venture. Of course, the Blockbuster deal never made a nickel but Enron counted the $115 million loan as a "profit." Wall Street analysts applauded and called Ken Lay, Enron's chairman, the "mastermind of the year."

Other partnerships, with names like Cheruco (named for Chewbacca, the *Star Wars* Wookie), Raptor, and Jedi, had similar effects, since the Force was clearly with Enron. Before the law caught up with him, the Force appeared to be with Andrew Fastow, Enron's chief financial officer, who made $30 million in fees for running what were supposedly independent partnerships. All the partnerships were kept off Enron's financial statements. This had the effect of inflating earnings, while keeping losses and enormous amounts of debt obscured from view. The accounting firm of Arthur Andersen certified the books as "fairly stating" Enron's financial condition. And Wall Street was delighted to collect lucrative fees from the creative partnerships that were established.

Deception appeared to be a way of life at Enron. The *Wall Street Journal* reported that Ken Lay and Jeff Skilling, Enron's top executives, were personally involved in establishing a fake trading room to impress Wall Street security analysts, in an episode employees referred to as "The Sting." The best equipment was purchased, employees were given parts to play arranging fictitious deals, and even the phone lines were painted black to make the operation look particularly slick. Rehearsals were held and Jeff Skilling, by personal choice, was given the role of Paul Newman's character in *The Sting*. The whole thing was an elaborate charade.

Lay and Skilling were particularly effective as promoters. They vigorously and consistently touted their stock as "undervalued," not only to the public at large but even to their own loyal employees. At the same time, they were selling hundreds of thousands of their own shares to an unsuspecting public and pocketing millions of dollars. When asked about such inconsistency at congressional hearings, Skilling opined that he knew of no difficulties—he thought all operations at Enron were just fine. Ken Lay took the Fifth Amendment. One employee, who lost his job and his retirement savings when Enron collapsed into bankruptcy, got some measure of revenge by starting a new company offering a product particularly attractive to former Enron employees, T-shirts with the message "I GOT LAY'D BY ENRON," which were sold on his Web site layoff.com.

But Enron was only one of a number of accounting frauds that were perpetrated on unsuspecting investors during the bubble. Various telecom companies overstated revenues through swaps of fiber-optic capacity at inflated prices. Tyco created "cookie jar" reserves and accelerated pre-merger outlays to "springload" earnings from acquisitions. And WorldCom admitted that it had overstated profits and cash flow by $7 billion, by classifying ordinary expenses that should have been charged against earnings as capital investments that were not deducted from the bottom line. In far too many cases corporate chief executive officers (CEOs) acted more like chief embezzlement officers and some chief financial officers (CFOs) could more appropriately be called corporate fraud officers. While analysts were praising stocks like Enron and WorldCom to the skies, some corporate officers were transforming the meaning of EBITDA from earnings before interest, taxes, depreciation, and amortization to "earnings before I tricked the dumb auditor." These scandals shook investors' faith in our corporate executives and in the watchdog functions provided by boards of directors, auditors, and the financial community. They also led to a number of reforms that should lessen the widespread conflicts of interest involving managers, accountants, boards, and security analysts.

Should We Have Known the Dangers?

Fraud aside, we should have known better. We should have known that investments in transforming technologies have often proved unrewarding for investors. In the 1850s, the railroad was widely expected to greatly increase the efficiency of communications and commerce. It certainly did so, but it did not justify the prices of railroad stocks, which increased to enormous speculative heights before collapsing in August

1857. Electricity in the early twentieth century had profound effects on the layout and design of factories and led to a large increase in the productive efficiency of the economy. But throughout the first two decades of the century, electric utilities were poor investments. In the early days of the automobile, we had close to 100 automobile companies, and most of them became roadkill. Similarly, the radio in the 1920s promised to create a revolution in communications and commerce. As we have seen, even the stock of RCA, the only company that successfully built a profitable business from radio, lost 97 percent of its value between 1929 and 1933. Similarly, airlines and television manufacturers transformed our country, but most of the early investors lost their shirts. The key to investing is not how much industry will affect society or even how much it will grow, but rather its ability to make and sustain profits.

And history tells us that eventually all excessively exuberant markets succumb to the laws of gravity. Moreover, the Internet itself is a destroyer of costs, and one of the costs that is destroyed is profits. While the Internet is an efficient revealer of prices in all products and services, there was no reason to think that Internet companies would be rewarded with large profits. Internet companies can only succeed with razor-thin margins. And one can't count on the power of the "first mover." Neither the first computer company (Univac) nor the first Internet service provider (Netcom) prevailed. The same low barriers that enabled Amazon to challenge traditional booksellers must make the present leaders of the Net vulnerable to low-cost upstarts. While the Internet can deliver billions of dollars of savings to consumers and businesses, investors in Net stocks had no reason to count on the same rewards. Amazon became a very successful retailer, but investors in Amazon's stock at the height of the bubble lost more than 90 percent of their capital when sanity returned to the stock market.

Why are memories so short? Why do such speculative crazes seem so isolated from the lessons of history? I have no apt answer to offer, but I am convinced that Bernard Baruch was correct in suggesting that a study of these events can help equip investors for survival. The consistent losers in the market, from my personal experience, are those who are unable to resist being swept up in some kind of tulip-bulb craze. It is not hard, really, to make money in the market. As we shall see later, an investor who simply buys and holds a broad-based portfolio of stocks can make reasonably generous long-run returns. What is hard to avoid is the alluring temptation to throw your money away on short, get-rich-quick speculative binges.

There were many villains in this morality tale: the fee-obsessed underwriters who should have known better than to peddle all of the crap they brought to market; the research analysts who were the cheerleaders for the banking departments and who were eager to recommend Net stocks that could be pushed by commission-hungry brokers; corporate executives using "creative accounting" to inflate their profits. But it was the infectious greed of individual investors and their susceptibility to get-rich-quick schemes that allowed the bubble to expand.

And yet the melody lingers on. I have a friend who built a modest investment stake into a small fortune with a diversified portfolio of bonds, real estate funds, and stock funds that owned a broad selection of blue-chip companies. But he was restless. At cocktail parties he kept running into people boasting about this Net stock that tripled or that telecom chipmaker that doubled. He wanted some of the action. Along came a stock called Boo.com, an Internet retailer that planned to sell with no discounts "urban chic clothing—that was so cool it wasn't even cool yet." In other words, Boo.com was going to sell clothes that people were not yet wearing at full price. But my friend had seen the cover of *Time* with the headline "Kiss Your Mall Goodbye: Online Shopping Is Faster, Cheaper, and Better." The prestigious firm of JP Morgan had invested millions in the company and *Fortune* called it one of the "cool companies of 1999."

My friend was hooked. "This Boo.com story will have all the tape watchers drooling with excitement and conjuring up visions of castles in the air. Any delay in buying would be self-defeating." And so my friend had to rush in before greater fools would tread.

The company blew through $135 million in two years before going bankrupt. The co-founder, answering charges that her firm spent too extravagantly, explained: "I only flew Concorde three times, and they were all special offers." Of course, my friend had bought in just at the height of the bubble, and he lost his entire investment when the firm declared bankruptcy. The ability to avoid such horrendous mistakes is probably the most important factor in preserving one's capital and allowing it to grow. The lesson is so obvious and yet so easy to ignore.

A Final Word

Probably more so than any other chapter in the book, this review of the Internet bubble seems inconsistent with the view that the stock market is rational and efficient. The lesson from this chapter, it seems to me, is not that markets occasionally can be irrational and, therefore, that we should abandon the firm-foundation theory. Rather, the clear conclusion is that, in every case, the market did correct itself. The market eventually corrects any irrationality—albeit in its own slow, inexorable fashion. Anomalies can crop up, markets can get irrationally optimistic, and often they attract unwary investors. But eventually, true value is recognized by the market, and this is the main lesson investors must heed.

I am also persuaded by the wisdom of Benjamin Graham, author of *Security Analysis*, who wrote that in the final analysis the stock market is not a voting mechanism but a weighing mechanism. Valuation metrics have not changed. Eventually, every stock can only be worth the value of the cash flow it is able to earn for the benefit of investors. In the final analysis, true value will win out.

5

The Firm-Foundation
Theory
of Stock Prices

The greatest of all gifts is the power to estimate things at their
true worth.
> —La Rochefoucauld, *Reflexions; ou sentences
> et maximes morales*

Investors can and should learn vicariously
from the stock market. The historical reviews in chapters 2, 3,
and 4 should provide sufficient warning to save you from the
traps that ensnare builders of castles in the air. Autopsies
should be as useful in the practice of investment as in medicine. At the same time, to be forewarned is not to be forearmed
in the investment world. Investors also need a sense of justification for market prices—a standard, even if only a very loose
one, with which to compare current market prices. Is there
such a thing? I happen to think so—though I believe it neither
rests on a firm foundation nor floats like a castle in the air.

The firm-foundation theorists, who include many of Wall
Street's best security analysts, know full well that purely psychic
support for market valuations has proved a most undependable
pillar, and skyrocketing markets have invariably succumbed to
the financial laws of gravity. Therefore, many security analysts
devote their energies to estimating a stock's firm foundation of
value. Let's see what lies behind such estimates.

The "Fundamental" Determinants of Stock Prices

What is it that determines the real or intrinsic value of a share? What are the so-called fundamentals that security analysts look at in estimating a security's firm foundation of value?

I said in the first chapter that firm-foundation theorists view the worth of any share as the present value of all dollar benefits the investor expects to receive from it. Remember that the word "present" indicates that a distinction must be made between dollars expected immediately and those anticipated later on, which must be "discounted." All future income is worth less than money in hand; for if you had the money now you could be earning interest on it. In a very real sense, time is money.

In arriving at their value estimates, firm-foundation theorists usually take the standpoint of a very long-term investor who buys his shares "for keeps." One may buy 100 shares of IBM at $75 per share hoping that someone will come along later to purchase them from you at $100. But far less speculative estimates of value can be made by looking at the long-run flow of IBM dividends.

During the great bull market of the late 1990s, however, dividends appeared far less important than capital gains to investors. Indeed, many corporations preferred to institute stock buy-back programs rather than increase their dividends. When a corporation buys back its stock, fewer shares are outstanding and thus earnings per share and price per share are likely to be higher. Hence, buybacks tend to increase capital gains and the growth rate of the company's earnings and stock price. Corporate managers who receive a major share of their compensation through stock options naturally favor the buyback approach because it makes their options more valuable. We shall see in the discussion that follows how this practice can be accommodated in arriving at intrinsic-value estimates. The starting point, however, focuses on the stream of cash dividends the company pays. The worth of a share is taken to be the present or discounted value of all the future dividends the firm is expected to pay.

Of course, the price of a common stock is dependent on a number of factors. I believe there are four determinants affecting share value, and I describe them below. For each, I give a broad rule that will help you determine the value of any stock you are considering. If you follow these rules consistently, firm-foundation theorists believe you will find yourself safe from the speculative crazes I have just described.

Determinant 1: The expected growth rate. Most people don't realize the implications of compound growth on financial decisions. Albert Einstein once described compound interest as the "greatest mathematical discovery of all time." It is often said that the Native American who sold Manhattan Island in 1626 for $24 was rooked by the white man. In fact, he may have been an extremely sharp salesman. Had he put his $24 away at 6 percent interest, compounded semiannually, it would now be worth about $100 billion, and with it his descendants could buy back much of the now-improved land. Such is the magic of compound growth!

Similarly, the implications of various growth rates for the size of future dividends may be surprising to many readers. As the table below shows, growth at a 15 percent rate means that dividends will double every five years.* Alternate rates are also presented.

Growth Rate of Dividends	Present Dividend	Dividend in 5 Years	Dividend in 10 Years	Dividend in 25 Years
5 %	$1.00	$1.28	$1.63	$ 3.39
15 %	1.00	2.01	4.05	32.92
25 %	1.00	3.05	9.31	264.70

The catch (and doesn't there always have to be at least one, if not twenty-two?) is that dividend growth does not go on forever. Corporations and industries have life cycles similar to most living things. There is, for corporations in particular, a high mortality rate at birth. Survivors can look forward to rapid growth, maturity, and then a period of stability. Later in the life cycle, companies eventually decline and either perish or undergo a substantial metamorphosis. Consider the leading corporations in the United States over 100 years ago. Such

---

*A handy rule for calculating how many years it takes dividends to double is to divide 72 by the long-term growth rate. Thus, if dividends grow at 15 percent per year, they will double in a bit less than five years (72 ÷ 15).

names as Eastern Buggy Whip Company, La Crosse and Minnesota Steam Packet Company, Lobdell Car Wheel Company,
Savanna and St. Paul Steamboat Line, and Hazard Powder
Company, the already mature enterprises of the time, would
have ranked high in a Fortune Top 500 list of that era. All are
now deceased.

Look at the industry record. Railroads, the most dynamic
growth industry a century ago, finally matured and enjoyed a
long period of prosperity before entering their recent period of
decline. The paper and aluminum industries provide more
recent examples of the cessation of rapid growth and the start
of a more stable, mature period in the life cycle. These industries were the most rapidly growing in the United States during
the 1940s and early 1950s. By the 1960s, they were no longer
able to grow any faster than the economy as a whole. Similarly,
the most rapidly growing industry of the late 1950s and 1960s,
electric equipment, had slowed to a crawl by the 1970s and
1980s. The manufacturers of personal computers and their
components, which grew rapidly during the late 1980s and
1990s, saw their growth rates begin to decline during the late
1990s.

And even if the natural life cycle doesn't get a company,
there's always the fact that it gets harder and harder to grow at
the same percentage rate. A company earning $1 million need
increase its earnings by only $100,000 to achieve a 10 percent
growth rate, whereas a company starting from a base of $10 mil-
lion in earnings needs $1 million in additional earnings to pro-
duce the same record.

The nonsense of relying on very high long-term growth
rates is nicely illustrated by working with population projections for the United States. If the populations of the nation and
of California continue to grow at their recent rates, 120 percent
of the United States population will live in California by the
year 2035! Using similar kinds of projections, it can be estimated that at the same time 240 percent of the people in the
country with venereal disease will live in California. As one
Californian put it on hearing these forecasts, "Only the former
projections make the latter one seem at all plausible."

As hazardous as projections may be, share prices must
reflect differences in growth prospects if any sense is to be

made of market valuations. Also, the probable length of the growth phase is very important. If one company expects to enjoy a rapid 20 percent growth rate for ten years, and another growth company expects to sustain the same rate for only five years, the former company is, other things being equal, more valuable to the investor than the latter. The point is that growth rates are general rather than gospel truths. And this brings us to the firm-foundation theorists' first rule for evaluating securities:

Rule 1: A rational investor should be willing to pay a higher price for a share the larger the growth rate of dividends and earnings.

To this is added an important corollary:

Corollary to Rule 1: A rational investor should be willing to pay a higher price for a share the longer an extraordinary growth rate is expected to last.

Determinant 2: The expected dividend payout. The amount of dividends you receive at each payout—as contrasted to their growth rate—is readily understandable as being an important factor in determining a stock's price. The higher the dividend payout, other things being equal, the greater the value of the stock. The catch here is the phrase "other things being equal." Stocks that pay out a high percentage of earnings in dividends may be poor investments if their growth prospects are unfavorable. Conversely, many companies in their most dynamic growth phase often pay out little or none of their earnings in dividends. And as noted above, many companies tend to buy back their shares rather than increasing their dividends. For two companies whose expected growth rates are the same, you are better off with the one whose dividend payout is higher.

Beware of the stock dividend. This provides no benefits whatever. The practice is employed on the pretext that the firm is preserving cash for expansion while providing dividends in the form of additional shares. Stockholders presumably like to receive new pieces of paper—it gives them a warm feeling that the firm's managers are interested in their welfare. Some even think that by some alchemy the stock dividend increases the worth of their holdings.

In actuality, only the printer profits from the stock dividend.

To distribute a 100 percent stock dividend, a firm must print one additional share for each share outstanding. But with twice as many shares outstanding, each share represents only half the interest in the company that it formerly did. Earnings per share and all other relevant per-share statistics about the company are now halved. This unit change is the only result of a stock dividend. Stockholders should not greet with any joy the declaration of stock splits or dividends—unless these are accompanied by higher cash dividends or news of higher earnings.

The only conceivable advantage of a stock split (or large stock dividend) is that lowering the price level of the shares might induce more public investors to purchase them. People like to buy in 100-share lots, and if a stock's price is very high many investors feel excluded. But 2 and 3 percent stock dividends, which are often declared, do no good at all.

The distribution of new certificates for stock dividends brings up the whole concept of actual certificates of ownership. This is an incredibly cumbersome and archaic system and should be eliminated. Records of ownership could easily be kept on the memory disks of large computers. Most bonds and some stocks are actually recorded that way now. If stockholders could rid themselves of their atavistic longing for pretty, embossed certificates, the securities industry could reduce its paperwork burden, and environmentalists could congratulate themselves on another victory.

Now that I've got that off my chest, let's sum up by printing the second rule:

> Rule 2: A rational investor should be willing to pay a higher price for a share, other things being equal, the larger the proportion of a company's earnings that is paid out in cash dividends.

Determinant 3: The degree of risk. Risk plays an important role in the stock market, no matter what your overeager broker may tell you. There is always a risk—and that's what makes it so fascinating. Risk also affects the valuation of a stock. Some people think risk is the only aspect of a stock to be examined.

The more respectable a stock is—that is, the less risk it has—the higher its quality. Stocks of the so-called blue-chip companies, for example, are said to deserve a quality premium.

(Why high-quality stocks are given an appellation derived from the poker tables is a fact known only to Wall Street.) Most investors prefer less risky stocks and, therefore, these stocks can command higher price-earnings multiples than their risky, low-quality counterparts.

Although there is general agreement that the compensation for higher risk must be greater future rewards (and thus lower current prices), measuring risk is well-nigh impossible. This has not daunted the economist, however. A great deal of attention has been devoted to risk measurement by both academic economists and practitioners. Indeed, risk measurement is so important that chapter 10 is largely devoted to this subject.

According to one well-known theory, the bigger the swings—relative to the market as a whole—in an individual company's stock prices (or in its total yearly returns, including dividends), the greater the risk. For example, a nonswinger such as Johnson & Johnson gets the *Good Housekeeping* seal of approval for "widows and orphans." That's because its earnings do not decline much if at all during recessions, and its dividend is secure. Therefore, when the market goes down 20 percent, J&J usually trails with perhaps only a 10 percent decline. Thus, the stock qualifies as one with less than average risk. Cisco Systems, on the other hand, has a very volatile past record and it characteristically falls by 40 percent or more when the market declines by 20 percent. It is called a "flyer," or an investment that is a "businessman's risk." The investor gambles in owning stock in such a company, particularly if he may be forced to sell out during a time of unfavorable market conditions.

When business is good and the market mounts a sustained upward drive, however, Cisco can be expected to outdistance J&J. But if you are like most investors, you value stable returns over speculative hopes, freedom from worry about your portfolio over sleepless nights, and limited loss exposure over the possibility of a downhill roller-coaster ride. You will prefer the more stable security, other things being the same. This leads to a third basic rule of security valuation:

Rule 3: A rational (and risk-averse) investor should be willing to pay a higher price for a share, other things being equal, the less risky the company's stock.

I should warn the reader that a "relative volatility" measure may not fully capture the relevant risk of a company. Chapter 10 will present a thorough discussion of this important risk element in stock valuation.

Determinant 4: The level of market interest rates. The stock market, no matter how much it may think so, does not exist as a world unto itself. Investors should consider how much profit they can obtain elsewhere. Interest rates, if they are high enough, can offer a stable, profitable alternative to the stock market. Consider periods such as the early 1980s when yields on prime-quality corporate bonds soared to close to 15 percent. Long-term bonds of somewhat lower quality were being offered at even higher interest rates. The expected returns from stock prices had trouble matching these bond rates; money flowed into bonds while stock prices fell sharply. Finally, stock prices reached such a low level that a sufficient number of investors were attracted to stem the decline. Again in 1987, interest rates rose substantially, preceding the great stock-market crash of October 19. To put it another way, to attract investors from high-yielding bonds, stock must offer bargain-basement prices.*

On the other hand, when interest rates are very low, fixed-interest securities provide very little competition for the stock market and stock prices tend to be relatively high. This provides justification for the last rule of the firm-foundation theory:

Rule 4: A rational investor should be willing to pay a higher price for a share, other things being equal, the lower are interest rates.

---

*The point can be made another way by noting that because higher interest rates enable us to earn more now, any deferred income should be "discounted" more heavily. Thus, the present value of any flow of future dividend returns will be lower when current interest rates are relatively high. The relationship between interest rates and stock prices is somewhat more complicated, however, than this discussion may suggest. Suppose investors expect that the rate of inflation will increase from 5 to 10 percent. Such an expectation is likely to drive interest rates up by about 5 percentage points to compensate investors for holding fixed-dollar-obligation bonds whose purchasing power will be adversely affected by greater inflation. Other things being the same, this should make stock prices fall. But with higher expected inflation, investors may reasonably project that corporate earnings and dividends will also increase at a faster rate, causing stock prices to rise. A fuller discussion of inflation, interest rates, and stock prices is contained in chapter 13.

Two Important Caveats

The four valuation rules imply that a security's firm-foundation value (and its price-earnings multiple) will be higher the larger the company's growth rate and the longer its duration; the larger the dividend payout for the firm; the less risky the company's stock; and the lower the general level of interest rates.

As I indicated earlier, economists have taken rules such as these and expressed in a mathematical formula the exact price (present value) at which shares should sell. In principle, such theories are very useful in suggesting a rational basis for stock prices and in giving investors some standard of value. Of course, the rules must be compared with the facts to see if they conform at all to reality, and I will get to that in a moment. But before we even think of using and testing these rules in a very precise way, there are two important caveats to bear in mind.

Caveat 1: Expectations about the future cannot be proven in the present. Remember, not even Jeane Dixon can accurately predict all of the future. Yet some people have absolute faith in security analysts' estimates of the long-term growth prospects of a company and the duration of that growth.

Predicting future earnings and dividends is a most hazardous occupation. It requires not only the knowledge and skill of an economist but also the acumen of a psychologist. On top of that, it is extremely difficult to be objective; wild optimism and extreme pessimism constantly battle for top place. During the early 1960s, when the economy and the world situation were relatively stable, investors had no trouble convincing themselves that the coming decade would be soaring and prosperous. As a result, very high growth rates were projected for a large number of corporations. Years later, in 1980, the economy was suffering from severe "stagflation" and an unstable international situation. The best that investors could do that year was to project modest growth rates for most corporations. During the Internet bubble, in the late 1990s, investors convinced themselves that a new era of high growth and unlimited prosperity was a foregone conclusion.

The point to remember is that no matter what formula you

use for predicting the future, it always rests in part on the indeterminate premise. Although many Wall Streeters claim to see into the future, they are just as fallible as the rest of us. As Samuel Goldwyn once said, "Forecasts are difficult to make— particularly those about the future."

Caveat 2: Precise figures cannot be calculated from undetermined data. It stands to reason that you can't obtain precise figures by using indefinite factors. Yet to achieve desired ends, investors and security analysts do this all the time. Here's how it's done.

Take a company that you've heard lots of good things about. You study the company's prospects, and suppose you conclude that it can maintain a high growth rate for a long period. How long? Well, why not ten years?

You then calculate what the stock should be "worth" on the basis of the current dividend payout, the expected future growth rate of dividends, and the general level of interest rates, perhaps making an allowance for the riskiness of the shares. It turns out to your chagrin that the price the stock is worth is just slightly less than its present market price.

You now have two alternatives. You could regard the stock as overpriced and refuse to buy it, or you could say, "Perhaps this stock could maintain a high growth rate for eleven years rather than ten. After all, the ten was only a guess in the first place, so why not eleven years?" And so you go back to your computer and lo and behold you now come up with a worth for the shares that is larger than the current market price. Armed with this "precise" knowledge, you make your sound purchase.

The reason the game worked is that the longer one projects growth, the greater is the stream of future dividends. Thus, the present value of a share is at the discretion of the calculator. If eleven years was not enough to do the trick, twelve or thirteen might well have sufficed. There is always some combination of growth rate and growth period that will produce any specific price. In this sense, it is intrinsically impossible, given human nature, to calculate the intrinsic value of a share.

J. Peter Williamson, author of an excellent textbook for financial analysts entitled *Investments*, provides another example. Williamson estimated the present (or firm-foundation) value of IBM shares by using the same general principle of valuation I have described above; that is, by estimating how fast IBM's dividends would grow and for how long. At the time IBM was one of the premier growth stocks in the country, Williamson first made the seemingly sensible assumption that IBM would grow at a fairly high rate for some number of years before falling into a much smaller mature growth rate. When he made his estimate, IBM was selling at a pre-split price of $320 per share.

> I began by forecasting growth in earnings per share at 16%. This was a little under the average for the previous ten years. . . . I forecast at 16% growth rate for 10 years, followed by indefinite growth at . . . 2%. . . . When I put all these numbers into the formula I got an intrinsic value of $172.94, about half of the current market value.

Since the intrinsic value and market value of IBM stock were so far apart, Williamson decided that perhaps his estimates of the future might not be accurate. He experimented further:

> It doesn't really seem sensible to predict only 10 years of above average growth for IBM, so I extended my 16% growth forecast to 20 years. Now the intrinsic value came to $432.66, well above the market.

Had Williamson opted for thirty years of above-average growth, he would be projecting IBM to generate a future sales volume of about half the then-current U.S. national income. In fact, we know that IBM stopped growing in the mid-1980s and that it reported some enormous losses in the early 1990s before a vigorous recovery started in 1994 under new management.

The point to remember from such examples is that the mathematical precision of the firm-foundation value formulas is based on treacherous ground: forecasting the future. The major fundamentals for these calculations are never known with certainty; they are only relatively crude estimates—perhaps one should say guesses—about what might happen in the future. And depending on what guesses you make, you can convince yourself to pay any price you want to for a stock.

There is, I believe, a fundamental indeterminateness about the value of common shares even in principle. God Almighty does not know the proper price-earnings multiple for a common stock.

Testing the Rules

With the rules and caveats in mind, let us take a closer look at stock prices and examine whether the rules seem to conform to actual practices. Let's start with Rule 1: the larger the anticipated growth rate, the higher the price of a share.

To begin, we'll reformulate the question in terms of price-earnings (P/E) multiples rather than the market prices themselves. This provides a good yardstick for comparing stocks— which have different prices and earnings—against one another. A stock selling at $100 per share with earnings of $10 per share would have the same P/E multiple (10) as a stock selling at $40 with earnings of $4 per share. It is the P/E multiple, not the dollar price, that really tells you how a stock is valued in the market.

Our reformulated question now reads: Are actual price-earnings multiples higher for stocks for which a high growth rate is anticipated? A major study by John Cragg and myself strongly indicates that the answer is yes.

It was easy to collect the first half of the data required. P/E multiples are printed daily in papers such as the *New York Times* and the *Wall Street Journal*. To obtain information on expected long-term growth rates, we surveyed eighteen leading investment firms whose business it is to produce the forecasts on which buy and sell recommendations are made. (I'll describe later how they make these forecasts.) Estimates were obtained from each firm of the five-year growth rates anticipated for a large sample of stocks.

I will not bore you with the details of the actual statistical study that was performed. The 2002 results are illustrated, however, for a few representative securities in the following chart. It is clear that, just as Rule 1 asserts, high P/E ratios are associated with high expected growth rates. This general pattern has held up in every year since the 1960s, when we began the study.

In addition to demonstrating how the market values different growth rates, the chart can also be used as a practical investment guide. Suppose you were considering the purchase of a stock with an anticipated 20 percent growth rate and you knew

High Expected Long-Term Growth Rates
Push Price-Earnings Multiple Up*

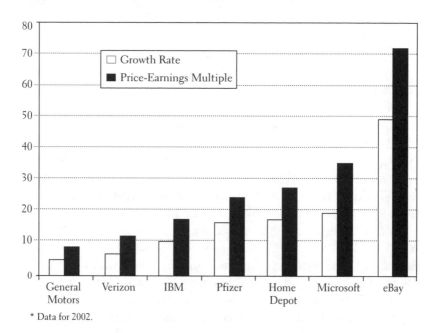

* Data for 2002.

that, on average, stocks with 20 percent growth sold, like Microsoft, at 36 times earnings. If the stock you were considering sold at a price-earnings multiple of 40, you might reject the idea of buying the stock in favor of one more reasonably priced in terms of current market norms. If, on the other hand, your stock sold at a multiple below the average in the market for that growth rate, the security is said to represent good value for your money. I'll return to the practical use of such techniques, as well as the pitfalls, at several later points.

How about rules 2, 3, and 4? Just as we were able to test for a relationship between earnings multiples and anticipated growth rates, it was also possible to collect the necessary data and find the ways in which not only growth, but dividend payout, risk, and interest rates influence price-earnings multiples in the market. The particular techniques used need not concern us. What is important to realize is that there does seem to be a logic to market valuations. Market prices seem to behave just as the four rules developed by the firm-foundation theorists would lead us to expect. It is comforting to know that at least to this extent there is an underlying rationality to the stock market.

One More Caveat

So market prices do seem to have an inherent logic. Stock prices are closely related to differential patterns of expected growth as well as to the other "fundamental" valuation influences so important to proponents of the firm-foundation theory. Yes, Virginia, it looks like there may be a firm foundation of value after all, and some jokers in Wall Street actually think you can make money knowing what it is.

Caveat 3: What's growth for the goose is not always growth for the gander. The difficulty comes with the value the market puts on specific fundamentals. It is always true that the market values growth, and that higher growth rates and larger multiples go hand in hand. But the crucial question is: How much more should you pay for higher growth?

There is no consistent answer. In some periods, as in the early 1960s and 1970s, when growth was thought to be especially desirable, the market has been willing to pay an enormous price for stocks exhibiting high-growth rates. At other times, such as the late 1980s and early 1990s, high-growth stocks commanded only a modest premium over the multiples of common stocks in general. By early 2000, the growth stocks making up the NASDAQ 100 Index sold at triple-digit price-earnings multiples. Growth can be as fashionable as tulip bulbs, as investors in growth stocks painfully learned.

From a practical standpoint, the rapid changes in market valuations that have occurred suggest that it would be very dangerous to use any one year's valuation relationships as an indication of market norms. However, by comparing how growth stocks are currently valued with historical precedent, investors should at least be able to isolate those periods when a touch of the tulip bug has smitten investors.

What's Left of the Firm Foundation?

A renowned rabbi, whose fame for adjudicating disputes had earned him the reputation of a modern-day Solomon, was asked to settle a long-standing argument between two philosophers. The rabbi listened intently as the first disputant vigorously presented his case. The rabbi reflected on the argument and finally pronounced, "Yes, you are correct." Then the second philosopher presented his case with equal vigor and persuasion and argued eloquently that the first philosopher could not be correct. The rabbi nodded his approval and indicated, "You are correct." A bystander, somewhat confused by this performance, accosted the rabbi to complain, "You told both philosophers they were right, but their arguments were totally contradictory. They both can't be correct." The rabbi needed only a moment to formulate his response: "Yes, you are indeed correct."

In adjudicating the dispute between the firm-foundation theorists and those who take a castle-in-the-air view of the stock market, I feel a little like the accommodating rabbi. It seems clear that so-called fundamental considerations do have a profound influence on market prices. We have seen that price-earnings multiples in the market are influenced by expected growth, dividend payouts, risk, and the rate of interest. Higher anticipations of earnings growth and higher dividend payouts tend to increase price-earnings multiples. Higher risk and higher interest rates tend to pull them down. There is a logic to the stock market, just as the firm foundationists assert.

Thus, when all is said and done, it appears that there is a yardstick for value, but one that is a most flexible and undependable instrument. To change the metaphor, stock prices are in a sense anchored to certain "fundamentals," but the anchor is easily pulled up and then dropped in another place. For the standards of value, we have found, are not the fixed and immutable standards that characterize the laws of physics, but rather the more flexible and fickle relationships that are consistent with a marketplace heavily influenced by mass psychology.

Not only does the market change the values it puts on the various fundamental determinants of stock prices, but the most important of these fundamentals are themselves liable to change depending on the state of market psychology. Stocks are bought on expectations—not on facts.

The most important fundamental influence on stock prices is the level and duration of the future growth of corporate earnings and dividends. But, as I pointed out earlier, future earnings growth is not easily estimated, even by market professionals. In times of great optimism, it is very easy for investors to convince themselves that their favorite corporations can enjoy substantial and persistent growth over an extended period of time. By raising his estimates of growth, even the most sober firm-foundation theorist can convince himself to pay any price whatever for a share.

During periods of extreme pessimism, many security analysts will not project any growth that is not "visible" to them over the very short run and hence will estimate only the most modest of growth rates for the corporations they follow. But if expected growth rates themselves and the price the market is willing to pay for this growth can both change rapidly on the basis of market psychology, then it is clear that the concept of a firm intrinsic value for shares must be an elusive will-o'-the-wisp. As an old Wall Street proverb runs: No price is too high for a bull or too low for a bear.

Dreams of castles in the air, of getting rich quick, may therefore play an important role in determining actual stock prices. And even investors who believe in the firm-foundation theory might buy a security on the anticipation that eventually the average opinion would expect a larger growth rate for the stock in the future. After all, investors who want to reap extraordinary profits may find that the most profitable course of action is to beat the gun and anticipate future changes in the intrinsic value of shares.

Still, this analysis suggests that the stock market will not be a perpetual tulip-bulb craze. The existence of some generally accepted principles of valuation does serve as a kind of balance wheel. For the castle-in-the-air investor might well consider that if prices get too far out of line with normal valuation standards, the average opinion may soon expect that others will anticipate a reaction. To be sure, these standards of value are extremely loose ones and difficult to estimate. But sooner or later in a skyrocketing market, some investors may begin to compare the growth rates that are implicit in current prices with more reasonable and dispassionate estimates of the growth likely to be achieved.

It seems eminently sensible to me that both views of security pricing tell us something about actual market behavior. But the important investment question is how you can use the theories to develop practically useful investment strategies. More about this in Part Two, where I take a close look at how the professionals use the two theories in their own investing, and in Part Three, where I examine the academic approach to investing.

PART TWO

How the Pros
Play the
Biggest Game
in Town

6
Technical and Fundamental Analysis

A picture is worth ten thousand words.

—Old Chinese proverb

On July 24, 2002, over 2.7 billion shares with a total market value of $75 billion were traded on the New York Stock Exchange. Exchanges of shares valued at $50 billion are now considered routine for a day's trading on the big board. And this is only part of the story. An even larger volume of trading is carried out on the NASDAQ market, and substantial numbers of shares are exchanged on the American Stock Exchange and on a variety of regional exchanges and electronic networks across the country. Professional investment analysts and counselors are involved in what has been called the biggest game in town.

If the stakes are high, so are the rewards. When Wall Street is having a good year, new trainees from the Harvard Business School routinely draw salaries of well more than $125,000 per year. Successful salesmen, euphemistically called "account executives" or "financial advisers" make considerably more. At the top of the salary scale are the high-profile securities analysts and the money managers themselves—the men and women who run the large mutual, pension, and trust funds. "Adam Smith," after writing *The Money Game*, boasted that he would make a quarter of a million dollars from his best-selling book. His Wall Street friends retorted, "You're only going to make as

much as a second-rate institutional salesman." It is fair to conclude that although not the oldest, the profession of high
finance is certainly one of the most generously compensated.

Part Two of this book concentrates on the methods and
results of the professionals of Wall Street, LaSalle Street, Mont-
gomery Street, and the various road-town financial centers. It
then shows how academics in towns like Princeton and Berke-
ley have analyzed these professional results and have concluded that they are not worth the money you pay for them.

Academicians are a notoriously picayune lot. With their
ringing motto, "Publish or perish," they keep themselves busy
by preparing papers demolishing other people's theories,
defending their own work, or constructing elaborate embel-
lishments to generally accepted ideas.

The efficient-market theory is a case in point. We now have
three versions—the "weak," the "semi-strong," and the
"strong." All three forms espouse the general idea that except
for long-run trends, future stock prices are difficult, if not
impossible, to predict. Therefore, stock investors can do no better than simply buying and holding a fund that owns a representative sample of all the stocks in the market. The weak form
says you cannot predict future stock prices on the basis of past
stock prices. This version asserts that stock prices behave very
much like a random walk. The semi-strong form says you cannot even utilize published information to predict future prices.
The strong version goes flat out and says that nothing—not
even unpublished developments—can be of use in predicting
future prices; everything that is known, or even knowable, has
already been reflected in present prices. The weak form attacks
the underpinnings of technical analysis, and the semi-strong
and strong forms argue against many of the beliefs held by
those using fundamental analysis.

Technical versus Fundamental Analysis

The attempt to predict accurately the future course of stock
prices and thus the appropriate time to buy or sell a stock must
rank as one of investors' most persistent endeavors. This search
for the golden egg has spawned a variety of methods ranging

from the scientific to the occult. There are people today who forecast future stock prices by measuring sunspots, looking at the phases of the moon, or measuring the vibrations along the San Andreas Fault. Most, however, opt for one of two methods: technical or fundamental analysis.

The alternative techniques used by the investment pros are related to the two theories of the stock market I covered in Part One. Technical analysis is the method of predicting the appropriate time to buy or sell a stock used by those believing in the castle-in-the-air view of stock pricing. Fundamental analysis is the technique of applying the tenets of the firm-foundation theory to the selection of individual stocks.

Technical analysis is essentially the making and interpreting of stock charts. Thus its practitioners, a small but abnormally dedicated cult, are called chartists. They study the past—both the movements of common stock prices and the volume of trading—for a clue to the direction of future change. Most chartists believe that the market is only 10 percent logical and 90 percent psychological. They generally subscribe to the castle-in-the-air school and view the investment game as one of anticipating how the other players will behave. Charts, of course, tell only what the other players have been doing in the past. The chartist's hope, however, is that a careful study of what the other players are doing will shed light on what the crowd is likely to do in the future.

Fundamental analysts take the opposite tack, believing the market is 90 percent logical and only 10 percent psychological. Caring little about the particular pattern of past price movement, fundamentalists seek to determine an issue's proper value. Value in this case is related to growth, dividend payout, interest rates, and risk, according to the rules of the firm-foundation theory outlined in the last chapter. By estimating such factors as the future growth for each company, the fundamentalist arrives at an estimate of a security's intrinsic value. If this is above the market price, then the investor is advised to buy. Fundamentalists believe that eventually the market will reflect accurately the security's real worth. Perhaps 90 percent of the Wall Street security analysts consider themselves fundamentalists. Many would argue that chartists are lacking in dignity and professionalism.

What Can Charts Tell You?

The first principle of technical analysis is that all information about earnings, dividends, and the future performance of a company is automatically reflected in the company's past market prices. A chart showing these prices and the volume of trading already comprises all the fundamental information, good or bad, that the security analyst can hope to know. The second principle is that prices tend to move in trends: A stock that is rising tends to keep on rising, whereas a stock at rest tends to remain at rest.

A true chartist doesn't even care to know what business or industry a company is in, as long as he or she can study its stock chart. A chart shaped in the form of an "inverted bowl" or "pennant" means the same for Microsoft as it does for Coca-Cola. Fundamental information on earnings and dividends is considered at best to be useless—and at worst a positive distraction. It is either of inconsequential importance for the pricing of the stock or, if it is important, it has already been reflected in the market days, weeks, or even months before the news has become public. For this reason, many chartists will not even read the newspaper except to follow the daily price quotations.

One of the original chartists, John Magee, operated from a small office in Springfield, Massachusetts, where even the windows were boarded up to prevent any outside influences from distracting his analysis. Magee was once quoted as saying, "When I come into this office I leave the rest of the world outside to concentrate entirely on my charts. This room is exactly the same in a blizzard as on a moonlit June evening. In here I can't possibly do myself and my clients the disservice of saying 'buy' simply because the sun is out or 'sell' because it is raining."

As shown in the figure opposite, you can easily construct a chart. You simply draw a vertical line whose bottom is the stock's low for the day and whose top is the high. This line is crossed to indicate the closing price for the day. In the figure, the stock had a range of quotations that day between 20 and 21 and closed at 20½. The process can be repeated for each trading day. It can be used for individual stocks or for one of the stock averages that you see in the financial pages of most newspapers.

Often the chartist will indicate the volume of shares of

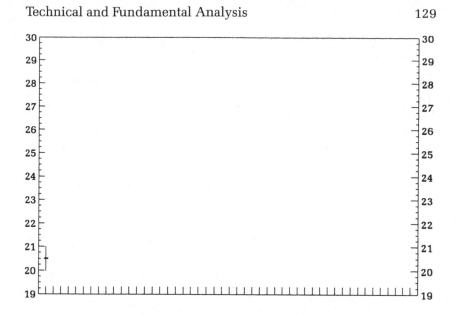

stock traded during the day by another vertical line at the bottom of the chart. Gradually, the highs and lows on the chart of the stock in question jiggle up and down sufficiently to produce patterns. To the chartist, these patterns have the same significance as X-ray plates to a surgeon.

One of the first things the chartist looks for is a trend. The figure below shows one in the making. It is the record of price

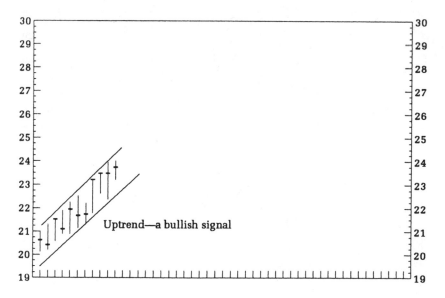

Uptrend—a bullish signal

changes for a stock over a number of days—and the prices are obviously on the way up. The chartist draws two lines connecting the tops and bottoms, creating a "channel" to delineate the uptrend. Because the presumption is that momentum in the market will tend to perpetuate itself, the chartist interprets such a pattern as a bullish augury—the stock can be expected to continue to rise. As Magee wrote in the bible of charting, *Technical Analysis of Stock Trends*, "Prices move in trends, and trends tend to continue until something happens to change the supply-demand balance."

Suppose, however, that at about 24, the stock finally runs into trouble and is unable to gain any further ground. This is called a resistance level. The stock may wiggle around a bit and then turn downward. One pattern, which chartists claim reveals a clear signal that the market has topped out, is a head-and-shoulders formation (shown in the next figure.)

The stock first rises and then falls slightly, forming a rounded shoulder. It rises again, going slightly higher, before once more receding, forming a head. Finally the right shoulder is formed, and chartists wait with bated breath for the sell signal, which sounds loud and clear when the stock "pierces the neckline." With the glee of Count Dracula surveying one of his victims, the chartists are off and selling, anticipating that a pro-

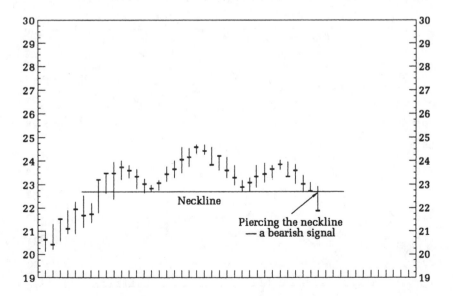

longed downtrend will follow as it allegedly has in the past. Of course, sometimes the market surprises the chartist. For example, the stock may make an end run up to 30 right after giving a bear signal, as shown in the following chart. This is called a bear trap or, to the chartist, the exception that tests the rule.

It follows from the technique that the chartist is a trader, not a long-term investor. The chartist buys when the auguries look favorable and sells on bad omens. He flirts with stocks just as some flirt with the opposite sex, and his scores are successful in-and-out trades, not rewarding long-term commitments. Indeed, the psychiatrist Don D. Jackson, author with Albert Haas, Jr., of *Bulls, Bears and Dr. Freud*, suggested that such an individual may be playing a game with overt sexual overtones.

When the chartist chooses a stock for potential investment there is typically a period of observation and flirtation before he commits himself, because for the chartist—as in romance and sexual conquest—timing is essential. There is mounting excitement as the stock penetrates the base formation and rises higher. Finally, if the affair has gone well, there is the moment of fulfillment—profit-taking, and the release and afterglow that follow. The chartist's vocabulary features such terms as "double bottoms," "breakthrough," "violating the lows," "firmed up," "big play," "ascending peaks," and "buying climax." And

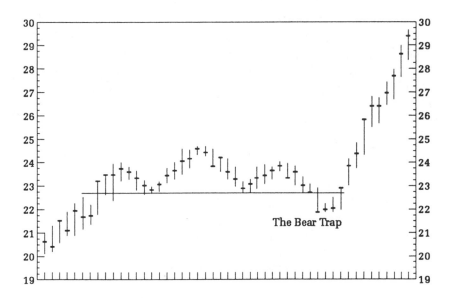

The Bear Trap

all this takes place under the pennant of that great symbol of sexuality: the bull.

The Rationale for the Charting Method

Probably the hardest question to answer is: Why is charting supposed to work? Some of my best friends are chartists and I have listened very carefully to their explanations, but I have yet really to understand them. Indeed, many chartists freely admit that they don't know why charting should work—history just has a habit of repeating itself. Even Magee, the chartist seer, went so far as to say that we can never hope to know "why" the market behaves as it does, we can only aspire to understand "how."

According to Magee, the situation in the stock market is analogous to that of a pig in a barn. The barn is all closed up on the ground floor, but it has a hayloft above with a large open door. The pig has a harness around his body to which is attached a long pole, the top of which is visible through the hayloft door. Of course, when the pig moves about, so will the pole. Magee supposed that we are perched in a nearby tree observing the motions of the top of the pole, which is all we can see. We must deduce from the pole's movement what is happening below, just as market participants must deduce what is happening in the market from the price movements they can observe. Magee went on to say that it is not important to know the color or size of the pig, or even whether it is a pig at all; it is only important to be able to make predictions about the next movement of the pole.

> Some of the watchers who are not comfortable with highly abstract symbols will assign "meanings" to the pole's movements. They will try to "interpret" these movements as corresponding to various assimilative, combative, copulative, etc., actions of the pig. Others [like Magee, the author], who might consider themselves "pure technicians," will watch the pole, and work entirely on the basis of what the pole has done, is doing, or might be expected to do according to trends, repetitive motions, extrapolations, etc.

Yet it is in our nature to ask why. To me, the following explanations of technical analysis appear to be the most plausible. Trends might tend to perpetuate themselves for either of two reasons. First, it has been argued that the crowd instinct of mass psychology makes it so. When investors see the price of a speculative favorite going higher and higher, they want to jump on the bandwagon and join the rise. Indeed, the price rise itself helps fuel the enthusiasm in a self-fulfilling prophecy. Each rise in price just whets the appetite and makes investors expect a further rise.

Second, there may be unequal access to fundamental information about a company. When some favorable piece of news occurs, such as the discovery of a rich mineral deposit, it is alleged that the insiders are the first to know and they act, buying the stock and causing its price to rise. The insiders then tell their friends, who act next. Then the professionals find out the news and the big institutions put blocks of the shares in their portfolios. Finally, the poor slobs like you and me get the information and buy, pushing the price still higher. This process is supposed to result in a rather gradual increase in the price of the stock when the news is good and a decrease when the news is bad. Chartists claim that this scenario is somewhat close to what actually happened in the notorious Texas Gulf Sulphur case, in which insiders profited on the basis of nonpublic information. Chartists are convinced that even if they do not have access to this inside information, observation of price movements alone enables them to pick up the scent of the "smart money" and permits them to get in long before the general public.

Chartists believe that another reason their techniques have validity is that people have a nasty habit of remembering what they paid for a stock, or the price they wish they had paid. For example, suppose a stock sold for about $50 a share for a long period of time, during which a number of investors bought in. Suppose then that the price drops to $40.

The chartists claim that the public will be anxious to sell out the shares when they rise back to the price at which they were bought, and thus break even on the trade. Consequently, the price of $50 at which the stock sold initially becomes a "resistance area." Each time the resistance area is reached and the stock turns down again, the theory holds that the resistance level becomes even harder to cross, because more and more investors get the idea that the market or the individual stock in question cannot go any higher.

A similar argument lies behind the notion of "support levels." Chartists say that many investors who failed to buy when the market fluctuated around a relatively low price level will feel they have missed the boat when prices rise. Presumably such investors will jump at the chance to buy when prices drop back to the original low level.

Chartists also believe that investors who sold shares when the market was low and then saw prices rise will be anxious to buy those shares back if they can get them again at the price for which they sold. The argument then is that the original low price level becomes a "support area," because investors will believe that prices will again rise above that level. In chart theory, a support area that holds on successive declines becomes stronger and stronger. So if a stock declines to a support area and then begins to rise, the traders will jump in believing the stock is just "coming off the pad." Another bullish signal is flashed when a stock finally breaks through a resistance area. In the lexicon of the chartists, the former resistance area becomes a support area, and the stock should have no trouble gaining further ground.

Why Might Charting Fail to Work?

It is easier for me to present the logical arguments against charting. First, it should be noted that the chartist buys in only after price trends have been established, and sells only after they have been broken. Because sharp reversals in the market may occur quite suddenly, the chartist often misses the boat. By the time an uptrend is signaled, it may already have taken place. Second, such techniques must ultimately be self-defeating. As more and more people use it, the value of any technique depreciates. No buy or sell signal can be worthwhile if everyone tries to act on it simultaneously.

Moreover, traders tend to anticipate technical signals. If they see a price about to break through a resistance area, they tend to buy before, not after, it breaks through. If it ever was profitable to use such charting techniques, it will now be possible only for those who anticipate the signals. This suggests that others will try to anticipate the signal still earlier. Of course, the earlier they anticipate, the less certain they are that the signal will occur, and in the scrambling to anticipate signals it is doubtful that any profitable technical trading rules can be developed.

Perhaps the most telling argument against technical methods comes from the logical implications of profit-maximizing behavior on the part of investors. Suppose, for example, that Universal Polymers is selling at around 20 when Sam, the chief research chemist, discovers a new production technique that promises to double the company's earnings and stock price. Now Sam is convinced that the price of Universal will hit 40 when the news of his discovery comes out. Because any purchases below 40 will provide a swift profit, he may well buy up all the stock he can until the price hits 40, a process that could take no longer than a few minutes.

Even if Sam doesn't have enough money to drive up the price himself, surely his friends and the financial institutions do have the funds to move the price so rapidly that no chartist could get into the act before the whole play is gone. The point is that the market may well be a most efficient mechanism. If some people know that the price will go to 40 tomorrow, it will go to 40 today. Of course, if Sam makes a public announcement of his discovery as the law requires, the argument holds with even greater force. Prices may adjust so quickly to new information as to make the whole process of technical analysis a futile exercise. In the next chapter, I'll examine whether the evidence supports such a pessimistic view of charting.

From Chartist to Technician

Although chartists are not held in high repute on Wall Street, their colorful methods, suggesting an easy way to get rich quick, have attracted a wide following. The companies that manufacture and distribute stock charts and the computer programmers who provide charting software for individuals, securities firms, and financial news networks such as CNBC, Bloomberg, and CNNfn have enjoyed a boom in their sales, and chartists themselves still find excellent employment opportunities with mutual funds and brokerage firms.

In the days before the computer, the laborious task of charting a course through the market was done by hand. Chartists were often viewed as peculiar people, with green eyeshades and carbon on their fingers, who were tucked away in a small closet at the back of the office. Now chartists have the services of a marvelous personal computer, hooked into a variety of data networks and replete with a large display terminal which, at the tap of a finger, can produce any conceivable chart one might want to see. The chartist (now always called a technician) can, with the glee of a little child playing with a new electric train, produce a complete chart of a stock's past performance, including measures of volume, the 200-day moving average (an average of prices over the previous 200 days recalculated each day), the strength of the stock relative to the market and relative to its industry, and literally hundreds of other averages, ratios, oscillators, and indicators. Moreover, individuals can gain easy access to a variety of charts for different time periods through Internet sites such as Yahoo!

The Technique of Fundamental Analysis

Fred Schwed, Jr., in his charming and witty exposé of the financial community in the 1930s, *Where Are the Customers' Yachts?*, tells of a Texas broker who sold some stock to a customer at $760 a share at the moment when it could have been purchased anywhere else at $730. When the outraged customer found out what had happened, he complained bitterly to the broker. The Texan cut him short. "Suh," he boomed, "you-all don't appreciate the policy of this firm. This heah firm selects investments foh its clients not on the basis of Price, but of Value."

In a sense, this story illustrates the difference between the technician and the fundamentalist. The technician is interested only in the record of the stock's price, whereas the fundamentalist's primary concern is with what a stock is really worth. The fundamentalist strives to be relatively immune to the optimism and pessimism of the crowd and makes a sharp distinction between a stock's current price and its true value.

In estimating the firm-foundation value of a security, the fundamentalist's most important job is to estimate the firm's future stream of earnings and dividends. To do this, he or she must estimate the firm's sales level, operating costs, corporate tax rates, depreciation policies, and the sources and costs of its capital requirements.

Basically, the security analyst must be a prophet without the benefit of divine inspiration. As a poor substitute, the analyst turns to a study of the past record of the company, a review of the company's income statements, balance sheets, and investment plans, and a firsthand visit to and appraisal of the company's management team. This yields a wealth of data. The analyst must then separate the important from the unimportant facts. As Benjamin Graham put it in *The Intelligent Investor*, "Sometimes he reminds us a bit of the erudite major general in 'The Pirates of Penzance,' with his 'many cheerful facts about the square of the hypotenuse.'"

Because the general prospects of a company are strongly influenced by the economic position of its industry, the obvious starting point for the security analyst is a study of industry prospects. Indeed, in almost all professional investment firms, security analysts specialize in particular industry groups. The fundamentalist hopes that a thorough study of industry conditions will produce valuable insights into factors that may be operative in the future but are not yet reflected in market prices.

A brief example will help illustrate what is involved. It involves a research study undertaken late in 1977 by the investment firm of Smith, Barney & Co. The analysis covered the international freight-forwarding industry and the prospects for a small company in the industry named the Harper Group. (Neither Smith, Barney nor Harper exists today in the same form. Smith, Barney merged with Salomon Brothers and is part of Citigroup. The former Harper is now part of EGL, Inc.)

The report first reviewed the international freight-forwarding industry. U.S. exports were benefiting from the recovery of the world economy and the revaluation of the dollar, which made U.S. exports increasingly competitive in world markets. The volume of international trade was therefore expanding more rapidly than that of the domestic economy. Also, the industry was described as highly fragmented, with no major operator having an entrenched position. This situation meant that a small company like Harper had a very good opportunity to increase its market share.

The report then turned to an analysis of the Harper Group. The past record of Harper suggested that it was precisely the kind of innovative company that could increase its market share in the rapidly expanding international freight-forwarding industry. Earnings had grown at a rate of better than 35 percent over the preceding five years, and the company appeared poised to continue that excellent record in the future.

First of all, a field analysis of the market indicated that Harper had installed the most modern computer technology to facilitate paperwork and to keep track at all times of the location of its shipments. It was adept at customs clearing, and its reputation for service was the best in the business. It had a strong financial position, with no debt in its capital structure, and clearly had sufficient cash flow to produce rapid expansion in the future.

The report went on to note the particular innovations made by Harper's management. Harper was a leader in obtaining large quantities of shipping space at wholesale prices and then consolidating cargo shipments so as to utilize the space. This consolidation not only provided lower rates to its customers but also enhanced profit margins. The company had plans to do the same kind of consolidating in air-freight forwarding, including the chartering of whole aircraft for its shipments. In addition, growth opportunities were present in areas such as container leasing, customshouse brokerage, and cargo insurance. Consequently, the report stated, the company would have substantial growth in both sales and profits. The report estimated that earnings and dividends should grow at a 25 percent rate over the next five years. On this basis, the report concluded that the market price of the Harper Group was below reasonable estimates of its firm foundation of value.

Recall that the first principle of valuation of the firm-foundation theory is that a stock is worth more—should sell at a higher price-earnings multiple—the larger its anticipated rate of growth. When the report was written, Harper sold at a price-earnings ratio of less than 7, while the price-earnings multiple for the market as a whole was approximately 9. The expected growth rate of earnings and dividends for the market as a whole was less than 10 percent, but Harper was expected to grow at a rate of 25 percent; hence, by our first valuation principle, it deserved to sell at a *higher* multiple than that of the market as a whole. Since the stock actually sold at a lower multiple, the report concluded that the stock was undervalued.

Of course, other principles of valuation mentioned in chapter 5 were also relevant. By the second principle, stocks are worth more to investors, other things being the same, if the company can finance its growth and still pay out a reasonable share of its earnings in dividends. On this score, one could probably justify a bit of a discount for Harper since its dividend yield was only about half of that for the market as a whole. Still, on balance, the extraordinary growth potential of the company had to be the dominant factor for valuation.

The firm-foundation theory also suggests that the riskier a stock, the lower the multiple it should sell at. While it is true that Harper was a small company and thus riskier than some of the more established blue-chip companies, other aspects of Harper's business actually made it less risky than the general market. Harper had a great deal of resistance to domestic recessions since its business was a function more of the world economy than of the U.S. economy. And as we shall learn in Part Three, stocks in a company like Harper, whose fortunes are affected by international rather than domestic considerations, play an important role in *reducing* the risk of a portfolio. Hence, on this score, Harper stock would deserve a premium multiple to the market.

It is also possible to use the empirical relationships discussed in chapter 5 to argue that Harper represented a good value. When the analysis was made, stocks for which a 25 percent rate of growth was expected sold, on average, at over 25 times earnings, more than 2½ times the multiple for the market as a whole. Harper's multiple was only 7. This further enhanced its appeal. For these reasons, Smith, Barney recommended purchase of the Harper Group.

The Smith, Barney report represents the technique of fundamental analysis at its finest. People who followed its "buy" advice found that Harper enjoyed much better performance than the market over the period that it existed as a separate company.

Why Might Fundamental Analysis Fail to Work?

Despite its plausibility and scientific appearance, there are three potential flaws in this type of analysis. First, the information and analysis may be incorrect. Second, the security analyst's estimate of "value" may be faulty. Third, the market may not correct its "mistake" and the stock price might not converge to its value estimate.

The security analyst traveling from company to company and consulting with industry specialists will receive a great deal of fundamental information. Some critics have suggested that, taken as a whole, this information will be worthless. What investors make on the valid news (assuming it is not yet recognized by the market) they lose on the bad information and, unfortunately, some of the information the analyst receives may be fraudulent. Moreover, the analyst wastes considerable effort in collecting the information, and investors pay heavy transactions fees in trying to act on it. To make matters even worse, the security analyst may be unable to translate correct facts into accurate estimates of earnings for several years into the future. A faulty analysis of valid information could throw estimates of the rate of growth of earnings and dividends far wide of the mark.

The second problem is that even if the information is correct and its implications for future growth are properly assessed, the analyst might make a faulty value estimate. We have already seen how difficult it is to translate specific estimates of growth and other valuation factors into a single estimate of intrinsic value. Recall the widely different estimates of the value for IBM shown in chapter 5. I have suggested earlier that the attempt to obtain a precise measure of intrinsic value may be an unrewarding search for a will-o'-the-wisp. Thus, even if the security analyst's estimates of growth are correct, this information may already be reflected accurately by the market, and any difference between a security's price and value may result simply from an incorrect estimate of value.

The final problem is that even with correct information and value estimates, the stock you buy might still go down. For example, suppose that Biodegradable Bottling Company is selling at 20 times earnings, and the analyst estimates that it can sustain a long-term growth rate of 25 percent. If, on average, stocks with 25 percent anticipated growth rates are selling at 30 times earnings, the fundamentalist might conclude that Biodegradable was a "cheap" stock and recommend purchase.

But suppose, a few months later, stocks with 25 percent growth rates are selling in the market at only 20 times earnings. Even if the analyst was absolutely correct in his growth-rate estimate, his customers might not gain because the market revalued its estimates of what growth stocks in general were worth. The market might correct its "mistake" by revaluing all stocks downward, rather than raising the price for Biodegradable Bottling.

Such changes in valuation are not extraordinary—these are the routine fluctuations in market sentiment that have been experienced in the past. Not only can the average multiple change rapidly for stocks in general but the market can also dramatically change the premium assigned to growth. Clearly, then, one should not take the success of fundamental analysis for granted.

Using Fundamental and Technical Analysis Together

Many analysts use a combination of techniques to judge whether individual stocks are attractive for purchase. One of the most sensible procedures can easily be summarized by the following three rules. The persistent, patient reader will recognize that the rules are based on principles of stock pricing I have developed in the previous chapters.

Rule 1: Buy only companies that are expected to have above-average earnings growth for five or more years. An extraordinary long-run earnings growth rate is the single most important element contributing to the success of most stock investments. Pfizer, Microsoft, the former Harper Group, and practically all the other really outstanding common stocks of the past were growth stocks. As difficult as the job may be, picking stocks whose earnings grow is the name of the game. Consistent growth not only increases the earnings and dividends of the company but may also increase the multiple that the market is willing to pay for those earnings. Thus, the purchaser of a stock whose earnings begin to grow rapidly has a chance at a potential double benefit—both the earnings and the multiple may increase.

Rule 2: Never pay more for a stock than its firm foundation of value. While I have argued, and I hope persuasively, that you can never judge the exact intrinsic value of a stock, many analysts feel that you can roughly gauge when a stock seems to be reasonably priced. Generally, the earnings multiple for the market as a whole is a helpful benchmark. Growth stocks selling at multiples in line with or not very much above this multiple often represent good value.

There are important advantages to buying growth stocks at very reasonable earnings multiples. If your growth estimate turns out to be correct, you may get the double bonus I mentioned in connection with Rule 1: The price will tend to go up simply because the earnings went up, but also the multiple is likely to expand in recognition of the growth rate that is established. Hence, the double bonus. Suppose, for example, you buy a stock earning $1 per share and selling at $7.50. If the earnings grow to $2 per share and if the price-earnings multiple increases from 7½ to 15 (in recognition that the company now can be considered a growth stock), you don't just double your money—you quadruple it. That's because your $7.50 stock will be worth $30 (15, the multiple, times $2, the earnings).

Now consider the other side of the coin. There are special risks involved in buying "growth stocks" when the market has already recognized the growth and has bid up the price-earnings multiple to a hefty premium over that accorded more run-of-the-mill stocks. The problem is that the very high multiples may already fully reflect the growth that is anticipated, and if the growth does not materialize and earnings in fact go down (or even grow more slowly than expected), you will take a very unpleasant bath. The double benefits that are possible if the earnings of low-multiple stocks grow can become double damages if the earnings of high-multiple stocks decline. When earnings fall, the multiple is likely to crash as well. But the crash won't be so loud if the multiple wasn't that high in the first place.

What is proposed, then, is a strategy of buying unrecognized growth stocks whose earnings multiples are not at any substantial premium over the market. Of course, it is very hard to predict growth. But even if the growth does not materialize and earnings decline, the damage is likely to be only single if the multiple is low to begin with, whereas the benefits may double if things do turn out as you expected. This is an extra way to put the odds in your favor.

Peter Lynch, the very successful but now retired manager of the Magellan Fund, used this technique to great advantage during the fund's early years. Lynch calculated each potential stock's growth-to-P/E ratio and would only buy for his portfolio those stocks with high growth relative to their P/Es. This was not simply a low P/E strategy, because a stock with a 50 percent growth rate and a P/E of 25 (growth-to-P/E ratio of 2) was deemed far better than a stock with 20 percent growth and a P/E of 20 (growth-to-P/E ratio of 1). If one is correct in one's growth projections, and for a while Lynch was, this strategy can produce eye-popping returns.

We can summarize the discussion thus far by restating the first two rules: *Look for growth situations with low price-earnings multiples. If the growth takes place, there's often a double bonus—both the earnings and the multiple rise, producing large gains. Beware of very high multiple stocks in which future growth is already discounted. If growth doesn't materialize, losses are doubly heavy—both the earnings and the multiple drop.*

Rule 3: Look for stocks whose stories of anticipated growth are of the kind on which investors can build castles in the air. I have stressed the importance of psychological elements in stock-price determination. Individual and institutional investors are not computers that calculate warranted price-earnings multiples and print out buy and sell decisions. They are emotional human beings—driven by greed, gambling instincts, hope, and fear in their stock-market decisions. This is why successful investing demands both intellectual and psychological acuteness.

Stocks that produce "good feelings" in the minds of investors can sell at premium multiples for long periods, even if the growth rate is only average. Those not so blessed may sell at low multiples for long periods, even if their growth rate is above average. To be sure, if a growth rate appears to be established, the stock is almost certain to attract some type of following. The market is not irrational. But stocks are like people—what stimulates one may leave another cold, and the multiple improvement may be smaller and slower to be realized if the story never catches on.

So Rule 3 says to ask yourself whether the story about your stock is one that is likely to catch the fancy of the crowd. Is it a story from which contagious dreams can be generated? Is it a story on which investors can build castles in the air—but castles in the air that really rest on a firm foundation?

You don't have to be a technician to follow Rule 3. You might simply use your intuition or speculative sense to judge whether the "story" on your stock is likely to catch the fancy of the crowd—particularly the notice of institutional investors. Technical analysts, however, would look for some tangible evidence before they could be convinced that the investment idea was, in fact, catching on. This tangible evidence is, of course, the beginning of an uptrend or a technical signal that could "reliably" predict that an uptrend would develop.

Although the rules I have outlined seem sensible, the important question is whether they really work. After all, lots of other people are playing the game, and it is by no means obvious that anyone can win consistently.

In the next two chapters, I shall look at the actual record. Chapter 7 asks the question: Does technical analysis work? Chapter 8 looks at the performance record of fundamentalists. Together they should help us evaluate how well professional investment people do their job and how much confidence we should have in their advice.

7

Technical Analysis
and the
Random-Walk Theory

Things are seldom what they seem.
Skim milk masquerades as cream.
—Gilbert and Sullivan, *H.M.S. Pinafore*

Not earnings, nor dividends, nor risk, nor gloom of high interest rates stay the chartists from their assigned task: studying the price movements of stocks. Such single-minded devotion to numbers has yielded the most colorful theories and folk language of Wall Street:

"Hold the winners, sell the losers," "Switch into the strong stocks," "Sell this issue, it's acting poorly," "Don't fight the tape." All are popular prescriptions of technical analysts as they cheerfully collect their brokerage fees for churning your account.

Technical analysts build their strategies upon dreams of castles in the air and expect their tools to tell them which castle is being built and how to get in on the ground floor. The question is: Do they work?

Holes in Their Shoes and Ambiguity in Their Forecasts

University professors are sometimes asked by their students, "If you're so smart, why aren't you rich?" The question usually rankles professors, who think of themselves as passing

up worldly riches to engage in such an obviously socially useful occupation as teaching. The same question might more
appropriately be addressed to technicians. For, after all, the
whole point of technical analysis is to make money, and one
would reasonably expect that those who preach it should practice it successfully in their own investments.

On close examination, technicians are often seen with
holes in their shoes and frayed shirt collars. I personally have
never known a successful technician, but I have seen the
wrecks of several unsuccessful ones. Curiously, however, the
broke technician is never apologetic. If you commit the social
error of asking him why he is broke, he will tell you quite
ingenuously that he made the all-too-human error of not
believing his own charts. To my great embarrassment, I once
choked conspicuously at the dinner table of a chartist friend of
mine when he made such a comment. I have since made it a
rule never to eat with a chartist. It's bad for digestion.

Although technicians might not get rich following their
own advice, their store of words is precious indeed. Consider
this advice offered by one technical service:

> The market's rise after a period of reaccumulation is a bullish
> sign. Nevertheless, fulcrum characteristics are not yet clearly
> present and a resistance area exists 40 points higher in the
> Dow, so it is clearly premature to say the next leg of the bull
> market is up. If, in the coming weeks, a test of the lows holds
> and the market breaks out of its flag, a further rise would be
> indicated. Should the lows be violated, a continuation of the
> intermediate term downtrend is called for. In view of the cur-
> rent situation, it is a distinct possibility that traders will sit in
> the wings awaiting a clearer delineation of the trend and the
> market will move in a narrow trading range.

If you ask me exactly what all this means, I'm afraid I cannot
tell you, but I think the technician probably had the following
in mind: "If the market does not go up or go down, it will
remain unchanged." Even the weather forecaster can do better
than that.

Obviously, I'm biased against the chartist. This is not only
a personal predilection but a professional one as well. Technical analysis is anathema to the academic world. We love to pick
on it. Our bullying tactics are prompted by two considerations:

(1) after paying transactions costs, the method does not do better than a buy-and-hold strategy for investors; and (2) it's easy to pick on. And while it may seem a bit unfair to pick on such a sorry target, just remember: It's your money we are trying to save.

Although the advent of the computer may have enhanced the standing of the technician for a time, it has ultimately proved to be his (or her) undoing. Just as fast as the technician creates charts to show where the market is going, the academic gets busy constructing charts showing where the technician has been. Because it's so easy to test all the technical trading rules on the computer, it has become a favorite pastime for academics to see if they really work.

Is There Momentum in the Stock Market?

The technician believes that knowledge of a stock's past behavior can help predict its probable future behavior. In other words, the sequence of price changes before any given day is important in predicting the price change for that day. This might be called "the wallpaper principle." The technical analyst tries to predict future stock prices just as we might predict that the pattern of wallpaper behind the mirror is the same as the pattern above the mirror. The basic premise is that there are repeatable patterns in space and time.

Chartists believe momentum exists in the market. Supposedly, stocks that have been rising will continue to do so, and those that begin falling will go on sinking. Investors should therefore buy stocks that start rising and continue to hold their strong stocks. Should the stock begin to fall or "act poorly," investors are advised to sell.

These technical rules have been tested exhaustively by using stock-price data on both major exchanges going back as far as the beginning of the twentieth century. The results reveal that past movements in stock prices cannot be used reliably to foretell future movements. The stock market has little, if any, memory. While the market does exhibit some momentum from time to time, it does not occur dependably and there is not enough persistence in stock prices to overwhelm the substantial transactions costs involved in undertaking trend-following strategies.

One set of tests, perhaps the simplest of all, compares the price change for a stock in a given period with the price change in a subsequent period. For example, technical lore has it that if the price of a stock rose yesterday it is more likely to rise today. It turns out that the correlation of past price movements with present and future price movements is slightly positive but very close to zero. Last week's price change bears little relationship to the price change this week, and so forth. Whatever slight dependencies have been found between stock price movements in different time periods are extremely small and economically insignificant. Although there is some short-term momentum in the stock market, as will be described more fully in chapter 11, any investor who pays transactions costs cannot benefit from it.

Economists have also examined the technician's thesis that there are often sequences of price changes in the same direction over several days (or several weeks or months). Stocks are likened to fullbacks who, once having gained some momentum, can be expected to carry on for a long gain. It turns out that this is simply not the case. Sometimes one gets positive price changes (rising prices) for several days in a row; but sometimes when you are flipping a fair coin you also get a long string of "heads" in a row, and you get sequences of positive (or negative) price changes no more frequently than you can expect random sequences of heads or tails in a row. What are often called "persistent patterns" in the stock market occur no more frequently than the runs of luck in the fortunes of any gambler playing a game of chance. This is what economists mean when they say that stock prices behave very much like a random walk.

Just What Exactly Is a Random Walk?

To many people this appears to be arrant nonsense. Even the most casual reader of the financial pages can easily spot patterns in the market. For example, look at the stock chart on the following page.

The chart seems to display some obvious patterns. After an initial rise the stock turned down, and once the decline got under way the stock headed persistently downhill. Happily for the bulls, the decline was arrested and the stock had another sustained upward move. One cannot look at a stock chart like this without realizing the self-evidence of these statements. How can the economist be so myopic that he cannot see what is so plainly visible to the naked eye?

The persistence of this belief in repetitive patterns in the stock market is due to statistical illusion. To illustrate, let me describe an experiment in which I asked my students to participate. The students were asked to construct a normal stock chart showing the movements of a hypothetical stock initially selling at $50 per share. For each successive trading day, the closing stock price would be determined by the flip of a fair coin. If the toss was a head, the students assumed that the stock closed ½ point higher than the preceding close. If the flip was a tail, the price was assumed to be down by ½. The chart below is actually the hypothetical stock chart derived from one of these experiments.

The chart derived from random coin tossings looks remarkably like a normal stock price chart and even appears to display cycles. Of course, the pronounced "cycles" that we

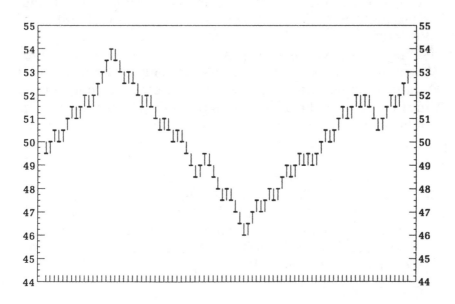

seem to observe in coin tossings do not occur at regular intervals as true cycles do, but neither do the ups and downs in the
stock market.

It is this lack of regularity that is crucial. The "cycles" in the
stock charts are no more true cycles than the runs of luck or
misfortune of the ordinary gambler. And the fact that stocks
seem to be in an uptrend, which looks just like the upward
move in some earlier period, provides no useful information on
the dependability or duration of the current uptrend. Yes, history does tend to repeat itself in the stock market, but in an infi-
nitely surprising variety of ways that confound any attempts to
profit from a knowledge of past price patterns.

In other simulated stock charts derived through student
coin-tossings, there were head-and-shoulders formations, triple
tops and bottoms, and other more esoteric chart patterns. One
of the charts showed a beautiful upward breakout from an
inverted head and shoulders (a very bullish formation). I
showed it to a chartist friend of mine who practically jumped
out of his skin. "What is this company?" he exclaimed. "We've
got to buy immediately. This pattern's a classic. There's no
question the stock will be up 15 points next week." He did not
respond kindly to me when I told him the chart had been produced by flipping a coin. Chartists have no sense of humor. I
got my comeuppance when *BusinessWeek* hired a technician,
who was adept at hatchet work, to review the first edition of
this book.

My students used a completely random process to produce
their stock charts. With each toss, as long as the coins used
were fair, there was a 50 percent chance of heads, implying an
upward move in the price of the stock, and a 50 percent chance
of tails and a downward move. Even if they flip ten heads in a
row, the chance of getting a head on the next toss is still 50 percent. Mathematicians call a sequence of numbers produced by
a random process (such as those on our simulated stock chart)
a random walk. The next move on the chart is completely
unpredictable on the basis of what has happened before.

To a mathematician, the sequence of numbers recorded on
a stock chart behaves no differently from that in the simulated
stock charts—with one clear exception. There is a long-run
uptrend in most averages of stock prices in line with the long-

run growth of earnings and dividends. After adjusting for this trend, there is very little difference. The next move in a series of stock prices is largely unpredictable on the basis of past price behavior. No matter what wiggle or wobble the prices have made in the past, tomorrow starts out roughly fifty-fifty. The next price change is no more predictable than the flip of a coin.

Now, in fact, the stock market does not quite measure up to the mathematician's ideal of the complete independence of present price movements from those in the past. There have been some dependencies found, as will be explained more fully in chapter 11. The market is not a perfect random walk. But any systematic relationships that exist are so small that they are not useful for an investor. The transactions charges involved in trying to take advantage of these dependencies are far greater than any advantage that might be obtained. Thus, an accurate statement of the "weak" form of the random-walk hypothesis goes as follows:

> The history of stock price movements contains no useful information that will enable an investor consistently to outperform a buy-and-hold strategy in managing a portfolio.

If the weak form of the random-walk hypothesis is a valid description of the stock market, then, as my colleague Richard Quandt says, "Technical analysis is akin to astrology and every bit as scientific."

I am not saying that technical strategies never make money. They very often do make profits. The point is rather that a simple "buy-and-hold" strategy (that is, buying a stock or group of stocks and holding on for a long period of time) typically makes as much or more money.

When scientists want to test the efficacy of some new drug, they usually run an experiment in which two groups of patients are administered pills—one containing the drug in question, the other a worthless placebo (a sugar pill). The results of the administration to the two groups are compared, and the drug is deemed effective only if the group receiving the drug did better than the group getting the placebo. Obviously, if both groups got better in the same period of time, the drug should not be given the credit, even if the patients did recover.

In the stock-market experiments, the placebo with which

the technical strategies are compared is the buy-and-hold strategy. Technical schemes often do make profits for their users, but so does a buy-and-hold strategy. Indeed, as we shall see later, a naive buy-and-hold strategy using a portfolio consisting of all the stocks in a broad stock-market index has provided investors with an average annual rate of return of over 10 percent over the past seventy-five years. Only if technical schemes produce better returns than the market can they be judged effective. To date, none has consistently passed the test.

Some More Elaborate Technical Systems

Devotees of technical analysis may argue with some justification that I have been unfair. The simple tests I have just described do not do justice to the "richness" of technical analysis. Unfortunately for the technician, even some of his more elaborate trading rules have been subjected to scientific testing. Because many of the systems tested are very popular, let's briefly examine a few in detail.

The Filter System

Under the popular "filter" system, a stock that has reached a low point and has moved up, say 5 percent (or any other percent you wish to name here and throughout this discussion), is said to be in an uptrend. A stock that has reached a peak and has moved down 5 percent is said to be in a downtrend. You're supposed to buy any stock that has moved up 5 percent from its low and hold it until the price moves down 5 percent from a subsequent high, at which time you sell the stock and, perhaps, even sell short. The short position is maintained until the price rises at least 5 percent from a subsequent low.

This scheme is very popular with brokers, and forms of it have been recommended in a variety of investment books. Indeed, the filter method is what lies behind the popular "stop-loss" order favored by brokers, where the client is advised to sell his stock if it falls 5 percent below his purchase price to "limit his potential losses." The argument is that presumably a stock that falls by 5 percent will be going into a downtrend anyway.

Exhaustive testing of various filter rules based on past price changes has been undertaken. The percentage drop or rise that filters out buy and sell candidates has been allowed to vary from 1 percent to 50 percent. The tests covered different time periods and involved individual stocks as well as stock indexes. Again, the results are remarkably consistent. When the higher transactions charges incurred under the filter rules are taken into consideration, these techniques cannot consistently beat a policy of simply buying the individual stock (or the stock index) and holding it over the period during which the test is performed. The individual investor would do well to avoid using any filter rule and, I might add, any broker who recommends it.

The Dow Theory

The Dow theory is a great tug-of-war between resistance and support. When the market tops out and moves down, that previous peak defines a resistance area, because people who missed selling at the top will be anxious to do so if given another opportunity. If the market then rises again and nears the previous peak, it is said to be "testing" the resistance area. Now comes the moment of truth. If the market breaks through the resistance area, it is likely to keep going up for a while and the previous resistance area becomes a support area. If, on the other hand, the market "fails to penetrate the resistance area" and instead falls through the preceding low where there was previous support, a bear-market signal is given and the investor is advised to sell.

The basic Dow principle implies a strategy of buying when the market goes higher than the last peak and selling when it sinks through the preceding valley. There are various wrinkles to the theory, such as penetration of a double or triple top being especially bullish, but the basic idea is followed by many chartists and is part of the gospel of charting.

Unhappily, the signals generated by the Dow mechanism have no significance for predicting future price movements. The market's performance after sell signals is no different from its performance after buy signals. Relative to simply buying and holding the representative list of stocks in the market averages, the Dow follower actually comes out a little behind, because the strategy entails a number of extra brokerage costs as the investor buys and sells when the strategy decrees.

The Relative-Strength System

In the relative-strength system, an investor buys and holds those stocks that are acting well, that is, outperforming the general market indices in the recent past. Conversely, the stocks that are acting poorly relative to the market should be avoided or, perhaps, even sold short. While there do seem to be some time periods when a relative-strength strategy would have outperformed a buy-and-hold strategy, there is no evidence that it can do so consistently. As indicated earlier, there is some evidence of momentum in the stock market. Nevertheless, a computer test of relative-strength rules over a twenty-five-year period suggests that such rules do not, after accounting for transactions charges, outperform the placebo of a buy-and-hold investment strategy.

Price-Volume Systems

Price-volume systems suggest that when a stock (or the general market) rises on large or increasing volume, there is an unsatisfied excess of buying interest and the stock can be expected to continue its rise. Conversely, when a stock drops on large volume, selling pressure is indicated and a sell signal is given.

Again, the investor following such a system is likely to be disappointed in the results. The buy and sell signals generated by the strategy contain no information useful for predicting future price movements. As with all technical strategies, however, the investor is obliged to do a great deal of in-and-out trading, and thus his transactions costs are far in excess of those necessitated in a buy-and-hold strategy. After accounting for these trading charges, the investor does worse than he would by simply buying and holding a diversified group of stocks.

Reading Chart Patterns

Perhaps some of the more complicated chart patterns, such as those described in the preceding chapter, are able to reveal the future course of stock prices. For example, is the downward penetration of a head-and-shoulders formation a reliable bearish omen? As one of the gospels of charting, *Technical Analysis*, puts it: "One does not bring instantly to a stop a heavy car moving at seventy miles per hour and, all within the same split second, turn it around and get it moving back down the road in the opposite direction." Before the stock turns around, its price movements are supposed to form one of a number of extensive reversal patterns as the smart-money traders slowly "distribute" their shares to the "public." Of course, we know some stocks do reverse directions in quite a hurry (this is called an "unfortunate V formation"), but perhaps these reversal patterns and other chart configurations can, like the Roman soothsayers, accurately foretell the future. Alas, the computer has even tested these more arcane charting techniques, and the technician's tool (magician's wand) has again betrayed him.

In one elaborate study, the computer was programmed to draw charts for 548 stocks traded on the New York Stock Exchange over a five-year period. It was instructed to scan all the charts and identify any one of thirty-two of the most popularly followed chart patterns. The computer was told to be on the lookout for heads and shoulders, triple tops and bottoms, channels, wedges, diamonds, and so forth. Because the machine is a very thorough (though rather dull) worker, we can be sure that it did not miss any significant chart patterns.

When the machine found that one of the bearish chart patterns such as a head and shoulders was followed by a downward move through the neckline toward décolletage (a most bearish omen), it recorded a sell signal. If, on the other hand, a triple bottom was followed by an upside breakout (a most favorable augury), a buy signal was recorded. The computer then followed the performance of the stocks for which buy and sell signals were given and compared them with the performance record of the general market.

Again, there seemed to be no relationship between the technical signal and subsequent performance. If you had bought only those stocks with buy signals, and sold on a sell signal, your performance after transactions costs would have been no better than that achieved with a buy-and-hold strategy.

Randomness Is Hard to Accept

Human nature likes order; people find it hard to accept the notion of randomness. No matter what the laws of chance might tell us, we search for patterns among random events wherever they might occur—not only in the stock market but even in interpreting sporting phenomena.

In describing an outstanding performance by a basketball player, reporters and spectators alike commonly use expressions such as "Alan Iverson has the hot hand" or "Kobe Bryant is a streak shooter." Those who play, coach, or otherwise follow basketball are almost universally convinced that if a player has successfully made his last shot, or last few shots, he is more likely to make his next shot. A study by a group of psychologists, however, suggests that the "hot hand" phenomenon is a myth.

The psychologists did a detailed study of every shot taken by the Philadelphia 76ers over a full season and a half. They found no evidence of any positive correlation between the outcomes of successive shots. Indeed, they found that a hit by a player followed by a miss was actually a bit likelier than the case of making two baskets in a row. Moreover, the researchers looked at sequences of more than two shots. Again, they found that the number of long streaks (that is, hitting of several baskets in a row) was no greater than could have been expected in a random set of data (such as flipping coins in which every event was independent of its predecessor). Although the event of making one's last two or three shots clearly influenced the player's perception of whether he would make his next shot, the hard evidence was that there was no effect. The researchers then confirmed their study by examining the free-throw records of the Boston Celtics and by conducting controlled shooting experiments with the men and women of the Cornell University varsity basketball teams. The outcomes of previous shots influenced players' predictions but not their performance.

These findings do not imply that basketball is a game of chance rather than skill. Obviously there are some players who are more adept at making baskets and free throws than others. The point is, however, that the probability of making a shot is independent of the outcome of previous shots. The psychologists conjecture that the persistent belief in the hot hand could be due to memory bias. If long sequences of hits or misses are more memorable than alternating sequences, observers are likely to overestimate the correlation between successive shots. When events sometimes do come in clusters and streaks, people look for explanations and patterns. They refuse to believe that they are random, even though such clusters and streaks do occur frequently in random data such as are derived from the tossing of a coin. So it is in the stock market as well.

A Gaggle of Other Technical Theories to Help You Lose Money

Once the academic world polished off most of the standard technical trading rules, it turned its august attention toward some of the more fanciful schemes. The world of financial analysis would be much quieter and duller without the chartists, as the following techniques amply demonstrate.

The Hemline Indicator

Not content with price movements, some technical analysts have broadened their investigations to include other movements as well. One of the most charming of these schemes has been called by the author Ira Cobleigh the "bull markets and bare knees" theory. Check the hemlines of women's dresses in any given year and you'll have an idea of the direction of stock prices. There does seem to be a loose tendency for bull markets to be associated with bare knees and depressed markets to be associated with bear markets for girl watchers, as the chart on page 158 reveals.

For example, in the late nineteenth and early part of the twentieth centuries, the stock market was rather dull, and so were hemlines. But then came rising hemlines and the great bull market of the 1920s, to be followed by long skirts and the crash of the 1930s. (Actually, the chart cheats a bit: hemlines fell in 1927, before the most dynamic phase of the bull market.)

Things did not work out as well in the post–World War II period. The market declined sharply during the summer of 1946, well in advance of the introduction of the "New Look"

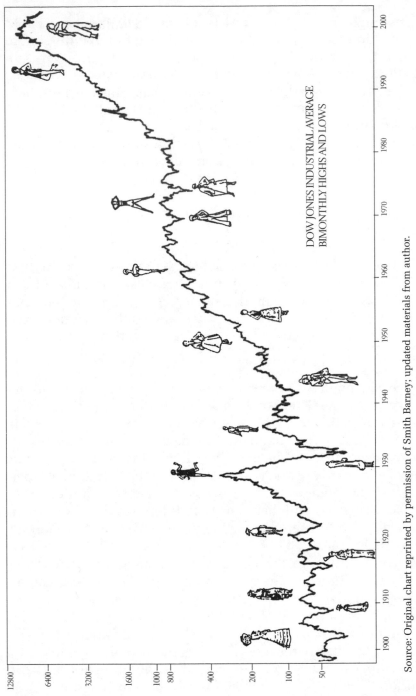

DOW JONES INDUSTRIAL AVERAGE
BIMONTHLY HIGHS AND LOWS

Source: Original chart reprinted by permission of Smith Barney; updated materials from author.

featuring longer skirt lengths in 1947. Similarly, the sharp stock-market decline that began at the end of 1968 preceded the introduction of the midiskirt, which was high fashion in 1969 and especially in 1970.

How did the theory work out during the crash of 1987? You might think the hemline indicator failed. After all, in the spring of 1987, when designers began shipping their fall lines, very short skirts were decreed as the fashion for the time. But along about the beginning of October, when the first chill winds began blowing across the country, a strange thing happened: Most women decided that miniskirts were not for them. As women went back to long skirts, designers quickly followed suit. "Short skirts now look ridiculous to me," declared Bill Blass. The rest is stock-market history.

And how about the severe bear market of the early 2000s? Unfortunately, you guessed it, Capri pants became the fashion at the turn of the century and women business leaders such as Hewlett Packard's Carly Fiorina always appeared in pants suits. Now we know the real culprit for the punishing bear market of the early 2000s.

Even though there does seem to be some evidence in favor of the theory, don't be too optimistic about expecting the hemline indicator to give you a leg up on market timing. No longer are women imprisoned by the tyranny of hemlines. As *Vogue* put it in 2002: you can now dress like a man or woman and all hemline lengths are okay now. I'm afraid this stock-market theory has undoubtedly outlived its usefulness.

The Super Bowl Indicator

Why did the market go down in 2002? That's easy to answer for a technical analyst who uses the Super Bowl indicator. The Super Bowl indicator forecasts how the stock market will perform based on which team wins the Super Bowl. A victory by an NFL team predicts a bull market in stocks, whereas a victory by a former AFL team is bad news for stock-market investors. In 2002 the New England Patriots (an original AFL team) defeated the (NFL) Saint Louis Rams and the market responded correctly by falling sharply. While the indicator failed in 2001 (the NFL Baltimore Ravens won the Super Bowl and the market fell), it has been correct far more often than it has been wrong. Naturally, it makes no sense. The results of the Super Bowl indicator simply illustrate nothing more than the fact that it's sometimes possible to correlate two completely unrelated events. Indeed, Mark Hulbert reports that stock-market researcher David Leinweber found that the indicator most closely correlated with the S&P 500 Index is the volume of butter production in Bangladesh.

The Odd-Lot Theory

The odd-lot theory holds that except for the investor who is always right, no person can contribute more to a successful investment strategy than an investor who is known to be invariably wrong. The "odd-lotter," according to popular superstition, is precisely that kind of person. Thus, success is assured by buying when the odd-lotter sells and selling when the odd-lotter buys.

Odd-lotters are the people who trade stocks in less than 100-share lots (called round lots). Many amateurs in the stock market cannot afford the $5,000 investment to buy a round lot (100 shares) of stock selling at $50 a share. They are more likely to buy, say, ten shares for a more modest investment of $500.

By examining the ratio of odd-lot purchases (the number of shares these amateurs bought during a particular day) to odd-lot sales (the number of shares they sold) and by looking at what particular stocks odd-lotters buy and sell, one can supposedly make money. These uninformed amateurs, presumably acting solely out of emotion and not with professional insight, are lambs in the street being led to slaughter. They are, according to legend, invariably wrong.

It turns out that the odd-lotter isn't such a stupendous dodo after all. A little stupid? Maybe. There is some indication that the performance of odd-lotters might be slightly worse than the stock averages. However, the available evidence indicates that knowledge of odd-lotter's actions is not useful for the formulation of investment strategies.

One of the available studies examines the theory that an investor can make use of data on odd-lot sales and odd-lot purchases in selecting stocks. Supposedly, a switch from net odd-lot buying (in which odd-lot shares purchased exceed odd-lot shares sold) to net odd-lot selling (odd-lot sales greater than odd-lot purchases) should be taken as a "buy" signal, because the boobs who sell odd-lots obviously don't know what they're doing. The data did not support this contention. Indeed, the rule failed to indicate the major turning points for individual stocks or for the market as a whole. Moreover, an investor who followed the strategy would incur very heavy transactions charges, which would eat substantially into his capital. Some professional investors have seriously suggested that a new odd-lot theory is applicable to today's institutionally dominated market. Instead of looking at the behavior of the little guy in the market, it is suggested that the yo-yos who run the big mutual funds and pension funds are the odd-lotters of today, and that investors should look at what they are doing and then do the opposite.

A Few More Systems

To continue this review of technical schemes would soon generate rapidly diminishing returns. Probably few people seriously believe that the sunspot theory of stock-market movements can make money for them. But do you believe that by following the ratio of advancing to declining stocks on the New York Stock Exchange you can find a reliable leading indicator of general stock-market peaks? A careful computer study says no. Do you think that a rise in short interest (the number of shares of a stock sold short) is a bullish signal (because eventually the stock will be repurchased by the short seller to cover his or her position)? Exhaustive testing indicates no relationship either for the stock market as a whole or for individual issues. Do you think that a moving-average system as espoused by some of the financial television networks (for example, buy a stock if its price goes higher than its average price over the past 200 days and sell it if it goes below the average) can lead you to extraordinary stock-market profits? Not if you have to pay transactions charges—to buy and sell!

Technical Market Gurus

Joseph Granville was one of the most widely followed forecasters of the early 1980s. His record had been good for a time in the late 1970s, and at his heyday he had the power to move markets. At 6:30 P.M. on January 6, 1981, Granville sent word to his 3,000 investor-subscribers around the world, "Sell the market—sell everything." The next morning brokerage houses were deluged with sell orders, and the Dow Jones Industrial Average dropped sharply, representing some $40 billion in paper losses, three times the dollar amount lost on Black Thursday in 1929. And Granville's sell signal in September 1981 touched off near panic on world financial markets. Think of the ego satisfaction. Public adulation for Granville resembled that accorded rock stars. His traveling seminars were always oversubscribed. Asked at one seminar how he stayed close to the market when traveling, he dropped his pants to reveal various stock quotes printed on his shorts. When Joseph Granville talked, investors really did listen—at least for a while.

Unfortunately for Granville, his forecast accuracy during the 1980s left much to be desired. The Granville market letter warned of stock-market disaster throughout the early 1980s. Indeed, with the Dow Jones Industrial Average at 800, Granville told subscribers we were in a stock-market crash. He opined that investors should not only sell all their stock, but sell short as well, to take advantage of the coming financial Armageddon. The market responded by rising to the 1,200 level. "The bull market has been just a bubble," Granville remarked in 1984, continuing to warn a somewhat smaller number of listeners that the crash was near at hand. Granville's followers missed the spectacular bull market of the 1980s. His reputation as a seer and a mover of markets had been severely damaged.

During the 1980s, Granville was succeeded as the most influential market guru by Robert Prechter. Prechter became interested in the parallels between social psychology and the stock market while a Yale undergraduate. After college, while Granville was making his reputation, Prechter spent four years playing drums in a rock band, after which he joined Merrill Lynch as a junior technical analyst. There Prechter stumbled on the work of an obscure accountant, R. N. Elliott, who had devised an arcane theory which he modestly entitled the Elliott wave theory. Elliott's premise was that there were predictable waves of investor psychology and that they steered the market with natural ebbs and flows. By watching them, Elliott believed one could call major shifts in the market. Prechter was so excited about this discovery that he quit Merrill Lynch in 1979 to write an investor newsletter from the unlikely location of Gainesville, Georgia.

Prechter's initial predictions were uncannily accurate. Early in the 1980s, he predicted a major bull market with the Dow expected to rise to the 3,600 level, after an interim stop at 2,700. Just when Granville's predictions were shown to be flat-out wrong, Prechter was the golden knight of the day by keeping his followers fully invested through October 1987.

Tarnish set in after October 1987. To Prechter's credit, he did say that there was "a 50/50 risk of a 10% decline" in the market on October 5, 1987, when the Dow was still selling above the 2,600 level, and he advised traders and investors with a short-term outlook to sell. Institutional investors were advised, however, to hang on for the ultimate target of 3,686 in the Dow. After the crash, with the Dow near 2,000, Prechter turned bearish for the long term and recommended holding Treasury bills. He predicted that "the great bull market is probably over" and that by the early 1990s the Dow Jones Industrial Average would plunge below 400. By not advising repurchase, Prechter missed out on the entire bull market of the 1990s. This was a mortal wound for a golden guru. Prechter remained a consistent bear, however, and did gain some renewed following during the market's meltdown of the early 2000s. This only proves that if one keeps predicting a market decline (or rise) one is bound to be correct at some time.

Prechter was succeeded by Elaine Garzarelli, an executive vice president of the investment firm of Lehman Brothers. Garzarelli was not a one-indicator woman. She plunged into the ocean of financial data and used no fewer than thirteen different indicators to predict the course of the market. Garzarelli always liked to study vital details. As a child, she would get animal organs from the local butcher and dissect them.

Garzarelli was the Roger Babson of the 1987 crash. Turning bearish in August, she was recommending by September 1 that her clients get completely out of the stock market. By October

11, she was almost certain that a crash was imminent. Two days later, in a forecast almost frighteningly prescient, she told *USA Today* that a drop of more than 500 points in the Dow Jones averages was coming. Within a week, her predictions were realized.

But the crash was Garzarelli's last hurrah. Just as the media were coronating her as the "Guru of Black Monday" and adulatory articles appeared in magazines from *Cosmopolitan* to *Fortune*, she drowned in her prescience—or her notoriety. After the crash she said she wouldn't touch the market and predicted that the Dow would fall another 200 to 400 points. Thus, Garzarelli missed the bounce-back in the market. Moreover, those who put money in her hands were sadly disappointed. The mutual fund that was launched in the summer of 1987 to capitalize on her fame and talent had a terrific start. From 1988 on, however, she badly underperformed the market each year until she left the management of the fund in 1994. In explaining her lack of consistency, she gave the time-honored explanation of technicians: "I failed to believe my own charts." Later in 1994, Garzarelli and Lehman parted company.

Perhaps the most colorful investment gurus of the mid-1990s were the homespun, grandmotherly (median age seventy) Beardstown Ladies. Called by publicists "the greatest investment minds of our generation," these celebrity grannies cooked up profits and hype, selling more than a million books and appearing frequently on national television shows and in weekly magazines. They mixed explanations of their investment success ("heartland" virtues of hard work and churchgoing) with yummy cooking recipes (such as stock-market muffins—guaranteed to rise). In their best-selling 1995 book, *The Beardstown Ladies Common-Sense Investment Guide*, they claimed their investment returns were 23.9 percent per year over the preceding decade, far eclipsing the 14.9 annual percent return of the S&P 500 index. They suggested that ordinary folks could do just as well following their advice. What a great story: Little old midwestern ladies using common sense could beat the pants off the overpaid investment pros of Wall Street and could even put index funds to shame.

Unfortunately, the ladies were discovered to be cooking the books as well. Apparently, the Beardstown group was counting their investment club dues as part of their stock-market profits. The accounting firm Price Waterhouse was called in, and they calculated the ladies' true investment return over the decade to be 9.1 percent per year—almost 6 points below the overall market. So much for getting rich by worshiping investment idols.

During the late 1990s, Abby Joseph Cohen of Goldman Sachs was the best known and most successful market strategist as she accurately forecast the great bull market of the 1990s. But her techniques were diametrically opposed to the technical gurus discussed above. Abby Cohen relied on sophisticated economic analysis, and her success came from accurately predicting the noninflationary growth in the U.S. economy. She never based her forecasts on a reading of stock charts. And while her strategy calls have been correct more often than wrong, she did not forecast the decline of the early 2000s.

The moral to the story is obvious. With large numbers of technicians predicting the market, there will always be some who have called the last turn or even the last few turns, but none will be consistently accurate. To paraphrase the biblical warning, "He who looks back at the predictions of market gurus dies of remorse."

Why Are Technicians Still Hired?

It seems very clear that under scientific scrutiny chart reading must share a pedestal with alchemy. There has been a remarkable uniformity in the conclusions of studies done on all forms of technical analysis. Not one has consistently outperformed the placebo of a buy-and-hold strategy. Technical methods cannot be used to make useful investment strategies. This is the fundamental conclusion of the random-walk theory.

A former colleague of mine, who believed that the capitalist system would be sure to weed out all useless growths such as the flourishing technicians, was convinced that the technical cult was just a passing fad. "The days of these modern-day soothsayers on Wall Street are numbered," he would say. "Brokers will soon learn they can easily do without the technicians' services."

The chartist's durability, and the fact that over the years they have been hired in increasing numbers, suggests that the capitalist system may garden like most of the rest of us. We like to see our best plants grow, but as summer wears on somehow the weeds often manage to get the best of us. And as I often tell my wife when she remarks about the abundance of weeds in our lawn, "At least they're green."

The point is, the technicians often play an important role in the greening of the brokers. Chartists recommend trades—almost every technical system involves some degree of in-and-out trading. Trading generates commissions, and commissions are the lifeblood of the brokerage business. The technicians do not help produce yachts for the customers, but they do help generate the trading that provides yachts for the brokers. Until the public catches on to this bit of trickery, technicians will continue to flourish.

Appraising the Counterattack

As you might imagine, the random-walk theory's dismissal of charting is not altogether popular among technicians. Academic proponents of the theory are greeted in some Wall Street quarters with as much enthusiasm as Enron's Kenneth Lay addressing the Better Business Bureau. Technical analysts consider the theory and its implications to be, in the words of one veteran professional, "just plain academic drivel." Let us pause, then, and appraise the counterattack by beleaguered technicians.

Perhaps the most common complaint about the weakness of the random-walk theory is based on a distrust of mathematics and a misconception of what the theory means. "The market isn't random," the complaint goes, "and no mathematician is going to convince me it is." Even so astute a commentator on the Wall Street scene as "Adam Smith" displays this misconception when he writes: "I suspect that even if the random walkers announced a perfect mathematic proof of randomness I would go on believing that in the long run future earnings influence present value, and that in the short run the dominant factor is the elusive *Australopithecus*, the temper of the crowd."

Of course earnings and dividends influence market prices, and so does the temper of the crowd. We saw ample evidence of this in earlier chapters of the book. But, even if markets were dominated during certain periods by irrational crowd behavior, the stock market might still well be approximated by a random walk. The original illustrative analogy of a random walk concerned a drunken man staggering around an empty field. He is not rational, but he's not predictable either.

Moreover, new fundamental information about a company (a big mineral strike, the death of the president, etc.) is also unpredictable. It will occur randomly over time. Indeed, successive appearances of news items must be random. If an item of news were not random, that is, if it were dependent on an earlier item of news, then it wouldn't be news at all. The weak form of the random-walk theory says only that stock prices cannot be predicted on the basis of past stock prices. Thus, criticisms of the type quoted above are not valid.

The technical analyst will also cite chapter and verse that the academic world has certainly not tested every technical scheme that has been devised. That is quite correct. No economist or mathematician, however skillful, can prove conclusively that technical methods can never work. All that can be said is that the small amount of information contained in stock-market pricing patterns has not been shown to be sufficient to overcome the transactions costs involved in acting on that information. Consequently, I have received a flood of letters condemning me for not mentioning, in my earlier editions of this book, a pet technical scheme that the writer is convinced actually works.

Being somewhat incautious, I will climb out on a limb and argue that no technical scheme whatever could work for any length of time. I suggest first that methods which people are convinced "really work" have not been adequately tested; and second, that even if they did work, the schemes would be bound to destroy themselves.

Each year a number of eager people visit the gambling parlors of Las Vegas and Atlantic City and examine the last several hundred numbers of the roulette wheel in search of some repeating pattern. Usually they find one. And so they stay until they lose everything because they do not retest the pattern.* The same thing is true for technicians.

If you examine past stock prices in any given period, you can almost always find some kind of system that would have worked in a given period. If enough different criteria for selecting stocks are tried, one will eventually be found that selects the best ones of that period.

Let me illustrate. Suppose we examine the record of stock prices and volume over the five-year period of 1998 through 2002 in search of technical trading rules that would have worked during that period. After the fact, it is always possible to find a technical rule that works. For example, it might be that you should have bought all stocks whose names began with the letters X or D, whose volume was at least 80,000 shares a day, and whose earnings grew at a rate of 10 percent or more during the preceding five-year period. The point is that it is obviously possible to describe, after the fact, which categories of stocks had the best performance. The real problem is, of course, whether the scheme works in a different time period. What most advocates of technical analysis usually fail to do is to test their schemes with market data derived from periods other than those during which the scheme was developed.

Even if the technician follows my advice, tests his scheme in many different time periods, and finds it a reliable predictor of stock prices, I still believe that technical analysis must ultimately be worthless. For the sake of argument, suppose the technician had found a reliable year-end rally, that is, every year stock prices rose between Christmas and New Year's Day. The problem is that once such a regularity is known to market participants, people will act in a way that prevents it from happening in the future.†

---

*Edward O. Thorp actually did find a method to win at blackjack. Thorp wrote it all up in *Beat the Dealer*. Since then, casinos switched to the use of several decks of cards to make it more difficult for card counters and, as a last resort, they banished the counters from the gaming tables.

†If such a regularity was known to only one individual, he would simply practice the technique until he had collected a large share of the marbles. He surely would have no incentive to share a truly useful scheme by making it available to others.

Any successful technical scheme must ultimately be self-defeating. The moment I realize that prices will be higher after New Year's Day than they are before Christmas, I will start buying before Christmas ever comes around. If people know a stock will go up tomorrow, you can be sure it will go up today. Any regularity in the stock market that can be discovered and acted upon profitably is bound to destroy itself. This is the fundamental reason why I am convinced that no one will be successful in using technical methods to get above-average returns in the stock market.

Implications for Investors

The past history of stock prices cannot be used to predict the future in any meaningful way. Technical strategies are usually amusing, often comforting, but of no real value. This is the weak form of the random-walk theory, and it is the consistent conclusion of research done at universities such as Chicago, Yale, Princeton, and Stanford. It has been published mainly in investment journals, but also in more esoteric ones such as *Kyklos* and *Econometrica*. Technical theories enrich only the people preparing and marketing the technical service or the brokerage firms who hire technicians in the hope that their analyses may help encourage investors to do more in-and-out trading and thus generate commission business for the brokerage firm.

Using technical analysis for market timing is especially dangerous. Because there is a long-term uptrend in the stock market, it can be very risky to be in cash. An investor who frequently carries a large cash position to avoid periods of market decline is very likely to be out of the market during some periods where it rallies smartly. Professor H. Negat Seybun of the University of Michigan found that 95 percent of the significant market gains over the thirty-year period from the mid-1960s through the mid-1990s came on 90 of the roughly 7,500 trading days. If you happened to miss those 90 days, just over 1 percent of the total, the generous long-run stock market returns of the period would have been wiped out. The point is that market timers risk missing the infrequent large sprints that are the big contributors to performance.

The implications of this analysis are simple. If past prices contain little or no useful information for the prediction of future prices, there is no point in following any technical trading rule for timing the purchases and sales of securities. A simple policy of buying and holding will be at least as good as any technical procedure. Discontinue your subscriptions to worthless technical services, and eschew brokers who read charts and are continually recommending the purchase or sale of securities.

There is another major advantage to a buy-and-hold strategy that I have not yet mentioned. Buying and selling, to the extent that it is profitable at all, tends to generate capital gains, which are subject to tax. Buying and holding enables you to postpone or avoid gains taxes. By following any technical strategy, you are likely to realize most of your capital gains and pay larger taxes (as well as paying them sooner) than you would under a buy-and-hold strategy. Thus, simply buying and holding a diversified portfolio suited to your objectives will enable you to save on investment expense, brokerage charges, and taxes; and, at the same time, to achieve an overall performance record at least as good as that obtainable using technical methods.

8

How Good Is
Fundamental
Analysis?

How could I have been so mistaken as to have trusted the
experts?
—John F. Kennedy after the Bay of Pigs fiasco

In the beginning he was a statistician. He wore
a white, starched shirt and threadbare blue suit. He quietly put
on his green eyeshade, sat down at his desk, and recorded
meticulously the historical financial information about the
companies he followed. The result: writer's cramp. But then a
metamorphosis began to set in. He rose from his desk, bought
blue button-down shirts and gray flannel suits, threw away his
eyeshade, and began to make field trips to visit the companies
that previously he had known only as a collection of financial
statistics. His title now became security analyst.

As time went on, his salary and perks attracted the attention
of his female cohorts and they too donned suits. And just about
everybody who was anybody was now flying first class and
talking money, money, money. The bright newcomers entering
the job market during the 1990s laughed at the old fogey forty-
year-olds and disdained their ways. The new generation was
hip and suits were out and Gucci shoes and Armani slacks were
in. They were so incredibly brilliant and knowledgeable that
portfolio managers relied on their recommendations and Wall

Street firms used them increasingly to cultivate investment banking clients. They were more than security analysts. They were equity research stars. Some, however, unkindly whispered that they were investment banking whores.

The Views from Wall Street and Academia

No matter what title, derogatory or otherwise, these highly paid individuals hold, the great majority are fundamentalists. Thus, the studies casting doubt on the efficacy of technical analysis would not be considered surprising by most professionals. At heart, the Wall Street pros are fundamentalists. The really important question is whether fundamental analysis is any good.

Two opposing views have been taken about the efficacy of fundamental analysis. Wall Streeters feel that fundamental analysis is becoming more powerful and skillful all the time. The individual investor has scarcely a chance against the professional portfolio manager and a team of fundamental analysts.

Many in the academic community sneer at such pomposity. Some academicians have gone so far as to suggest that a blindfolded monkey throwing darts at the *Wall Street Journal* can select stocks with as much success as professional portfolio managers. They have argued that fund managers and their fundamental analysts can do no better at picking stocks than a rank amateur. Many have concluded that the value of professional stock picking advice is downright financially harmful to investors.

My own view of the matter is not as extreme as that taken by many of my academic colleagues. Nevertheless, an understanding of the large body of research on these questions is essential for any intelligent investor. This chapter will recount the major battle in an ongoing war between academics and market professionals and why it is important to your wallet.

Are Security Analysts Fundamentally Clairvoyant?

Forecasting future earnings is the security analysts' *raison d'être*. As a top Wall Street professional put it in his fraternity magazine, *Institutional Investor*: "Expectation of future earnings is still the most important single factor affecting stock prices." As we have seen, growth (in earnings and therefore in the ability to pay dividends or to engage in stock buybacks) is the key element needed to estimate a stock's firm foundation of value. The analyst who can make accurate forecasts of the future will be richly rewarded. "If he is wrong," *Institutional Investor* puts it, "a stock can act precipitously, as has been demonstrated time and time again. Earnings are the name of the game and always will be."

To predict future directions, analysts generally start by looking at past wanderings. "A proven score of past performance in earnings growth is," one analyst told me, "a most reliable indicator of future earnings growth." If management is really skillful, there is no reason to think it will lose its Midas touch in the future. If the same adroit management team remains at the helm, the course of future earnings growth should continue as it has in the past, or so the argument goes. While it sounds suspiciously like an argument used by technical analysts, fundamentalists pride themselves on the fact that it is based on specific, proven company performance.

Such thinking flunks in the academic world. Calculations of past earnings growth are no help in predicting future growth. If you had known the growth rates of all companies during, say, the 1980–90 period, this would not have helped you at all in predicting what growth they would achieve in the 1990–2000 period. And knowing the fast growers of the 1990s has not helped analysts find the fast growers of the early twenty-first century. This startling result was first reported by British researchers for companies in the United Kingdom in an article charmingly titled "Higgledy Piggledy Growth." Learned academicians at Princeton and Harvard applied the British study to U.S. companies—and, surprise, the same was true here!

"IBM," the cry immediately went up, "remember IBM." I do remember IBM: a steady high grower for decades. For a while it was a glaring exception. But after the mid-1980s, even the mighty IBM failed to continue its dependable growth pattern. I also remember Polaroid, Apple Computer, Nortel Networks, Xerox, Cisco, and dozens of other firms that chalked up consistent large growth rates until the roof fell in. I hope you remember not the current exceptions, but rather the rule: Many in Wall Street refuse to accept the fact that no reliable pattern can be discerned from past records to aid the analyst in predicting future growth. Even during the boom years of the 1990s, only one in eight large companies managed to achieve consistent yearly growth. And not even one continued to enjoy growth into the first years of the New Millennium. Analysts can't predict consistent long-run growth because it does not exist.

A good analyst will argue, however, that there's much more to predicting than just examining the past record. Some will even admit the past record is not a perfect measurement. Rather than examine every factor that goes into the actual forecasting process, John Cragg and I decided to concentrate on the end result: the prediction itself.

Donning our cloak of academic detachment, we wrote to nineteen major Wall Street firms engaged in fundamental analysis. The nineteen firms, which asked to remain anonymous, included some of the major brokerage firms, mutual-fund management companies, investment advisory firms, and banks engaged in trust management. They are among the most respected names in the investment business.

We requested—and received—past earnings predictions on how these firms felt earnings for specific companies would behave over both a one-year and a five-year period. These estimates, made at several different times, were then compared with actual results to see how well the analysts forecast short-run and long-run earnings changes. The results were surprising.

Bluntly stated, the careful estimates of security analysts (based on industry studies, plant visits, etc.) do little better than those that would be obtained by simple extrapolation of past trends, which we have already seen are no help at all. Indeed, when compared with actual earnings growth rates, the five-year estimates of security analysts were actually worse than the predictions from several naive forecasting models.

For example, one placebo with which the analysts' estimates were compared was the assumption that every company in the economy would enjoy a growth in earnings approximating the long-run rate of growth of the national income. It often turned out that if you used this naive forecasting model, you would make smaller errors in forecasting long-run earnings growth than by using the professional forecasts of the analysts.

Our method of determining the efficacy of the security analyst's diagnoses of his companies is exactly the same as was used before in evaluating the technicians' medicine. We compared the results obtained by following the experts with the results from some naive mechanism involving no expertise at all. Sometimes these naive predictors work very well. For example, if you want to forecast the weather tomorrow, you will do a pretty good job by predicting that it will be exactly the same as today. Although this system misses every one of the turning points in the weather, for most days it is quite reliable. How many weather forecasters do you suppose do any better?

When confronted with the poor record of their five-year growth estimates, the security analysts honestly, if sheepishly, admitted that five years ahead is really too far in advance to make reliable projections. They protested that although long-term projections are admittedly important, they really ought to be judged on their ability to project earnings changes one year ahead. Believe it or not, it turned out that their one-year forecasts were even worse than their five-year projections.

The analysts fought back gamely. They complained that it was unfair to judge their performance on a wide cross section of industries, because earnings for high-tech firms and various "cyclical" companies are notoriously hard to forecast. "Try us on utilities," one analyst confidently asserted. At the time they were considered among the most stable group of companies because of government regulation. So we tried it and they didn't like it. Even the forecasts for the stable utilities were far off the mark. This led to the second major finding of our study: Not one industry is easy to predict.

Moreover, no analysts proved consistently superior to the others. Of course, in each year some analysts did much better than average, but no consistency in their pattern of performance was found. Analysts who did better than average one year were no more likely than the others to make superior forecasts in the next year.

My findings with Cragg have been confirmed by several other researchers. For example, Michael Sandretto of Harvard and Sudhir Milkrishnamurthi of MIT completed a massive study of the one-year forecasts of the 1,000 most widely followed companies. The staggering conclusion of the study was that the error rates each year were remarkably consistent and that the average annual error of the analysts was 31.3 percent over a five-year period. Financial forecasting appears to be a science that makes astrology look respectable.

Amidst all these accusations is a deadly serious message: Security analysts have enormous difficulty in performing their basic function of forecasting company earnings prospects. Investors who put blind faith in such forecasts in making their investment selections are in for some rude disappointments.

Why the Crystal Ball Is Clouded

It is always somewhat disturbing to learn that a group of highly trained and well-paid professionals may not be terribly skillful at their calling. Unfortunately, this is hardly unusual. Similar types of findings could be made for most groups of professionals. There is, for example, a classic example in medicine. At a time when tonsillectomies were very fashionable, the American Child Health Association surveyed a group of 1,000 children, eleven years of age, from the public schools of New York City, and found that 611 of these had had their tonsils removed. The remaining 389 were then examined by a group of physicians, who selected 174 of these for tonsillectomy and declared the rest had no tonsil problem. The remaining 215 were reexamined by another group of doctors, who recommended 99 of these for tonsillectomy. When the 116 "healthy" children were examined a third time, a similar percentage were told their tonsils had to be removed. After three examinations, only 65 children remained who had not been recommended for tonsillectomy. These remaining children were not examined further because the supply of examining physicians ran out.

Numerous studies have shown similar results. Radiologists have failed to recognize the presence of lung disease in about 30 percent of the X-ray plates they read, despite the clear presence of the disease on the X-ray film. Another experiment proved that professional staffs in psychiatric hospitals could not tell the sane from the insane. The point is that we should not take for granted the reliability and accuracy of any judge, no matter how expert. When one considers the low reliability of so many kinds of judgments, it does not seem too surprising that security analysts, with their particularly difficult forecasting job, should be no exception.

There are, I believe, five factors that help explain why security analysts have such difficulty in predicting the future. These are (1) the influence of random events, (2) the production of dubious reported earnings through "creative" accounting procedures, (3) the basic incompetence of many of the analysts themselves, (4) the loss of the best analysts to the sales desk or to portfolio management, and (5) the conflicts of interest facing securities analysts at firms with large investment banking operations. Each factor deserves some discussion.

1. The Influence of Random Events

Many of the most important changes that affect the basic prospects for corporate earnings are essentially random, that is, unpredictable.

Take the utility industry, to which I referred earlier. Presumably it is one of the most stable and dependable groups of companies. But, in fact, many important unpredictable events made earnings even for this industry enormously difficult to forecast. Throughout the late 1900s, unexpected unfavorable rulings of state public utility commissions often made it impossible for utilities to translate rapid growth in demand into higher profits. Other unpredictable events compounded the problem. In the 1970s, forecasts were very wide of the mark as analysts failed to predict the increased fuel costs resulting from the tenfold increase in the international price of oil. In the early 1980s, analysts failed to appreciate the effect of the 1979 accident at Three Mile Island on the later performance of utilities with uncompleted nuclear power plants. And in the 1990s, analysts failed to appreciate the extent to which deregulation and competition would reduce the profit margins of the telephone and electric utilities. Thus, even the "stable" utility industry has proved extraordinarily difficult to predict.

Forecasting problems have been even more difficult in other industries. As we saw in chapter 4, growth forecasts made in early 2000 for a wide variety of high-tech and telecom companies were egregiously wrong. U.S. government budgetary, contract, legal, and regulatory decisions can have enormous implications for the fortunes of individual companies. So can the incapacitation of key members of management, the discovery of a major new product, the finding of defects in a current product, a major oil spill, industrial accidents, terrorist attacks, the entry of new competitors, price wars, and natural disasters such as floods and hurricanes, among others. The stories of unpredictable events affecting earnings are endless.

2. The Production of Dubious Reported Earnings through "Creative" Accounting Procedures

A firm's income statement may be likened to a bikini—what it reveals is interesting but what it conceals is vital. Enron, one of the most ingeniously corrupt companies I have come across, led the beauty parade in this regard. Alas, Enron was far from unique. During the great bull market of the late 1990s, companies increasingly used aggressive fictions to report the soaring sales and earnings needed to propel their stock prices upward.

In the hit musical *The Producers*, Leo Bloom decides he can make more money from a flop than from a hit. He says, "It's all a matter of creative accounting." Bloom's client Max Bialystock sees the potential immediately. Max fleeces buckets of money from rich widows to finance a Broadway musical, *Springtime for Hitler*. Hoping for a total flop, he spends all the money on himself and assumes that no one will ask questions about where the money went.

Actually, Bloom doesn't begin to match the tricks that have been used by companies to pump up earnings and to fool investors and security analysts alike. In chapter 3, I described how Barry Minkow's late 1980's carpet-cleaning empire, ZZZZ Best, was built on a mosaic of phony credit card holdings and fictitious contracts. But accounting abuses appear to have become even more frequent during the 1990s and early twenty-first century. Failing dot-coms, high-tech leaders, and even old economy blue chips all tried to hype earnings and mislead the investment community. As he left the chairmanship of the SEC in 2001, Arthur Levitt warned, "We see greater evidence of [accounting] illusions or tricks than has ever been true of the past."

Here's but a brief number of examples of how companies

have often stretched accounting rules like taffy to mislead analysts and the public as to the true state of their operations.

- In September 2001, Enron and Qwest, the big telecom company, had a problem that revenues and profits needed to be increased. They figured out a great way to make their statements look like business was proceeding well. They swapped fiber-optic network capacity at an exaggerated value of $500 million and each company recorded the transaction as a sale. This inflated profits and masked a deteriorating position for both companies. Qwest already had a surfeit of capacity and, with an enormous glut of fiber in the market, the valuation put on the trade had no justification.

- Motorola, Lucent, and Nortel all boosted sales and earnings by lending large amounts to their customers. Many of these accounts became uncollectable and had to be written off later.

- Xerox boosted its profits in the short term by allowing its overseas units in Europe and Latin America, as well as Canada, to book as one-time revenue all the cash to be paid over several years for long-term copier leases.

- "Chainsaw Al" Dunlap, the CEO of Sunbeam, needed a boost during the winter quarter to satisfy Wall Street's need for steadily growing earnings. He hit upon the ingenious idea of convincing retailers to buy backyard grills in the middle of winter. Chainsaw sweetened the deal by saying that the retailer would not have to actually pay for the grills until later and, furthermore, he would see to it that all purchases would be stored in Sunbeam warehouses. Eventually, he ran out of tricks and Dunlap fled, leaving a cut-up wreck that finally went bankrupt.

- Eastman Kodak availed itself of the "big bash" accounting write-offs. Kodak took six "extraordinary" charges during the 1990s totaling $4.5 billion, equal to all the company's profits over the preceding eight years. Of course, by charging off years of expenses all at once, future earnings look all that much better. It's like an individual making several years of mortgage payments in advance and then claiming that his income has grown.

- Mergers provided lucrative opportunities for accounting tricks. After Worldcom's $37 billion deal for MCI in 1998, they announced a $6 to $7 billion special charge for "in process research" underway at MCI. By taking this high write-off, rather than writing off the research as "goodwill" over forty years, Worldcom could boost its earnings by at least $100 million annually for years to come. "Goodwill" is an accounting term for the premium paid in a merger above the value on the books of the acquired company. Later, under pressure from the SEC, Worldcom reduced the charge to $3 billion. Eventually, Worldcom needed even cruder tricks to boost earnings. In 2002, it admitted to overstating profits by $7 billion by labeling ordinary expenditures as "capital investments" that were recorded as assets of the company.

- Then there is the pension gambit. Many companies in the late 1990s estimated that their pension plans were over-funded and therefore they eliminated the companies' contribution to the plans, thus boosting profits. Often these gains were hidden in the footnotes. When the market suffered a sharp decline during the early 2000s, the companies discovered that their plans were actually underfunded and what investors assumed were sustainable profits turned out to be transitory.

- Other companies treated pending sales as if they had already occurred or reported sales without promised rebates. Airlines, for example, sold first-class tickets to far-away places giving "double miles" as an incentive. They booked the total price of the ticket as revenue but neglected to deduct any liability for the free trips they owe on the accumulated mileage.

But the major problem the analyst has in interpreting current and in projecting future earnings is the tendency of companies to report so-called pro forma earnings as opposed to actual earnings computed in accordance with generally accepted accounting principles. In pro forma earnings, companies decide to ignore certain costs that are considered unusual; in fact, no rules or guidelines exist. Pro forma earnings are often called "earnings before all the bad stuff," and give firms license to exclude any expenses they deem to be "special," "extraordinary," and "non-recurring." Depending on what expenses are considered to be improperly ignored, companies can report a substantial overstatement of earnings. Small wonder that security analysts have extraordinary difficulty estimating what future earnings are likely to be.

3. The Basic Incompetence of Many of the Analysts Themselves

To be perfectly blunt, many security analysts are not particularly perceptive, critical, or competent. I learned this early in the game as a young Wall Street trainee. In attempting to learn the techniques of the pros, I tried to duplicate some analytic work done by a metals specialist named Louie. Louie had figured that for each 1¢ increase in the price of copper, the earnings for a particular copper producer would increase by $1 per share. Because he expected a 5¢ increase in the price of copper, he reasoned that this particular stock was "an unusually attractive purchase candidate."

In redoing the calculation, I found that Louie had misplaced a decimal point. A penny increase in the price of copper would increase earnings by 10¢, not by $1. When I pointed this out to Louie (feeling sure he would want to put out a correction immediately), he simply shrugged his shoulders and declared, "Well, the recommendation sounds more convincing if we leave the report as is." Attention to detail was clearly not the forte of this particular analyst. Alas, Louie was not lonely in this regard.

Louie's lack of attention to detail pointed out his lack of understanding of the industry he was covering. But, he was not unique. In an article written for *Barron's* in early 2000, Dr. Lloyd Kriezer, a plastic surgeon, examined some reports written by biotech analysts. Kriezer paid particular attention to analysts' coverage of those biotech companies that were creating artificial skin for use in the treatment of chronic wounds and burns—a field in which he had considerable expertise. He found the security analysts' diagnoses of stocks far wide off the mark. First, he added the assumptions made of the share of the market predicted for competing companies. The predicted shares of the five biotech companies competing in the market for artificial skin added up to well over 100 percent. Moreover, the analysts' prediction of the absolute size of the potential market bore little relationship to data on the number of actual burn victims, even though accurate data were easily available. Moreover, in examining the various analyst reports on the companies, Dr. Kriezer concluded that "They clearly did not understand the industry." One is reminded of a quote from the legendary baseball manager Casey Stengel: "Can't anybody here play this game?"

Many analysts emulate Louie. Generally too lazy to make their own earnings projections, they prefer to copy the forecasts of other analysts or to swallow the ones released by corporate managements without even chewing. Then it's very easy to know whom to blame if something goes wrong. "That ***!!! treasurer gave me the wrong dope." And it's much easier to be wrong when your professional colleagues all agreed with you. As Keynes put it, "Worldly wisdom teaches that it is better for reputation to fail conventionally than to succeed unconventionally."

Corporate management goes out of its way to ease the forecasting task of the analyst. Let me give you a personal example: A two-day field trip was arranged by a major corporation to brief a whole set of Wall Street security analysts on its operations and future programs.

We were picked up in the morning by the company's private plane for visits and briefings at three of the company's plants. In the evening, we were given first-class accommodations and royally wined and dined. After two more plant visits the next day, we had a briefing, replete with slide show, indicating a "most conservative five-year forecast" of robustly growing earnings.

At each stop, we were showered with gifts—and not only the usual souvenir mock-ups of the company's major products. We also received a variety of desk accessories for the office, a pen and pencil set, leather billfold, tie bar, cufflinks, and a tasteful piece of jewelry to "take home to the wife or mistress, as the case may be." Throughout each day liquor and wine flowed in abundance. As one bleary-eyed analyst confided at the end of the trip, "It's very hard not to have a warm feeling for this company."

I do not mean to imply that most Wall Street analysts do nothing more than to parrot back what managements tell them. But I do imply that the average analyst is just that—a well-paid and usually highly intelligent person who has an extraordinarily difficult job and does it in a rather mediocre fashion. Analysts are often misguided, sometimes sloppy, perhaps self-important, and at times susceptible to the same pressures as other people. In short, they are really very human beings.

4. The Loss of the Best Analysts to the Sales Desk or to Portfolio Management

My fourth argument against the profession is a paradoxical one: Many of the best security analysts are not paid to analyze securities. They are often very high-powered institutional salespeople or they are promoted to the prestigious position of portfolio manager.

Brokerage houses that pride themselves on their research prowess project an aura of respectability by sending a security analyst to chaperone the regular salesperson on a call to a financial institution. Institutional investors like to hear about a new investment idea right from the horse's mouth, and so the regular salesperson usually sits back and lets the analyst do the talking. Thus, most of the articulate analysts find their time is spent with institutional clients, not with financial reports and corporate treasurers. They also find that their monetary rewards are heavily dependent on their ability to bring commission business to the firm.

Moreover, many analysts are seduced away from research work into portfolio management. It's far more exciting, prestigious, and remunerative to "run money" in the line position of portfolio manager than only to advise in the staff position of security analyst. Small wonder that many of the best-respected security analysts do not remain long in their jobs.

5. The Conflicts of Interest between Research and Investment Banking Departments

The analyst's goal is to ring as many cash registers as possible, and the fullest cash registers for the major brokers are to be found in the investment banking division. It wasn't always that way. In the 1970s, before the demise of fixed commissions and the introduction of "discount" brokerage firms, the retail brokerage operation paid the tab and analysts could feel they were really working for their customers—the retail and institutional investors. But that profit center faded in importance with competitive commissions and the only gold mine left was the underwriting of new issues for new or existing firms (where fees can run to hundreds of millions of dollars) and advising firms on borrowing facilities, restructuring, acquisitions, etc. And so it came to pass that "ringing the cash registers" meant helping the brokerage firm obtain and nurture banking clients. And that's how the conflicts arose. Analysts' salaries and bonuses were determined in part by their role in assisting the underwriting department. When such business relationships existed, critics assert the analyst became nothing more than a tool of the investment banking division.

One indication of the tight relationship between security analysts and their investment banking operations is the paucity of sell recommendations. There has always been some bias in the ratio of buy to sell recommendations since analysts do not want to offend the companies they cover for fear that the companies will cut them off from the flow of information. But as investment banking revenues became the major source of profits for the major brokerage firms, research analysts were increasingly paid to be bullish rather than accurate. In one celebrated incident, an analyst who had the chutzpah to recommend that Trump's Taj Mahal bonds should be sold because they were unlikely to pay their interest was summarily fired by his firm after threats of legal retaliation from "The Donald" himself. (Later, the bonds did default.) This is far from an isolated incident. An analyst from BNP Paribas alleged that he was forced out of his job after a sell recommendation on Enron. And a bank stock analyst at Credit Suisse First Boston alleged he was canned after he issued a sweeping recommendation to sell bank stocks. Small wonder that most analysts have purged their prose of negative comments that might give offense to current or prospective investment banking clients. In the 1990s, the ratio of buy to sell recommendations climbed to 100 to 1, particularly for brokerage firms with large investment banking businesses.

To be sure, when an analyst says "buy" he may mean "hold," and when he says "hold" he probably means this as a euphemism for "dump this piece of crap as soon as possible." But investors should not need a course in deconstruction semantics to understand the recommendations and most individual investors sadly took the analysts at their words during the Internet bubble.

There is convincing evidence that analyst recommendations are tainted by the very profitable investment banking relationships of the brokerage firms. Several studies have assessed the accuracy of analysts' stock selections. Brad Barber of the University of California studied the performance of the "strong buy" recommendations of Wall Street analysts and found it nothing short of "disastrous." Indeed, the analysts' strong buy recommendations underperformed the market as a whole by 3 percent per month while their sell recommendations outperformed the markets by 3.8 percent per month. Even worse, researchers at Dartmouth and Cornell found that stock recommendations of Wall Street firms without investment banking relationships did much better than the recommendations of brokerage firms that were involved in profitable investment banking relationships with the companies they covered. Another study from Investors.com found that investors lost over 50 percent when they followed the advice of an analyst employed by a Wall Street firm that managed or co-managed the initial public offering of the recommended stock. Research analysts were basically paid to tout the stocks of the firm's underwriting clients. And analysts lick the hands that feed them.

In 2002, the attorney general of the state of New York, Eliot Spitzer, found a smoking gun. While Henry Blodgett and other analysts at Merrill Lynch were officially recommending a number of Internet and New Economy stocks, the same analysts were referring to the stocks disparagingly in e-mail messages as "junk," "dogs," or less attractive epithets. Merrill did not admit guilt, but it settled with New York and other states for $100 million. Merrill also promised certain reforms such as not directly tying analysts' pay to investment banking revenues, clarifying its stock recommendations, and better disclosing potential conflicts of interest. Other firms such as Goldman Sachs and Salomon Smith Barney quickly embraced the Merrill proposals. As this edition goes to press, however, both regulators and Wall Street firms are still searching for more effective solutions.

Do Security Analysts Pick Winners?—The Performance of the Mutual Funds

I can almost hear the chorus in the background as I write these words. It goes something like this: The real test of the analyst lies in the performance of the stocks he recommends. Maybe "Sloppy Louie," the copper analyst, did mess up his earnings forecast with a misplaced decimal point, but if the stocks he recommended made money for his clients, his lack of attention to detail can surely be forgiven. "Analyze investment performance," the chorus is saying, "not earnings forecasts."

Fortunately, the records of one group of professionals—the mutual funds—are publicly available. Better still for my argument, many of the men and women at the funds are the best analysts and portfolio managers in the business. They stand at the pinnacle of the investment profession.

They allegedly are the first to learn and act on any new fundamental information that becomes available. By their own admission they can clearly make above-average returns. As one investment manager recently put it: "It will take many years before the general level of competence rises enough to overshadow the startling advantage of today's aggressive investment manager." "Adam Smith" echoes a similar statement:

> All the players in the Game are getting rapidly more professional. . . . The true professionals in the Game—the professional portfolio managers—grow more skilled all the time. They are human and they make mistakes, but if you have your money managed by a truly alert mutual fund or even by one of the better banks, you will have a better job done for you than probably at any time in the past.

Statements like these were just too tempting to the lofty-minded in the academic world. Given the wealth of available data, the time available to conduct such research, and the overwhelming desire to prove academic superiority in such matters, it was only natural that academia would zero in on mutual-fund performance.

Again, the evidence from several studies is remarkably uniform. Investors have done no better with the average mutual fund than they could have done by purchasing and holding an unmanaged broad stock index. In other words, over long periods of time mutual-fund portfolios have not outperformed randomly selected groups of stocks. Although funds may have very good records for certain short time periods, there is generally no consistency to superior performance and there is no way to predict in advance how funds will perform in any given future period.

The table below shows the returns from the average large capitalization equity mutual fund over different periods to December 31, 2001. As a comparison, the Standard & Poor's 500-Stock Index is used to represent the market. The table shows that the average mutual fund underperformed the S&P index by almost 2 percentage points per year. Similar results have been found for different time periods and for pension-fund managers as well as mutual-fund managers. Simply buying and holding the stocks in a broad-market index is a strategy that is very hard for the professional portfolio manager to beat.

Mutual Funds vs. the Market Index

	Median total returns (%) ending Dec. 31, 2001		
	10 Years	15 Years	20 Years
Large Cap Equity Funds	10.98	11.95	13.42
S&P 500 Index	12.94	13.74	15.24

Source: Lipper Analytical, Wilshire Associates, Standard & Poor's, and The Vanguard Group.

In addition to the scientific evidence that has been accumulated, several less formal tests have verified this finding. For example, in the early 1990s, the *Wall Street Journal* started a dartboard contest in which each month the selections of four experts were pitted against the selections of four darts. The *Journal* kindly let me throw the darts for the first contest. By the early 2000s, the experts appeared to be somewhat ahead of the darts. If, however, the performance of the experts was measured from the day their selections and their attendant publicity was announced in the *Journal* (rather than from the preceding day), the darts were actually slightly ahead. Does this mean that the wrist is mightier than the brain? Perhaps not, but I think *Forbes* magazine raised a very valid question when one journalist concluded: "It would seem that a combination of luck and sloth beats brains."

How can this be? Every year one can read the performance

rankings of mutual funds. These always show many funds beating the averages—some by significant amounts. The problem is that there is no consistency to performances. Just as past earnings growth cannot predict future earnings, neither can past fund performance predict future results. Fund managements are also subject to random events: they may grow fat, become lazy, or break up. An investment approach that works very well for one period can easily turn sour the next. One is tempted to conclude that a very important factor in determining performance ranking is our old friend Lady Luck.

This conclusion is not a recent one. It has held throughout the past forty years, a period of great change in the market and in the percentage of the general public holding stocks. Again and again yesterday's star fund has proven to be today's disaster. During the late 1960s the go-go funds with their youthful gunslingers turned in spectacular results and their fund managers were written up like sports celebrities. But when the next bear market hit from 1969 through 1976 it was fly now, pay later. The top funds of 1968 had a perfectly disastrous subsequent performance.

The Mates Fund, for example, was number one in 1968. At the end of 1974, the Mates Fund had lost 93 percent of its 1968 value and Fred Mates finally threw in the towel. He then left the investment community to enter a business catering to a new fad. In New York City he started a singles' bar, appropriately named "Mates." Indeed, most of the top performing funds of the late 1960s were out of business by the mid-1970s.

The illustration from the late 1960s appeared in the first edition of this book. Similar examples can be found for subsequent years. The following table presents the 1980 to 1990 performance for the twenty top funds of the 1970–80 period. Again, there is no consistency. Many of the top funds of the 1970s ranked close to the bottom over the next decade. Although the top twenty funds almost doubled the average fund return during the 1970s (19.0 percent versus 10.4 percent), those same funds did worse than average (11.1 percent versus 11.7 percent) over the next decade., There was, however, one striking exception. The Magellan Fund, managed by Peter Lynch, was a superior performer in both the 1970s and 1980s. But Lynch retired in 1990 at the ripe old age of forty-six and we will never know if he would have continued to beat the Street.

How the Top 20 Equity Funds of the 1970s Performed During the 1980s

	Average Annual Return	
	1970s	1980s
Top 20 funds of the 1970s	+19.0%	+11.1%
Average of all equity funds	+10.4%	+11.7%

In case you think the picture changed during the decade of the 1990s, the next table shows the top twenty mutual-fund performers of the decade of the 1980s and how their performance deteriorated into the 1990s. The results are distressingly similar. Note that while the new top twenty of the 1980s were racking up 18 percent yearly gains, the top twenty from the 1970s recorded returns of only 11.1 percent. Financial magazines and newspapers will keep singing the praises of particular mutual-fund managers who have recently produced above-average returns. As long as there are averages, some managers will outperform. But good performance in one period does not predict good performance in the next.

How the Top 20 Equity Funds of the 1980s Performed During the 1990s

	Average Annual Return	
	1980s	1990s
Top 20 funds of the 1980s	+18.0%	+13.7%
S&P 500-Stock Index	+14.1%	+14.9%

An even more dramatic example entitled "Getting Burned by Hot Funds" looks at the best performing general equity funds during the 1998–99 period. We find that the top twenty funds earned rates of return during the last two years of the 1990s that were on average over three times as great as the S&P return. Some had rates of return of approximately 100 percent—implying that an investor would double her money in each of the two years. These were the fund managers adoringly interviewed on CNBC as geniuses and the subject of feature articles in investment magazines. In fact, these funds had simply loaded up their portfolios with New Economy stocks and had ridden the Internet bubble up. When the bubble burst, these same funds had disastrous returns. On average, these same funds were about three times worse than the market as a whole during 2000 and 2001. Investors tragically learned that if even if they made 100 percent one year but lost 50 percent the next, they were not ahead. Their stake ended up exactly where it began. And as these funds continued to plummet during 2002, the picture continued to darken dramatically and investors suffered punishing losses.

In any activity in which large numbers of people are

Getting Burned by Hot Funds

| | 1998–1999 | | 2000–2001 | |
	Rank	Average Annual Return (%)	Rank	Average Annual Return (%)
Fund Name				
Van Wagoner: Emerging Growth	1	105.52	1106	-43.54
Rydex: OTC Fund; Investor Shares	2	93.43	1103	-36.31
TCW Galileo: Aggressive Growth: Institutional	3	92.78	1098	-34.00
RS Investor Shares: Emerging Growth	4	90.19	1055	-26.17
PBHG: Large Capitalization 20	5	84.56	1078	-29.03
Janus Olympus Fund	6	77.24	1061	-27.03
Van Kampen Aggressive Growth: A	7	76.70	1067	-28.04
Janus Mercury	8	76.31	1057	-26.35
PBHG: Selected Equity	9	76.21	1097	-33.19
WM: Growth: A	10	74.77	1046	-25.82
Berger New Generation; Investor Shares	11	73.31	1107	-45.96
Janus Enterprise	12	72.28	1101	-35.40
Janus Venture	13	72.22	1091	-30.89
Fidelity Aggressive Growth	14	70.56	1105	-38.02
Janus Twenty	15	69.09	1090	-30.83
American Century: New Opportunity	16	67.64	1033	-24.11
Morgan Stanley Small Capitalization Growth: B	17	66.59	1102	-35.96
Van Kampen Emerging Growth: A	18	65.67	1021	-22.70
TCW Galileo: Small Capitalization Growth: Institutional	19	64.87	1099	-34.77
BlackRock: Mid-Capitalization Growth: Institutional	20	64.44	1009	-22.18
Average Fund Return		76.72		-31.52
S&P 500 Return		**24.75**		**-10.50**

Source: Bogle Financial Research Center.

engaged, although the average is likely to predominate, the unexpected is bound to happen. The very small number of really good performers we find in the investment management business actually is not at all inconsistent with the laws of chance. Indeed, as I mentioned earlier, the fact that good past performance of a mutual fund is generally no help in predicting future performance only serves to emphasize this point.

Perhaps the laws of chance should be illustrated. Let's engage in a coin-flipping contest. Those who can consistently flip heads will be declared winners. The contest begins and 1,000 contestants flip coins. Just as would be expected by chance, 500 of them flip heads and these winners are allowed to advance to the second stage of the contest and flip again. As might be expected, 250 flip heads. Operating under the laws of chance, there will be 125 winners in the third round, 63 in the fourth, 31 in the fifth, 16 in the sixth, and 8 in the seventh.

By this time, crowds start to gather to witness the surprising ability of these expert coin-flippers. The winners are overwhelmed with adulation. They are celebrated as geniuses in the art of coin-flipping, their biographies are written, and people urgently seek their advice. After all, there were 1,000 contestants and only 8 could consistently flip heads. The game continues and some contestants eventually flip heads nine and ten times in a row.* The point of this analogy is not to indicate that investment-fund managers can or should make their decisions by flipping coins, but that the laws of chance do operate and they can explain some amazing success stories.

It is the nature of an average that some investors will beat it. With large numbers of players in the money game, chance will—and does—explain some extraordinary performance. The very great publicity given occasional success in stock selection reminds me of the story of the doctor who claimed he had developed a cure for cancer in chickens. He proudly announced that in 33 percent of the cases tested remarkable improvement was noted. In another one-third of the cases, he admitted, there seemed to be no change in condition. He then rather sheepishly

---

*If we had let the losers continue to play (as mutual-fund managers do, even after a bad year), we would have found several more contestants who flipped eight or nine heads out of ten and were therefore regarded as expert coin-flippers.

added, "And I'm afraid the third chicken ran away."

Although the preceding discussion has focused on mutual funds, it should not be assumed that the funds are simply the worst of the whole lot of investment managers. In fact, the mutual funds have had a somewhat better performance record than many other professional investors. The records of life insurance companies, property and casualty insurance companies, pension funds, foundations, college endowments, state and local trust funds, personal trusts administered by banks, and individual discretionary accounts handled by investment advisers all have been studied. This research suggests that no sizable differences in the investment performance of common stock portfolios exist among these professional investors or between these groups and the market as a whole. As in the case of the mutual funds, there are some exceptions, but again they are very rare. No scientific evidence has yet been assembled to indicate that the investment performance of professionally managed portfolios as a group has been any better than that of a broad-based index.

Can Any Fundamental System Pick Winners?

Research has also been done on whether above-average returns can be earned by using trading systems based on press announcements of new fundamental information. The answer seems to be a clear no. Systems have been devised in which a news event such as the announcement of an unexpectedly large increase in earnings or a stock split triggers a buy signal. But the evidence points mainly toward the efficiency of the market in adjusting so rapidly to new information that it is impossible to devise successful trading strategies on the basis of such news announcements.* Research indicates that, on average, stock prices react well in advance of unexpectedly good or unexpectedly bad earnings reports. In other words, the

---

*These tests are often referred to as tests of the "semi-strong" form of the efficient-market hypothesis. As mentioned earlier, the "weak" form asserts that past price information cannot be exploited to develop successful trading strategies. The "semi-strong" form says that no publicly announced news event can be exploited by investors to obtain above-average returns.

market is usually sufficiently efficient at anticipating published earnings announcements that investment strategies
involving purchases or sales of stocks after the publication of
those announcements do not appear to offer any help to the
general investor. Although it is true that some studies have
found that stock prices sometimes underreact to earnings
announcements, whatever abnormalities exist do not occur
consistently over time. Indeed, stock prices overreact to earnings news about as often as they underreact.

Similarly, no new information is obtained from announcements of stock splits. Although it is true that companies
announcing stock splits have generally enjoyed rising stock
prices in the period before the announcement of the splits, the
relative performance of the stocks after the announcement
turns out to be precisely in line with that of the general market.
The research indicates that splits are a consequence, not a
cause, of rising stock prices and that no useful investment strategy can be undertaken on the basis of news of impending stock
splits. These studies lend support to the old Wall Street maxim,
"A pie doesn't grow through its slicing."

A good deal of research has also been done on the usefulness
of dividend increases as a basis for selecting stocks that will give
above-average performance. The argument is that an increase in
a stock's dividend is a signal by management that it anticipates
strong future earnings. Dividend increases, in fact, are usually
an accurate indicator of increases in future earnings. There is
also some tendency for a strong price performance to follow the
dividend announcement. However, any rise in price resulting
from the dividend increase, although perhaps not immediately
reflected in the price of stock, was reflected reasonably completely by the end of the announcement month.

The Verdict on Market Timing

Many professional investors move money from cash to equities or to long-term bonds based on their forecasts of fundamental economic conditions. Indeed, this is one reason many
brokers give to support their belief in professional money management. The words of John Bogle, founder of The Vanguard

Group of Investment Companies, are closest to my views on the subject of market timing. Bogle said: "In 30 years in this business, I do not know anybody who has done it successfully and consistently, nor anybody who knows anybody who has done it successfully and consistently. Indeed, my impression is that trying to do market timing is likely, not only not to add value to your investment program, but to be counterproductive."

Bogle's point may be very well illustrated by an examination of the chart shown on page 195. The chart shows the percentage of total assets held in cash of all equity mutual funds from 1970 to 2002. It shows that mutual-fund managers have been incorrect in their allocation of assets into cash in essentially every market cycle during this period. Note that caution on the part of mutual-fund managers (as represented by a very high cash allocation) coincides almost perfectly with troughs in the market. Peaks in mutual funds' cash positions have coincided with market troughs during 1970, 1974, 1982, and the end of 1987 after the great stock-market crash. Another peak in cash positions occurred in late 1990, just before the market rallied during 1991, and in 1994, just before the greatest six-year rise in stock prices in market history. Conversely, the allocation to cash of mutual-fund managers was almost invariably at a low during peak periods in the market. For example, the cash position of mutual funds was near an all time low in March 2000, just before the market began its sharp decline. Clearly the ability of mutual-fund managers to time the market has been egregiously poor.

Remember, over the past fifty-four years the market has risen in thirty-five years, been even in three years, and declined in only fifteen. Thus, the odds of being successful when you are in cash rather than stocks are almost three to one against you. An academic study by Professors Richard Woodward and Jess Chua of the University of Calgary shows that holding on to your stocks as long-term investments works better than market timing because your gains from being in stocks during bull markets far outweigh the losses in bear markets. The professors conclude that a market timer would have to make correct decisions 70 percent of the time to outperform a buy-and-hold investor. I've never met anyone who can bat .700 in calling market turns.

Equity Mutual Funds' Cash–to–Total Assets Ratio and the S&P 500

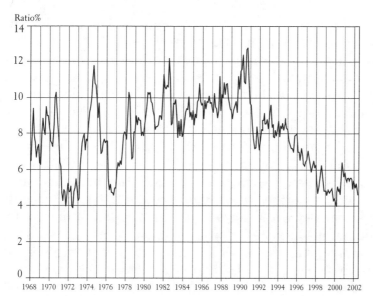

S&P 500*

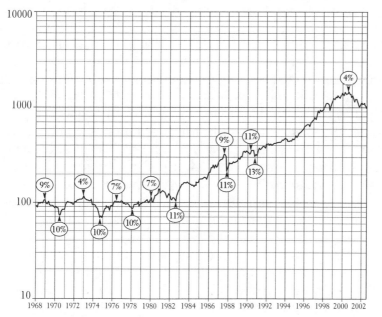

*The circled numbers are the cash–to–total assets ratios

The Semi-strong and Strong Forms of the Efficient-Market Theory

The academic community had rendered its judgment. Fundamental analysis is no better than technical analysis in enabling investors to capture above-average returns. Nevertheless, given its propensity for splitting hairs, the academic community soon fell to quarreling over the precise definition of fundamental information. Some said it was what is known now; others said it extended to the hereafter. It was at this point that what began as the strong form of the efficient-market theory split into two. As we have seen, the "semi-strong" form says that no published information will help the analyst to select undervalued securities. The argument here is that the structure of market prices already takes into account any public information that may be contained in balance sheets, income statements, dividend declarations, and so forth; professional analyses of these data will at best be useless. The "strong" form says that absolutely nothing that is known or even knowable about a company will benefit the fundamental analyst. Not only all the news that is public but also all the information that it is possible to know about the company has already been reflected in the price of the stock. According to the strong form of the theory, not even "inside" information can help the investors.

The strong form of the theory is obviously an overstatement if it does not admit the possibility of gaining from inside information. Nathan Rothschild made millions in the market when his carrier pigeons brought him the first news of Wellington's victory at Waterloo before other traders were aware of the victory. But today, the information superhighway carries news far more swiftly than carrier pigeons. And the SEC has promulgated Regulation FD (Fair Disclosure), which requires companies to make prompt public announcements of any material news items that may affect the price of its stock. The adjustment of market prices to such major news items is immediate. Moreover, insiders who do profit from trading on the basis of nonpublic information are breaking the law. Nobel laureate Paul Samuelson sums up the situation as follows:

> If intelligent people are constantly shopping around for good value, selling those stocks they think will turn out to be over-

valued and buying those they expect are now undervalued, the result of this action by intelligent investors will be to have existing stock prices already have discounted in them an allowance for their future prospects. Hence, to the passive investor, who does not himself search out for under- and overvalued situations, there will be presented a pattern of stock prices that makes one stock about as good or bad a buy as another. To that passive investor, chance alone would be as good a method of selection as anything else.

This is a statement of the efficient-market theory. The "narrow" (weak) form of the theory says that technical analysis—looking at past stock prices—could not help investors. Prices move from period to period very much like a random walk. The "broad" (semi-strong and strong) forms state that fundamental analysis is not helpful either: All that is known concerning the expected growth of the company's earnings and dividends, all of the possible favorable and unfavorable developments affecting the company that might be studied by the fundamental analyst, is already reflected in the price of the company's stock. Thus, purchasing a fund holding all the stocks in a broad-based index will produce a portfolio that can be expected to do as well as any managed by professional security analysts. In a nutshell, the broad form of the theory states: Fundamental analysis cannot produce investment recommendations that will enable an investor consistently to outperform a strategy of buying and holding an index fund.

The efficient-market theory does not, as some critics have proclaimed, state that stock prices move aimlessly and erratically and are insensitive to changes in fundamental information. On the contrary, the reason prices move in a random walk is just the opposite: The market is so efficient—prices move so quickly when new information does arise—that no one can consistently buy or sell quickly enough to benefit. And real news develops randomly, that is, unpredictably. It cannot be predicted by studying either past technical or fundamental information.

Even the legendary Benjamin Graham, heralded as the father of fundamental security analysis, reluctantly came to the conclusion that fundamental security analysis could no longer be counted on to produce superior investment returns. Shortly before he died in 1976, he was quoted in an interview in the

Financial Analysts Journal as saying: "I am no longer an advo-
cate of elaborate techniques of security analysis in order to find
superior value opportunities. This was a rewarding activity,
say, 40 years ago, when Graham and Dodd was first published;
but the situation has changed. . . . [Today] I doubt whether such
extensive efforts will generate sufficiently superior selections
to justify their cost. . . . I'm on the side of the 'efficient market'
school of thought." And Peter Lynch, just after he retired from
managing the Magellan Fund, as well as the legendary Warren
Buffett, admitted that most investors would be better off in an
index fund rather than investing in an actively managed equity
mutual fund.

The Middle of the Road: A Personal Viewpoint

Let's first briefly recap the diametrically opposed view-
points about the functioning of the stock market. The view of
most investment managers is that professionals certainly outperform all amateur and casual investors in managing money.
Much of the academic community, on the other hand, believes
that professionally managed investment portfolios cannot outperform randomly selected portfolios of stocks with equivalent
risk characteristics. Random walkers claim that the stock market adjusts so quickly and perfectly to new information that
amateurs buying at current prices can do just as well as the
pros. Thus, the value of professional investment advice is nil—
at least insofar as it concerns choosing a stock portfolio.

I walk a middle road. I believe that investors might recon-
sider their faith in professional advisers, but I am not as ready
as many of my academic colleagues to damn the entire field.
Although it is abundantly clear that the pros do not consistently beat the averages, I must admit that exceptions to the
rule of the efficient market exist. Well, a few. Although the
preponderance of statistical evidence supports the view that
market efficiency is high, some gremlins are lurking about
that harry the efficient-market theory and make it impossible
for anyone to state that the theory is conclusively demonstrated. Finding inconsistencies in the efficient-market theory
became such a cottage industry during the late 1980s and 1990s

that I will devote an entire chapter (chapter 11) to the market anomalies and so-called predictable patterns that have been uncovered.

Moreover, I worry about accepting all the tenets of the efficient-market theory, in part because the theory rests on several fragile assumptions. The first is that perfect pricing exists. As the quote from Paul Samuelson indicates, the theory holds that, at any time, stocks sell at the best estimates of their intrinsic values. Thus, uninformed investors buying at the existing prices are really getting full value for their money, whatever securities they purchase.

This line of reasoning is uncomfortably close to that of the "greater fool" theory. We have seen ample evidence in Part One that stocks sometimes do not sell on the basis of anyone's estimate of value (as hard as this is to measure)—that purchasers are often swept up in waves of frenzy. It is true that the market pros were largely responsible for several twentieth-century speculative crazes, including the turn-of-the-century Internet bubble. But the existence of such psychological influences on market prices at least raises the possibility that investors may not want to accept the current tableau of market prices as being the best reflection of intrinsic values.

Another fragile assumption is that news travels instantaneously. I doubt that there will ever be a time when all useful inside information is immediately disclosed to everybody. Indeed, even if it can be argued that all relevant news for the major stocks followed by institutional investors is quickly reflected in their prices, it may well be that this is not the case for all the thousands of small companies that are not closely followed by the pros. Moreover, the efficient-market theory implies that no one possesses monopolistic power over the market and that stock recommendations based on unfounded beliefs do not lead to large buying. But firms specializing in research services and various institutional investors wield considerable power in the market and can direct tremendous money flows in and out of stocks. In this environment, it is quite possible that erroneous beliefs about a stock by some professionals can for a considerable time be self-fulfilling.

Finally, there is the enormous difficulty of translating known information about a stock into an estimate of true value.

We have seen that the major determinants of a stock's value concern the extent and duration of its growth path far into the future. Estimating this is extraordinarily difficult, and there is considerable scope for an individual with superior intellect and judgment to turn in a superior performance.

But although I believe in the possibility of superior professional investment performance, I must emphasize that the evidence we have thus far does not support the view that such competence exists; and although I may be excommunicated from some academic sects because of my only lukewarm endorsement of the semi-strong and particularly the strong form of the efficient-market theory, I make no effort to disguise my heresy in the financial church. It is clear that if there are exceptional financial managers, they are very rare, and there is no way of telling in advance who they will be. This is a fact of life with which both individual and institutional investors have to deal.

PART THREE

The New Investment Technology

9

A New Walking Shoe: Modern Portfolio Theory

> . . . Practical men, who believe themselves to be quite exempt from any intellectual influence, are usually the slaves of some defunct economist. Madmen in authority, who hear voices in the air, are distilling their frenzy from some academic scribbler of a few years back.
>
> —J. M. Keynes, *The General Theory of Employment, Interest and Money*

Throughout this book, I have attempted to explain the theories used by professionals—simplified as the firm-foundation and castle-in-the-air theories—to predict the valuation of stocks. As we have seen, many academics have earned their reputations by attacking these theories. Although not denying that these theories tell us a good deal about how stocks are valued, the academics maintain that they cannot be relied on to yield extraordinary profits.

As graduate schools continued to grind out bright young economists and statisticians, the attacking academics became so numerous that it seemed obvious—even to them—that a new strategy was needed; ergo, the academic community busily went about erecting its own theories of stock-market valuation. That's what this part of the book is all about: the rarified world of the "new investment technology" created within the towers of academy. One insight—modern portfolio theory (MPT)—is so basic that it is now widely followed on the Street. The others remain controversial enough to continue to generate thesis material for students and hefty lecture fees for their advisers.

In this chapter, I describe the origins and applications of modern portfolio theory. Using these insights, you'll be able to reduce risk while possibly earning a higher return. In chapter 10, I describe how some academics have gained press coverage by saying that investors can increase their returns by assuming a certain kind of risk. Then, in chapter 11, I cover the arguments of some academics and practitioners who conclude that there is no such thing as a random walk and that markets are not efficient: they argue that a large number of investment strategies can be followed to "beat the market" and that, to a considerable extent, market prices are predictable. Then, I conclude by showing how wrong they are. I do this, in part, by using the best example of the efficient-market application—a common-stock index fund—and show that, despite all the journal publications and learned conferences, it remains the undisputed champion in taking the most profitable stroll through the market.

The Role of Risk

Efficient-market theory explains why the random walk is possible. It holds that the stock market is so good at adjusting to new information that no one can predict its future course in a superior manner. Because of the actions of the pros, the prices of individual stocks quickly reflect all the news that is available. Thus, the odds of selecting superior stocks or anticipating the general direction of the market are even. Your guess is as good as that of the ape, your stockbroker, or even mine.

Hmmm. "I smell a rat," as Samuel Butler wrote long ago. Money is being made on the market; some stocks do outperform others. Common sense attests that some people can and do beat the market. It's not all chance. Many academics agree; but the method of beating the market, they say, is not to exercise superior clairvoyance but rather to assume greater risk. Risk, and risk alone, determines the degree to which returns will be above or below average, and thus decides the valuation of any stock relative to the market.

Defining Risk: The Dispersion of Returns

Risk is a most slippery and elusive concept. It's hard for investors—let alone economists—to agree on a precise definition. The American Heritage Dictionary defines risk as the possibility of suffering harm or loss. If I buy one-year Treasury bills to yield 5 percent and hold them until they mature, I am virtually certain of earning a 5 percent monetary return, before income taxes. The possibility of loss is so small as to be considered nonexistent. If I hold common stock in my local power and light company for one year on the basis of an anticipated 6 percent dividend return, the possibility of loss is greater. The dividend of the company may be cut and, more important, the market price at the end of the year may be much lower, causing me to suffer a serious net loss. Investment risk, then, is the chance that expected security returns will not materialize and, in particular, that the securities you hold will fall in price.

Once academics accepted the idea that risk for investors is related to the chance of disappointment in achieving expected security returns, a natural measure suggested itself—the probable variability or dispersion of future returns. Thus, financial risk has generally been defined as the variance or standard deviation of returns. Being long-winded, we use the accompanying exhibit to illustrate what we mean. A security whose returns are not likely to depart much, if at all, from its average (or expected) return is said to carry little or no risk. A security whose returns from year to year are likely to be quite volatile (and for which sharp losses are typical in some years) is said to be risky.

Illustration: Expected Return and Variance Measures of Reward and Risk

This simple example will illustrate the concept of expected return and variance and how they are measured. Suppose you buy a stock from which you expect the following overall returns (including both dividends and price changes) under different economic conditions:

Business Conditions	Possibility of Occurrence	Expected Return
"Normal" economic conditions	1 chance in 3	10 %
Rapid real growth without inflation	1 chance in 3	30 %
Recession with inflation (stagflation)	1 chance in 3	−10 %

If, on average, a third of past years have been "normal," another third characterized by rapid growth without inflation, and the remaining third characterized by "stagflation," it might be reasonable to take these relative frequencies of past events and treat them as our best guesses (probabilities) of the likelihood of future business conditions. We could then say that an investor's expected return is 10 percent. One-third of the time the investor gets 30 percent, another one-third 10 percent, and the rest of the time she suffers a 10 percent loss. This means that, on average, her yearly return will turn out to be 10 percent.

Expected return $= \frac{1}{3}(0.30) + \frac{1}{3}(0.10) + \frac{1}{3}(-0.10) = 0.10$.

The yearly returns will be quite variable, however, ranging from a 30 percent gain to a 10 percent loss. The "variance" is a measure of the dispersion of returns. It is defined as the average squared deviation of each possible return from its average (or expected) value, which we just saw was 10 percent.

Variance $= \frac{1}{3}(0.30-0.10)^2 + \frac{1}{3}(0.10-0.10)^2 + \frac{1}{3}(-0.10-0.10)^2$
$= \frac{1}{3}(0.20)^2 + \frac{1}{3}(0.00)^2 + \frac{1}{3}(-0.20)^2 = 0.0267$.

The square root of the variance is known as the standard deviation. In this example, the standard deviation equals 0.1634.

Dispersion measures of risk such as variance and standard deviation have failed to satisfy everyone. "Surely riskiness is not related to variance itself," the critics say. "If the dispersion results from happy surprises—that is, from outcomes turning out better than expected—no investors in their right minds would call that risk."

It is, of course, quite true that only the possibility of downward disappointments constitutes risk. Nevertheless, as a practical matter, as long as the distribution of returns is symmetric— that is, as long as the chances of extraordinary gain are roughly the same as the probabilities for disappointing returns and losses—a dispersion or variance measure will suffice as a risk measure. The greater the dispersion or variance, the greater the possibilities for disappointment.

Although the pattern of historical returns from individual securities has not usually been symmetric, the returns from well-diversified portfolios of stocks do seem to be distributed approximately symmetrically. The following chart shows the distribution of monthly security returns for a portfolio invested in the S&P 500-Stock Index over more than sixty years. It was constructed by dividing the range of returns into equal intervals (of approximately 1¼ percent) and then noting the frequency (the number of months) with which the returns fell within each interval. On average, the portfolio returned close to 1 percent per month or about 11 percent per year. In periods when the market declined sharply, however, the portfolio also plunged, losing as much as 20 percent in a single month.

For reasonably symmetric distributions such as this one, a helpful rule of thumb is that two-thirds of the monthly returns tend to fall within one standard deviation of the average return

Distribution of Monthly Returns for a Portfolio Invested in the S&P 500-Stock Index, January 1940–June 2002

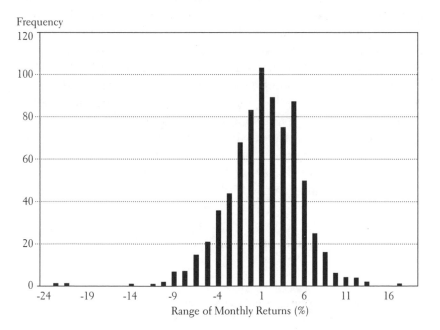

and 95 percent of the returns fall within two standard deviations. Recall that the average return for this distribution was close to 1 percent per month. The standard deviation (our measure of portfolio risk) turns out to be about 4½ percent per month. Thus, in two-thirds of the months the returns from this portfolio were between 5½ percent and –3½ percent, and 95 percent of the returns were between 10 percent and –8 percent. Obviously, the higher the standard deviation (the more spread out are the returns), the more probable it is (the greater the risk) that at least in some periods you will take a real bath in the market. That's why a measure of variability such as standard deviation* is so often used and justified as an indication of risk.

Documenting Risk: A Long-Run Study

One of the best documented propositions in the field of finance is that, on average, investors have received higher rates of return for bearing greater risk. The most thorough study has been done by Ibbotson Associates. Their data cover the period 1926 through 2001, and the results are shown in the following table. Appearances notwithstanding, the table was not designed to show one Manhattan skyline and a series of Eiffel Towers. What Ibbotson Associates did was to take several different investment vehicles—stocks, bonds, and Treasury bills—as well as the consumer price index, and measure the percentage increase or decrease each year for each item. A rectangle or bar was then erected on the baseline to indicate the number of years the returns fell between 0 and 5 percent; another rectangle indicated the number of years the returns fell between 5 and 10 percent; and so on, for both positive and negative returns. The result is a series of bars showing the dispersion of returns and from which the standard deviation can be calculated.

A quick glance shows that over long periods of time, common stocks have, on average, provided relatively generous total

*Standard deviation and its square, the variance, are used interchangeably as risk measures. They both do the same thing and it's purely a matter of convenience which one we use.

Basic Series: Summary Statistics of Annual Total Returns from 1926 to 2001

Series	Geometric Mean	Arithmetic Mean	Standard Deviation	Distribution
Large-company stocks	10.4%	12.4%	20.8%	
Small-company stocks*	12.1	17.5	35.3	
Long-term corporate bonds	5.4	5.7	8.5	
Long-term government bonds	4.8	5.1	8.6	
Intermediate-term government bonds	5.1	5.3	5.6	
U.S. Treasury bills	3.7	3.8	3.4	
Inflation	3.1	3.2	4.7	

–90%   0%   90%

Source: Ibbotson Associates.
*The 1993 small-company stock total return was 142.9 percent.

rates of return. These returns, including dividends and capital gains, have exceeded by a substantial margin the returns from long-term bonds, Treasury bills, and the inflation rate as measured by the annual rate of increase in consumer prices. Thus, stocks have tended to provide positive "real" rates of return, that is, returns after washing out the effects of inflation.* The data show, however, that common-stock returns are highly variable, as indicated by the standard deviation and the range of annual returns, shown in adjacent columns of the table. Returns from equities have ranged from a gain of more than 50

*Similar returns have been earned over even longer periods. For example, Jeremy Siegel finds that since 1871, U.S. common stocks have provided an average annual rate of return of close to 9 percent. The average inflation rate was only 2 percent over that same period.

percent (in 1933) to a loss of almost the same magnitude (in 1931). Clearly, the extra returns that have been available to investors from stocks have come at the expense of assuming considerably higher risk. Note that small company stocks have provided an even higher rate of return since 1926 but the dispersion (standard deviation) of those returns has been even larger than for equities in general. Again, we see that higher returns have been associated with higher risks.

There have been several periods of five years or longer when common stocks have actually produced negative rates of return. The early 1930s were extremely poor for stock-market investors. The early 1970s also produced negative returns. The one-third decline in the broad stock-market averages during October 1987 is the most dramatic change in stock prices during a brief period since the 1930s. And stock investors know only too well how poorly stocks performed in the early years of the 2000s. Still, over the long haul, investors have been rewarded with higher returns for taking on more risk. However, given the rate of return they seek, there are ways in which investors can reduce the risks they take. This brings us to the subject of modern portfolio theory, which has revolutionized the investment thinking of professionals.

Reducing Risk: Modern Portfolio Theory (MPT)

Portfolio theory begins with the premise that all investors are like my wife—they are risk-averse. They want high returns and guaranteed outcomes. The theory tells investors how to combine stocks in their portfolios to give them the least risk possible, consistent with the return they seek. It also gives a rigorous mathematical justification for the time-honored investment maxim that diversification is a sensible strategy for individuals who like to reduce their risks.

The theory was invented in the 1950s by Harry Markowitz, and for his contribution he was awarded the Nobel Prize in Economics in 1990. His book, *Portfolio Selection*, was an outgrowth of his Ph.D. dissertation at the University of Chicago. His experience has ranged from teaching at UCLA to designing a computer language at RAND Corporation and helping Gen-

eral Electric solve manufacturing problems by computer simu-
lations. He has even practiced money management, serving as
president of Arbitrage Management Company, which ran a
"hedge fund." What Markowitz discovered was that portfolios
of risky (volatile) stocks might be put together in such a way
that the portfolio as a whole could be less risky than the individual stocks in it.

The mathematics of modern portfolio theory (also known
as MPT) is recondite and forbidding; it fills the journals and,
incidentally, keeps a lot of academics busy. That in itself is no
small accomplishment. Fortunately, there is no need to lead
you through the labyrinth of quadratic programming for you to
understand the core of the theory. A single illustration will
make the whole game clear.

Let's suppose we have an island economy with only two
businesses. The first is a large resort with beaches, tennis
courts, a golf course, and the like. The second is a manufacturer
of umbrellas. Weather affects the fortunes of both. During sunny
seasons, the resort does a booming business and umbrella sales
plummet. During rainy seasons, the resort owner does very
poorly, while the umbrella manufacturer enjoys high sales and
large profits. The table below shows some hypothetical returns
for the two businesses during the different seasons:

	Umbrella Manufacturer	Resort Owner
Rainy season	50%	−25%
Sunny season	25%	50%

Suppose that, on average, one-half of the seasons are sunny
and one-half are rainy (i.e., the probability of a sunny or rainy
season is ½). An investor who bought stock in the umbrella
manufacturer would find that half the time he earned a 50 percent return and half the time he lost 25 percent of his investment. On average, he would earn a return of 12½ percent. This
is what we have called the investor's expected return. Similarly, investment in the resort would produce the same results.
Investing in either one of these businesses would be fairly
risky, however, because the results are quite variable and there
could be several sunny or rainy seasons in a row.

Suppose, however, that instead of buying only one security,

an investor with two dollars diversified and put half his money in the umbrella manufacturer's and half in the resort owner's business. In sunny seasons, a one-dollar investment in the resort would produce a 50-cent return, whereas a one-dollar investment in the umbrella manufacturer would lose 25 cents. The investor's total return would be 25 cents (50 cents minus 25 cents), which is 12½ percent of his total investment of two dollars.

Note that during rainy seasons, exactly the same thing happens—only the names are changed. Investment in the umbrella manufacturer produces a good 50 percent return while the investment in the resort loses 25 percent. Again, however, the diversified investor makes a 12½ percent return on his total investment.

This simple illustration points out the basic advantage of diversification. Whatever happens to the weather, and thus to the island economy, by diversifying investments over both of the firms an investor is sure of making a 12½ percent return each year. The trick that made the game work was that although both companies were risky (returns were variable from year to year), the companies were affected differently by weather conditions. (In statistical terms, the two companies had a negative covariance.)* As long as there is some lack of parallelism in the fortunes of the individual companies in the economy, diversification will always reduce risk. In the present case, where there is a perfect negative relationship between the companies' fortunes (one always does well when the other does poorly), diversification can totally eliminate risk.

---

*Statisticians use the term "covariance" to measure what I have called the degree of parallelism between the returns of the two securities. If we let R stand for the actual return from the resort and $\bar{R}$ be the expected or average return, whereas U stands for the actual return from the umbrella manufacturer and $\bar{U}$ is the average return, we define the covariance between U and R (or COV_{UR}) as follows:

$$\text{COV}_{UR} = \text{Prob. rain}\,(U, \text{if rain} - \bar{U})\,(R, \text{if rain} - \bar{R}) + \text{Prob. sun}\,(U, \text{if sun} - \bar{U})\,(R, \text{if sun} - \bar{R}).$$

From the preceding table of returns and assumed probabilities, we can fill in the relevant numbers:

$$\text{COV}_{UR} = \tfrac{1}{2}(0.50 - 0.125)\,(-0.25 - 0.125) + \tfrac{1}{2}(-0.25 - 0.125)\,(0.50 - 0.125) = -0.141.$$

Whenever the returns from two securities move in tandem (when one goes up the other always goes up), the covariance number will be a large positive number. If the returns are completely out of phase, as in the present example, the two securities are said to have negative covariance.

Of course, there is always a rub, and the rub in this case is that the fortunes of most companies move pretty much in tandem. When there is a recession and people are unemployed, they may buy neither summer vacations nor umbrellas. Therefore, one should not expect in practice to get the neat kind of total risk elimination just shown. Nevertheless, because company fortunes don't always move completely in parallel, investment in a diversified portfolio of stocks is likely to be less risky than investment in one or two single securities.

It is easy to carry the lessons of this illustration to actual portfolio construction. Suppose you were considering combining General Motors and its major supplier of new tires in a stock portfolio. Would diversification be likely to give you much risk reduction? Probably not. It may not be true that "as General Motors goes, so goes the nation" but it surely does follow that if General Motors' sales slump, GM will be buying fewer new tires from the tire manufacturer. In general, diversification will not help much if there is a high covariance (high correlation) between the returns of the two companies.

On the other hand, if General Motors were combined with a government contractor in a depressed area, diversification might reduce risk substantially. It usually has been true that as the nation goes, so goes General Motors. If consumer spending is down (or if an oil crisis comes close to paralyzing the nation), General Motors' sales and earnings are likely to be down and the nation's level of unemployment up. Now, if the government makes a habit during times of high unemployment of giving out contracts to the depressed area (to alleviate some of the unemployment miseries there), it could well be that the returns of General Motors and those of the contractor do not move in phase. The two stocks might have very little covariance or, better still, negative covariance.

The example may seem a bit strained, and most investors will realize that when the market gets clobbered, just about all stocks go down. Still, at least at certain times, some stocks and some classes of assets do move against the market; that is, they have negative covariance or, what is the same thing, they are negatively correlated with each other.*

---

*The correlation coefficient is the major factor determining covariance.

The Correlation Coefficient and the Ability
of Diversification to Reduce Risk

Correlation Coefficient	Effect of Diversification on Risk
+1.0	No risk reduction is possible.
0.5	Moderate risk reduction is possible.
0	Considerable risk reduction is possible.
−0.5	Most risk can be eliminated.
−1.0	All risk can be eliminated.

Now comes the real kicker; negative correlation is not necessary to achieve the risk reduction benefits from diversification. Markowitz's great contribution to investors' wallets was
his demonstration that anything less than perfect positive correlation can potentially reduce risk. His research led to the
results presented in the preceding table. As shown, it demonstrates the crucial role of the correlation coefficient in determining whether adding a security or an asset class can reduce risk.

Diversification in Practice

To paraphrase Shakespeare, can there be too much of a
good thing? In other words, is there a point at which diversification is no longer a magic wand safeguarding returns? Numerous studies have demonstrated that the answer is a resounding
yes. Of course, economists qualify that straightforward answer.

As shown in the following chart, the golden number for
American xenophobes—those fearful of looking beyond our
national borders—is at least fifty equal-sized and well-diversified
U.S. stocks (clearly, fifty oil stocks or fifty electric utilities
would not produce an equivalent amount of risk reduction).
With such a portfolio, the total risk is reduced by over 60 percent. And that's where the good news stops, as further
increases in the number of holdings do not produce much additional risk reduction.

Those with a broader view—investors who recognize that
the world has changed considerably since Markowitz first
enunciated his theory—can reap even greater protection
because the movement of foreign economies is not always syn-
chronous with that of the U.S. economy. The oil crisis of the

The Benefits of Diversification

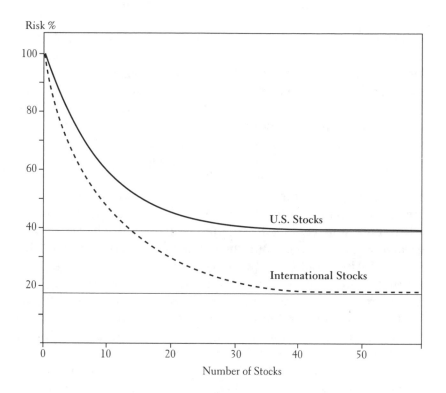

1970s, for example, had a more devastating effect on oil-poor Europe and Japan than on the United States, which is at least partially self-sufficient in oil. On the other hand, the tenfold increase in the price of oil had a very positive effect on Indonesia, Venezuela, and oil-producing countries in the Middle East. Similarly, increases in mineral and other raw material prices have positive effects on nations rich in natural resources and negative effects on many developed manufacturing countries.

It turns out that about fifty is also the golden number for global-minded investors. Such investors, however, get more protection for their money, as shown in the preceding chart. Here, the stocks are drawn not simply from the U.S. stock market but from the international markets as well. As expected, the international diversified portfolio tends to be less risky than the one of corresponding size drawn purely from U.S. stocks.

The benefits of international diversification have been well documented. The figure on page 217 shows the gains realized over a more than thirty year period from 1970 through mid-2002. During this time period, foreign stocks (as measured by the Morgan Stanley EAFE [Europe, Australia, and Far East] Index of developed foreign countries) had an average annual return that was slightly higher than the U.S. stocks in the S&P 500 Index. U.S. stocks, however, were safer in that their year-to-year returns were less volatile. The correlation between the returns from the two indexes during this time period was around 0.5—positive but only moderately high. The figure shows the different combinations of return and risk (volatility) that could have been achieved if an investor had held different combinations of U.S. and EAFE (developed foreign country) stocks. At the right-hand side of the figure, we see the higher return and higher risk level (greater volatility) that would have been achieved with portfolio of only EAFE stocks. At the left-hand side of the figure, the return on and risk level of a totally domestic portfolio of U.S. stocks are shown. The solid dark line indicates the different combinations of return and volatility that would result from different portfolio allocations between domestic and foreign stocks.

Note that as the portfolio shifts from a 100 percent domestic allocation to one with gradual additions of foreign stocks, the return tends to increase because EAFE stocks produced a slightly higher return than domestic stocks over this period. The significant point, however, is that adding some of these riskier securities actually reduces the portfolio's risk level—at least for a while. Eventually, however, as larger and larger proportions of the riskier EAFE stocks are put into the portfolio, the overall risk rises with the overall return.

The paradoxical result of this analysis is that overall portfolio risk is reduced by the addition of a small amount of riskier foreign securities. Good returns from Japanese automakers, for example, balanced out poor returns from domestic ones during a time when the Japanese share of the U.S. market increased. On the other hand, good returns from U.S. manufacturing firms balanced out poor returns from foreign manufacturers when the dollar became more competitive and Japan and Europe remained in a recession as the U.S. economy boomed. It is precisely these offsetting movements that reduced the overall volatility of the portfolio.

Diversification of U.S. and Developed
Foreign Country Stocks
January 1970–June 2002
Over a 32-year period, the mix that provided the highest return available
with the least risk was 24% in foreign and 76% in U.S. stocks.

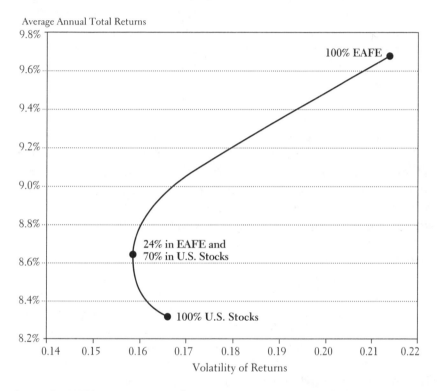

Source: DATASTREAM (Morgan Stanley).

It turns out that the portfolio with the least risk had 24 percent foreign securities and 76 percent U.S. securities. Moreover, adding 24 percent EAFE stocks to a domestic portfolio also tended to increase the portfolio return. In this sense, international diversification provided the closest thing to a free lunch available in our world securities markets. When higher portfolio returns can be achieved with lower risk by adding international stocks, no individual or institutional portfolio manager should fail to take notice.

International stocks will not always provide higher returns than U.S. stocks. During the 1990s, the U.S. market, as measured by the S&P 500, far outdistanced the stock markets of

Europe and Japan. Nevertheless, the risk-reduction benefits of diversification remain no matter which markets do best. As long as correlations among markets remain in less than a perfect lockstep relationship, investors will gain considerable benefits from international diversification.

Investors may do even better by including stocks from emerging markets in their overall mix. Despite the fact that emerging stock markets are wildly volatile—having bucked up and down much more violently than the U.S. stock market and suffering punishing losses during 1997 and early 1998—some further diversification into these markets can actually reduce overall portfolio volatility. Correlations between broad indexes of emerging market stocks and the U.S. stock market are generally lower than those of the U.S. stock market with developed foreign markets. Moreover, correlations between emerging market returns and those of developed European and Asian markets are also low. Most Americans are global consumers: they buy cars from Japan and Germany, television sets from Asia, and a variety of goods from emerging market countries—from nearby Mexico to far-off Thailand. Just as consumers benefit from the global marketplace, so too can investors benefit from global investing.

It has been possible to achieve greater returns and less risk from a portfolio of common stocks drawn from both developed and emerging foreign markets as well as from the U.S. market. But as readers of this book should know only too well, what worked in the past does not necessarily work in the future. Can you continue to expect a free lunch from international diversification? Many analysts think not. They feel that the globalization of the world economies has blunted the benefits of international diversification.

The figure on page 219 shows that the correlations between markets have tended to rise over time throughout the 1990s. The top panel shows the correlations between the EAFE and S&P 500 indexes. Every three years a correlation coefficient between quarterly EAFE returns and U.S. stock returns was calculated, and the three-year correlation coefficients were plotted over time. The figure shows that the correlations between the U.S. and developed foreign markets have risen to almost 1 at the turn of the century, suggesting that diversification benefits for international investing may be substantially reduced.

Correlation of Foreign Developed and
Emerging Markets with the U.S. Stock Market*

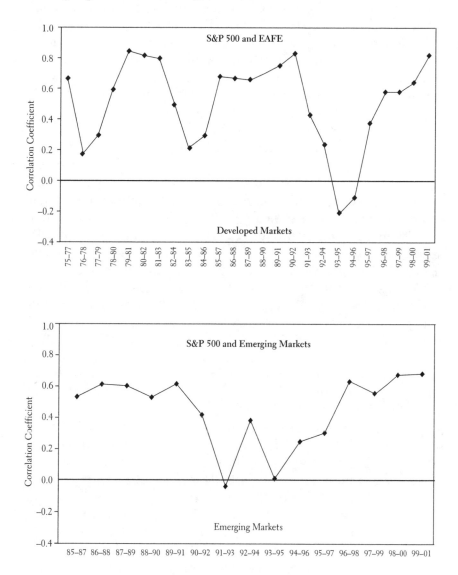

*The dots are the measured correlation coefficients for quarterly returns for various three-year periods from 1975 (for developed markets) and 1985 (for emerging markets) through 2001. Remember that a correlation of (+) 1 implies no benefit from diversification. A correlation of zero implies considerable benefit from diversification.

Moreover, the correlations during times when the U.S. market declines tend to be even higher. When the U.S. market catches cold, foreign markets often develop pneumonia and diversification can fail us just when we need it most.

While we should not get too enthusiastic about the benefits of international diversification, we also should not reject the potential benefits. Correlations jump around a good deal (they have been around 0.8 during some earlier periods) and international markets should not continue to move in lock step, particularly as currency relationships change. Over half of the world's capitalization exists outside the United States and we should not ignore the many dynamic and innovative companies domiciled outside the United States. Moreover, correlations between the United States and emerging markets tended to be lower than was the case with developed markets.

There are also compelling reasons to diversify a portfolio with other asset classes. As will be more fully described in Part Four, real estate investment trusts (REITs), which are marketable stocks mostly traded on the New York Stock Exchange, enable investors to buy portfolios of commercial real estate properties. REITs provide attractive diversification benefits for portfolios. Real estate returns don't move in tandem with other assets. For example, during periods of accelerating inflation, properties tend to do much better than other common stocks. Thus, adding real estate to a portfolio tends to reduce its overall volatility.

Another asset class that belongs in most portfolios is bonds. In Part Four, I describe the advantages of bonds in more detail, but here I note their diversification benefits. Movements in long-term bonds and especially Treasury inflation-protection securities (more fully discussed in chapter 12) do not mirror those of other assets, and tend to provide relatively stable returns when held to maturity. The two charts on page 221 show that three-year correlations of U.S. real estate and various bonds with the U.S. market are sufficiently low to provide important diversification benefits and have shown no tendency to become less favorable over time. In Part Four, I will rely on this discussion of portfolio theory to craft appropriate asset allocations for individuals in different age brackets and with different risk tolerances.

Correlation of U.S. Real Estate Market (REITs) with the U.S. Stock Market*

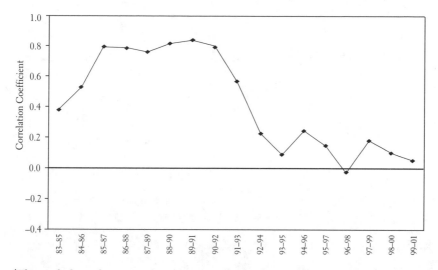

*The graph shows the measured correlation coefficients for quarterly returns for various three-year periods from 1983 through 2001. Remember that a correlation of (+)1 implies no benefit from diversification. A correlation of zero implies considerable benefit from diversification.

Correlation of U.S. Bond Market (30-Year Treasury Bonds) with the U.S. Stock Market*

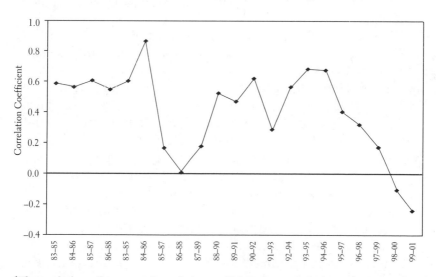

*The graph shows the measured correlation coefficients for quarterly returns for various three-year periods from 1979 through 2001. Remember that a correlation of (+)1 implies no benefit from diversification. A correlation of zero imples considerable benefit from diversification.

10
Reaping Reward
by Increasing
Risk

Theories that are right only 50 percent of the time are less eco-
nomical than coin-flipping.
—George J. Stigler, *The Theory of Price*

As every reader should know by now, risk has
its rewards. Thus, both within academia and on the Street,
there has long been a scramble to exploit risk to reap greater
riches. That's what this chapter covers: the creation of analytical tools to measure risk and, with such knowledge, reap greater
rewards.

We begin with a refinement to modern portfolio theory. As
I mentioned in the last chapter, diversification cannot eliminate all risk—as it did in my mythical island economy—
because all stocks tend to move up and down together. Thus,
diversification in practice reduces some but not all risk. Three
academics—Stanford professor William Sharpe and the late
finance specialists John Lintner and Fischer Black—focused
their intellectual energies in determining what part of a security's risk can be eliminated by diversification and what part
cannot. The result is known as the capital-asset pricing model.
Sharpe received a Nobel Prize for his contribution to this work
at the same time Markowitz was honored in 1990.

The basic logic behind the capital-asset pricing model is
that there is no premium for bearing risks that can be diversified away. Thus, to get a higher average long-run rate of return

in a portfolio, you need to increase the risk level of the portfolio that cannot be diversified away. According to this theory, savvy investors can outperform the overall market and win the profit race simply by adjusting their portfolios by a risk measure known as beta.

Beta and Systematic Risk

Beta? How did a Greek letter enter this discussion? Surely it didn't originate with a stockbroker. Can you imagine any stockbroker saying, "We can reasonably describe the total risk in any security (or portfolio) as the total variability (variance or standard deviation) of the returns from the security"? But we who teach say such things often. We go on to say that part of total risk or variability may be called the security's *systematic risk* and that this arises from the basic variability of stock prices in general and the tendency for all stocks to go along with the general market, at least to some extent. The remaining variability in a stock's returns is called *unsystematic risk* and results from factors peculiar to that particular company; for example, a strike, the discovery of a new product, and so on.

Systematic risk, also called *market risk*, captures the reaction of individual stocks (or portfolios) to general market swings. Some stocks and portfolios tend to be very sensitive to market movements. Others are more stable. This relative volatility or sensitivity to market moves can be estimated on the basis of the past record, and is popularly known by—you guessed it—the Greek letter beta.

You are now about to learn all you ever wanted to know about beta but were afraid to ask. Basically, beta is the numerical description of systematic risk. Despite the mathematical manipulations involved, the basic idea behind the beta measurement is one of putting some precise numbers on the subjective feelings money managers have had for years. The beta calculation is essentially a comparison between the movements of an individual stock (or portfolio) and the movements of the market as a whole.

The calculation begins by assigning a beta of 1 to a broad market index, such as the S&P 500. If a stock has a beta of 2, then on average it swings twice as far as the market. If the market goes up 10 percent, the stock tends to rise 20 percent. If a stock has a beta of 0.5, it tends to be more stable than the market (it will go up or down 5 percent when the market rises or declines 10 percent). Professionals often call high-beta stocks aggressive investments and label low-beta stocks as defensive.

Now the important thing to realize is that *systematic risk cannot be eliminated by diversification*. It is precisely because all stocks move more or less in tandem (a large share of their variability is systematic) that even diversified stock portfolios are risky. Indeed, if you diversified perfectly by buying a share in the Total Stock Market Index (which by definition has a beta of 1) you would still have quite variable (risky) returns because the market as a whole fluctuates widely.

Unsystematic risk is the variability in stock prices (and therefore, in returns from stocks) that results from factors peculiar to an individual company. Receipt of a large new contract, the finding of mineral resources on the company's property, labor difficulties, accounting fraud, the discovery that the corporation's treasurer has had his hand in the company till—all can make a stock's price move independently of the market. The risk associated with such variability is precisely the kind that diversification can reduce. The whole point of portfolio theory is that, to the extent that stocks don't move in tandem all the time, variations in the returns from any one security tend to be washed away or smoothed out by complementary variation in the returns from other securities.

The chart below, similar to the one on page 215, illustrates the important relationship between diversification and total risk. Suppose we randomly select securities for our portfolio that tend on average to be just as volatile as the market (the average betas for the securities in our portfolio will always be equal to 1). The chart shows that as we add more and more securities, the total risk of our portfolio declines, especially at the start.

When thirty securities are selected for our portfolio, a good deal of the unsystematic risk is eliminated, and additional diversification yields little further risk reduction. By the time sixty well-diversified securities are in the portfolio, the unsystematic risk is substantially eliminated and our portfolio (with

How Diversification Reduces Risk

Risk of Portfolio (Standard Deviation of Return)

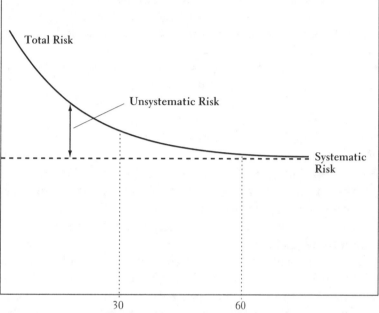

30   60
Number of Securities in Portfolio

a beta of 1) will tend to move up and down essentially in tandem with the market. Of course, we could perform the same experiment with stocks whose average beta is 1½. Again, we would find that diversification quickly reduced unsystematic risk, but the remaining systematic risk would be larger. A portfolio of sixty or more stocks with an average beta of 1½ would tend to be 50 percent more volatile than the market.

Now comes the key step in the argument. Both financial theorists and practitioners agree that investors should be compensated for taking on more risk with a higher expected return. Stock prices must, therefore, adjust to offer higher returns where more risk is perceived, to ensure that all securities are held by someone. Obviously, risk-averse investors wouldn't buy securities with extra risk without the expectation of extra reward. But not all of the risk of individual securities is rele-

vant in determining the premium for bearing risk. The unsystematic part of the total risk is easily eliminated by adequate
diversification. So there is no reason to think that investors will
receive extra compensation for bearing unsystematic risk. The
only part of total risk that investors will get paid for bearing is
systematic risk, the risk that diversification cannot help. Thus,
the capital-asset pricing model says that returns (and, therefore, risk premiums) for any stock (or portfolio) will be related
to beta, the systematic risk that cannot be diversified away.

The Capital-Asset Pricing Model (CAPM)

The proposition that risk and reward are related is not new.
Finance specialists have agreed for years that investors do need
to be compensated for taking on more risk. What is different
about the new investment technology is the definition and
measurement of risk. Before the advent of the capital-asset
pricing model, it was believed that the return on each security
was related to the total risk inherent in that security. It was
believed that the return from a security varied with the instability of that security's particular performance, that is, with the
variability or standard deviation of the returns it produced. The
new theory says that the *total* risk of each individual security is
irrelevant. It is only the systematic component that counts as
far as extra rewards go.

Although the mathematical proof of this proposition is forbidding, the logic behind it is fairly simple. Consider a case in
which there are two groups of securities—Group I and Group
II—with sixty securities in each. Suppose that the systematic
risk (beta) for each security is 1; that is, each of the securities in
the two groups tends to move up and down in tandem with the
general market. Now suppose that, because of factors peculiar to
the individual securities in Group I, the total risk for each of
them is substantially higher than the total risk for each security
in Group II. Imagine, for example, that in addition to general
market factors the securities in Group I are also particularly susceptible to climatic variations, to changes in exchange rates, and
to natural disasters. The specific risk for each of the securities
in Group I will, therefore, be very high. The specific risk for

each of the securities in Group II, however, is assumed to be very low, and, hence, the total risk for each of them will be very low. Schematically, this situation appears as follows:

Group I (60 Securities)	Group II (60 Securities)
Systematic risk (beta) = 1 for each security	Systematic risk (beta) = 1 for each security
Specific risk is high for each security	Specific risk is low for each security
Total risk is high for each security	Total risk is low for each security

Now, according to the old theory, commonly accepted before the advent of the capital-asset pricing model, returns should be higher for a portfolio made up of Group I securities than for a portfolio made up of Group II securities, because each security in Group I has a higher total risk, and risk, as we know, has its reward. With a wave of their intellectual wands, the academics changed that sort of thinking. Under the capital-asset pricing model, returns from both portfolios should be equal. Why?

First, remember the preceding chart on page 225. (The forgetful can turn the page back to take another look.) There we saw that as the number of securities in the portfolio approached sixty, the total risk of the portfolio was reduced to its systematic level. All of the unsystematic risk had been eliminated. The conscientious readers will now note that in the schematic illustration, the number of securities in each portfolio is sixty. That means that the unsystematic risk has essentially been washed away: An unexpected weather calamity is balanced by a favorable exchange rate, and so forth. What remains is only the systematic risk of each stock in the portfolio, which is given by its beta. But in these two groups, each of the stocks has a beta of 1. Hence, a portfolio of Group I securities and a portfolio of Group II securities will perform exactly the same with respect to risk (standard deviation), even though the stocks in Group I display higher total risk than the stocks in Group II.

The old and the new views now meet head on. Under the old system of valuation, Group I securities were regarded as offering a higher return because of their greater risk. The capital-asset pricing model says there is no greater risk in holding

Group I securities if they are in a diversified portfolio. Indeed, if the securities of Group I did offer higher returns, then all rational investors would prefer them over Group II securities and would attempt to rearrange their holdings to capture the higher returns from Group I. But by this very process, they would bid up the prices of Group I securities and push down the prices of Group II securities until, with the attainment of equilibrium (when investors no longer want to switch from security to security), the portfolio for each group had identical returns, related to the systematic component of their risk (beta) rather than to their total risk (including the unsystematic or specific portions). Because stocks can be combined in portfolios to eliminate specific risk, only the undiversifiable or systematic risk will command a risk premium. Investors will not get paid for bearing risks that can be diversified away. This is the basic logic behind the capital-asset pricing model.

In a big fat nutshell, the proof of the capital-asset pricing model (henceforth to be known as CAPM because we economists love to use letter abbreviations) can be stated as follows:

> If investors did get an extra return (a risk premium) for bearing unsystematic risk, it would turn out that diversified portfolios made up of stocks with large amounts of unsystematic risk would give larger returns than equally risky portfolios of stocks with less unsystematic risk. Investors would snap at the chance to have these higher returns, bidding up the prices of stocks with large unsystematic risk and selling stocks with equivalent betas but lower unsystematic risk. This process would continue until the prospective returns of stocks with the same betas were equalized and no risk premium could be obtained for bearing unsystematic risk. Any other result would be inconsistent with the existence of an efficient market.

The key relationship of the theory is shown in the following diagram. As the systematic risk (beta) of an individual stock (or portfolio) increases, so does the return an investor can expect. If an investor's portfolio has a beta of zero, as might be the case if all her funds were invested in a government-guaranteed bank savings certificate (beta would be zero because the returns from the certificate would not vary at all with swings in the stock market), the investor would receive some modest rate of return,

Risk and Return According to the Capital-Asset Pricing Model*

Rate of Return

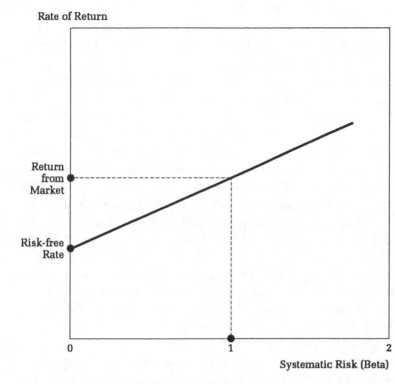

*Those who remember their high school algebra will recall that any straight line can be written as an equation. The equation for the straight line in the diagram is

Rate of Return = Risk-free Rate + Beta (Return from Market – Risk-free Rate).

Alternately, the equation can be written as an expression for the risk premium, that is, the rate of return on the portfolio of stock over and above the risk-free rate of interest:

Rate of Return – Risk-free Rate = Beta (Return from Market – Risk-free Rate).

The equation says that the risk premium you get on any stock or portfolio increases directly with the beta value you assume. Some readers may wonder what relationship beta has to the covariance concept that was so critical in our discussion of portfolio theory. The beta for any security is essentially the same thing as the covariance between that security and the market index as measured on the basis of past experience.

which is generally called the risk-free rate of interest. As the individual takes on more risk, however, the return should increase. If the investor holds a portfolio with a beta of 1 (as, for example, holding a share in one of the broad stock-market averages), her return will equal the general return from common stocks. This return has over long periods of time exceeded the risk-free rate of interest, but the investment is a risky one. In certain periods, the return is much less than the risk-free rate and involves taking substantial losses. This, as we have said, is precisely what is meant by risk.

The diagram shows that a number of different expected returns are possible simply by adjusting the beta of the portfolio. For example, suppose the investor put half of her money in a savings certificate and half in a share of the market averages. In this case, she would receive a return midway between the risk-free return and the return from the market and her portfolio would have an average beta of 0.5.* The CAPM then asserts very simply that to get a higher average long-run rate of return, you should just increase the beta of your portfolio. An investor can get a portfolio with a beta larger than 1 either by buying high-beta stocks or by purchasing a portfolio with average volatility on margin (see the preceding diagram and the following table). One fund proposed by a West Coast bank would have allowed an investor to buy the S&P average on margin, thus increasing both his risk and potential reward. Of course, in times of rapidly declining stock prices, such a fund would have enabled an investor to lose his shirt in a hurry. This may explain why the fund found few customers.

Just as stocks had their fads, so beta came into high fashion by the early 1970s. The *Institutional Investor*, the glossy prestige magazine that spent most of its pages chronicling the accomplishments of professional money managers, put its imprimatur on the movement in 1971 by featuring on its cover the letters BETA on top of a temple and including as its lead story "The Beta Cult! The New Way to Measure Risk." The magazine noted that money men whose mathematics hardly went beyond long division were now "tossing betas around with the abandon of Ph.D.s in statistical theory." Even the SEC gave beta its approval as a risk measure in its *Institutional Investors Study Report*.

On Wall Street, the early beta fans boasted that they could earn higher long-run rates of return simply by buying a few high-beta stocks. Those who thought they were able to time the

---

*In general, the beta of a portfolio is simply the weighted average of the betas of its component parts.

Illustration of Portfolio Building*

Desired Beta	Composition of Portfolio	Expected Return from Portfolio
0	$ 1 in risk-free asset	10%
½	$ .50 in risk-free asset	½ (0.10) + ½ (0.15) = 0.125,
	$ .50 in market portfolio	or 12½%†
1	$ 1 in market portfolio	15%
1½	$ 1.50 in market portfolio	1½ (0.15) − ½ (0.10) = 0.175,
	borrowing $.50 at an	or 17½%
	assumed rate of 10 percent	

*Assuming expected market return is 15 percent and risk-free rate is 10 percent.

†We can also derive the figure for expected return using directly the formula that accompanies the preceding chart:

$$\text{Rate of Return} = 0.10 + \tfrac{1}{2}\,(0.15 - 0.10) = 0.125 \text{ or } 12\tfrac{1}{2}\%.$$

market thought they had an even better idea. They would buy high-beta stocks when they thought the market was going up, switching to low-beta ones when they feared the market might decline. To accommodate the enthusiasm for this new investment idea, beta measurement services proliferated among brokers, and it was a symbol of progressiveness for an investment house to provide its own beta estimates. Today, you can obtain beta estimates from brokers such as Merrill Lynch and investment advisory services such as Value Line and Morningstar. The beta boosters on the Street oversold their product with an abandon that would have shocked even the most enthusiastic academic scribblers intent on spreading the beta gospel.

Let's Look at the Record

In Shakespeare's *Henry IV Part I*, Glendower boasts to Hotspur, "I can call spirits from the vasty deep." "Why, so can I, or so can any man," says Hotspur, unimpressed. "But will they come when you do call for them?" Anyone can theorize about how security markets work, and the capital-asset pricing model is just another theory. The really important question is: Does it work?

Certainly many institutional investors have embraced the beta concept, if only in an attempt to play down the flamboyant excesses of the past. Beta is, after all, an academic creation.

What could be more staid? Simply created as a number that describes a stock's risk, it appears almost sterile in nature. True, it requires large investments in computer programs, but the closet chartists love it. Even if you don't believe in beta, you have to speak its language because, back on the nation's campuses, my colleagues and I have been producing a long line of PhD's and MBA's who spout its terminology. They have gone professional and now use beta as a method of evaluating a portfolio manager's performance. If the realized return is larger than that predicted by the overall portfolio beta, the manager is said to have produced a positive alpha. Lots of money in the market sought out the manager who could deliver the largest alpha.

But is beta a useful measure of risk? Is it true that high-beta portfolios will provide larger long-term returns than lower-beta ones, as the capital-asset pricing model suggests? Does beta alone summarize a security's total systematic risk, or do we need to consider other factors as well? In short, does beta really deserve an alpha? These are subjects of intense current debate among practitioners and academics.

In a study published in 1992, Eugene Fama and Kenneth French divided all traded stocks on the New York, American, and NASDAQ exchanges into deciles according to their beta measures over the 1963–90 period. Decile 1 contained the 10 percent of all stocks that had the lowest betas; decile 10 contained the 10 percent that had the highest betas. The remarkable result, shown in the chart on page 233, is that there was essentially no relationship between the return of these decile portfolios and their beta measures. I have done a similar study showing the relationship between return and beta for mutual funds. The chart on page 234 presents the results for mutual funds during the 1980s. It appears that there is no relationship between returns for stocks or portfolios and their beta measures of risk, confirming the Fama-French results.

Because their comprehensive study covered a period of almost thirty years, Fama and French concluded that the relationship between beta and return is essentially flat. Beta, the key analytical tool of the capital-asset pricing model, is not a useful measure to capture the relationship between risk and return. And so, by the mid-1990s, not only practitioners but

Average Monthly Return vs. Beta: 1963–90
(Fama and French Study)

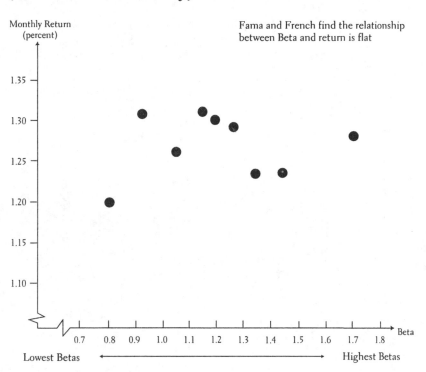

Monthly Return
(percent)

Fama and French find the relationship
between Beta and return is flat

Beta

Lowest Betas ←——————————————————→ Highest Betas

even many academics as well were ready to assign beta to the scrap heap. The financial press, which earlier had chronicled the ascendancy of beta, now ran feature stories with titles such as "The Death of Beta," "Bye, Bye Beta," and "Beta Beaten." Typical of the times was a letter quoted in the *Institutional Investor* from a writer known only as "Deep Quant."* The letter began: "There is a very big story breaking in money management. The Capital-Asset Pricing Model is dead." The magazine went on to quote one "turncoat quant" as follows: "Advanced mathematics will become to investors what the *Titanic* was to sailing." And so the whole set of tools making

---

*"Quant" is the Wall Street nickname for the quantitatively inclined financial analyst who devotes attention largely to the new investment technology.

Average Quarterly Returns vs. Beta: 271 Mutual Funds 1981–91 (Malkiel Study)

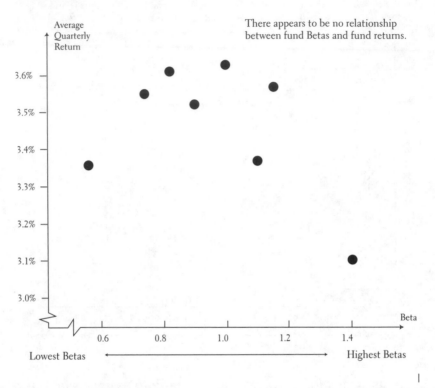

up the new investment technology—including even modern portfolio theory—came under a cloud of suspicion.

An Appraisal of the Evidence

My own guess is that the "turncoat quant" is wrong. The unearthing of serious cracks in the CAPM will not lead to an abandonment of mathematical tools in financial analysis and a return to traditional security analysis. Moreover, I am not quite ready to write an obituary for beta at this time. There are many reasons, I believe, to avoid a rush to judgment.

First, it is important to remember that stable returns are

"Does it bother you at all that when you say MPT quickly it comes out 'empty'?"

preferable, that is, less risky than very volatile returns. Clearly, if one could earn only the same rate of return drilling for oil as could be obtained from a riskless government security, only those who loved gambling for gambling's sake alone would drill for oil. If investors really did not worry at all about volatility, the multitrillion-dollar derivative-securities markets would not be thriving as they are. Thus, the beta measure of relative volatility does capture at least some aspects of what we normally think of as risk. And portfolio betas from the past do a reasonably good job of predicting relative volatility in the future.

Secondly, as Professor Richard Roll of UCLA has argued, we must keep in mind that it is very difficult (indeed probably impossible) to measure beta with any degree of precision. The S&P 500 Index is not "the market." The total stock market contains many thousands of additional stocks in the United States and thousands more in foreign countries. Moreover, the total market includes bonds, real estate, precious metals, and other commodities and assets of all sorts, including one of the most important assets any of us has—the human capital built up by education, work, and life experiences. Depending on exactly how you measure the "market," you can obtain very different beta values. One's conclusions about the capital-asset pricing model and the usefulness of beta as a measure of risk depend very much on how you measure beta. Two economists from the University of Minnesota, Ravi Jagannathan and Zhenyu Wang, find that when the market index (against which we measure beta) is redefined to include human capital and when betas are allowed to vary with cyclical fluctuations in the economy, the support for the CAPM and beta as a predictor of returns is quite strong. Third, there is some evidence that returns are positively related to beta when measured over a much longer period, such as 1927 to the present. Moreover, beta did a reasonably good job of predicting relative returns during the decade of the 1990s.

Finally, investors should be aware that even if the long-run relationship between beta and return is flat, beta can still be a useful investment management tool. Were it in fact the case that low-beta stocks will *dependably* earn rates of return at least as large as high-beta stocks (a very big "if" indeed), then beta as an investment tool is even more valuable than it would be if the capital-asset pricing model held. Investors should scoop up *low*-beta stocks and earn returns as attractive as for the market as a whole but with much less risk. And investors who do wish to seek higher returns by assuming greater risk should buy and hold low-beta stocks on margin, thereby increasing their risk and returns. Moreover, beta may be a useful risk measure during sharp market swings. High-beta stocks did tend to fall more than low-beta stocks in all of the bear market periods during the past fifty years. High beta tech stocks took a particularly painful beating during the bear market of the early 2000s. What is clear, however, is that beta, as it is usually measured, is not a substitute for brains and cannot be relied on as a simple predictor of long-run future returns. Nevertheless, reports of beta's total demise are, in my judgment, premature.

The Quant Quest for Better Measures of Risk: Arbitrage Pricing Theory

If beta is badly damaged as an effective quantitative measure of risk, is there anything to take its place? One of the pioneers in the field of risk measurement is Stephen Ross. Ross has developed a theory of pricing in the capital markets called arbitrage pricing theory (APT). APT has had wide influence both in the academic community and in the practical world of portfolio management. To understand the logic of the newest APT work on risk measurement, one must remember the correct insight underlying the CAPM: The only risk that investors should be compensated for bearing is the risk that cannot be diversified away. Only systematic risk will command a risk premium in the market. But the systematic elements of risk in particular stocks and portfolios may be too complicated to be capturable by a measure of beta—the tendency of the stocks to move more or less than the market. This is especially so because any particular stock index is a very imperfect representative of the general market. Hence, many quants now feel that beta fails to capture a number of important systematic elements of risk.

Let's take a look at several of these other systematic risk elements. Changes in national income, for one, may affect returns from individual stocks in a systematic way. This was shown in our illustration of a simple island economy in chapter 9. Also, changes in national income mirror changes in the personal income of individuals, and the systematic relationship between security returns and salary income can be expected to have a significant effect on individual behavior. For example, the laborer in a GM plant will find a holding of GM common stock particularly risky, because job layoffs and poor returns from GM stock are likely to occur at the same time. Changes in national income may also reflect changes in other forms of property income and may, therefore, be relevant for institutional portfolio managers as well.

Changes in interest rates also systematically affect the returns from individual stocks and are important nondiversifiable risk elements. To the extent that stocks tend to suffer as interest rates go up, equities are a risky investment, and those stocks that are particularly vulnerable to increases in the general level of interest rates are especially risky. Thus, some stocks and fixed-income investments tend to move in parallel, and these stocks will not be helpful in reducing the risk of a bond portfolio. Because fixed-income securities are a major

part of the portfolios of many institutional investors, this systematic risk factor is particularly important for some of the
largest investors in the market. Clearly, then, investors who
think of risk in its broadest and most meaningful sense will be
sensitive to the tendency of certain stocks to be particularly
affected by changes in interest rates.

Changes in the rate of inflation will similarly tend to have
a systematic influence on the returns from common stocks.
This is so for at least two reasons. First, an increase in the rate
of inflation tends to increase interest rates and thus tends to
lower the prices of some equities, as just discussed. Second, the
increase in inflation may squeeze profit margins for certain
groups of companies—public utilities, for example, which
often find that rate increases lag behind increases in costs. On
the other hand, inflation may benefit the prices of common
stocks in the natural resource industries. Thus, again there are
important systematic relationships between stock returns and
economic variables that may not be captured adequately by a
simple beta measure of risk.

Statistical tests of the influence on security returns of several systematic risk variables have shown somewhat promising
results. Better explanations than those given by the CAPM can
be obtained for the variation in returns among different securities by using, in addition to the traditional beta measure of risk,
a number of systematic risk variables, such as sensitivity to
changes in national income, in interest rates, and in the rate of
inflation. Of course, the APT measures of risk are beset by some
of the same problems faced by the CAPM beta measure. It is not
yet certain how these new theories will stand up to more extensive examination.

If, however, one wanted for simplicity to select the one risk
measure most closely related to expected returns, the traditional beta measure would not be most analysts' first choice. In
my own work with John Cragg, the best single risk proxy turned
out to be the extent of disagreement among security analysts'
forecasts for each individual company. Companies for which
there is a broad consensus with respect to the growth of future
earnings in dividends seem to be considered less risky (and
hence have lower expected returns) than companies for which
there is little agreement among security analysts. It is possible

to interpret this result as contradicting modern asset pricing theory, which suggests that individual security variability per se will not be relevant for valuation. The dispersion of analysts' forecasts, however, may actually serve as a particularly useful proxy for a variety of systematic risks.

Although we still have much to learn about the market's evaluation of risk, I believe it is fair to conclude that risk is unlikely to be captured adequately by a single beta statistic (the risk measure of the CAPM). It appears that several other systematic risk measures affect the valuation of securities. In addition, as will be indicated in the next chapter, there is some evidence that security returns are related to size (smaller firms tend to have higher rates of return) and also to price-earnings multiples (firms with low P/Es tend to produce higher returns) and price-book value ratios (stocks that are cheap relative to their book values tend to earn higher total returns). All three of these measures may be effective proxies for systematic risk. Whether individual risk plays any role at all in the valuation process is still, however, an open question.

My results with Cragg can be interpreted as showing that individual security variability does play a role in the valuation process. This would not be hard to explain. Because of transactions and information costs, a large number of individual portfolios may not be diversified. Individuals own a significant fraction of all NYSE stocks and an even larger fraction of stocks traded on other exchanges. Thus, these security holders might well be concerned with the variability of individual stocks. Even well-diversified institutional investors may worry about the behavior of individual stocks when they must report to finance committees the breakdown of their performance results over the preceding period. It is not easy for investment managers to explain to supervisory committees why they bought stock in companies like Enron and WorldCom, which later went bankrupt. Still, there is a powerful argument on the other side. Any role in the valuation process that may consistently be provided by individual security variability will create an arbitrage opportunity for investors able to diversify widely. It is difficult to believe that these arbitrage opportunities will not eventually be exploited. Returning to the theme we played earlier, eventually "true value will out."

A Summing Up

Chapters 9 and 10 have been an academic exercise in the modern theory of capital markets. The stock market appears to be an efficient mechanism that adjusts quite quickly to new information. Neither technical analysis, which analyzes the past price movements of stocks, nor fundamental analysis, which analyzes more basic information about the prospects for individual companies and the economy, seems to yield consistent benefits. It appears that the only way to obtain higher long-run investment returns is to accept greater risks.

Unfortunately, a perfect risk measure does not exist. Beta, the risk measure from the capital-asset pricing model, looks nice on the surface. It is a simple, easy-to-understand measure of market sensitivity. Alas, beta also has its warts. The actual relationship between beta and rate of return has not corresponded to the relationship predicted in theory during long periods of the twentieth century. Moreover, betas for individual stocks are not stable over time, and they are very sensitive to the market proxy against which they are measured.

I have argued here that no single measure is likely to capture adequately the variety of systematic risk influences on individual stocks and portfolios. Returns are probably sensitive to general market swings, to changes in interest and inflation rates, to changes in national income, and, undoubtedly, to other economic factors such as exchange rates. And if the best single risk estimate were to be chosen, the traditional beta measure is unlikely to be everyone's first choice. The mystical perfect risk measure is still beyond our grasp.

To the great relief of assistant professors who must publish or perish, there is still much debate within the academic community on risk measurement, and much more empirical testing needs to be done. Undoubtedly, there will yet be many improvements in the techniques of risk analysis, and the quantitative analysis of risk measurement is far from dead. My own guess is that future risk measures will be even more sophisticated—not less so. Nevertheless, we must be careful not to accept beta or any other measure as an easy way to assess risk and to predict future returns with any certainty. You should know about the best of the modern techniques of the new investment technology—they can be useful aids. But there is never going to be a handsome genie who will appear and solve all our investment problems. And even if he did, we would probably foul it up—as did the little old lady in the following favorite story of Robert Kirby of Capital Guardian Trust:

> She was sitting in her rocking chair on the porch of the retirement home when a little genie appeared and said, "I've decided to grant you three wishes."
>
> The little old lady answered, "Buzz off, you little twerp, I've seen all the wise guys I need to in my life."
>
> The genie answered, "Look, I'm not kidding. This is for real. Just try me."
>
> She shrugged and said, "Okay, turn my rocking chair into solid gold."
>
> When, in a puff of smoke, he did it, her interest picked up noticeably. She said, "Turn me into a beautiful young maiden."
>
> Again, in a puff of smoke, he did it. Finally, she said, "Okay, for my third wish turn my cat into a handsome young prince."
>
> In an instant, there stood the young prince, who then turned to her and asked, "Now aren't you sorry you had me fixed?"

11

Potshots at the Efficient-Market Theory and Why They Miss

> The clairvoyant society of London will not meet Tuesday because of unforeseen circumstances.
>
> —An advertisement in the *Financial Times*

During a three-week period in July 2002, the Dow Jones average of thirty industrial stocks fell 1,500 points, from 9,250 to 7,750, a decline of over 16 percent. In surveying the carnage, financial reporters were quick to point out that it wasn't quite as bad as it was fifteen years earlier in October 1987, when the Dow lost approximately one-third of its value in that single month. This is efficient? To many observers and shocked investors, these events blatantly exposed the failings of the efficient-market theory. Did the stock market really accurately reflect all relevant information about stocks and the economy in early October 1987 or early July 2002? Had fundamental information about the economic prospects of major U.S. corporations changed enough to justify such rapid declines in the value of the Dow?

Critics believe that such events stretch the credibility of the efficient-market theory beyond the breaking point. The financial press has been unambiguous in its judgment. Just after the crash of 1987, the *Wall Street Journal* opined that the efficient-market theory was "the most remarkable error in the history of economic theory." A bit later, *BusinessWeek* described the theory as a "failure."

Some academic economists came to similar conclusions. Lawrence Summers, whose résumé includes secretary of the Treasury and president of Harvard University, claimed that "the stock in the efficient market hypothesis . . . crashed along with the rest of the market on October 19, 1987." Robert Shiller concluded from a longer history of stock market fluctuations that stock prices show far "too much variability" to be explained by an efficient-market theory of pricing, and that one must look to behavioral considerations and to crowd psychology to explain the actual process of price determination in the stock market.

During the late 1980s and early 1990s, those who believed that psychological considerations are an essential feature of our stock markets developed a new field that came to be called behavioral finance. As was indicated in Part One, there have always been both logical and psychological theories of stock prices, and earlier generations of economists, such as John Maynard Keynes, stressed the importance of the fallibility of human decision making. The efficient-market theory was developed on the assumption that market participants are highly rational. But particularly during the 1990s and early 2000s, psychologists such as Daniel Kahneman and financial economists in increasing numbers have argued that the decisions of many investors are strongly influenced by behavioral characteristics such as overconfidence, overreaction, attraction to fashions and fads, and even hubris. Often these characteristics can lead to predictable patterns of stock-price movements and can be used by savvy investors to implement successful investment strategies—or so behavioralists such as Richard Thaler argue. The behavioralists chide their efficient-market brethren for blindly accepting that people in the stock market always behave rationally while at the same time readily agreeing that the people they observe most often (their spouses, their colleagues, and certainly their deans) quite often do not.

The work of the behavioralists has been buttressed by a large number of statistical studies that confirmed several predictable patterns of stock prices. Indeed, the new mantra in the academic community is that the stock market is at least partially predictable. One of the brightest of the new wave of financial economists, Andrew Lo of the Massachusetts Institute of Technology, published a book in the late 1990s entitled *A Non-Random Walk Down Wall Street.* And in *What Works on Wall Street,* a best-selling book published in 1997, James O'Shaughnessy, a money manager with a statistical bent, documents a large number of investment strategies that he believes have "beaten" the market and can be depended on to continue to do so in the years ahead.

That's what this chapter is about: the attempts to show that the market, as demonstrated above, is not efficient and that there is no such thing as a profitable random walk through it. I will review all the recent research proclaiming the demise of the efficient-market theory and purporting to show that market prices are, in fact, predictable. My conclusion is that such obituaries are greatly exaggerated and that the extent to which the stock market is usefully predictable has been vastly overstated. And then when all is said and done, I will show that following the tenets of the efficient-market theory—that is, buying and holding a broad-based market index fund—is still the only game in town. Although the market may not always be rational in the short run, it always is over the long haul. That, plus the fact that no one, or no technique, can consistently predict the future, represents to me (and I hope to you) a resounding confirmation of the efficient-market approach.

What Do We Mean by Saying Markets Are Efficient?

At the outset, I feel it important to review what I mean by the term "efficient." I'd like to relate it to a well-known story that tells of a finance professor and a student who come across a $100 bill lying on the ground. As the student stops to pick it up, the professor says, "Don't bother—if it were really a $100 bill, it wouldn't be there." The story well illustrates what financial economists usually mean when they say that markets are efficient. Markets can be efficient even if they sometimes make egregious errors in valuation, as was certainly true during the 1999–early 2000 Internet bubble. Markets can be efficient even if many market participants are quite irrational. Markets can be efficient even if stock prices exhibit greater volatility than can apparently be explained by fundamentals such as earnings and dividends. Many of us economists who believe in efficiency do so because we view markets as amazingly successful devices for reflecting new information rapidly and, for the most part, accurately. Above all, we believe that financial markets are efficient because they don't allow investors to earn above-average returns without accepting above-average risks. In short, we believe that $100 bills are not lying around for the taking, either by the professional or the amateur investor.

While there are some who agree that there are no $100 bills lying around, an even greater number insist that there's still lots of loose change. The debate on just how much loose change there is, and whether there is any dependable way to pick it up, is a subject that has made many academic careers. For the record, here's what I hold to be true, a conviction that has only grown more steadfast over time:

> *No one can consistently predict either the direction of the stock market or the relative attractiveness of individual stocks and thus no one can consistently obtain better overall returns than the market. And while there are undoubtedly profitable trading opportunities that occasionally appear, these are quickly wiped out once they become known. No one person or institution has yet to produce a long-term, consistent record of finding money-making, risk-adjusted individual stock-trading opportunities, particularly if they pay taxes and incur transactions costs.*

I put it more colorfully in the first edition of my book when I wrote that a blindfolded chimpanzee throwing darts at the *Wall Street Journal* could select a portfolio that would do as well as the experts. Of course, the advice was not literally to throw darts but instead to throw a towel over the stock pages, that is, to buy a broad-based index fund that simply bought and held all the stocks in the market and that charged very low expenses.

I am more convinced than ever of the wisdom of that advice and I am persuaded that those who take potshots at the market's random walk inevitably miss their target. Or, to put it another way, the efficient-market theory is quite efficient at dodging slings and arrows.

Potshots That Completely Miss the Target

Some attempts to discredit the unpredictability of the market are so ridiculous that perhaps they should earn the sobriquet of "greater fool" theories. Among these are the Super Bowl and the Hemline indicators, both described in chapter 7. If nothing else, these theories do at least have colorful names. Under close examination, other picturesque potshots also misfire completely. These include the Dogs of the Dow, the January Effect, the "Thank God It's Monday Afternoon" Pattern, and the Hot News Response.

Dogs of the Dow

This interesting strategy became popular during the mid-1990s. It capitalized on a general contrarian style of investing consistent with the idea that out-of-favor stocks eventually tend to reverse direction. The strategy entailed buying each year the ten stocks in the Dow Jones 30-Stock Industrial Average that had the highest dividend yields. The idea was that these ten stocks were the most out of favor, so they typically had low price-earnings multiples and low price-to-book-value ratios as well. The theory is attributed to a money manager named Michael O'Higgins, who publicized the technique in his book, *Beating the Dow*, published in 1991. James O'Shaughnessy tested the theory as far back as the 1920s; he found that the "Dogs of the Dow" had beaten the overall index by about 2 to 3 percentage points per year, and argued that the strategy had not involved any additional risk.

The canine contingent of Wall Street analysts raised their ears and brought to market a large number of mutual funds based on the principle. By the mid-1990s, more than $20 billion of investment-fund dollars were placed in "Dogs of the Dow" funds sold by such prestigious firms as Morgan Stanley, Dean Witter, and Merrill Lynch. And then, just as might be expected, once a lot of investors started playing the game, success bit the dogs. The Dogs of the Dow consistently underperformed the overall market during the last half of the 1990s. As "Dogs" star Michael O'Higgins opined, "the strategy became too popular" and ultimately self-destructed. The Dogs of the Dow no longer hunt.

January Effect

A number of researchers have found that January has been a very unusual month for stock-market returns. Stock-market returns have tended to be especially high during the first two weeks of January. The effect appears to be particularly strong for smaller firms. Even after adjusting for risk, small firms appear to offer investors abnormally generous returns—with the excess returns largely produced during the first few days of the year. Such an effect has also been documented for several foreign stock markets. This led to the publication of one book with the provocative title *The Incredible January Effect*. Investors and especially stockbrokers, with visions of large commissions dancing around in their heads, designed strategies to capitalize on this "anomaly" believed to be so dependable.

One possible explanation for a "January Effect" is that tax effects are at work. Some investors may sell securities at the end of the calendar year to establish short-term capital losses for income tax purposes. If this selling pressure depresses stock prices before the end of the year, it would seem reasonable that the bounce-back during the first week in January could create abnormal returns during that period. Although this effect could be applicable for all stocks, it would be larger for small firms because stocks of small companies are more volatile and less likely to be in the portfolios of tax-exempt institutional investors and pension funds. One might suppose that traders would take advantage of any excess returns during this period. Unfortunately, however, the transactions costs of trading in the stocks of small companies are substantially higher than for larger companies (because of the higher bid-asked spreads) and there appears to be no way a commission-paying ordinary investor could exploit this anomaly. Moreover, the effect is not dependable in each year. In other words the January "loose change" costs too much to pick up and in some years it turns out to be a mirage.

"Thank God It's Monday Afternoon" Pattern

Another "predictable" pattern, suggesting that a walk down Wall Street may not be perfectly random, is the so-called weekend effect—negative average stock returns from the close of trading on Friday to the close of trading on Monday. In other words, there is some justification for the expression "blue Monday on Wall Street." According to this line of thinking, you should buy your stocks on Monday afternoon at the close, not on Friday afternoon or Monday morning, when they tend to be selling at slightly higher prices.

Again, the effect is small relative to the transactions costs involved to exploit it. Moreover, consider how the strategy fared during the three-month period May–July 2002. Those following such a strategy might have concluded that it put the investor ahead eight out of the thirteen weekends. While few would fly on planes that landed safely only eight out of thirteen times, there may perhaps be naive investors who feel being ahead more than half the time is not all that bad. Of course, these people would have completely missed the Monday, July 29, rally when the blue-chip Dow soared 447.49 points, racking up its third biggest point gain ever. That gain completely wiped out any (pre-transactions-cost) profit to be made from, as well as any relevance to, the "Thank God It's Monday Afternoon" Pattern.

Hot News Response

Skeptics of the inherent unpredictability of the market often point to the fact that the market is simply incapable of quickly absorbing information and then automatically repricing itself in response. Some academics believe that stock prices underreact to news events and, therefore, purchasing (selling) stocks where good (bad) news comes out will produce abnormal returns. Those who explore this aspect of the market are said to engage in "event studies."

In 1998, Eugene Fama surveyed the considerable body of empirical work in this area to determine if stock prices do indeed respond efficiently to information. The "events" included such announcements as earnings surprises, stock splits, dividend actions, mergers, new exchange listings, and initial public offerings. Fama found that apparent underreaction to information is about as common as overreaction, and post-event continuation of abnormal returns is as frequent as post-event reversals. He also showed that many of the return "anomalies" tend to disappear when exposed to different models for expected "normal" returns, different methods to adjust for risk, and when different statistical approaches are used to measure them. He concluded that most of the anomalies discovered by researchers "can reasonably be attributed to chance." Certainly they do not appear to offer investors a dependable way to earn abnormal returns.

Why the Aim Is So Bad

It should be obvious by now that any truly repetitive and exploitable pattern that can be discovered in the stock market and can be arbitraged away will self-destruct. At one time, there may have been a truly dependable and exploitable January Effect in which the stock market—especially stocks of small companies—generated extraordinary returns during the first five days of January. What would investors do with the finding? Easy. They would buy on the last day of December, and sell on January 5. But then investors would find that the market rallied on the last day of December and so they would need to begin to buy on the next to last day of December; and because there is so much "profit taking" on January 5, investors would have to sell on January 4 to take advantage of this effect. Thus, to beat the gun, investors will have to be buying earlier and earlier in December and selling earlier and earlier in January so that eventually the pattern would self-destruct. Indeed, the January Effect became undependable after it received considerable publicity. As one wag put it, "The January Effect sometimes occurs on the previous Thanksgiving week."

Similarly, suppose there is a general tendency for stock prices to underreact to certain new events, leading to abnormal returns to investors who exploit the lack of full immediate adjustment—a finding publicized by behavioralists Werner De Bondt and Richard Thaler and researchers John Campbell, Andrew M. Lo, and A. Craig MacKinlay. "Quantitative" investment managers will then develop strategies in an attempt to exploit the pattern. Indeed, the more potentially profitable a discoverable pattern is, the less likely it is to survive.

Moreover, many of the predictable patterns that have been discovered may simply be the result of data mining. The ease of experimenting with financial data banks of almost every conceivable dimension makes it quite likely that investigators

will find some seemingly significant but wholly spurious correlation between financial variables or among financial and
nonfinancial data sets. Given enough time and massaging of
data series, it is possible to tease almost any pattern out of
most data sets. Moreover, the published literature is likely to
be biased in favor of reporting such results. Significant effects
are likely to be published in professional journals while negative results, or boring confirmations of previous findings, are
relegated to the file drawer or discarded. Data-mining problems are unique to nonexperimental sciences, such as financial economics, which rely on statistical analysis for their
insights and cannot test hypotheses by running repeated controlled experiments.

Potshots That Get Close but Still Miss the Target

Ever mindful that they need either theories or strategies to
nail down tenure or bonuses, both academics and analysts
have come up with slightly more accurate shots aimed at
destroying the essential unpredictability of the stock market.
These can be grouped into three categories: those that seek to
nail down the market's direction; those that purport to find
superior longer-run market returns; and those that attempt to
single out the most profitable stocks. Economists refer to the
first two categories as time series strategies and include under
these the Trend Is Your Friend, the Dividend Jackpot Approach,
the Initial P/E Predictor, and the "Back We Go Again" Strategy.
Theories in the third category come under the aegis of cross-
sectional studies and include the Smaller Is Better Effect and
the claim that Value Will Win. While all of these strategies have
some merit, and some more than others, not one—as explained
below—is able to consistently penetrate the veil of unpredictability cloaking the market.

The Trend Is Your Friend (Otherwise Known as Short-Term Momentum)

The original empirical work supporting the notion of randomness in stock prices supported the view that the stock
market has no memory—the way a stock price behaved in the

past is not useful in divining how it will behave in the future. Just because a stock has been rising, that doesn't mean it will keep on rising. Several later studies have been inconsistent with this pure random-walk model. They show that there is some degree of momentum in the stock market and that price changes measured over short periods of time do tend to persist. For example, researchers Lo and MacKinlay found that for two decades broad portfolio stock returns for weekly and monthly holding periods showed positive serial correlation. In other words, a positive return in one week is more likely than not to be followed by a positive return in the next week. Moreover, Lo and others have suggested that some of the stock-price patterns used by so-called technical analysts may actually have some modest predictive power.

Economists and psychologists in the field of behavioral finance find such short-run momentum to be consistent with psychological feedback mechanisms. Individuals see a stock price rising and are drawn into the market in a kind of "bandwagon effect." As mentioned in chapter 4, Robert Shiller described the rise in the U.S. stock market during the late 1990s as the result of psychological contagion leading to irrational exuberance. As behavioral finance became more prominent as a branch of the study of financial markets, momentum, as opposed to randomness, seemed entirely reasonable to many investigators.

I believe there are two factors that should prevent us from interpreting the empirical results reported above as an indication that markets are inefficient. While the stock market may not be a perfect random walk, it is important to distinguish statistical significance from economic significance. The statistical dependencies giving rise to momentum, in fact, are extremely small and are not likely to permit investors to realize excess returns. Anyone who pays transactions costs is unlikely to find a trading strategy based on momentum that will beat a buy and hold strategy. Indeed, work by another behavioral economist, Terrance Odean, suggested that momentum investors do not realize excess returns. Quite the opposite—a sample of such investors suggests that these traders did far worse than buy-and-hold investors even during a period where there was clear statistical evidence of positive momentum.

We also need to ask whether such patterns of serial correlation are consistent over time. Momentum strategies (buying stocks that appear to be in an uptrend and/or displaying positive relative strength) appeared to produce positive relative returns during some periods of the late 1990s but highly negative relative returns during 2000. It is far from clear that any stock-price patterns are in fact useful for investors in fashioning an investment strategy that will dependably earn excess returns.

William Schwert raises the interesting question that since many predictable patterns seem to disappear after they are published in the finance literature, they may simply reflect a bias in the data samples selected and the normal tendency of researchers to focus on results that challenge perceived wisdom. Alternatively, perhaps practitioners learn quickly about any true predictable pattern and exploit it to the extent that it becomes no longer profitable.

The Dividend Jackpot Approach

This technique for outguessing the market rests on the logical assumption that if stocks in general are providing above-average dividend yields, then the total future returns investors receive will be relatively generous. Two academic studies—one by Eugene Fama and Kenneth French and the other by John Campbell and Robert Shiller—concluded that one can indeed hit the jackpot with such an approach, thereby negating the randomness of the market. Depending on the forecast horizon involved, as much as 40 percent of the variability in future market returns can be predicted on the basis of the initial dividend yield of the market as a whole.

An interesting way of presenting the results is shown in the diagram below. The diagram was produced by measuring the dividend yield of the broad U.S. stock market (in this case, the Standard & Poor's 500-Stock Index) each quarter since 1926 and then calculating the market's subsequent ten-year total return through the year 2001. The observations were then divided into deciles depending upon the level of the initial dividend yield. In general, the exhibit shows that investors have earned higher total rates of return from the stock market when the initial dividend yield of the market portfolio was relatively high, and relatively low future rates of return when stocks were purchased at low dividend yields.

The Future Ten-Year Rates of Return When Stocks Are Purchased at Alternative Initial Dividend Yields (D/P)

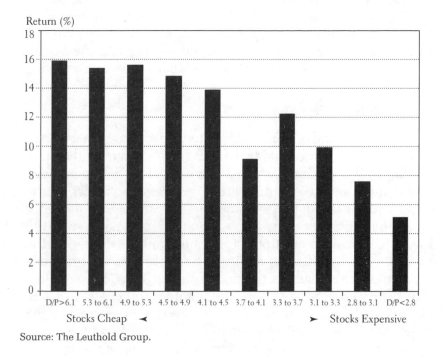

Return (%)

Stocks Cheap ◄   ► Stocks Expensive

Source: The Leuthold Group.

These findings are not necessarily inconsistent with efficiency. Dividend yields of stocks tend to be high when interest rates are high, and they tend to be low when interest rates are low. Consequently, the ability of initial yields to predict returns may simply reflect the adjustment of the stock market to general economic conditions. Moreover, the dividend behavior of U.S. corporations may have changed over time. Companies in the twenty-first century may be more likely to institute a share repurchase program rather than increase their dividends. Thus, dividend yield may not be as meaningful as in the past. Further, it is worth pointing out that dividend yields were unusually low and the stock market appeared irrationally exuberant at the start of 1995 when the Dow Jones Industrial Average was selling at the 5,000 level. The Dow went on to peak near 11,000, and even after the punishing decline in stock prices during the early 2000s the return from the market portfolio was still generous. Indeed, even from the time of Federal

Reserve Chairman Alan Greenspan's famous "irrational exuberance" speech in December 1996, returns from the market portfolio were approximately 7 percent through mid-2002.

Finally, it is worth noting that this phenomenon does *not* work consistently with individual stocks. Investors who simply purchase a portfolio of individual stocks with the highest dividend yields in the market will *not* earn a particularly high rate of return.

The Initial P/E Predictor

The same kind of predictability for the market as a whole, as was demonstrated for dividends, has been shown for the price-earnings ratio of the market as a whole. The data are shown below and are presented in a decile analysis similar to that described for dividend yields above. Investors have tended to earn larger future returns when purchasing stocks at relatively low price-earnings multiples. Campbell and Shiller report that over 40 percent of the variability in long-horizon returns can be predicted on the basis of the initial market P/E. They conclude that equity returns have been predictable in the past to a considerable extent. As we will see in the diagram on page 262, there is also some evidence that individual stocks with low P/Es *relative* to the market may produce higher rates of return.

Two points should be made about these findings, which suggest a great deal of forecast ability of stock prices. First, such findings may be perfectly consistent with an efficient-market view of security price determination. For example, stock prices are low relative to earnings when interest rates are high and thus required returns for all financial assets are high. P/Es were very low during the early 1980s when U.S. government bonds had double-digit yields. Moreover, blind reliance on these patterns can lead to large investment mistakes. In 1992 the P/E for the market was unusually high (well above 20). As you can see from the diagram on page 255, the ten-year average annual rate of return was forecasted to be only 5 percent. In fact, the ten-year rate of return for the S&P 500 from 1992 through 2001 was in the double digits. I have a colleague who switched his retirement plan entirely into bonds during the early 1990s because P/E ratios were so high. Over the next ten years, he was very

The Future Ten-Year Rates of Return When Stocks Are Purchased at Alternative Initial Price-to-Earnings (P/E) Multiples

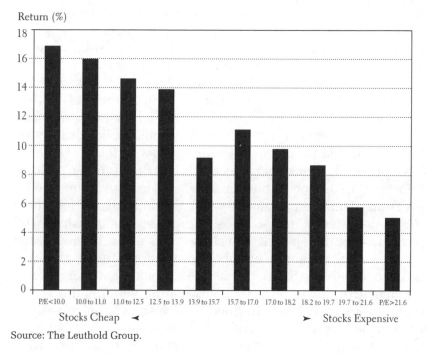

Source: The Leuthold Group.

sorry for his decision and far less certain that it is easy to predict stock returns.

The "Back We Go Again" Strategy (Otherwise Known as Long-Run Return Reversals)

Buying stocks that performed poorly during the past three years or so is likely to give you above-average returns over the next three years. This is the finding of research carried out by Eugene Fama and Kenneth French as well as by James Poterba and Lawrence Summers and by Werner De Bondt and Richard Thaler. In research jargon, they say that although stock returns over short horizons such as a week or a month may be positively correlated, stock returns over longer horizons, such as two years or more, display negative serial correlation. I have confirmed that this result continued to hold into the 1990s. Thus, a contrarian investment strategy—that is, buying those stocks that have had relatively poor recent performance— might be expected to outperform a strategy of buying those stocks that recently produced superior returns. The implicit advice to investors is that the market often overreacts, as the behavioralists argue, and therefore it is wise to shun fashionable stocks and concentrate on those out of favor.

Of all the predictable patterns that have been uncovered or alleged, this one strikes me not only as one of the most believable but also as potentially most beneficial for investors. Certainly, the evidence in Part One of this book shows clearly that fads and fashions can play a role in stock pricing. At times, large blue-chip stocks have been all the rage; in other periods, Internet stocks or biotechnology securities have caught investors' fancies. No matter what the fad, all carried stock prices to extremes and led to severe losses for investors who purchased at the apex. If investors could avoid buying at the top of an unwarranted bubble, serious investment mistakes could be avoided. Similarly, if those stocks that were overly popular turn out to be poor investments, perhaps the stocks that have recently been shunned by investors—the ugly ducklings of the investment world—will eventually come out from under their cloud. Particularly when such a contrarian approach is wedded to a fundamental-value approach (to avoid buying stocks simply because they are unpopular), investors may well benefit from such a strategy.

The psychological explanation for such reversals in realized stock returns suggests the dominance of "castle-in-the-air" builders among investment decision makers. If stock prices were always influenced by fads and fashions that tended to arise and then decay over time, such reversals in security returns would be expected. Hence, many investigators have concluded that the evidence concerning reversals in returns is inconsistent with the efficient-market hypothesis. Well— maybe yes, but maybe no. There are both logical and statistical reasons to continue to stand by the theory of efficient markets.

Return reversals over different time periods are often rooted in solid economic facts rather than psychological swings. The volatility of interest rates constitutes a prime economic influence on share prices. Because bonds—the front-line reflectors of interest-rate direction—compete with stocks for the investor's dollars, one should logically expect systematic relationships between interest rates and stock prices. Specifically, when interest rates go up, share prices should fall, other things being the same, so as to provide larger expected stock returns in the future. Only if this happens will stocks be competitive with higher-yielding bonds. Similarly, when interest rates fall, stocks should tend to rise, because they can promise a lower total return and still be competitive with lower-yielding bonds.

It's easy to see how fluctuations in interest rates can produce return reversals in stocks. Suppose interest rates go up. This causes both bond and stock prices to fall and tends to produce low and often negative rates of return over the time periods when the interest rates rose. Suppose now that interest rates fall back to their original level. This causes bond and stock prices to rise and tends to produce very high returns for stockholders. Thus, over a cycle of interest-rate fluctuations, we will tend to see relatively large stock returns following low stock returns—that is, exactly the kinds of return reversals found by investigators. The point is that such return reversals need not be due to fads that decay over time. They can also result from the very logical and efficient reaction of stock-market participants to fluctuations in interest rates.

Obviously, in any given period there are many influences on stock prices apart from interest rates, so one should not expect to find a perfect correspondence between movements of interest rates and stock prices. Nevertheless, the tendency of interest rates to influence stock prices could account for the sorts of return reversals that have been found historically, and such a relationship is perfectly consistent with the existence of highly efficient markets.

Statistically, there are also reasons to doubt the "robustness" of this finding concerning return reversals. It turns out that correlations of returns over time are much lower in the period since 1940 than they were in the period before 1940. Thus, the use of simple contrarian investment strategies is no guarantee of success. And even if fads are partially responsible for some return reversals (as when a particular group of stocks comes in and out of favor), fads don't occur all the time.

Finally, it may not be possible to profit from the tendency for individual stocks to exhibit patterns of return reversals. Although such reversals may be statistically significant, they may only represent reversion to the mean rather than predictable opportunities to earn above-average returns. Zsuzsanna Fluck, Richard Quandt, and I simulated an investment strategy of buying stocks that had experienced relatively poor recent two- or three-year performance. We found that during the 1980s and 1990s, those stocks did enjoy improved returns in the next period of time, but they recovered only to the average stock-market performance. Thus, there was a statistically strong pattern of return reversal, but not one that you could make money on. And even if the recent "losers" did produce extraordinary subsequent returns, this does not imply that stock prices systematically "overshoot" their appropriate levels. Stocks that have gone down sharply after some unfavorable business reversals exhibit heightened uncertainty and volatility and, therefore, greater risk for investors. Because investors require higher returns for bearing greater risk, a finding that future returns in these stocks are relatively generous is quite consistent with the efficient functioning of markets. Moreover, my belief that prices do not systematically overact is reinforced by the fact that we do not find significant price reversals after sharp runups in prices.

So, what's an investor to do? As the careful reader knows, I believe the stock market is fundamentally logical. I also recognize that the market does get carried away with popular fads or fashions. Similarly, pessimism can often be overdone. Thus, "value" investors operating on the firm-foundation theory will often find that stocks that have produced very poor recent returns may provide very generous returns in the future. Knowing that careful statistical work also supports this tendency, at least to some extent, should give investors an additional measure of comfort in undertaking a contrarian investment strategy coupled with a firm-foundation approach. But remember that the statistical relationship is a loose one and that some unpopular stocks may be justly unpopular and undoubtedly somewhat riskier. Certainly some companies that have been going downhill may continue to go down the tubes, as investors in Enron and WorldCom painfully learned during 2002. The relationships are sufficiently loose and uncertain that one should be very wary of expecting sure success from any simple contrarian strategy.

The Smaller Is Better Effect

Probably one of the strongest patterns in stock returns that investigators have found is the tendency over long periods of time for smaller company stocks to generate larger returns than those of large company stocks. Since 1926, small company stocks in the United States have produced rates of return over 1½ percentage points larger than the returns from large stocks, as was shown in chapter 9.

The diagram on page 260 shows the work of Fama and French, who divided stocks into deciles according to their size. They found that decile 1, the 10 percent of stocks with the smallest total capitalization,* produced the largest rates of return, whereas decile 10, the largest stocks in terms of market capitalization, produced the smallest rate of return. Moreover, small firms tended to outperform larger firms with the same beta levels.

Nevertheless, we need to remember that, first, small stocks may be riskier than larger stocks and deserve to give investors a higher rate of return. Thus, even if the "small firm effect" was to persist in the future, it's not at all clear that such a finding would violate market efficiency. A finding that small company stocks outperform the stocks of larger companies on a risk-adjusted basis depends importantly on how one measures risk. We have seen that beta, the risk measure typically used in the studies that have found "excess" returns from small firms, may be a very poor measure of risk. Thus, it is impossible to distinguish if the abnormal returns are truly the result of inefficiencies or result instead because of inadequacies in our measure of risk. The higher returns for smaller companies may simply be the requisite reward owed to investors for assuming a greater risk of disappointment in the investment returns they expect, just as larger returns are achieved over the long run from investing in relatively volatile long-term bonds than from more

---

*Total capitalization is one way to measure a company's size. It is simply the price per share multiplied by the number of shares outstanding.

Average Monthly Returns vs. Size: 1963–90

*Portfolios of smaller firms have tended to produce
higher rates of return than portfolios of larger firms.*

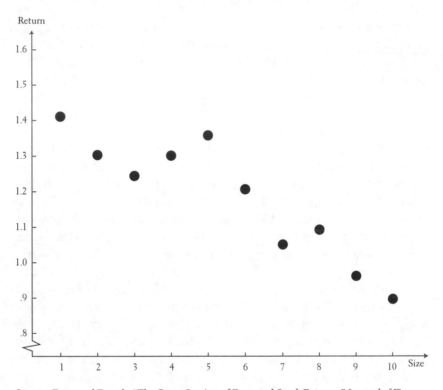

Source: Fama and French, "The Cross-Section of Expected Stock Returns," *Journal of Finance*
(June 1992).

predictable short-term Treasury bills. Moreover, it is also possible that the small firm effect found in some studies is simply
a result of what is called "survivorship bias" in currently available computer tapes of past returns. Today's list of companies
includes only small firms that have survived—not the small
firms that later went bankrupt.

Finally, the dependability of the small firm effect continuing is open to considerable question. Certainly during the
1990s there was little to gain from holding smaller stocks.
Indeed, in most world markets it was the larger capitalization
stocks that produced larger rates of return. It may be that the

growing institutionalization of the market led portfolio managers to prefer larger companies with more liquidity to smaller companies where it would be difficult to liquidate significant blocks of stock. Clearly, buying a portfolio of small firms is hardly a surefire technique to enable an investor to earn abnormally high, risk-adjusted returns.

The "Value Will Win" Record

In 1934, David L. Dodd and Benjamin Graham published a manifesto for individual investors that has attracted strong adherents, including the legendary Warren Buffett, to this day. They basically argued that value always wins over time. And, in order to find value, investors should look for stocks with low price-earning ratios and with low prices relative to their book values. In this scenario, value is based on current realities rather than future growth projections. The resulting theory is consistent with the views of behavioralists (such as Kahneman and Thaler) that investors tend to be overconfident of their ability to project high earnings growth and thus overpay for "growth" stocks.

Stocks with Low Price-Earnings Multiples Outperform Those with High Multiples

I have considerable intellectual sympathy with this approach. One of my cardinal rules of stock selection is to look for companies with reasonable growth prospects that have yet to be discovered by the stock market and thus are selling at relatively low earnings multiples. I have also warned investors repeatedly about the dangers of very high multiple stocks that may be the current favorites of the investment community. Particularly because earnings growth is so hard to forecast, it's far better to be in low-multiple stocks; if growth does materialize, both the earnings and the earnings multiple will likely increase, giving the investor a double benefit. Buying a high-multiple stock whose earnings growth fails to materialize subjects investors to a double whammy. Both the earnings and the multiple can fall.

There is some evidence that a portfolio of stocks with relatively low earnings multiples (as well as low multiples of cash flow and of sales) has often produced above-average rates of return even after adjusting for risk. This strategy was tested by Sanjoy Basu in the late 1970s and has been confirmed by several researchers over the next twenty years. For example, the figure below shows the returns during the 1980s from ten equal-sized groups of exchange-traded stocks, ranked by their P/E ratios. Group 1 had the lowest P/Es, Group 2 the second lowest, and so on. The figure shows that as the P/E of a group of stocks increased, the return decreased.

This "P/E effect," however, appears to vary over time—it is certainly not dependable over every specific investment period. And even if it can be shown to persist on average over a long period of time, one can never be sure if the excess returns are due to increased risk or to market abnormalities. The studies that have documented abnormal returns have used

Average Quarterly Returns during the 1980s vs. P/E Ratio

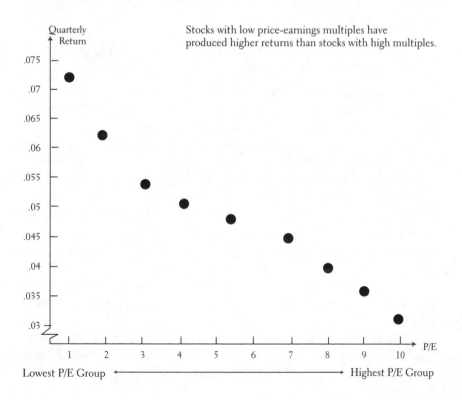

beta to measure risk. To the extent that one believes beta to be a far from perfect, or even a useful, risk measure, one cannot claim that the low P/E pattern indicates a market inefficiency. And don't forget that low P/Es are often justified. Often, companies on the verge of some financial disaster will sell at very low multiples of reported earnings. The low multiples might reflect not value but a profound concern about the viability of the companies.

Another illustration will show how difficult it is to implement a low P/E strategy. Suppose two identical banks have $10 per share in earnings for the year, half of which represents "pay-in-kind" interest from financially weak, less developed countries (LDCs). The LDCs can't pay their interest but instead just write a new IOU for the unpaid interest. Bank One reports the whole $10 in earnings, whereas Bank Two reports only $5 as earnings, preferring to set up the more questionable extra $5 "pay-in-kind" interest as a reserve against future potential defaults. Which bank will show the higher P/E multiple? Most likely it will be the more conservative Bank Two, which reported the lower earnings. If both banks sold at $50 per share (and by assumption they are identical except for their accounting policies), then the conservative Bank Two would have a P/E multiple of 10, whereas Bank One, which set up no reserves and just called everything "earnings," would have a multiple of only 5. It's easy to see how a low P/E criterion could in some instances give a poor measure of true value.

Stocks That Sell at Low Multiples of Their Book Values Tend to Produce Higher Subsequent Returns

Another predictable pattern of return is the relationship between the ratio of a stock's price to its book value (the value of the company's assets as recorded on its books) and its later return. Stocks that represent good value in the sense that they sell at low ratios of price to book value tend to produce higher future returns. This pattern appears to hold for both U.S. and many foreign stock markets, as has been shown by Fama and French.

Behavioralists argue that such results raise questions about the efficiency of the market if one accepts beta as the appropriate measure of risk. But these findings do not necessarily imply inefficiency. Price-to-book-value ratios (P/BV) may simply reflect another risk factor that is priced into the market. Companies in some degree of financial distress, for example, are likely to sell at low prices relative to book values. Fama and French argue that a three-factor risk model (including P/BV and size as well as beta as measures of risk) is the appropriate benchmark against which any supposed inefficiencies should be measured.

But Does "Value" Really Trump Growth on a Consistent Basis?

We also need to keep in mind that the results of published studies—even those done over decades—may still be time-dependent and to ask whether the return patterns of academic studies can actually be generated with real money. The chart opposite presents average actual returns generated by mutual funds classified by either their "growth" or "value" objectives. "Value" funds are so classified if they buy stocks with P/E multiples and P/BV ratios that are below the averages for the whole stock market. We see that over a period running back to the 1930s, it does not appear that investors could actually have realized higher rates of return from mutual funds specializing in "value" stocks. Indeed, the chart suggests that the period studied by Fama and French from the early 1960s through 1990 may have been a unique period in which value stocks rather consistently produced higher rates of return.

William Schwert points out that the investment firm of Dimensional Fund Advisors actually began a mutual fund that selected value stocks quantitatively according to the Fama-French criteria. The excess-risk-adjusted return of such a portfolio was a negative 0.2 percent per month over the 1993–98 period (using beta as the measure of risk). This is consistent with the results from "actively managed" value mutual funds shown in the preceding chart.

Why Even Close Shots Miss

Another "market pathology" often cited by behavioralists as clear evidence that markets are not efficient describes the turn-

Reversion to the Mean:
Relative Performance of "Value" vs. "Growth" Mutual Funds 1937–2002

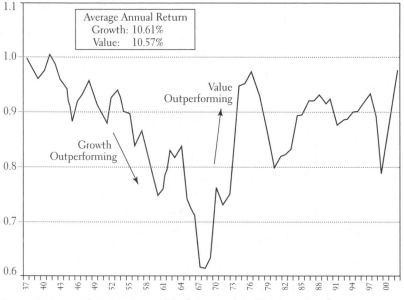

Source: Lipper Analytic Services and Bogle Research Institute.

of-the-century Internet bubble in chapter 4. Surely, the remarkable market values assigned to Internet and related high-tech companies seem totally inconsistent with rational valuation. I do have some sympathy with behavioralists in this instance, and in reviewing Robert Shiller's *Irrational Exuberance*, I agreed that it was in the high-tech sector of the market that his thesis could most plausibly be supported. But even here, when we know *ex post* (after the collapse) that major errors were made, there were certainly no clear *ex ante* (while it was going on) arbitrage opportunities available to rational investors. As convinced as I was that a bubble was expanding, I did not want to take the risk of selling Internet stocks short because no one could know how many greater fools would come around and push prices even higher.

Equity valuations rest on uncertain future forecasts. Even if all market participants rationally price common stocks as the present value of all future cash flows expected therefrom, it is still possible for clear excesses to develop. We know now, with the benefit of hindsight, that the outlandish claims that were being made regarding the growth of the Internet (and the related telecommunications structure needed to support it) were unsupportable. We know now that projections for the rates of growth and the stability and duration of those growth rates for so-called New Economy companies were unsustainable. But interestingly, it was the sharp-penciled professional investors who argued that the valuations of high-tech companies were proper. It was a top security analyst from the venerable Wall Street firm of Morgan Stanley who became the doyenne of the Internet by recommending Net stocks to the firm's institutional and individual clients. And it was the professional pension-fund and mutual-fund managers who overweighted their portfolios with high-tech stocks.

While it is now clear in retrospect that such professionals were egregiously wrong, there was certainly no obvious arbitrage opportunity available. One could disagree with the projected growth rates of security analysts. But who could be absolutely sure, with the use of the Internet then doubling every several months, that the extraordinary growth rates that could justify stock valuations were impossible? After all, even Alan Greenspan was singing the praises of the New Economy. Nothing is ever as clear in prospect as it is in retrospect.

And even when clear mispricing arbitrage opportunities seem to have existed, there was no way to exploit them. Recall the illustration in chapter 4 when 3Com spun off 5 percent of the shares of PalmPilot stock it owned, announcing its intention to spin off the remaining 95 percent later. Irrational exuberance pushed the price of Palm's stock so high that if you bought 3Com, which still owned 95 percent of Palm, you could have effectively bought Palm stock for less than the price at which it was selling in the market. The 95 percent of Palm that 3Com owned was worth $25 billion more than the total market capitalization of 3Com at going market prices. Here was a clear case of mispricing and an apparently profitable arbitrage opportunity. The clear arbitrage in case (borrow PalmPilot stock and sell it short and buy 3Com) could not be undertaken. There was not enough Palm stock outstanding to make it possible to borrow the stock. The "anomaly" disappeared once 3Com spun off more of Palm stock. Moreover, the potential profits from name or ticker symbol confusion described in chapter 4 were extremely small relative to the transactions costs that would be required to exploit them. Thus, none of these illustrations should shake our faith in the long-run efficiency of our stock markets. Perhaps the more important anomaly today is why so many investors buy high-expense, actively managed mutual funds instead of low-cost index funds.

And the Winner Is . . .

It's now time to see how the findings just discussed actually perform in practice. If predictable patterns are present and if mispricings frequently exist, then clearly professional investment managers ought to be able to use them to beat a simple index fund. So let's take a careful look at the results racked up by professionally managed portfolios.

The Performance of Professional Investors

For me, the most direct and most convincing tests of market efficiency are direct tests of the ability of professional fund managers to outperform the market as a whole. Surely, if market prices were determined by irrational investors and systematically deviated from rational estimates of the present value of corporations, and if it was easy to spot predictable patterns in security returns or anomalous security prices, then professional fund managers should be able to beat the market. Direct tests of the actual performance of professionals, who are richly incentivized to outperform the market, should represent the most compelling evidence of market efficiency.

There is a remarkably large body of evidence suggesting that professional investment managers are not able to outperform index funds that simply buy and hold the broad stock-market portfolio. We covered much of this work in chapter 8. For the twenty years ending December 31, 2001, the average actively managed large capitalization mutual fund underperformed the Standard & Poor's 500 large cap index by almost 2 percentage points per year. In decade after decade, two-thirds to three-quarters of professionally managed funds are beaten by funds that simply buy and hold a broad-based stock-market index. The table below shows the results for the ten-year period ending June 30, 2002. Similar results can be shown for different time periods and using different indexes for comparison. Results are also the same for international markets as well as for different asset classes such as bonds and real estate investment trusts.

Percent of Large Capitalization Equity Funds Outperformed by Index Ending June 30, 2002

	1 year	3 years	5 years	10 years
S&P 500 vs. Large Cap Equity Funds	63%	56%	70%	79%
Wilshire 5,000 vs. Large Cap Equity Funds	72%	64%	69%	74%

To be sure, there are always hot funds that beat the market in some particular period of time. And there have been academic studies claiming that mutual-fund returns are predictable. They claim that funds that have been superior (inferior) performers in one period predictably perform better (or worse) in a subsequent period, at least over the near term. Thus, investors could earn significantly better returns by purchasing recently good-performing funds, apparently contradicting the efficient-market hypothesis.

Naturally, I have followed this work with great interest. And I am convinced that many studies have been flawed by the phenomenon of "survivorship bias," that is, including in their studies only the successful funds that survived over a long period of time, while excluding from the analysis all the unsuccessful funds that fell by the wayside. Commonly used data sets of mutual-fund returns, such as those available from the Morningstar Service, typically show the past records of all funds currently in existence. Clearly, today's investors are not interested in the records of funds that no longer exist. This creates the possibility of significant biases in the return figures calculated from most of the available data sets.

Mutual funds that are unsuccessful with big risky bets usually do not survive. You are not alone in being reluctant to buy a mutual fund with a poor record. Mutual-fund complexes (those with large numbers of funds) typically allow such a fund

The Records of Surviving Funds Overstates the Success of Active Management

As poor-performing stock funds are killed off, the average for the surviving funds looks better and better.

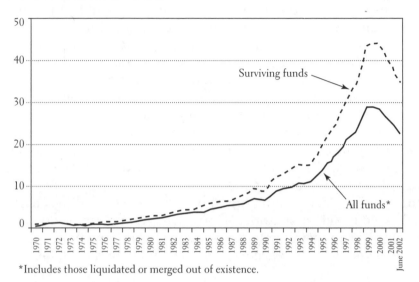

*Includes those liquidated or merged out of existence.

Source: Lipper Analytic services and Bogle Research Institute as compiled by The Vanguard Group.

to suffer a painless death by merging it into a more successful fund in the complex, thereby burying the bad fund's record. Thus, there will be a tendency for only the more successful funds to survive, and measures of the returns of such funds will tend to overstate the success of mutual-fund management. Moreover, it may appear that high returns will tend to persist because funds whose bets were unsuccessful will tend to drop out of the sample. The problem for investors is that at the beginning of any period they can't be sure which funds will be successful and survive.

Another little known factor in the behavior of mutual-fund management companies also leads to the conclusion that survivorship bias may be quite severe. A number of mutual-fund management complexes employ the practice of starting "incubator" funds. A complex may start ten small new equity funds with different in-house managers and wait to see which ones

are successful. Suppose after a few years only three funds produce total returns better than the broad-market averages. The
complex begins to market those successful funds aggressively,
dropping the other seven and burying their records. The full
records from inception of the successful funds will be the only
ones to appear in the usual publications of mutual-fund returns.

To get a handle on the possible magnitude of this bias, I
obtained from Lipper Analytic Services, a company that publishes information on mutual-fund returns, more than twenty
years of data on the records of all mutual funds that were available to the public each year, whether or not they survived.
What I found was that surviving funds earned returns that were
1½ percentage points greater than the returns for all mutual
funds that were in existence each year. The Vanguard Group of
Investment Companies plotted the data for a period of over
thirty years. The results are shown in the preceding chart.
When you read press stories of how well mutual funds do, it is
likely you are seeing only the records of surviving funds. And
no one knows in advance who the surviving funds will be.

The Odds of Success:
Returns of Surviving Mutual Funds 1970–Dec. 31, 2001

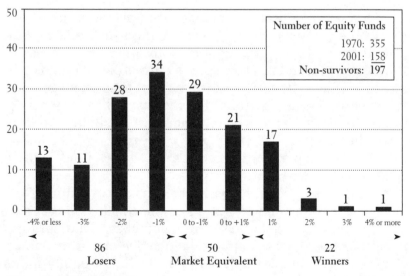

Source: Bogle Research Institute.

When all mutual funds sold to the public are considered, the original thesis propounded by the first edition of *A Random Walk Down Wall Street* in 1973 holds up remarkably well. Over the entire thirty-year period since the first edition of this book, about two-thirds of the funds proved inferior to the market as a whole. The same result also holds for professional pension-fund managers. Most managers of the equity portfolios of mutual funds and pension funds could have substantially improved their performance by casting their lot with the efficient-market theory and not trying to outguess the market. Indeed, if the S&P and Wilshire indexes were athletes, we would probably be testing them for steroids.

We see that managed funds are regularly outperformed by a broad index fund with equivalent risk. Moreover, as was demonstrated in chapter 8, those funds that do appear to produce excess returns in one period are not likely to do so in the next. There is no dependable persistence in performance when one considers all mutual funds, not simply the survivors. Recall that it was the hot funds of the late 1990s that failed so miserably in the early 2000s. Over the long run, the results are even more devastating to active managers. One can count on the fingers of one hand the number of professional portfolio managers who have managed to beat the market by any significant amount, as is shown in the chart on page 270. And you can be sure the non-surviving funds did even worse. The record of professionals does not suggest that sufficient predictability exists in the stock market or that there are enough recognizable irrationalities to produce exploitable opportunities to earn excess returns over the market average.

A Summing Up

I have emphasized that market valuations rest on both logical and psychological factors. The theory of valuation depends on the projection of a long-term stream of dividends whose growth rate is extraordinarily difficult to estimate. Thus, fundamental value is never a definite number. It is a fuzzy band of possible values, and prices can move sharply within this band whenever there is increased uncertainty or confusion. Moreover, the appropriate risk premiums for common equities are changeable and far from obvious either to investors or to financial economists. Thus, there is room for the hopes, fears, and favorite fashions of market participants to play a role in the valuation process. Indeed, I emphasized in early chapters how history provides extraordinary examples of markets in which psychology seemed to dominate the pricing process, as in the tulip-bulb mania in seventeenth-century Holland and the Internet bubble at the turn of the twenty-first century. Thus, I harbor some doubts that we should consider that the current array of market prices always represents the best estimate available of appropriate discounted value.

Nevertheless, one has to be impressed with the substantial volume of evidence suggesting that stock prices display a remarkable degree of efficiency. Information contained in past prices or any publicly available fundamental information is rapidly assimilated into market prices. Prices adjust so well to reflect all-important information that a randomly selected and passively managed portfolio of stocks performs as well as or better than the portfolios selected by the experts. If some degree of mispricing exists, it does not persist for long. "True value will always out" in the stock market. To paraphrase Benjamin Graham, ultimately the market is a weighing mechanism, not a voting mechanism. Moreover, whatever mispricing there is usually is only recognizable after the fact, just as we always know Monday morning the correct play the quarterback should have called.

With respect to the evidence reviewed in this chapter indicating that future returns are, in fact, somewhat predictable, there are several points to make in summary. First, there are considerable questions regarding the long-run dependability of these effects. Many could be the result of "data snooping," letting the computer search through the data sets of past securities prices in the hopes of finding some relationships. With the availability of fast computers and easily accessible stock-market data, it is not surprising that some statistically significant correlations have been found, especially because published work is probably biased in favor of reporting anomalous results rather than boring confirmations of randomness. Thus, many of the predictable patterns that have been discovered may simply be the result of data mining—the result of beating the data set in every conceivable way until it finally confesses. There may be little confidence that these relationships will continue in the future.

Second, even if there is a dependable predictable relationship, it may not be exploitable by investors. For example, the transaction costs involved in trying to capitalize on the January Effect are sufficiently large that the predictable pattern is not economically meaningful. Third, the predictable pattern that has been found, such as the dividend yield effect (what I called the Dividend Jackpot Approach), may simply reflect general economic fluctuations in interest rates or, in the case of the small firm effect, an appropriate premium for risk. Finally, if the pattern is a true anomaly, it is likely to self-destruct as profit-maximizing investors seek to exploit it. Indeed, the more profitable any return predictability appears to be, the less likely it is to survive.

An exchange during the 1990s between Robert Shiller, a skeptic about market efficiency, and Richard Roll, an academic economist who also is a businessman running billions of dollars of investment funds, is quite revealing. After Shiller stressed the importance of fads and inefficiencies in the pricing of stocks, Roll responded as follows:

> I have personally tried to invest money, my client's money and my own, in every single anomaly and predictive device that academics have dreamed up. . . . I have attempted to exploit the so-called year-end anomalies and a whole variety of strategies supposedly documented by academic research. And I have yet to make a nickel on any of these supposed market inefficiencies. . . . I agree with Bob that investor psychology plays an important role. But, I have to keep coming back to my original point that a true market inefficiency ought to be an exploitable opportunity. If there's nothing investors can exploit in a systematic way, time in and time out, then it's very hard to say that information is not being properly incorporated into stock prices. . . . Real money investment strategies don't produce the results that academic papers say they should.

Roll's final point was underscored for me during a recent exchange I had with a portfolio manager who used the most modern quantitative methods to run his portfolio and who followed closely all the statistical work done by academics and practitioners. His method was to use, in combination, a large number of the statistical predictabilities I have outlined above. He "back-tested" his technique with historical data from the past twenty years and found that it outperformed the Standard & Poor's 500-Stock Index by 3 percentage points per year over the twenty-year period. But his actual results running real money were quite different. Over the twenty-year period he had barely managed to equal the S&P return after expenses. This was an extraordinary performance and ranked him in the top 10 percent of all money managers. Yet the results make abundantly clear that techniques that work on paper do not necessarily work when investing real money and incurring the large transactions costs that are involved in the real world of investing. As this portfolio manager sheepishly told me, "I have never met a back test I didn't like." But let's never forget that academic back tests are not the same thing as managing real money.

As long as there are stock markets there will be mistakes made by the collective judgment of investors. And undoubtedly, some market participants are demonstrably less then rational. As a result, pricing irregularities and predictable patterns in stock returns can appear over time and even persist for short periods. Undoubtedly, with the passage of time and with the increasing sophistication of our databases and empirical techniques, we will document further apparent departures from efficiency and further patterns in the development of stock returns. But I suspect that the end result will not be an abandonment of the belief of many in the profession that the stock market is remarkably efficient in its utilization of information and that whatever patterns or *ex post* irrationalities have existed are unlikely to persist and will not provide investors with a method to obtain extraordinary returns. If there are any $100 bills lying around, they will not be there for long.

A Practical Guide for Random Walkers and Other Investors

12
A Fitness Manual
for
Random Walkers

In investing money, the amount of interest you want should
depend on whether you want to eat well or sleep well.
—J. Kenfield Morley, *Some Things I Believe*

Part Four is a how-to-do-it guide for your random walk down Wall Street. In this chapter, I shall offer general investment advice that should be useful to all investors, even if they don't believe that security markets are highly efficient. In chapter 13, I try to explain the recent fluctuations that have occurred in stock and bond returns and show how you might estimate what the future holds. I also indicate how you can at least roughly gauge the long-run returns you are likely to achieve from different investment programs. In chapter 14, I present a life-cycle investment guide indicating how the stage of your life plays an important role in determining the mix of investments that is most likely to enable you to meet your financial goals.

In the final chapter, I outline three specific strategies for equity investors who believe at least partially in the efficient-market theory or who are convinced that even if real expertise does exist, they are unlikely to find it. I have yet to see any compelling evidence that past stock prices can be used to predict future stock prices, and I am convinced that new information quickly gets reflected in market prices. But if you are sensible, you will take your random walk only after you have made detailed and careful plans with regard to all your investments, including your cash reserves. Even if stock prices move randomly, you shouldn't. Think of the advice that follows as a set of warm-up exercises that will enable you to reduce your income taxes and risk and at the same time increase your returns.

Exercise 1: Cover Thyself with Protection

Disraeli once wrote that "patience is a necessary ingredient of genius." It's also a key element in investing; you can't afford to pull your money out at the wrong time. You need staying power to increase your odds of earning attractive long-run returns. That's why it is so important for you to have noninvestment resources, such as medical and life insurance, to draw on should any emergency strike you or your family.

There are two broad categories of life insurance products available: high-premium policies that combine an insurance scheme with a type of savings plan, and low-premium term insurance that provides death benefits only, with no buildup of cash value.

The high-premium policies do have some advantages. Earnings on the part of the insurance premiums that go into the savings plan accumulate tax-free and this can be advantageous for some wealthy individuals who have maxed out on their tax-deferred retirement savings plans. Moreover, individuals who will not regularly and constantly save may find that the periodic premium bills provide the discipline necessary for them to make sure that a certain amount will be available for their families if they die and that a cash value builds up on the investment part of the program. But these kinds of policies entail high sales charges, and early premiums go mainly for sales commissions and other overhead rather than for buildup of cash value. Thus, not all your money goes to work. Hence, for most people, I favor the do-it-yourself approach. Buy term insurance for protection—invest the difference yourself (preferably in tax-deferred plans such as IRAs).

My advice is to buy renewable term insurance; you can keep renewing your policy without the need for a physical examination. So-called decreasing term insurance, renewable for progressively lower amounts, should suit many families best, because as time passes (and the children and family resources grow), the need for protection usually diminishes. You should understand, however, that term-insurance premiums escalate sharply when you reach the age of sixty or seventy or higher. If you still need insurance at that point, you will find that term insurance has become prohibitively expensive. But the major risk at that point is not premature death; it is that you will live too long and outlive your assets. You can increase those assets more effectively by buying term insurance and using the money you save for the investments I'll discuss below.

Take the time to shop around for the best deal. There is considerable variation in insurance company rates. It is wise to use either telephone quote services or the Internet to ensure that you are getting the best deal. I recommend that you do not buy insurance from any company with an A. M. Best rating of less than A. A lower premium will not compensate you for taking any risk that your insurance company will get into financial difficulty and be unable to pay its claims.

In addition, you should keep some reserves in safe and liquid investments. That, surely, is to many the antithesis of investing. Why put money in a safe place when you could be picking the next winner on the stock market? To cover unforeseen emergencies, that's why! It's the height of folly to gamble that nothing will happen to you. Every family should have a reserve of several months of living expenses to pay an unexpected medical bill or to provide a cushion during a time of unemployment. Moreover, any large future expenditures (such as junior's college tuition bill) should be funded with short-term investments whose maturity matches the date on which the funds will be needed.

Exercise 2: Know Your Investment Objectives

Determining clear goals is a part of the investment process that too many people skip, with disastrous results. You must decide at the outset what degree of risk you are willing to assume and what kinds of investments are most suitable to your tax bracket. The securities markets are like a large restaurant with a variety of products, suitable for different tastes and needs. Just as there is no one food that is best for everyone, so there is no one investment that is best for all investors.

We would all like to double our capital overnight, but how many of us can afford to see half our capital disintegrate just as quickly? J. P. Morgan once had a friend who was so worried about his stock holdings that he could not sleep at night. The friend asked, "What should I do about my stocks?" Morgan replied, "Sell down to the sleeping point." He wasn't kidding. Every investor must decide the trade-off he or she is willing to make between eating well and sleeping well. The decision is up to you. High investment rewards can be achieved only at the cost of substantial risk-taking. This has been one of the fundamental lessons of this book. So what's your sleeping point? Finding the answer to this question is one of the most important investment steps you must take.

To help raise your investment consciousness, I've prepared a sleeping scale on investment risk (see pages 282 and 283) and expected rate of return, as of the early part of the twenty-first century. At the stultifying end of the spectrum are a variety of short-term investments. A bank account appears to be the safest investment of all. You are certain to be able to withdraw every dollar you put in. The dollar value of your investment will never fluctuate. But even this investment does have a risk, because with inflation, you are, unfortunately, just about certain to lose out in real purchasing power even with the interest added, especially if you pay taxes on the interest. Next come money-market funds and six-month certificates—somewhat less flexible, but far more likely to offer inflation protection. If this is your sleeping point, you'll be interested in the information on these kinds of investments in Exercise 4.

Treasury inflation-protection securities (TIPS) come next in the safety scale. These bonds promise a low guaranteed rate that is augmented each year by the rate of increase of the consumers' price index. Because they are long-term bonds, they can fluctuate in price with changes in real interest rates (stated interest rates reduced by the rate of inflation). But if held to maturity, they are guaranteed to preserve real purchasing power. In Exercise 5, I'll discuss the advantages of having a small portion of your portfolio invested in these bonds.

Corporate bonds are somewhat riskier, and some dreams will start intruding in your sleep pattern if you choose this form of investment. In the early 2000s, the yield on good-quality, long-term bonds was around 6½ to 7 percent when held to maturity. Should you sell before then, your return will depend on the level of interest rates at the time of sale. If interest rates rise, your bonds will fall to a price that makes their yield competitive with new bonds offering a higher stated interest rate. Thus, there is a chance of loss. Your capital loss could be enough to eat up a whole year's interest—or even more. On the other hand, if interest rates fall, the price of your bonds will rise and you will get not only the promised percent interest but also a capital gain. Thus, if you sell prior to maturity, your actual yearly return could vary considerably, and that is why bonds are riskier than short-term instruments, which carry almost no risk of principal fluctuation. Generally, the longer a bond's term to maturity, the greater the risk and the greater the resulting yield.* You will find some useful information on how to buy both short- and long-term bonds in exercises 4 and 5.

No one can say for sure what the returns on common stocks will be. But the stock market, as Oskar Morgenstern once observed, is like a gambling casino where the odds are rigged in favor of the players. Although stock prices do plummet, as they did so disastrously during October 1987 and again during the early 2000s, the overall return during the entire twentieth century was about 9 percent per year, including both dividends and capital gains. I believe that a portfolio of domestic common stocks such as those that make up a typical mutual fund will have nearly similar average annual rates of return during the twenty-first century. Comparable returns are likely from the

---

*This isn't always the case. During some periods of unusually high interest rates in the 1980s, for example, short-term securities actually yielded more than long-term bonds. The catch was that investors could not count on continually reinvesting their short-term funds at such high rates, and by later in the decade, short-term rates had declined sharply. Thus, investors can reasonably expect that continual investment in short-term securities will not produce as high a return as investment in long-term bonds. In other words, there is a reward for taking on the risk of owning long-term bonds even if short-term rates are temporarily above long-term rates.

The Sleeping Scale of Major Investments

Sleeping Point	Type of Asset	2002 Expected Rate of Return before Income Taxes (%)	Length of Time Investment Must Be Held to Get Expected Rate of Return	Risk Level
Semicomatose state	Bank accounts	1–3	No specific investment period required. Many thrift institutions calculate interest from day of deposit to day of withdrawal.	No risk of losing what you put in. Deposits up to $100,000 guaranteed by an agency of the federal government. An almost sure loser with high inflation, however.
Long afternoon naps and sound night's sleep	Money-market deposit accounts	1–3	No specific investment period required, but check withdrawals limited to three per month.	No risk of losing what you put in. Deposits guaranteed as above. Rates geared to expected inflation and will vary over time.
Sound night's sleep	Money-market funds	1–4	No specific investment period required. Most funds provide check-writing privileges.	Very little risk because most funds are invested in government securities and bank certificates. Not usually guaranteed. Rates vary with expected inflation
	Special six-month certificates	1½–4	Money must be left on deposit for the entire six months to take advantage of higher rate.	Early withdrawals subject to penalty. Rates geared to expected inflation and will vary.
	Treasury inflation-protection securities (TIPS)	3¾+ inflation rate	These are long-term securities maturing in five years or longer.	Prices can vary if sold before maturity.
An occasional dream or two—some possibly unpleasant	High-quality corporate bonds (prime-quality public utilities)	6½–7	Investments must be held until maturity (20–30 years) to be assured of the stated rate. (The bonds also need to be protected against redemption.) The bonds may be sold at any time, but market prices vary with interest rates.	Very little risk if held to maturity. Moderate to substantial fluctuations can be expected in realized return if bonds are sold before maturity. Rate geared to expected long-run inflation rate. "Junk bonds" promise much higher returns but with much higher risk.

The Sleeping Scale of Major Investments (continued)

Sleeping Point	Type of Asset	2002 Expected Rate of Return before Income Taxes (%)	Length of Time Investment Must Be Held to Get Expected Rate of Return	Risk Level
Some tossing and turning before you doze, and vivid dreams before awakening	Diversified portfolios of blue-chip U.S. or developed foreign country common stocks	8–9	No specific investment period required and stocks may be sold at any time. The average expected return assumes a fairly long investment period and can only be treated as a rough guide based on current conditions.	Moderate to substantial risk. In any one year, the actual return could in fact be negative. Diversified portfolios have at times lost 25% or more of their actual value. Contrary to some opinions, a good inflation hedge over the long run.
	Real estate	Similar to common stocks	Same as for common stocks in general if purchase is made through REITs.	Same as above but REITs are good diversifiers and can be a good inflation hedge.
Nightmares not uncommon but, over the long run, well rested	Diversified portfolios of relatively risky stocks of smaller growth companies	9–10	Same as above. The average expected return assumes a fairly long investment period and can only be treated as a rough guide based on current conditions.	Substantial risk. In any one year the actual return could be negative. Diversified portfolios of very risky stocks have at times lost 50% or more of their value. Good inflation hedge.
Vivid dreams and occasional nightmares	Diversified portfolios of emerging-market stocks	±11	Plan to hold for at least 10 years. Projected returns impossible to quantify precisely.	Fluctuations up or down of 50% to 75% in a single year are not uncommon but have diversification benefits.
Bouts of insomnia	Gold	Impossible to predict	High returns could be earned in any new speculative craze as long as there are greater fools to be found.	Substantial risk. Believed to be a hedge against doomsday and hyperinflation. Can play a useful role in balancing a diversified portfolio, however.

major companies in developed foreign markets. The actual yearly return in the future can and probably will deviate substantially from this target—in down years you may lose as much as 25 percent or more. Can you stand the sleepless nights in the bad years?

How about dreams in full color with quadraphonic sound? You may want to choose a portfolio of somewhat riskier (more volatile) stocks, like those in aggressive growth-oriented mutual funds. These are the stocks in younger companies in newer technologies, where the promise of greater growth exists. Such companies are likely to be more volatile performers, and portfolios of these issues can easily lose half of their value in a bad market year. But your average future rate of return for the twenty-first century could be over 9 percent per year. Portfolios of smaller stocks have tended to outperform the market averages by small amounts. If you have no trouble sleeping during bear markets, and if you have the staying power to stick with your investments, an aggressive common-stock portfolio—made up of smaller companies—may be just right for you. Even greater returns, as well as greater market swings, are likely from portfolios of stocks from many emerging markets that have tremendous growth potential in the twenty-first century.

Commercial real estate has been an unattainable investment for many individuals. Nevertheless, the returns from real estate have been quite generous, similar to those from common stocks. I'll argue in Exercise 6 that individuals who can afford to buy their own homes are well advised to do so. In Exercise 7, I will discuss how it is much easier today for individuals to invest in commercial real estate. I believe that real estate investment trusts (REITs) deserve a position in a well-diversified investment portfolio.

I realize that my table slights gold and omits art objects, venture capital, hedge funds, commodities, and other more exotic investment possibilities. Many of these have done very well, and can serve a useful role in balancing a well-diversified portfolio of paper assets. Because of their substantial risk, and thus extreme volatility, it's impossible to describe them in the kind of terms applied to other investments; Exercise 8 reviews them in greater detail.

In all likelihood, your sleeping point will be greatly influenced by the way in which a loss would affect your financial survival. That is why the typical "widow" is often viewed in investment texts as unable to take on much risk. The widow has neither the life expectancy nor the ability to earn, outside her portfolio, the income she would need to recoup losses. Any loss of capital and income will immediately affect her standard of living. At the other end of the spectrum is the "aggressive young businesswoman." She has both the life expectancy and the earning power to maintain her standard of living in the face of any financial loss. At what stage you are in the "life cycle" is so important that I have devoted a special chapter (chapter 13) to this determinant of how much risk is appropriate for you.

In addition, your psychological makeup will influence the degree of risk you are willing to assume. One investment adviser suggests that you consider what kind of Monopoly player you once were (or still are). Were you a plunger? Did you construct hotels on Boardwalk and Park Place? True, the other players seldom landed on your property, but when they did, you could win the whole game in one fell swoop. Or did you prefer the steadier but moderate income from the orange monopoly of St. James Place, Tennessee Avenue, and New York Avenue? The answers to these questions may give you some insight into your psychological makeup with respect to investing and may help you to choose the right categories of securities for you. Or perhaps the analogy breaks down when it comes to real money. In any event, it is critical that you understand yourself before choosing specific securities for investment. Perhaps the most important question to ask yourself is how you felt during a period of sharply declining stock markets. If you became physically ill and even sold out all your stocks rather than staying the course with a diversified investment program, then a heavy exposure of common stocks is not for you.

A second key step is to review how much of your investment return goes to Uncle Sam and how much current income you need. Check last year's income tax form (1040) and the taxable income you reported for the year. For those in a high marginal tax bracket (the rate paid on the last dollar of income) there is a substantial tax advantage from municipal (tax-exempt) bonds. If you are in a high tax bracket, with little need for current income, you will prefer bonds that are tax-exempt and stocks that have low dividend yields but promise favorably taxed long-term capital gains (on which taxes do not have to be paid until gains are realized—perhaps never, if the stocks are part of a bequest). On the other hand, if you are in a low tax bracket and need a high current income, you will be better off with taxable bonds and high-dividend-paying common stocks, so that you don't have to incur the heavy transactions charges involved in selling off shares periodically to meet current income needs.

The two steps in this exercise—finding your risk level, and identifying your tax bracket and income needs—seem obvious. But it is incredible how many people go astray by mismatching the types of securities they buy with their risk tolerance and their income and tax needs. The confusion of priorities so often displayed by investors is not unlike that exhibited by a young woman whose saga was recently written up in a London newspaper:

RED FACES IN PARK

London, Oct. 30

Secret lovers were locked in a midnight embrace when it all happened.

Wedged into a tiny two-seater sports car, the near-naked man was suddenly immobilised by a slipped disc, according to a doctor writing in a medical journal here.

Trapped beneath him his desperate girlfriend tried to summon help by sounding the hooter button with her foot. A doctor, ambulancemen, firemen and a group of interested passers-by quickly surrounded the couple's car in Regents Park.

Dr. Brian Richards of Kent said: "The lady found herself trapped beneath 200 pounds of a pain-racked, immobile man.

"To free the couple, firemen had to cut away the car frame," he added.

The distraught girl, helped out of the car and into a coat, sobbed: "How am I going to explain to my husband what has happened to his car?"

—Reuters

Investors are often torn by a similar confusion of priorities.

You can't seek safety of principal and then take a plunge with investment into the riskiest of common stocks. You can't shelter your income from high marginal tax rates and then lock in returns of for 8 percent from taxable corporate bonds, no matter how attractive these may be. Yet the annals of investment counselors are replete with stories of investors whose security holdings are inconsistent with their investment goals.

Exercise 3: Dodge Uncle Sam Whenever You Can

One of the best ways to obtain extra investment funds is to avoid taxes legally. We've already discussed tax-exempt bonds and the tax advantages of unrealized capital gains. But did you know that you pay no income taxes on the earnings from money invested in a retirement plan until you actually retire and use the money? And if your income is not high, you can deduct contributions to an Individual Retirement Account (IRA). When you retire, you may be in a lower tax bracket. Even if you are not in a lower bracket, you will have paid no taxes on your retirement savings over the years. This exercise makes you fit enough to reap these benefits.

Pension Plans and IRAs

First, check to see if your employer has a pension or profit-sharing plan, such as a 401(k) or 403(b)7 savings plan. If so, you are home free. But what if your employer doesn't have such a plan? If you're single, as of 2003 you can contribute up to $3,000 of your annual income a year to an Individual Retirement Account. If you're married and both you and your spouse work, you can contribute $6,000. Contribution limits are scheduled to rise in subsequent years. Although the contribution to your IRA is not tax-deductible if your income is high, the IRA account is still a good deal because the interest earnings on your contributions compound free of tax. The chart on page 288 compares a $2,000 annual contribution to an IRA, where the interest earnings are not taxed, with the equivalent contribution to a taxable (a 30 percent rate is assumed) investment. The chart assumes funds are invested at an 8 percent interest rate and that contributions are made for a forty-year

The Advantage of Tax-Deferred Compounded Earnings

$559,562

$295,762

Investment
Account
without
Tax Deferral

IRA
Account
with
Tax Deferral

Source: *www.vanguard.com*
The Vanguard Group Personal Investors, Planning & Advice.

period. Although it is true that the earnings withdrawn from a tax-deferred account will ultimately be taxed,* a forty-year deferral of taxes paid implies more than a $263,000 advantage for the IRA account, as the chart shows. If your income is low enough to qualify for a deduction on the IRA contributions as well, you will be even further ahead.

Keogh Plans

For self-employed people, Congress has created the Keogh plan. All self-employed individuals—from accountants to Avon ladies, barbers to real estate brokers, doctors to decorators—are permitted to establish such a plan, to which they can contribute as much as 20 percent of their income, up to $30,000 annually. If you moonlight from your regular job, you can establish a Keogh for the income you earn on the side. The

*As will be explained below, moneys can be withdrawn from Roth IRAs tax-free.

money paid into a Keogh is deductible from taxable income, and the earnings are not taxed until they are withdrawn. If you qualify for this plan, you'll be making a big mistake not to take advantage of this perfectly legal way to checkmate the Internal Revenue Service and maximize your retirement savings to help you cope with the effects of inflation.

Millions of taxpayers are currently missing what is one of the truly good deals around. My advice is to save as much as you can through these tax-sheltered means. Use up any other savings you may have for current living expenses, if you must, so you can contribute the maximum allowed.

Is there a fly in the ointment? Yes. As the favorite expression of economists goes, "There ain't no such thing as a completely free lunch." You can't touch IRA or Keogh funds before turning fifty-nine and a half or becoming disabled. If you do, the amount withdrawn is taxed, and you must pay an additional 10 percent penalty on it. But even with this catch, I believe IRAs and Keoghs are a good deal. The advantages of staying in the plan for a few years far outweigh the penalty, even if you do withdraw some funds.

The important point is that if you plan to have any money saved up by the time you are fifty-nine and a half, you may as well do your saving by means of a tax-free retirement fund. Whatever your savings and investment decisions, it's always better to keep the sums involved tax-free.

What can Keogh and IRA funds be invested in? You name it—stocks, bonds, mutual funds, savings certificates, annuity contracts, and other investments. Your choice should depend on your risk preferences as well as the composition of your other investment holdings. You can choose from a wide variety of plans offered by savings institutions, securities dealers, insurance companies, and mutual funds. My own preference would be stock and bond funds, and I'll give you specific advice later for choosing the best vehicle for you. You certainly don't want to invest in lower-yield tax-exempt securities, however, because your retirement fund will accumulate tax-free anyway, and when you take the money out, you will pay taxes on what should have been tax-free income.

Any further questions regarding the plans? You can call your local office of the Internal Revenue Service for answers to specific questions. Also, the IRS has special publications covering all the detailed regulations.

Roth IRAs

During the late 1990s an additional form of individual retirement account called a Roth IRA became available to investors whose income is below certain levels. The traditional IRA offers "jam today" in the form of an immediate tax deduction (provided you are eligible). Once in the account, the money and its earnings are only taxed when taken out at retirement. The Roth IRA offers "jam tomorrow"—you don't get an upfront tax deduction, but your withdrawals (including investment earnings) are tax-free. In addition, you can Roth and roll. You can roll your regular IRA into a Roth IRA if you are within the certain income limits. You will need to pay tax on all the funds converted, but then neither future investment income nor withdrawals at retirement will be taxed. Moreover, there are no lifetime minimum distribution requirements for a Roth IRA and contributions can continue to be made after age seventy and a half. Thus significant amounts can be accumulated tax-free for the benefit of future generations.

The decision of which IRA is best for you and whether to convert can be a tough call. Important factors influencing the decision are whether you are likely to be in a higher or lower tax bracket at retirement, whether you have sufficient funds outside your IRA to pay conversion taxes, your age and life expectancy, and to what extent you will need your IRA funds during retirement. Fortunately, the financial services industry offers free software to analyze whether or not conversion makes sense for you. Many mutual-fund companies and brokers have Roth analyzers that are reasonably easy to use. I can offer a rule of thumb to suggest whether further investigation is likely to be useful. If you are close to retirement and your tax bracket is likely to be lower in retirement, you probably shouldn't convert, especially if conversion will push you into a higher bracket now. On the other hand, if you are far from retirement and are in a lower tax bracket now, you are very likely to come out well ahead with a Roth IRA. If your income is too high to allow you to take a tax deduction on a regular IRA but low enough to qualify for a Roth, then there is no question that a Roth is right for you since your contribution is made after tax in any event.

Tax-Deferred Annuities

Another strategy to foil the tax collector is the use of tax-deferred annuities. This instrument is useful if you have exceeded the limitations involved in other tax-advantaged savings programs. A tax-deferred annuity is a contract between you and an insurance company, purchased with one or more payments; the funds deposited accumulate tax-deferred interest, and the money is used to provide regular income payments at some later time. Usually, this type of contract involves no risk to your principal; the insurance company guarantees return of your original deposit at any time. Alternatively, variable annuities are usually invested in equity funds and their returns will depend on how well the particular investment you choose performs in the years ahead.

As with the IRA and the Keogh plan, you pay no income tax on the interest, dividends, or gains accrued during the accumulation period. Thus, all of your interest—as well as the principal—keeps working for you. When you start receiving payments from your annuity, a portion of each payment is considered to be a return of principal and is, therefore, tax-free. Furthermore, if—like most people—you use the annuity to provide a regular income during retirement, you will possibly be in a lower tax bracket when you finally do pay the taxes. A deferred annuity can also avoid the cost and delay of probate in the event of death, because your funds pass automatically to your beneficiaries. But make sure you check the fee tables published at the front of each annuity prospectus. With some very expensive deferred annuities, what you gain in tax deferral you can lose in extra fees. In general, annuities are more expensive than IRAs and Keoghs invested in mutual funds. Therefore, you should invest in an annuity only after you have placed the maximum amount in a regular retirement plan, such as a 401(k), 403(b)7, Keogh, or IRA. Finally, remember the age-old maxim that has served investors well over the past years: "Never buy anything from someone who is out of breath."

Saving for College: As Easy as 529

"529" college savings accounts allow parents and grandparents to give gifts to children that can later be used for college education. Named after the provision of the tax code that sanctioned them, the gifts can be invested in stocks and bonds and no federal taxes will be imposed on the investment earnings as long as the withdrawals are made for qualified higher education purposes. Moreover, as of 2002, the plans allow an individual donor to contribute as much as $55,000 to a 529 plan without gift taxes and without reducing estate tax credits. For couples, the amount doubles to $110,000. If you have kids or grandchildren who plan to go to college and you can afford to contribute to a 529 plan, the decision to establish such a plan is a no-brainer.

Are there pitfalls to avoid? You bet. Most of the salespeople pushing these plans receive hefty commissions that eat into investment returns. Be an educated consumer and contact a company such as TIAA-CREF or Vanguard for a no-load low-expense alternative. While it's always nice to stiff the tax man, some high-expense 529 plans could end up shortchanging you. Also note that these 529 plans are sanctioned by individual states and some states allow you to take a tax deduction on your state income tax return for at least part if not all of your contribution. Thus, if you live in New York State (which allows a $5,000 per person deduction), you will want to be sure to get a New York plan. On the other hand, Massachusetts does not allow a state tax deduction for its own 529 plan, so residents there can readily join a different state's plan. Moreover, if you don't use the proceeds of 529 plans for qualified education expenses (including midcareer retooling or even post-retirement education), withdrawals are not only subject to income tax but carry a 10 percent penalty as well.

Keep in mind that colleges are likely to consider 529 assets in determining need-based financial aid. Thus, if you believe you will be eligible for financial aid when your child goes to college, parents could be better off keeping the assets in their own names. Of course, if you won't qualify for need-based aid in any case, by all means establish a low-expense 529.* Finally,

---

* Comprehensive information about 529 plans, as well as other tax-advantaged savings vehicles such as Coverdell ESAs, can be found at *www.savingforcollege.com*.

remember Exercise 1: If you are establishing a 529 for a teenager who will be going to college in a few years, you will probably want to weight your investments toward bonds with short- to intermediate-term maturities.

Exercise 4: Be Competitive—Let the Yield on Your Cash Reserve Keep Pace with Inflation

As I've already pointed out, some ready assets are necessary for pending expenses, such as college tuition, possible emergencies, or even psychological support. Thus, you have a real dilemma. You know that if you keep your money in a savings bank and get, say, 2 percent interest in a year in which the inflation rate exceeds 2 percent, you will lose real purchasing power. In fact, the situation's even worse because the interest you get is subject to regular income taxes. So what's a small saver to do?

The investor of substantial means has many options. He or she can buy Treasury bills (short-term IOUs issued by the U.S. government) or large certificates of deposit (short-term IOUs issued by banks, called bank CDs), some of which are issued only in large denominations. If you have only a small amount of liquid assets, you can't get into this market directly. So how does the small saver avoid getting shafted? How do you get a rate of return that protects you against inflation? That is what this exercise is all about.

There are four short-term investment instruments that can at least help you stand up to inflation. These are (1) money-market mutual funds; (2) money-market deposit accounts; (3) bank certificates; and (4) tax-exempt money-market funds.

Money-Market Mutual Funds

In my judgment, money-market mutual funds (or money funds) provide the best instrument for many investors' needs. They combine safety, high yields, and the right to withdraw money with no penalty attached. Most funds allow you to write large checks against your fund balance, generally in amounts of at least $250. Interest earnings continue until the checks clear. These money funds are the best alternative to bank accounts, and they have been extraordinarily popular. You can find the addresses, telephone numbers, and detailed pertinent financial information for some low-expense funds in the Random Walker's Address Book at the end of this book.

These money funds invest in large bank CDs, commercial paper (short-term corporate IOUs), government securities, and other instruments. Their yield, therefore, fluctuates fairly closely with the available yield on these short-term securities. To date, this yield has usually outpaced—by a significant margin—the interest offered on cash savings accounts. Because they pool the funds of many small investors, the money funds can buy larger issues, beyond the individual's financial reach. The funds sell for a dollar a share and have been able to keep that principal constant. Although there's no guarantee against a loss of principal, you shouldn't have trouble sleeping nights if you invest in any of the funds in my Address Book.

For those who deep in their hearts prefer the semicomatose state of safety that government guarantees provide, a new class of money-market funds has been formed. These are funds that invest only in Treasury bills or government agency securities. As you might expect, they tend to yield less than comparable funds investing in bank obligations. Is the yield sacrifice worth the extra safety? The answer depends on your psychological makeup.

My personal answer is to go with the higher-yielding regular funds. Although I would be the first to agree that money saved for a rainy day should not be allowed to go down the drain, I think that the risk of the prime-quality funds is, as my lawyer friends like to put it, *de minimis*.

Money-Market Deposit Accounts

The money funds became so popular that hundreds of billions of dollars were drained out of bank deposits into these higher-yielding mutual funds. Needless to say, the banks sought ways to compete. And so, in another example of how deregulation benefits the consumer, the banks were allowed to offer money-market deposit accounts to individuals. At the outset, banks offered promotional rates that were well above the yields offered by the money funds. Savvy consumers, chasing the prettiest rate in the market, deserted the money funds in droves.

But once the banks had reestablished themselves, they qui-

Copyright © Randy Jones. Reprinted by permission.

etly reduced the rates they were offering so that the money funds then had an advantage over the deposit accounts. Money began to return to the funds and now both types of investments have hundreds of billions of consumers' dollars.

How should you decide between the two? Each has its own advantages. The banks enjoy important attractions. First, like other bank deposits, money-market deposit accounts are insured by an agency of the federal government. Thus, they score at the top of the scale for worried insomniacs. In addition, it's convenient to invest in money-market deposit accounts because banks have branches, whereas money funds only have post office boxes, toll-free telephone numbers, and Internet addresses. But the money funds have their own advantages. Their yields tend to be higher than the bank accounts. In addition, the money funds allow an unlimited number of checks to be written against balances (although each check must usually be written for at least $250). The deposit accounts usually allow only three checks per month (for any amount). Money funds also offer wire transfer facilities that permit money to be moved around overnight. Moreover, because money funds are typically part of a large mutual fund or brokerage complex, they are an ideal place to "park" cash and earn interest while awaiting movement into more permanent investments. Finally, it is possible to find money funds that invest only in tax-exempt securities so that high-bracket investors can earn considerably higher after-tax yields. I'll discuss these tax-exempt money funds below.

Bank Certificates

Banks also offer certificates of deposit with a variety of periods to maturity. Yields on these instruments are typically higher than those on either money-market deposit accounts or money funds. These certificates are government-insured up to $100,000 per buyer ($200,000 with your spouse). Thus, the certificates are even safer than the money funds and are an excellent medium for investors who can tie up their liquid funds for at least six months.

The certificates do have a number of disadvantages, however. First, you need to have a substantial nest egg—usually $10,000—before you can buy. Second, you can't write checks against the certificates as you can with shares in the money funds. Most important, as in other aspects of life, there is a substantial penalty for premature withdrawal. If you redeem your certificate before maturity, you will lose some interest as a

penalty. Fourth, the yield on bank certificates is subject to state and local taxes (Treasury bills, which can now be obtained direct from the Treasury, are exempt from these).

Tax-Exempt Money-Market Funds

Tax-exempt money-market funds may be useful for some investors, particularly those who pay taxes at the top marginal rate and who live in states with high income tax rates. A disadvantage of all the vehicles previously described is that the interest is fully taxable. This situation led to the establishment of tax-exempt money-market funds.

These funds invest in portfolios of short-term, high-quality, tax-exempt issues. They produce daily tax-exempt income, instant liquidity, and free checking for large bills ($250 or more). Some sample funds are listed in the Random Walker's Address Book. The yields on tax-exempt funds are considerably lower than those on taxable funds. Nevertheless, individuals in the highest tax brackets will find the earnings from this investment more attractive than the after-tax yield of the regular money funds.

If you live in a state that has high income tax rates, you will want to consider a fund that only holds securities issued by entities within your home state. Tax-exempt bonds issued, for example, by New York municipalities are taxable in other states. Thus, the only way for, say, a Californian to avoid both federal and state taxes is to buy a fund that holds only California securities. Fortunately, there are now tax-exempt money funds (as well as bond funds) available that invest in the securities of a single state. These are not available for all states. You should call one of the mutual-fund complexes such as Fidelity or Vanguard to check on the availability of a fund that invests in securities of the state in which you pay taxes.

Exercise 5: Investigate a Promenade through Bond Country

Let's face it, bonds were a lousy place to put your money from World War II until the early 1980s. Inflation had eaten away at the real value of the bonds with a vengeance. For example, savers who bought U.S. savings bonds for $18.75 in the early 1970s and redeemed them five years later for $25 found, much to their dismay, that they had actually lost real purchasing power. The trouble was that, although the $18.75 invested in such a bond five years before might have filled one's gas tank twice, the $25 obtained at maturity did little more than fill it once. In fact, an investor's real return was negative, as inflation had eroded purchasing power faster than interest earnings were compounding. Small wonder many investors view the bond as an unmentionable four-letter word.

In fact, the U.S. savings bond program, with its touching appeals to patriotism and good citizenship, has been a monumental rip-off. Interest rates on series EE savings bonds were far below the inflation rates of the 1970s and only about half what the government was paying on bonds sold on the open market. Fortunately, the government improved the terms of U.S. savings bonds so that they can pay 85 percent of the rate the Treasury pays for funds in the open market. The bonds also have some tax advantages. Still, as I'll show you below, far more attractive investment opportunities are available.

Of course, other bonds were also poor investments during the 1960s and 1970s, because the interest rates they carried did not offer adequate inflation protection. Investors thirty years ago simply did not realize how high inflation could go. But remember Part Two. Markets are reasonably efficient, and investors now refuse to buy bonds unless their yields offer a reasonable degree of compensation for the expected loss in the dollar's purchasing power. In the early 2000s, good-quality long-term bonds were yielding 6½ to 7 percent in the open market. This yield translates freely into protection against a long-term inflation rate of 2 percent (the actual rate during the late 1990s and early 2000s) and provides a real rate of return above that inflation of 4½ to 5 percent. Of course, the actual long-run rate of inflation may be considerably greater than 2 percent. But the 4½ to 5 percent real return they promise gives a reasonably generous margin of safety, as I will argue in the next chapter.

In my view, there are four kinds of bond purchases you may especially want to consider: (1) zero-coupon bonds (which allow you to lock in high yields for a predetermined length of time); (2) no-load bond mutual funds (which permit you to buy shares in bond portfolios); (3) tax-exempt bonds and bond funds (for those who are fortunate enough to be in high tax brackets); and (4) U.S. Treasury inflation-protection securities (TIPS).

Zero-Coupon Bonds Can Generate Large Future Returns

Suppose you were told you could invest $10,000 now and be guaranteed by the government that you would get back double that amount in ten years. The ability to do so is possible through the use of zero-coupon securities.

These securities are called zero coupons or simply zeros because owners receive no periodic interest payments as they do in a regular interest-coupon-paying bond. Instead, these securities are purchased at deep discounts from their face value (for example, 50 cents on the dollar) and gradually rise to their face or par values over the years. If held to maturity, the holder is paid the full stated amount of the bond. These securities are available on maturities ranging from a few months to over twenty years. They are excellent vehicles for putting money aside for required expenditures on specific future dates.

The principal attraction of zeros is that the purchaser is faced with no reinvestment risk. A zero-coupon Treasury bond guarantees an investor that his or her funds will be continuously reinvested at the yield to maturity rate. Thus, the zeros offer a convenient way to lock in high yields for many years to come.

The main disadvantage of zeros is that the Internal Revenue Service requires that taxable investors declare annually as income a pro rata share of the dollar difference between the purchase price and the par value of the bond. This is not required, however, for investors who hold zeros in IRAs or Keogh plans. Here the investor can defer all taxes until retirement. Thus, zero-coupon securities are a superb vehicle for retirement plans.

Two warnings are in order. Often brokers will charge small investors fairly large commissions for the purchase of zero-coupon bonds in small denominations. As I will discuss in Exercise 9 below, commission rates are not random and some comparison shopping could improve your net yield. In addition, you should know that redemption at face value is guaranteed only if you hold the bonds to maturity. In the meantime, prices can be highly variable as interest rates change.

No-Load Bond Funds Are Appropriate Vehicles for Individual Investors

Open-end bond (mutual) funds give some of the long-term advantages of the zeros but are much easier and less costly to buy or sell. Those that I have listed in the Address Book all invest in long-term securities. Although there is no guarantee that you can reinvest your interest at constant rates, these funds do offer long-run stability of income and are particularly suitable for investors who plan to live off their interest income.

Bond mutual funds typically hold a diversified portfolio of high-quality bonds. Purchasers of shares in such a fund in essence buy a pro rata share in all of the assets of the fund and are entitled to a pro rata share of the income. Thus, a small investor would be able to obtain the same kind of broad-scale diversification available to a large institutional investor.

Because bond markets tend to be at least as efficient as stock markets, I recommend low-expense bond index funds. Bond index funds, which just buy and hold a broad variety of bonds, generally outperform actively managed bond funds. In no event should you even buy a load fund (a fund with a commission fee). There's no point in paying for something if you can get it free.

The Address Book lists several types of funds: those specializing in corporate bonds, those that buy a portfolio of GNMA mortgage-backed bonds, those investing in tax-exempt bonds (which I will discuss in the next section), as well as some riskier high-yield funds appropriate for investors willing to accept extra risk in return for higher expected returns.

For investors who are very risk averse, I favor GNMA funds. These funds invest exclusively in GNMA (Ginnie Mae) mortgage pass-through securities. These are bonds backed by a pool of government-insured mortgages (either VA or FHA) and are, therefore, a general obligation of the U.S. government. Interest and principal payments on the bonds come from the interest and principal repayments of the underlying mortgages. Not only is the security on these bonds of the highest quality, but also the yields are comparable to those on corporate bonds. Mortgage bonds have one disadvantage in that when interest rates fall, many homeowners refinance their high-rate mortgages and some high-yielding mortgage bonds get repaid early. It is that potential disadvantage that makes the yield on government-guaranteed mortgage bonds so high. Mutual funds that diversify among mortgage bonds backed by mortgages issued at many different initial rates do offer some protection, however, against premature redemption.

Tax-Exempt Bonds Are Useful for High-Bracket Investors

If you are in a very high tax bracket, taxable money funds, zeros, and taxable bond funds may be suitable only within your retirement plan. Otherwise, you need the tax-exempt bonds issued by state and local governments and by various governmental authorities, such as port authorities or toll roads. The interest from these bonds doesn't count as taxable income on your federal tax form, and bonds from the state in which you live are typically exempt from any state income taxes.

By now, if you've carefully followed Exercise 2, you know whether municipal bonds are compatible with your tax bracket and your income needs. In the early 2000s, good-quality long-term corporate bonds were yielding 6½ to 7 percent, and tax-exempt issues of comparable quality yielded 5 to 5¼ percent. Suppose your tax bracket (the rate at which your last dollar of income is taxed—not your average rate) is about 36 percent, including both federal and state taxes. The following table shows that the after-tax income is $77 higher on the tax-exempt security, which is clearly the better investment for a person in your tax bracket. Even if you are in a lower tax bracket, tax-exempts may still pay, depending on the exact yields available in the market when you make your purchase.

Tax-Exempt vs. Taxable Bonds ($10,000 Face Value)

Type of Bond	Interest Paid	Applicable Taxes (36% Rate)	After-Tax Income
5¼% tax-exempt	$525	$0	$525
7% taxable	700	252	448

If you buy bonds directly (rather than indirectly through mutual funds), I suggest that you buy new issues rather than already outstanding securities. New-issue yields are usually a bit sweeter than the yields of seasoned outstanding bonds and you avoid paying transactions charges on new issues. I also think you should keep your risk within reasonable bounds by sticking with issues rated at least A by Moody's and Standard & Poor's rating services. Long-term bonds usually mature in twenty years or more, but they often enjoy a good trading market after they have been issued. Thus, if you want to sell the bonds later, you can do so with reasonable ease, particularly if you own at least $10,000 worth of a single issue.

For those who sleep poorly at night, consider guaranteed tax-exempt bonds that are insured against default by a consortium of banks, insurance companies, and securities firms. Their yields are only a bit lower, and they generally carry a AAA rating. Also consider so-called AMT bonds. These bonds are subject to the alternative minimum (income) tax and, therefore, are not attractive to individuals who have sheltered a significant part of their income from tax. But if you are not subject to the alternative minimum tax, you can get some extra yield from holding AMT bonds.

It is usually wise to avoid shorter-term serial bonds. These are usually tougher to sell than long-term bonds if you have to raise funds before their maturity. Also, yields on serial issues (especially the shorter-term ones) usually tend to be lower in part because they are particularly attractive to institutions, like banks, that pay taxes at high corporate rates. Unless you have funds to invest for some specific period of time and want to match the maturity of the bond you buy with the timing of your fund requirements, these bonds are best left to institutional buyers. So ask your broker how the "new-issue calendar" looks. By waiting a week or so until a new high-yielding revenue term bond comes out, you may be able to improve your interest return substantially.

There is one nasty "heads I win, tails you lose" feature of bonds that you should know about. If interest rates go up, the price of your bonds will go down, as I noted earlier. But if interest rates go down, the issuer can often "call" the bonds away from you (repay the debt early) and then issue new bonds at lower rates. To protect yourself, make sure your bonds have a ten-year call-protection provision that prevents the issuer from calling your bonds to issue new ones at lower rates.

There are good tax-exempt bond funds available that are listed in the Address Book. If you have substantial funds to invest in tax-exempts ($25,000 or more), however, I see little reason for you to make your tax-exempt purchases through a fund and pay the management fees involved. If you follow the rules already presented and confine your purchases to a few high-quality bonds, particularly those that are insured, there is little need for you to diversify. And you'll get more interest return if you invest directly. On the other hand, if you have just a few thousand dollars to invest, you will find it costly to buy and sell small lots of bonds, and a fund will provide convenient liquidity and diversification for you. In addition to the bond funds listed in the table, there are funds available that confine their purchases to the bonds of a single state so that you can avoid both state and federal income taxes.

Hot TIPS: Inflation-Indexed Bonds

We know that unanticipated inflation is devastating to bondholders. Inflation tends to increase interest rates and, as they go up, bond prices fall. And there's more bad news: Inflation also reduces the real value of a bond's interest and principal payments. Now a lead shield is available to investors in the form of Treasury inflation-protection securities (TIPS). These securities are immune to the erosion of inflation if held to maturity and guarantee investors that their portfolios will retain their purchasing power. The bonds pay a basic interest rate between 3 and 3½ percent. But in contrast to old-fashioned Treasuries, the interest payment is based on a principal amount that rises with the Consumer Price Index (CPI). If the price level were to rise 3 percent next year, the $1,000 face value would increase to $1,030 and the semiannual interest payment would increase as well. When the TIPS mature, the investor gets a principal payment equal to the inflation-adjusted face value at that time. Thus, TIPS provide a guaranteed real rate of return and a repayment of principal in an amount that preserves its real purchasing power.

No other financial instrument available today provides

investors a reliable inflation hedge. Although real assets often hold their value during periods of inflation, gold, diamonds, and other commodities have not provided competitive long-run rates of return and do not dependably rise in price along with the general price level. Although common stocks have bestowed generous long-run returns, they usually suffer during inflationary periods. TIPS also are great portfolio diversifiers. When inflation accelerates, TIPS will offer higher nominal returns, whereas stock and bond prices are likely to fall. Thus, TIPS have low correlations with other portfolio assets and are uniquely effective diversifiers and provide a very effective insurance policy for the white-knuckle crowd of investors.

TIPS do have a nasty tax feature, however, that limits their usefulness. Taxes on TIPS returns are due on both the coupon payment and the increase in principal amount reflecting inflation. The problem is that the Treasury does not pay out the increase in principal until maturity. If inflation were high enough, the small coupon payments might be insufficient to pay the taxes and the imbalance would worsen at higher rates of inflation. Thus, TIPS are far from ideal for taxable investors and are best used only in tax-advantaged retirement plans.

Should You Be a Bond-Market Junkie?

Is the bond market immune to the maxim that investment risk and reward are related? Not at all! During most periods, so-called junk bonds (lower credit quality, higher-yielding bonds) have given investors a net rate of return at least 2 percentage points higher than the rate that could be earned on "investment-grade" bonds with high-quality credit ratings. In the early 2000s, investment-grade bonds yielded 6½ to 7 percent, whereas "junk" bonds often yielded 9 percent or more. Thus, even if 2 percent of the lower-grade bonds defaulted on their interest and principal payments and produced a total loss, a diversified portfolio of low-quality bonds would still produce a larger net return than would be available from a high-quality bond portfolio. For this reason, many investment advisers have recommended well-diversified portfolios of high-yield bonds as sensible investments. They find the higher yields quite tempting and offering more than adequate compensation for the moderately larger investment risk involved.

There is, however, another school of thought which advises investors to "Just Say No" to junk bonds. These people view the risks involved as far too large. Most junk bonds have been issued since the mid-1980s as a result of a massive wave of corporate mergers, acquisitions, and leveraged (mainly debt-financed) buyouts. The junk-bond naysayers point out that lower credit bonds are most likely to be serviced in full only during good times in the economy. But watch out, they say, if the economy falters. Moreover, in some industries such as telecommunications, massive overbuilding led to bond defaults even during good economic times.

So what's a thoughtful investor to do? There's no easy solution. Again, the answer depends in part on how well you sleep at night when you assume substantial investment risk. Clearly, high-yield or junk-bond portfolios are not for insomniacs. Even with diversification, there is substantial risk in these investments. Moreover, they are not for investors who depend solely on high-yield bond payments as their major source of income. And they are certainly not for any investors who do not adequately diversify their holdings either through direct investment or through the medium of mutual funds. However, the gross yield premium from junk bonds is substantial and, at least historically, it has more than compensated for actual default experience

Exercise 6: Begin Your Walk at Your Own Home— Renting Leads to Flabby Investment Muscles

Remember Scarlett O'Hara? She was broke at the end of the Civil War, but she still had her beloved plantation, Tara. A good house on good land keeps its value no matter what happens to money. As long as the world's population continues to grow, the demand for real estate will be among the most dependable inflation hedges available.

One hundred years ago, Henry George sounded the call for real estate investment:

> Go, get yourself a piece of ground, and hold possession. . . .
> You need do nothing more. You may sit down and smoke your
> pipe; you may lie around like the lazzaroni of Naples or the

leperos of Mexico; you may go up in a balloon, or down a hole in the ground and without doing one stroke of work, without adding one iota to the wealth of the community, in ten years you will be rich.

By and large, George's advice turned out to be pretty good.

Although the calculation is tricky, it appears that the long-run returns on residential real estate have been quite generous. But the real estate market is less efficient than the stock market. There may be hundreds of knowledgeable investors who study the worth of every common stock. Perhaps only a handful of prospective buyers assess the worth of a particular real estate property. Hence, individual pieces of property are not always appropriately priced. Finally, real estate returns seem to be higher than stock returns during periods when inflation is accelerating, but do less well during periods of disinflation. In sum, real estate has proved to be a good investment providing generous returns and excellent inflation-hedging characteristics.

The natural real estate investment for most people is the single-family home or the condominium. You have to live somewhere, and buying has several tax advantages over renting. Because Congress wanted to encourage home ownership and the values associated with this, it gave the homeowner two important tax breaks: (1) Although rent is not deductible from income taxes, the two major expenses associated with home ownership—interest payments on your mortgage and property taxes—are fully deductible; (2) realized gains in the value of your house up to substantial amounts are tax-exempt. In addition, ownership of a house is a good way to force yourself to save, and a house provides enormous emotional satisfaction. My advice is: Own your own home if you can possibly afford it.

Exercise 7: Beef Up with Real Estate Investment Trusts

One of the major changes in U.S. financial markets during the late 1990s was the packaging of ownership interests in real property into trusts called real estate investment trusts, or REITs (pronounced "reets"). Properties from apartment houses to office buildings to shopping malls were packaged into REIT portfolios and managed by professional real estate operators. The REITs themselves are like any other common stock and are actively traded on the major stock exchanges. This has afforded an excellent opportunity for individuals to add commercial real estate to their investment portfolios.

If you want to move your portfolio toward terra firma, I strongly suggest you invest some of your assets in REITs. There are many reasons why they should play a role in your investment program.

First, ownership of real estate has produced comparable rates of return to common stocks over the past thirty years. Equally important, real estate is an excellent vehicle to provide the benefits of diversification described in chapter 9. Because real estate returns have relatively little correlation with other assets, putting some share of your portfolio into real estate can reduce the overall risk of your investment program. Moreover, real estate is probably a more dependable hedge against inflation than common stocks in general. Finally, most REITs have generous dividends and in some cases the dividends are partially tax exempt.

Unfortunately, the job of sifting through the hundreds of outstanding REITs is a daunting one for the individual investor. Moreover, a single-equity REIT is unlikely to provide the necessary diversification across property types and regions of the country. And, certainly, individuals could stumble badly by purchasing the wrong REIT. Now, however, investors have a rapidly expanding group of real estate mutual funds that are more than willing to do the job for them. The funds cull through the available offerings and put together a diversified portfolio of REITs, ensuring that a wide variety of property types and regions are represented. Moreover, investors have the ability to liquidate their fund holdings whenever they wish. There are also low-expense-indexed REIT funds (listed in the Address Book) and I believe these funds will continue to produce the best net returns for investors. I believe all investors should have a portion of their portfolios invested in REITs.

Before we leave the subject of real estate, a special note of caution should be raised about those late-night cable television real estate gurus who promise unlimited wealth by buying real estate with "nothing down." Don't buy their books and manuals and by all means avoid their get-rich-quick schemes that could lead you to personal bankruptcy and even jail. The gifted financial columnist Jane Bryant Quinn studied a group of these programs and the materials they sold and came to the following conclusion:

> I found them misleading, fantastical, false, and in some cases, flatly illegal. The dream they sell—that you can buy profitable property with no credit, no job, no experience, even with a bankruptcy behind you—shouldn't pass anyone's first-round BS test. Gurus earn their Rolls-Royces and their diamond pinky rings not by extracting value from real estate but by extracting cash from you.

Exercise 8: Tiptoe through the Fields of Gold, Collectibles, and Other Investments

In the early editions of this book, I took a very negative view of gold and other "things" as investment vehicles. At the start of the 1980s, gold had risen past $800 an ounce. Diamonds glittered, metals such as copper and silver shone, and collectibles such as art, rugs, and porcelains all became popular investment vehicles.

Publishers jumped on this golden bandwagon and a number of "how-to-beat-inflation" books came out, touting investments in "things" rather than paper securities. The premise was that because you and everybody else consume things, if you want to preserve real purchasing power, you can do so by owning specific commodities.

The problem is that things often don't yield a stream of benefits, such as dividend returns. Gold, for example, is a sterile investment in a rational world. It does not yield dividends and can be costly to store and protect. Moreover, the sharp run-up in prices in 1979–80 was uncomfortably close in my mind to the price increases during the tulip-bulb craze described in chapter 2.

I said in 1980 that I am not panning gold for all time. In early 2002, gold was selling at less than $300 an ounce, and I am slightly more positive about gold as an investment, but far from enthusiastic. Although I would recommend against

"I'm putting all my money into 'things.'"

putting a major proportion of your assets into gold, there is a modest role for gold in a well-diversified portfolio. Returns from gold tend to be very little correlated with the returns from paper assets. Hence, even modest holdings (say, 5 percent of the portfolio) can be of help to an investor in reducing the variability of the total portfolio, as was clearly shown in chapter 9. And if inflation were to reemerge, gold would likely produce acceptable returns. Small gold holdings can easily be obtained now by purchasing shares in one of the specialized mutual funds concentrating on gold.

The volatile movements in gold prices remind me of the story of the wily Chinese merchant who made an excellent living trading in sardines. His business was so successful that he hired a bright young college graduate to assist him in his endeavors. One day, when the young man was entertaining his in-laws for dinner, he decided to bring home a couple of cans of sardines to have as an appetizer. On opening the first can, he found, to his great chagrin, that the can was filled with sand. He then opened the second can and found that it, too, was filled with sand. When he informed the Chinese merchant of his experience the next day, the wily trader simply smiled and said, "Oh, those cans are for trading, not for eating."

In a sense, this story is very similar to the situation that occurs in gold trading. Practically all gold trading is for the purpose of hoarding or speculating so that the bullion can be sold later at a higher price. Almost none of the gold is actually used. Although there is some small demand for such uses as dentalwork, jewelry, and a few other specialized industrial needs, the current inventory of gold is some fifty times its annual industrial requirement—not to mention the large amounts of yet-to-be-mined metal stored below ground. In this kind of market, no one can tell where prices will go. Prudence suggests—at best—a limited role for gold as a vehicle for obtaining broader diversification.

What about other collectibles? Diamonds, for example, are often described as everybody's best friend. But there are enormous risks and disadvantages for individual investors. One must remember that buying diamonds involves large commission costs. Furthermore, there are fads in the way diamonds are cut. Despite assurances to the contrary, you will seldom be able to buy at true wholesale prices. It's also extraordinarily hard for an individual to judge quality, and I can assure you that the number of telephone calls you get from folks wishing to sell diamonds will greatly exceed the calls from those who want to buy them.

Another popular current strategy is investment in collectibles. Thousands of salesmen are touting everything from Renoir to rugs, Tiffany lamps to rare stamps, Art Deco to airsick bags. And eBay has made buying and selling collectibles much more efficient. I think there's nothing wrong in buying things you can love—and God knows people do have strange tastes—but my advice is buy those things because you love them, not because you expect them to appreciate in value.

Ask yourself why everyone is so willing to part with things whose value is supposedly increasing. And don't forget that fakes and forgeries are common. A portfolio of collectibles also

often requires hefty insurance premiums and endless mainte-
nance charges—so you are making payments instead of receiving dividends or interest. To earn money collecting, you need
great originality and taste. You must buy first-class objects
when no one else wants them, not inferior schlock when a vast
uninformed public enthusiastically bids it up. In my view,
most people who think they are collecting profit are really collecting trouble.

Another popular instrument these days is the commodities
futures contract. You can buy not only gold but also contracts
for the delivery of a variety of commodities from grains to metals as well as foreign exchange. It's a fast market where professionals can benefit greatly, but individuals who don't know
what they are doing can easily get clobbered. My advice to the
nonprofessional investor: Don't go against the grain. I would
also steer clear of "hedge funds." These can be great money
makers for the hedge-fund managers who pocket large management fees and 20 percent of the profits, but the individual
investor usually fails to benefit.

Exercise 9: Remember That Commission Costs Are Not Random; Some Are Cheaper than Others

With the advent of competitive commission rates, it has
now become possible to buy your brokerage services at wholesale prices. A number of brokers today will execute your stock
orders at discounts of as much as 90 percent off the standard
commission rates charged by the leading brokerage houses.
The discount broker usually provides a plain-pipe-rack service.
If you want your hand held, if you want opinions on individual
stocks and general portfolio advice and investment suggestions, the discount broker may *not* be for you. If, however, you
know exactly what you want to buy, the discount broker can get
it for you at much lower commission rates than the standard
full-service house. Do make sure that your discount broker is
actually transacting your orders for stocks like IBM or Exxon on
the New York Stock Exchange. Some discounters do the transactions off the exchange and the net price you end up paying is
actually higher than that charged by a full-service broker.

It's not too hard to find discount brokers. Just read the financial pages of your daily or Sunday paper and you'll find their ads with such catchy headlines as "Full commissions are for the herds" and "There's nothing discount about [our service] except [our] commission rates." Purely for the execution of stock-market orders, you can use an honest discounter. The discounters all belong to the Security Investors Protection Corporation, which insures all accounts up to $100,000.

If you are truly ready to make all your decisions yourself, you can do so with your own personal computer and make security trades electronically. Electronic trading enables you to buy and sell hundreds of shares of stocks for as little as $7.95 per trade. Trading stocks online is easy and cheap. But let me warn you, few investors who try to trade in and out of stocks each day make profits. Don't let low commission rates seduce you into becoming one of the legion of unsuccessful former day traders.

While on the subject of commission costs, you should be aware of a 1990s Wall Street innovation called the "wrap account." For a single fee, your broker obtains the services of a professional money manager, who then selects for you a portfolio of stocks, bonds, and perhaps real estate. Brokerage commissions and advisory fees are "wrapped" into the overall fee. One problem is that it is difficult, or impossible, for you to assess the manager selected by your broker. More important, the costs involved in wrap accounts are extremely high. Annual fees can be as high as 3 percent per year, and there may be additional execution fees and fund expenses (if the manager uses mutual funds or REITs). With those kinds of expenses, it will be virtually impossible for you to beat the market. My advice here is: Avoid taking the wrap.

Exercise 10: Diversify Your Investment Steps

In these warm-up exercises, we have discussed a number of investment instruments. The most important part of our walk down Wall Street will take us to the corner of Broad Street—to a consideration of sensible investment strategies with respect to common stocks. A guide to this part of our walk is contained in the final three chapters, because I believe common stocks should form the cornerstone of most portfolios. Nevertheless, in our final warm-up exercise we recall the important lesson of modern portfolio theory—the advantages of diversification.

A biblical proverb states that "in the multitude of counselors there is safety." The same can be said of investments. Diversification reduces risk and makes it far more likely that you will achieve the kind of good average long-run return that meets your investment objective. Therefore, within each investment category you should hold a variety of individual issues, and although common stocks should be a major part of your portfolio, they should not be the sole investment instrument. Just remember the teary-eyed ex-Enron employees who held nothing but Enron stock in their retirement plans. When Enron went under, they lost not only their jobs but all their retirement savings as well. Whatever the investment objectives, the investor who's wise diversifies.

A Final Checkup

Now that you have completed your warm-up exercises, let's take a moment for a final checkup. The theories of valuation worked out by economists and the performance recorded by the professionals lead to a single conclusion: There is no sure and easy road to riches. High returns can be achieved only through higher risk-taking (and perhaps through acceptance of lesser degrees of liquidity).

The amount of risk you can tolerate is partly determined by your sleeping point. The next chapter discusses the risks and rewards of stock and bond investing and will help you determine the kinds of returns you should expect from different financial instruments. But the risk you can assume is also significantly influenced by your age and by the sources and dependability of your noninvestment income. Chapter 14—A Life-Cycle Guide to Investing—will give you a clearer notion of how to decide what portion of your capital should be placed in common stocks, bonds, and short-term investments. The final chapter presents specific stock-market strategies that will enable amateur investors to achieve results as good as or better than those of the most sophisticated professionals.

13

Handicapping the Financial Race: A Primer in Understanding and Projecting Returns from Stocks and Bonds

No man who is correctly informed as to the past will be disposed to take a morose or desponding view of the present.
—Thomas B. Macaulay, *History of England*

This is the chapter where you learn how to become a financial bookie. Reading it will still leave you unable to predict the future—no one can do that—but you will be able to better the odds of constructing a winning portfolio. Although the price levels of stocks and bonds, the two most important determinants of net worth, will undoubtedly fluctuate beyond your control, my general methodology will serve you well in realistically projecting long-run returns and adapting your investment program to your financial needs.

What Determines the Returns from Stocks and Bonds?

Very long run returns from common stocks are driven by two critical factors: the dividend yield at the time of purchase, and the future growth rate of earnings and dividends. In principle, for the buyer who holds his or her stocks forever, a share of common stock is worth the "present" or "discounted" value of its stream of future dividends. Recall that this "discounting" reflects the fact that a dollar received tomorrow is worth less than a dollar in hand today. A stock buyer purchases an ownership interest in a business and hopes to receive a growing stream of dividends. Even if a company pays very small dividends today and retains most (or even all) of its earnings to reinvest in the business, the investor implicitly assumes that such reinvestment will lead to a more rapidly growing stream of dividends in the future or alternatively to greater earnings that can be used by the company to buy back its stock.

The discounted value of this stream of dividends (or funds returned to shareholders through stock buybacks) can be shown to produce a very simple formula for the long-run total return for either an individual stock or the market as a whole:

Long-Run Equity Return = Initial Dividend Yield + Growth Rate

From 1926 through 2002, for example, common stocks provided an average annual rate of return of about 10½ percent. The dividend yield for the market as a whole on January 1, 1926, was a bit above 5 percent. The long-run rate of growth of earnings and dividends was also approximately 5 percent. Thus, adding the initial dividend yield to the growth rate gives a close approximation of the actual rate of return.

Over shorter periods, such as a year or even several years, a third factor is critical in determining returns. This factor is the change in valuation relationships—specifically, the change in the price-dividend or price-earnings multiple. (Increases or decreases in the price-dividend multiple tend to move in the same direction as the more popularly used price-earnings multiple.)

Price-dividend and price-earnings multiples vary widely from year to year. For example, in times of great optimism, such as early March 2000, stocks sold at price-earnings multiples well above 30. The price-dividend multiple was over 80. At times of great pessimism, such as 1982, stocks sold at only 8 times earnings. The price-earnings multiple is also influenced by interest rates. When interest rates are low, stocks, which compete with bonds for an investor's savings, tend to sell at low dividend yields and/or high price-earnings multiples. When interest rates are high, stock yields rise to be more competitive and stocks stand to sell at low price-earnings multiples. As we will see below, one of the worst recent periods for common stocks was from 1968 to 1982, when returns were only about 5½ percent per year. Stocks sold at a dividend yield of 3 percent at the start of the period and earnings and dividend growth was 6 percent per year, a bit above the long-run average. Had price-earnings multiples (and dividend yields) remained constant, stocks would have produced a 9 percent annual return, with the 6 percent dividend growth translated into 6 percent capital appreciation per year. But a large increase in dividend yields (a large fall in price-earnings multiples) reduced the average annual return by about 3½ percentage points per year. The figure on page 317 shows the price-dividend multiple for stocks from 1926 to the present.

Many analysts question whether dividends are as relevant during the 2000s as they were in the past. They argue that firms increasingly prefer distributing their growing earnings to stockholders through stock repurchases rather than dividend increases. Two reasons are offered for such behavior—one serves shareholders and the other management. The shareholder benefit was created by tax laws. The tax rate on long-term capital gains is only a fraction of the maximum income tax rate on dividends. Firms that buy back stock tend to reduce the number of shares outstanding and therefore increase earnings per share and, thus, share prices. Hence, stock buybacks tend to create capital gains that are more lightly taxed. Moreover, capital-gains taxes can be deferred until the stocks are sold, or even avoided completely if the shares are later bequeathed. Thus, managers acting in the interest of the shareholder will prefer to engage in buybacks rather than increasing dividends.

The flip side of stock repurchases is more self-serving. A large part of management compensation is derived from stock options, which become valuable only if earnings and the price of the stock rise. Stock repurchases are an easy way to bring this about. Larger appreciation benefits the managers by enhancing the value of their stock options, whereas larger dividends go into the pockets of current shareholders. From the 1940s until the 1970s, earnings and dividends grew at about the same rate. During the last decades of the twentieth century, however, earnings have been growing faster than dividends. To

The Price of $1.00 of Dividends (S&P 500)*
(The Price-Dividend Multiple)

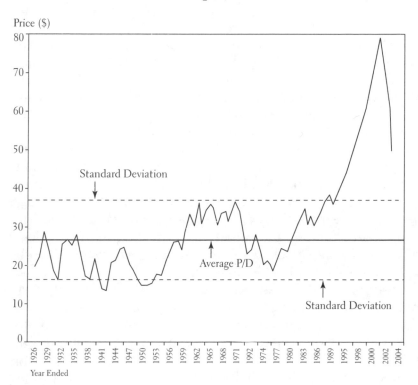

Price ($)

Standard Deviation

Average P/D

Standard Deviation

Year Ended

*The solid line is the average since 1926. The dashed lines above and below represent a range of one standard deviation above and below the average.

put it another way, the dividend payout ratio (the percentage of earnings paid out in dividends) has been declining.

For ease of reading, I have elected to do my analysis in terms of earnings growth rather than dividend growth. Nevertheless, it is worth questioning whether dividends have in fact gone out of style for all time. For one thing, the tax argument is irrelevant for the vast majority of stockholders who are either tax-exempt institutions or pension funds or individuals who own most of their stocks in retirement plans where dividends are not taxed. Moreover, many buybacks do not result in a fewer number of shares outstanding—they only match the amount of new stock issued to managers who exercise their stock options. Finally, dividends appeared far more important to investors during the early 2000s when the stock market fell than was the case during the ebullient 1990s.

Long-run returns from bonds are easier to calculate than those from stocks. Over the long run, the yield that a bond investor receives is approximated by the yield to maturity of the bond at the time it is purchased. For a zero-coupon bond (a bond that makes no periodic interest payments, but simply returns a fixed amount at maturity), the yield at which it is purchased is precisely the yield that investor will receive, assuming no default and assuming it is held to maturity. For a coupon-paying bond (a bond that does make periodic interest payments), there could be a slight variation in the yield that is earned over the term of the bond depending on whether and at what interest rates the coupon interest is reinvested and whether interest rates rise or fall, producing capital losses or gains. Nevertheless, the initial yield on the bond provides a quite serviceable estimate of the yield that will be obtained by an investor who holds the bond until maturity.

Estimating bond returns becomes murky when bonds are not held until maturity. Changes in interest rates (bond yields) then become a major factor in determining the net return received over the period during which the bond is held. When interest rates rise, bond prices fall so as to make existing bonds competitive with those that are currently being issued at the higher interest rates. When rates fall, bond prices increase. The principle to keep in mind is that bond investors who don't hold to maturity will have their return increased or decreased depending on what happens to interest rates in the interim. Bond investors suffer to the extent that interest rates rise and gain to the extent that rates fall.

Inflation is the dark horse in any handicapping of financial returns. In the bond market, an increase in the inflation rate is unambiguously bad. To see this, suppose that there was no inflation and bonds sold on a 5 percent yield basis, providing investors with a real (that is, after inflation) return of 5 percent. Now assume that the inflation rate increases from zero to 5 percent per year. If investors still require a 5 percent real rate of return, then the bond interest rate must rise to 10 percent. Only then will investors receive an after-inflation return of 5 percent. But this will mean that bond prices fall and those who previously purchased 5 percent long-term bonds will suffer a substantial capital loss. Except for the holder of the inflation-protected bonds recommended in chapter 12, inflation is the deadly enemy of the bond investor.

In principle, common stocks should be an inflation hedge and stocks are not supposed to suffer with an increase in the inflation rate. In theory at least, if the inflation rate rises by 1 percentage point, all prices should rise by 1 percentage point, including the values of factories, equipment, and inventories. Consequently, the growth rate of earnings and dividends should rise with the rate of inflation. Thus, even though bond yields will rise with inflation and so will the required return on common stocks, to make them competitive with bonds, no change in dividend yields (or the price-earnings ratio) will be required. This is so because expected growth rates should rise along with increases in the expected inflation rate. Whether this happens in practice we will examine below.

Three Eras of Financial Market Returns

Let's now study three recent periods of stock and bond market history and see if we can make sense of how investors fared in terms of the determinants of returns discussed above. The three eras coincide with the three broad swings in stock market returns over the post–World War II period. The table below indicates the three eras and the average annual returns earned by stock and bond investors:

An Era View of U.S. Stock and Bond Returns
(Average Annual Returns)

Assest Class	Era I Jan. 1946– Dec. 1968 The Age of Comfort	Ear II Jan. 1969– Dec. 1981 The Age of Angst	Era III Jan. 1982– March 2000 The Age of Exuberance
Common stocks (S&P 500)	14.0%	5.6%	18.3%
Bonds (high-quality, long-term corporates)	1.8	3.8	13.5
Average annual inflation rate	2.3	7.8	3.3

Era I, the Age of Comfort, as I call it, covers the years of growth after World War II. Stockholders made out extremely well after inflation, whereas the meager returns earned by bondholders were substantially below the average inflation rate. I call Era II the Age of Angst: widespread rebellion by the millions of teenagers produced during the baby boom, economic and political instability created by the Vietnam War, and various inflationary oil and food shocks combined to create an inhospitable climate for investors. No one was exempt: neither stocks nor bonds fared well. During our third era, the Age of Exuberance, the boomers matured, peace reigned, and a non-inflationary prosperity set in. It was a golden age for stockholders and bondholders. Never before had they earned such generous returns.

With these broad time periods set, let us now look at how the determinants of returns developed during those eras and look especially at what might have been responsible for changes in valuation relationships and in interest rates. Recall that stock returns are determined by (1) the initial dividend yield at which the stocks were purchased; (2) the growth rate of earnings; and (3) changes in valuation in terms of price-earnings (or price-dividend) ratios. And bond returns are determined by (1) the initial yield to maturity at which the bonds were purchased and (2) changes in interest rates (yields) and therefore in bond prices for bond investors who do not hold to maturity.

Era I: The Age of Comfort

Consumers celebrated the end of World War II with a spending spree. They had gone without cars, refrigerators, and countless other goods during the war, and they forked over their liquid savings with abandon, creating a mini-boom with some inflation. It was hard, however, to forget the Great Depression of the 1930s. Economists (those dismal scientists) were worried as demand began to slacken and became convinced that deep recession, or perhaps a depression, was just around the corner. President Harry Truman was responsible for a widely used definition of the difference between the two: "A recession is when you're out of work. A depression is when I'm out of work." Investors in the stock market noted the economists' gloom and were clearly worried. Dividend yields at the start of 1947 were unusually high at 5 percent and P/E multiples, which were around 12, were well below their long-term average.

It turned out that the economy did not sink into the depression many had feared. Although there were periods of mild recession, the economy grew at a quite reasonable rate through the 1950s and 1960s. President Kennedy had proposed a large tax cut in the early 1960s, which was enacted in 1964 after his death. With the stimulus from the tax cut and the increase in government spending for the Vietnam War, the economy was robust, with high employment levels. Inflation was generally not a problem until the very end of the period. Investors became progressively more confident and, by 1968, P/Es were above 18 and the yield on the S&P stock index had fallen to 3 percent. This truly created comfortable conditions for common stock investors: their initial dividends were high; both earnings and dividends grew at reasonably robust rates of 6½ to 7 percent; and valuations became richer, further augmenting capital gains. The following table shows the different components of the returns from stocks and bonds over the 1947–68 period.

The Development of Stock and Bond Returns
(January 1947–December 1968)

Stocks	Initial dividend yield	5.0
	Growth in earnings	6.6
	Change in valuation (increase in P/E ratio)	2.4
	Average annual return	14.0
Bonds	Initial yield	2.7
	Effect of increase in interest rates	−0.9
	Average annual return	1.8

Unfortunately, bond investors did not fare nearly as well. For starters, initial bond yields were low in 1947. Thus, bond returns were destined to be low even for investors who held to maturity. During World War II, the United States pegged long-term government-bond interest rates and did not allow those rates to exceed 2½ percent. The policy was implemented to permit the government to finance the war cheaply with low-interest borrowing, and it continued after the war until 1951, when rates were allowed to rise. Therefore, bond investors suffered a double whammy during the period. Not only were interest rates artificially low at the start of the period, but bond-holders suffered capital losses when interest rates were allowed to rise. As a result, bondholders received nominal rates of return below 2 percent over the period and real returns (after inflation) that were negative.

Era II: The Age of Angst

From the late 1960s through the early 1980s, accelerating inflation made an unexpected appearance and became the major influence on securities markets. In the mid-1960s, inflation was essentially unnoticeable—running at a rate of just more than 1 percent. When our involvement in Vietnam increased in the late 1960s, however, we had classic, old-fashioned "demand-pull" inflation—too much money chasing too few goods—and the rate of inflation spurted forward to something like 4 or 4½ percent.

Then the economy was beset by the oil and food shocks of 1973–74. It was a classic case of Murphy's Law at work—whatever could go wrong did. OPEC contrived to produce an artificial shortage of oil and Mother Nature produced a real shortage of foodstuffs through poor grain harvests in North America and disastrous ones in the Soviet Union and sub-Saharan Africa. When even the Peruvian anchovy crop mysteriously disappeared (anchovies are a major source of protein), it appears that O'Toole's commentary had come into play. (It was O'Toole who suggested that "Murphy was an optimist.") Again, the inflation rate ratcheted up to 6½ percent. Then in 1978 and 1979, a combination of policy mistakes—leading to considerable excess demand in certain sectors—and another 125 percent increase in the price of oil kicked the inflation rate up again, taking with it wage costs. By the early 1980s, the inflation rate went above 10 percent and there was considerable fear that the economy was out of control.

Finally, the Federal Reserve, under the leadership of its chairman at the time, Paul Volcker, took decisive action. The Fed initiated an extremely tight monetary policy designed to rein in the economy and kill the inflationary virus. Inflation did begin to subside in time, but the economy almost died as well. We suffered the sharpest economic decline since the 1930s and unemployment soared. By the end of 1981, the U.S.

economy suffered not only from double-digit inflation but from double-digit unemployment as well.

The table below shows the fallout in financial markets from the inflation and instability in the economy. Although nominal returns for both stockholders and bondholders were meager, the real returns, after factoring out the 7.8 percent inflation rate, were actually negative. On the other hand, hard assets such as gold, collectibles, and real estate provided generous double-digit returns.

The Development of Stock and Bond Returns
(January 1969–December 1981)

Stocks	Initial dividend yield	3.1
	Growth in earnings	8.0
	Change in valuation	−5.5
	Average annual return	5.6
Bonds	Initial yield	5.9
	Effect of increase in interest rates	−2.1
	Average annual return	3.8

Because the inflation was unanticipated and allowance for it was not incorporated into yields, investors in bonds suffered disastrous results. In 1968, for example, thirty-year long-term bonds offered a yield to maturity of about 6 percent. This provided protection against the going inflation rate of about 3 percent and an anticipated after-inflation real rate of return of 3 percent. Unfortunately, the actual rate of inflation over the period 1969–81 was almost 8 percent, wiping out any positive real rate of return. That's the good news part of this dreary story. The bad news was that there were capital losses. Who wanted to buy a bond yielding 6 percent in the late 1970s, when the rate of inflation was in double digits? No one! If you had to sell your bonds, you sold at a loss so the new buyer could get a yield consonant with the higher rate of inflation. Yields rose even further as the risk premium on bonds rose to take into account their increased volatility. To make matters worse, the tax system delivered the unkindest blow of all to bond investors. Even though bond investors often actually earned negative pre-tax rates of return, their bond coupons were taxed at regular income tax rates.

The failure of bonds to protect investors against an unanticipated inflationary episode is hardly surprising. The common-
stock flop was something else. Because stocks represent claims
on real assets that presumably rise in value with the price level,
stock prices—according to this line of logic—should have risen
also. It's like the story of the small boy on his first trip to an art
museum. When told that a famous abstract painting was supposed to be a horse, the boy asked wisely, "Well, if it is supposed
to be a horse, why isn't it a horse?" If common stocks were supposed to be an inflation hedge, then why weren't they?

Many different explanations involving faltering dividends
and earnings growth have been offered that simply don't hold
up under careful analysis. One common explanation was that
inflation had caused corporate profits to shrink drastically,
especially when reported figures were adjusted for inflation.
Inflation was portrayed as a kind of financial neutron bomb,
leaving the structure of corporate enterprise intact, but destroying the lifeblood of profits. Many saw the engine of capitalism
as running out of control, so that a walk down Wall Street—
random or otherwise—could prove extremely hazardous.

The facts are, however, that there was no evidence that profits had been "sliding down a pole greased by cruel and inexorable inflation," as some in the financial community believed
in the early 1980s. As the preceding table shows, profit growth
accelerated over the 1969–81 period and grew at an 8 percent
rate, comfortably ahead of inflation. Even dividends held their
own, rising at close to the same rate as inflation.

Movie buffs may recall the marvelous final scene from
Casablanca. Humphrey Bogart stands over the body of a Luft-
waffe major, a smoking gun in his hand. Claude Rains, a cap-
tain in the French colonial police, turns his glance from Bogart
to the smoking gun to the dead major and finally to his assistant, and says, "Major Strasser has been shot. Round up the
usual suspects." We, too, have rounded up the usual suspects,
but we have yet to focus on who shot the stock market.

The major reason for the poor equity returns during the
1970s was that investors' evaluations of dividends and earnings—the number of dollars they were willing to pay for a dollar
of dividends and earnings—fell sharply. Stocks failed to provide

investors with protection against inflation, not because earnings and dividends failed to grow with inflation, but rather because price-earnings multiples quite literally collapsed over the period.

The graph on page 317 showed the collapse in price-dividend multiples. The price-earnings multiple for the S&P index was cut by almost two-thirds during the 1969–81 period. It was this decline in multiples that produced such poor returns for investors in the 1970s and that prevented stock prices from reflecting the real underlying progress most companies made in earnings and dividend growth. Some financial economists concluded that the market was simply irrational during the 1970s and early 1980s—that multiples had fallen too far.

It is, of course, quite possible that stock investors may have become irrationally pessimistic in the early 1980s, just as they were possibly irrationally optimistic in the mid-1960s. But although I do not believe the market is always perfectly rational, if forced to choose between the stock market and the economics profession, I'd put my money on the stock market every time. I suspect that stock investors weren't irrational when they caused a sharp drop in price-dividend and earnings multiples—they were just scared. In the mid-1960s, inflation was so modest as to be almost unnoticeable, and investors were convinced that economists had found the cure for serious recessions—even mild downturns could be "fine-tuned" away. No one would have imagined in the 1960s that the economy could experience either double-digit unemployment or double-digit inflation, let alone that both could appear simultaneously. Clearly, we learned that economic conditions were far less stable than had previously been imagined.

We also realized more fully that inflation is not a benign phenomenon, as it used to be described in some textbooks. When prices rise by 10 percent, all prices do not rise by the same amount. Rather, relative prices (and the relationship between input and output prices) are far more variable at higher levels of inflation. Furthermore, the higher the rate of inflation, the more variable and unpredictable inflation becomes. Thus, more volatile levels of real output and higher inflation rates, as well as the accompanying greater volatility of interest rates, increased uncertainty throughout the economy. Equity securities (dare I say equity insecurities) were, therefore, considered riskier and deserving of higher risk compensation.*

The market provides higher-risk premiums through a drop in prices relative to earnings and dividends; this produces larger returns in the future consistent with the new riskier environment. Paradoxically, however, the same adjustments that produced very poor returns in the late 1960s and throughout the 1970s created some very attractive price levels in the early 1980s, as I argued in earlier editions of this book. The experience makes clear, however, that if one wants to explain the generation of returns over a decade, a change in valuation relationships plays a critical role. The growth rate of earnings did compensate for inflation during 1969–81, but the drop in price-dividend and price-earnings multiples, which I believe reflected increased perceived risk, is what killed the stock market.

Era III: The Age of Exuberance

Let us now turn to the third era—the golden age of financial asset returns from 1982 through early 2000. At the start of the period, both bonds and stocks had fully adjusted—perhaps even overadjusted—to the changed economic environment. Stocks and bonds were priced not only to provide adequate protection against the likely rate of inflation, but also to give unusually generous real rates of return.

Indeed, in late 1981, the bond market was in disgrace. *The Bawl Street Journal*, in its 1981 annual comedy issue, wrote: "A bond is a fixed-rate instrument designed to fall in price." At the time, the yield on high-quality corporate bonds was around 13 percent. The underlying rate of inflation (as measured by the growth of unit labor costs) was then about 8 percent. Thus, corporate bonds provided a prospective real rate of return of about 5 percent, a rate unusually generous by past historical standards. (The long-term real rate of return on corporate bonds

---

*Economists often put the proposition in terms of the risk premium—that is, the extra return you can expect from an investment over and above the return from perfectly predictable short-term investments. According to this view, the risk premiums in the 1960s were very small, perhaps 1 or 2 percentage points. During the early 1980s, risk premiums demanded by investors to hold both stocks and bonds expanded to a range of probably 4 to 6 percentage points, as I shall show below.

was only 2 percent.) To be sure, bond prices had become volatile and, thus, it was reasonable to suppose that bonds ought to offer a somewhat larger risk premium than before. But panic-depressive institutional investors probably overdiscounted the risks of bond investments. Like generals fighting the last war, investors had been loath to touch bonds because experience over the past fifteen years had been so disastrous. Thus, the initial conditions were such that bond investors could expect very generous returns in the years ahead.

What about stocks? As I mentioned above, it is possible to calculate the anticipated long-run rate of return on stocks by adding the dividend yield of the average to the anticipated growth of earnings per share. The calculations I performed during 1980 suggested a total expected rate of return from common stocks of more than 13 percent—a rate well above the core rate of inflation and very generous by historical standards.

Common stocks were also selling at unusually low multiples of cyclically depressed earnings, at below-average price-dividend multiples, and at prices that were only a fraction of the replacement value of the assets they represented. Small wonder we saw so many corporate takeovers during the 1980s. Whenever assets can be bought in the stock market at less than the cost of acquiring them directly, there will be a tendency for firms to purchase the equities of other firms, as well as to buy back their own stocks. Thus, I argued that in the early 1980s, we were presented with a market situation where paper assets had adjusted and perhaps overadjusted to inflation and the greater uncertainty associated with it. The following table shows how returns developed during the 1982–2000 period.

The Development of Stock and Bond Returns
(January 1982–March 2000)

Stocks	Initial dividend yield	5.8
	Growth in earnings	6.8
	Change in valuation (increase in P/E ratio)	5.7
	Average annual return	18.3
Bonds	Initial yield	13.0
	Effect of decrease in interest rates	0.6
	Average annual return	13.6

This was truly an age of investor exuberance, with both stocks and bonds producing unusually generous rates of return. Although the nominal growth in earnings and dividends was not any greater during this period than in the unsatisfactory period of the 1970s, two factors contributed to produce spectacular stock-market returns. First, initial dividend yields of nearly 6 percent were unusually generous. Second, market sentiment went from despair to euphoria. Price-earnings multiples in the market more than tripled from 8 to almost 30, dividend yields fell to just over 1 percent. It was the change in valuation that lifted stock returns from unusually good to absolutely extraordinary.

Similarly, the initial yield of 13 percent in the bond market guaranteed that long-term holders would achieve double-digit returns. As I have said, what yield long-term holders see is what they get. In addition, interest rates fell, augmenting the returns further. Moreover, because the inflation rate moderated to the 3 percent level, real returns (returns after inflation) were well above their long-term average. The 1982–early 2000 period was a once-in-a-lifetime period to be invested in financial assets. Meanwhile, hard assets such as gold and oil produced negative rates of return.

The Age of the Millennium

So what's ahead? How can you judge returns from financial assets for the years ahead? Although I remain convinced that no one can predict short-term movements in securities markets, I do believe it is possible to estimate the likely range of long-run rates of return investors can expect from financial assets. And it seems very clear that it would be unrealistic to anticipate that the generous double-digit returns earned by stock and bond investors during the 1980s and 1990s can be expected during the early decades of the twenty-first century.

We know that the Age of Exuberance was followed by a crushing bear market, which took the major averages such as the Standard & Poor's 500 Index down 40 percent by mid-2002. The NASDAQ Index, highly weighted with tech stocks, did even worse, falling 75 percent, from over 5,000 to below the 1,300 level in mid-2002. Moreover, the terrorist attacks of September 11, 2001, and the well-publicized accounting scandals including Enron, Global Crossing, Tyco, and WorldCom created a crisis of confidence among investors. The stock market of the new millennium seemed much riskier than it did in early 2000 and investors demanded larger risk premiums to induce them to hold common stocks. Valuation relationships changed accordingly, and by mid-2002, the dividend yield on the S&P 500 had risen from just over 1 percent to close to 2 percent. Price-earnings multiples (based on projected earnings) fell from about 30 to 20. What then are the reasonable long-run expectations for returns? The same methods as I have used in the past can be used today. I will illustrate the long-run return projections as of late 2002. The reader can perform similar calculations by using data appropriate for the time the projection is made.

Looking first at the bond market, as of mid-2002 we can get a very good idea of the returns that will be gained by long-term holders. Holders of good-quality corporate bonds will earn approximately 6½ to 7 percent if the bonds are held to maturity. Holders of long-term zero-coupon Treasury bonds until maturity will earn about 5¼ percent. Those who buy and hold long-term TIPS (the Treasury's inflation-protection securities) will earn a real (after-inflation) return of 3¼ percent. Such a real return is almost double the actual real return bondholders have earned from 1926 through 2002. So although the double-digit returns of the 1982–2002 period will not be repeated, bonds should be a serviceable investment for the start of the new century.

What kinds of returns can we project for common stocks as of mid-2002? We can make reasonable estimates of at least the first two determinants of equity returns. We know that the 2002 dividend yield for the S&P 500 Index was about 2 percent. It is reasonable to assume that earnings can grow at about 6.5 percent over the long term, a rate consistent with historical rates during periods of restrained inflation and similar to estimates made by Wall Street securities firms late in 2002. Adding the initial yield and growth rate together, we get a projected total return for the S&P 500 of 8½ percent per year—slightly higher than bond yields but somewhat below the long-term average since 1926, which had been about 10½ percent.

Of course, the major determinants of stock returns over short periods of time will be changes in the ways equities are valued in the market, that is, changes in market price-earnings multiples. Here I must refer back to my conclusions in chapter 11, where I suggested that none of the statistical methods of predicting valuation changes is dependable. I suspect that even God Almighty does not know what the "proper" P/E multiple is for the market, nor can future changes in the multiple be forecast. Changes in valuations are fundamentally unpredictable. Thus, all we can do is estimate what returns the market is likely to give us if valuation relationships do not change. And that figure is probably quite close to the 8½ percent estimate I arrived at above.

Investors should ask themselves, however, whether the valuation levels in the market during the summer of 2002 will in fact hold up. Price-earnings multiples during the summer of 2002 were still at historically high levels. Also, dividend yields at 2 percent were lower than they have been over the twentieth century, as can be seen from the following chart:

S&P 500 Index: Dividend Yields

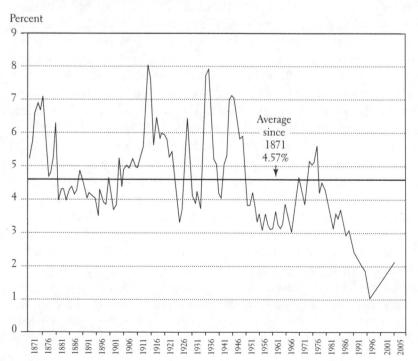

To be sure, interest rates and inflation were both relatively low during 2002. When interest rates (and inflation) are low, somewhat higher price-earnings multiples and lower dividend yields are justified. Still, we can't simply assume that rates will always be so low and that inflation will always be benign.

It is well to remember that our smartest economists were claiming in the mid-1960s that inflation (then at 1 percent) was dead and that even minor fluctuations in economic activity could easily be offset. And remember also that in the early 1990s, the financial press was replete with stories touting the wonders of the Japanese economic system and management techniques and insisting that the extraordinary multiples in the Japanese stock market were justified. And the horrific events of September 11, 2001, remind us that we live in a perilously unstable world, suggesting that investors should quite rationally expect to receive meaningful risk premiums if they are to accept the risks of equity ownership. The unexpected frequently happens.

The point is, don't invest with a rearview mirror. Don't simply project the returns from the Age of Exuberance into the new millennium. This age, in Alan Greenspan's famous description, undoubtedly became somewhat "irrational" at its close. The bear market of the early 2000s will end, as bear markets always do. But the returns from both stocks and bonds will undoubtedly be lower than the returns realized in the 1980s and 1990s. The most likely estimates we can make for the stock market when dividend yields are in the vicinity of 2 percent is that the total rate of return over the longer run will be in high single digits.

Does my expectation for high single-digit long-run rates of return imply a prediction of what the market will do during any specific period of time? Not at all! It is well to remember that we have lived through fairly long periods (such as the late 1960s through the early 1980s) when common stocks provided only 5½ percent annual rates of return that were actually lower than the rate of inflation. If your expected investment period is only for a decade or less, no one can predict the returns you will receive with any degree of accuracy.

As a random walker on Wall Street, I am skeptical that anyone can predict the course of short-term stock-price movements, and perhaps we are better off for it. I am reminded of one of my favorite episodes from the marvelous old radio serial *I Love a Mystery*. This mystery was about a greedy stock-market investor who wished that just once he would be allowed to see the paper, with its stock-price changes, twenty-four hours in advance. By some occult twist his wish was granted, and early in the evening he received the late edition of the next day's paper. He worked feverishly through the night planning early-morning purchases and late-afternoon sales that would guarantee him a killing in the market. Then, before his elation had diminished, he read through the remainder of the paper—and came upon his own obituary. His servant found him dead the next morning.

Because I, fortunately, do not have access to future newspapers, I cannot tell how stock and bond prices will behave in any particular period ahead. Nevertheless, I am convinced that the moderate long-run estimates of bond and stock returns presented here are the most reasonable ones that can be made for investment planning decades into the twenty-first century.

14
A Life-Cycle Guide to Investing

There are two times in a man's life when he should not speculate:
when he can't afford it, and when he can.
                                          —Mark Twain, *Following the Equator*

Investment strategy must be keyed to a life
cycle. It is simple common sense to say that a thirty-four-year-
old and a sixty-four-year-old saving for retirement may prudently use different financial instruments to accomplish their
goals. The thirty-four-year-old—just beginning to enter the
peak years of salaried earnings—can use wages to cover any
losses from increased risk. The sixty-four-year-old, on the other
hand, does not have the long-term luxury of relying on salary
income and cannot afford to lose money that will be needed in
the near future.

In essence, these strategic considerations have to do with a
person's capacity for risk. Heretofore, most of the discussion
about risk in this book has dealt with one's attitude toward risk.
Although the thirty-four-year-old and the sixty-four-year-old
may both invest in a certificate of deposit, the younger will do
so because of an attitudinal aversion to risk and the older
because of a reduced capacity to accept risk. In the first case,
one has more choice in how much risk to assume; in the second, one does not.

The most important investment decision you will probably
ever make concerns the balancing of asset categories (stocks,

bonds, real estate, money-market securities, etc.) at different stages of your life. According to Roger Ibbotson, who has spent a lifetime measuring returns from alternative portfolios, more than 90 percent of an investor's total return is determined by the asset categories that are selected and their overall proportional representation. Less than 10 percent of investment success is determined by the specific stocks or mutual funds that an individual chooses. In this chapter, I will show you that whatever your aversion to risk—whatever your position on the eat-well, sleep-well scale—your age, income from employment, and specific responsibilities in life go a long way toward helping you determine the mix of assets in your portfolio.

Four Asset-Allocation Principles

Before we can determine a rational basis for making asset-allocation decisions, certain principles must be kept firmly in mind. We've covered some of them implicitly in earlier chapters, but treating them explicitly here should prove very helpful. The key principles are:

1. History shows that risk and return are related.

2. The risk of investing in common stocks and bonds depends on the length of time the investments are held. The longer an investor's holding period, the lower the risk.

3. Dollar-cost averaging can be a useful, though controversial, technique to reduce the risk of stock and bond investment.

4. You must distinguish between your attitude toward and your capacity for risk.

The risks you can afford to take depend on your total financial situation, including the types and sources of your income exclusive of investment income.

1. Risk and Reward Are Related

Although you may be tired of hearing that investment rewards can be increased only by the assumption of greater risk, no lesson is more important in investment management.

This fundamental law of finance is supported by centuries of historical data. The table below, summarizing Ibbotson data presented earlier, illustrates the point.

Total Annual Returns for Basic Asset Classes, 1926–2001

	Average Annual Return	Risk Index (Year-to-Year Volatility of Returns)
Small company common stocks	12.1%	35.3%
Large company common stocks	10.4	20.8
Long-term corporate bonds	5.4	8.6
U.S. Treasury bills	3.7	3.4

Common stocks have clearly provided very generous long-run rates of return. It has been estimated that if George Washington had put just one dollar aside from his first presidential salary and invested it at the rate of return earned by common stocks, his heirs would have been millionaires more than seven times over by 2002. Roger Ibbotson estimates that stocks have provided a compounded rate of return of more than 8 percent per year since 1790. (As the table shows, returns have been even more generous since 1926, when common stocks in general earned about 10½ percent.) But this return came only at substantial risk to investors. Total returns were negative in about three years out of ten. So as you reach for higher returns, never forget that "There ain't no such thing as a free lunch." Higher risk is the price one pays for more generous returns.

2. Your Actual Risk in Stock and Bond Investing Depends on the Length of Time You Hold Your Investment

Your "staying power," the length of time you hold on to your investment, plays a critical role in the actual risk you assume from any investment decision. Thus, your stage in the life cycle is a critical element in determining the allocation of your assets. Let's see why the length of your holding period is so important in determining your capacity for risk.

We saw in the preceding table that long-term bonds have provided an average 5.8 percent annual rate of return over a seventy-two-year period. The risk index, however, showed that in any single year this rate could stray far from the yearly average. Indeed, in many individual years, it was actually negative.

What if I told you that you could invest in a 5½ percent, twenty-year bond and that if you promise to hold it for exactly twenty years you will earn exactly 5½ percent. Impossible, you say? Not at all. If you bought a twenty-year U.S. government bond in early 2002 and if you hold it until maturity, you will earn exactly 5½ percent—no more, no less—all guaranteed by the U.S. Treasury. Of course, the rub is that if you find you have to sell it next year, your rate of return could be 20 percent, 0 percent, or even a substantial loss if interest rates rise sharply with existing bond prices falling to adjust to the new higher interest rates. I think you can see why your age and the likelihood that you can stay with your investment program not only affect the risks you can assume but even determine the amount of risk involved in any specific investment program.

What about investing in common stocks? Could it be that the risk of investing in stocks also decreases with the length of time they are held? The answer is yes. A substantial amount (but not all) of the risk of common-stock investment can be eliminated by adopting a program of long-term ownership and sticking to it through thick and thin (the buy-and-hold strategy discussed in earlier chapters).

The picture opposite is worth a thousand words, so I can be brief in my explanation. Note that if you held a diversified stock portfolio (such as the Standard & Poor's 500-Stock Index) during the period from 1926 through the early 2000s, you would earn, on average, a quite generous return of over 10½ percent. But the range of outcomes is certainly far too wide for an investor who has trouble sleeping at night. In one year, the rate of return from a typical stock portfolio was more than 52 percent, whereas in another year it was negative by more than 26 percent. Clearly, there is no dependability of earning an adequate rate of return in any single year. If you have money to invest for only a single year and you want to be certain that you will earn a positive rate of return, a one-year U.S. Treasury security or a one-year government-guaranteed certificate of deposit is the investment for you.

But note how the picture changes if you hold on to your common-stock investments for twenty-five years. Although there is some variability in the return achieved depending on the exact twenty-five-year period in question, that variability is

Range of Annual Returns on Common Stocks for Various Time Periods, 1950–2002

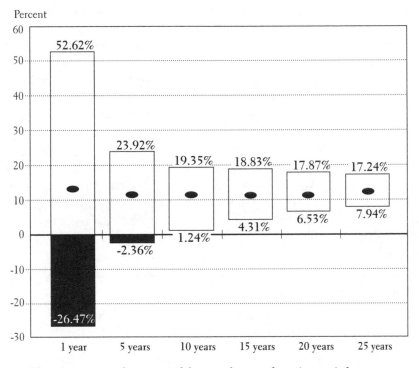

The ● represents the average of the annual returns for various periods.

not large. On average, investments over all twenty-five-year periods covered by this figure have produced a rate of return of close to 10½ percent. This long-run expected rate of return was reduced by only about 3 percentage points, if you happened to invest during the worst twenty-five-year period since 1950. It is this fundamental truth that makes a life-cycle view of investing so important. *The longer the time period over which you can hold on to your investments, the greater should be the share of common stocks in your portfolio.* In general, you are reasonably sure of earning the generous rates of return available from common stocks only if you can hold them for relatively long periods of time, such as twenty years or more. Moreover, these returns are gained by the steady strategy of *buying and holding* a diversified portfolio. Switching your investments around in a futile attempt to time the market will only involve extra commissions for your broker, extra taxes for the government, and poorer net performance.*

Moreover, the longer an individual's investment horizon, the more likely it is that stocks will outperform bonds. Over any single-year period, there is a one-out-of-three chance that bonds or money-market funds will outperform stocks. But if one looks instead at different twenty- or twenty-five-year holding periods, stocks are the performance winners every time. These data further support the advice that younger people should have a larger proportion of their assets in stocks than older people.

Finally, perhaps the most important reason for investors to become more conservative with age is that they have fewer years of labor income ahead of them. Thus, they cannot count on salary income to sustain them should the stock market have a period of negative returns. Reverses in the stock market could then directly affect an individual's standard of living and the steadier—even if smaller—returns from bonds represent the more prudent investment stance. Hence, stocks should comprise a smaller proportion of their assets.

3. Dollar-Cost Averaging Can Reduce the Risks of Investing in Stocks and Bonds

If, like most people, you will be building up your investment portfolio slowly over time with the accretion of yearly savings, you will be taking advantage of dollar-cost averaging. This technique is controversial, but it does help you avoid the risk of putting all your money in the stock or bond market at the wrong time.

Don't be alarmed by the fancy-sounding name. Dollar-cost averaging simply means investing the same fixed amount of money in, for example, the shares of some mutual fund at regular intervals—say, every month or quarter—over a long period of time. Periodic investments of equal dollar amounts in common stocks can reduce (but not avoid) the risks of equity investment by ensuring that the entire portfolio of stocks will not be purchased at temporarily inflated prices. The investor

---

*Technically, the finding that risk is reduced by longer holding periods depends on the mean-reversion phenomenon described in chapter 11. The interested reader is referred to Paul Samuelson's article "The Judgment of Economic Science on Rational Portfolio Management" in the *Journal of Portfolio Management* (Fall 1989).

who makes equal dollar investments will buy fewer shares when prices are high and more shares when prices are low. As illustrated in the following table, the average cost per share is actually lower than the average of the share prices during the period when the investments are made.

In this example, I assume you put $150 per period into a mutual fund whose share price fluctuates between $25 and $75. By the process of dollar-cost averaging, you have purchased eleven shares, now worth $50 apiece, for a total market value of $550. You have invested only $450 over the period. In other words, your average share cost ($450/11 = $40.91) is lower than the average ($50) of the market price of the fund's shares during the periods in which they are accumulated. So you've actually made money, despite the fact that the average price at which you bought is the same as the current price. It works because you bought more shares when they were cheap and fewer when they were dear.

Don't think that dollar-cost averaging will solve all of your investment problems. No plan can protect you against a loss in market value during declining stock markets. And a critical feature of the plan is that you have both the cash and the courage to continue to invest during bear markets as regularly as you do in better periods. No matter how pessimistic you are (and everybody else is), and no matter how bad the financial and world news is, you must not interrupt the automatic pilot nature of the plan or you will lose the important benefit of ensuring that you buy at least some of your shares after a sharp market decline.

Period	Investment	Price of Fund Shares	Shares Purchased
1	$150	$75	2
2	150	25	6
3	150	50	3
Total cost	$450		
Average price		$50	
Total shares owned			11
Average cost: approximately $41			

One potential drawback to dollar-cost averaging is that brokerage commissions are relatively high on small purchases, even when you use a discount broker. For that reason, it is usually advisable to buy larger blocks of securities over longer time intervals. For example, it is cheaper to buy $150 worth of stock each quarter, or $300 semi-annually, than to invest $50 each month. Of course, if you pick a no-load mutual fund (such as I used in my example) for your dollar-cost averaging, this problem disappears. You can invest as little as $50 per month in most no-load funds, with no brokerage charges at all. Another way to get some of the advantages of dollar-cost averaging is to join the dividend-reinvestment programs of those companies that have them. You can buy your shares at zero or only nominal brokerage costs, and some companies even price their shares at a discount for stockholders who reinvest their dividends.

The drawback to the technique, stressed by the economic profession, is that dollar-cost averaging is unlikely to provide the highest investment returns for an investor who has just received a lump sum of money, say, from an inheritance. It is true that putting it all in the stock market at once runs the risk that the funds are invested just before a substantial market correction, and the investor will suffer substantial regret. Not only does the investor lose money, but she feels like an idiot. Such an experience could turn an individual away from the stock market for life, as behavioralists stress. Had the investor planned to put some portion of the money in at periodic intervals, she would not feel so awful if the first installment proved unprofitable. But because the stock market has enjoyed a long-run uptrend, it is likely that putting the money to work in, say, twenty-four equal monthly installments will lead to investments being made at higher average prices than would be the case if the lump sum was invested in stocks all at once. Of course, for most people who will be accumulating an investment program through a retirement plan at work or through periodic savings in an IRA, dollar-cost averaging will happen automatically. For most people, the real issue is whether they will be willing to continue the program of common-stock investing during periods of market decline, when pessimism appears to be ubiquitous. There would certainly be no benefit to the program if investors failed to stick with it during a market decline.

To further illustrate the benefits of dollar-cost averaging, let's move from a hypothetical to a real example. The following table shows the results (ignoring taxes) of a $500 initial investment made on January 1, 1978, and thereafter $100 per month, in the shares of the Vanguard 500 Index mutual fund.

Illustration of Dollar-Cost Averaging with Vanguard's 500 Index Fund

Year Ended December 31	Total Cost of Cumulative Investments	Total Value of Shares Acquired
1978	$ 1,600	$ 1,657
1979	2,800	3,241
1980	4,000	5,680
1981	5,200	6,564
1982	6,400	9,386
1983	7,600	12,639
1984	8,800	14,705
1985	10,000	20,665
1986	11,200	25,634
1987	12,400	27,901
1988	13,600	33,691
1989	14,800	45,584
1990	16,000	45,283
1991	17,200	60,301
1992	18,400	66,049
1993	19,600	73,833
1994	20,800	75,914
1995	22,000	105,718
1996	23,200	131,238
1997	24,400	176,147
1998	25,600	227,928
1999	26,800	277,285
2000	28,000	253,298
2001	29,200	224,018

Source: Vanguard Group of Investment Companies.

$500 initial investment on January 1, 1978, and $100 monthly investment thereafter. All dividends and capital gains distributions were reinvested.

Of course, no one can be sure that the next quarter century will provide the same returns as in the past. But the table does illustrate the tremendous potential gains possible from consistently following a dollar-cost averaging program. But remember, because there is a long-term uptrend in common-stock prices, this technique is not necessarily appropriate if you need to invest a lump sum such as a bequest.

If possible, keep a small reserve (in a money fund) to take advantage of market declines and buy a few extra shares if the market is down sharply. I'm not suggesting for a minute that you try to forecast the market. However, it's usually a good time to buy after the market has fallen out of bed and no one can think of any reason why it should rise. Just as hope and greed can sometimes feed on themselves to produce speculative bubbles, so do pessimism and despair react to produce market panics. The greatest market panics are just as unfounded as the most pathological speculative explosions. No matter how bleak the outlook has been in the past, things usually got better. For the stock market as a whole, Newton's law has always worked in reverse: What goes down must come back up. But this does not necessarily hold for individual stocks, just for the market in general.

4. Distinguishing between Your Attitude toward and Your Capacity for Risk

As I mentioned at the beginning of this chapter, the kinds of investments that are appropriate for you depend significantly on your sources of income other than those derived from your investment portfolio. Your earning ability outside your investments, and thus your capacity for risk, is usually related to your age. Three illustrations will help you understand this concept.

Mildred G. is a recently widowed sixty-four-year-old. She has been forced to give up her job as a registered nurse because of her increasingly severe arthritis. Her modest house in Homewood, Illinois, is still mortgaged. Although this fixed-rate home mortgage was taken out some time ago at a relatively low rate, it does involve a substantial monthly payment. Apart from monthly Social Security payments, all Mildred has to live on are the earnings on a $250,000 group insurance policy of which she is the beneficiary and a $50,000 portfolio of small-growth stocks that had been accumulated over a long number of years by her late husband.

It is clear that Mildred's capacity to bear risk is severely constrained by her financial situation. She has neither the life expectancy nor the physical ability to earn income outside her portfolio. Moreover, she has substantial fixed expenditures on her mortgage. She would have no ability to recoup a loss on her portfolio. A portfolio of safe investments that can generate substantial income is what is appropriate for Mildred. Bonds and high-dividend-paying stocks as from an index fund of real estate investment trusts are the kinds of investments that are suitable. Risky (often non-dividend-paying) stocks of small-growth companies—no matter how attractive their prices may be—do not belong in Mildred's portfolio.

Tiffany B. is an ambitious, single twenty-six-year-old who was recently graduated from the Graduate School of Business at Stanford and has just entered a training program that will lead to a position as a loan officer at San Francisco's Bank of America. She has just inherited a $50,000 legacy from her grandmother's estate. Her goal is to build a sizable portfolio that in later years could finance the purchase of a home and be available as a retirement nest egg.

For Tiffany, one can safely recommend an "aggressive young businesswoman's" portfolio. She has both the life expectancy and the earning power to maintain her standard of living in the face of any financial loss. Although her personality will determine the precise amount of risk exposure she is willing to undertake, it is clear that Tiffany's portfolio belongs toward the far end of the risk-reward spectrum. Mildred's portfolio of small-growth stocks would be far more appropriate for Tiffany than for a sixty-four-year-old widow who is unable to work.

Carl P., a forty-three-year-old foreman at a General Motors production plant in Pontiac, Michigan, makes over $70,000 per year. His wife, Joan, has a $12,500 annual income from selling Avon products. The Ps have four children ranging in age from six to fifteen. Carl and Joan would like to see all the children attend college. They realize that private colleges are probably beyond their means but do hope that an education within the excellent Michigan state university system will be feasible. Fortunately, Carl has for some time been saving money regularly through the GM payroll savings plan and has chosen the option of purchasing GM stock under the plan. He has accumulated GM stock worth $219,000. He has no other assets but does have substantial equity in a modest house with only a small mortgage remaining to be paid off.

Carl and Joan have the resources to meet their financial needs. They have a most inappropriate portfolio, however, especially in view of their major source of income. First, the portfolio is completely undiversified. A negative development that caused a sharp loss in GM's common stock would directly affect the value of the portfolio. There would be no offsetting effects from other common stocks or other types of securities. Moreover, a serious negative development at GM could affect Carl's livelihood as well. It might not be true that "as General Motors goes so goes the nation," as a self-aggrandizing former chief executive officer of GM once suggested. But it certainly is true that as GM goes so go the fortunes of Carl and Joan. A serious depression in the auto industry could subject Carl to a double whammy—it could cost Carl his job as well as his investment portfolio. Carl and Joan's investment portfolio should be diversified, and it should not take on the same risks that attach to Carl's major source of income. Remember the sad lesson learned by many Enron employees who lost not only their jobs but all their savings in Enron stock when the company went under.

Three Guidelines to Tailoring a Life-Cycle Investment Plan

Now that I have set the stage, this section and the next present a life-cycle guide to investing. We will look here at some general rules that will be serviceable for most individuals at different stages of their lives, and in the next section I will summarize them in an investment guide. Of course, no guide will fit every individual case just as no general game plan will prove appropriate for the same sports team during every game of the season. Any game plan will require some alteration to fit the individual circumstances. This section reviews three broad guidelines that will help you tailor an investment plan to your particular circumstances.

1. Specific Needs Require Dedicated Specific Assets

Always keep in mind: A specific need must be funded with specific assets dedicated to that need. Suppose, for example, we are planning the investment strategy for a young couple in their twenties attempting to build a retirement nest egg. The advice in the life-cycle investment guide that follows is certainly appropriate to meet those long-term objectives.

But suppose also that the couple expects to need a $30,000 down payment to purchase a house in one year's time. That $30,000 to meet a specific need should be invested in a safe security, maturing when the money is required, such as a one-year certificate of deposit. Similarly, if college tuitions will be needed in three, four, five, and six years, funds might be invested in zero-coupon securities of the appropriate maturity or in intermediate-term bond mutual funds.

2. Recognize Your Tolerance for Risk

By far the biggest individual adjustment to the general guidelines suggested concerns your own attitude toward risk. It is for this reason that successful financial planning is more of an art than a science. General guidelines can be extremely helpful in determining what proportion of a person's funds should be deployed among different asset categories. But the key to whether any recommended asset allocation works for you is whether you are able to sleep at night. Risk tolerance is an essential aspect of any financial plan and only you can evaluate your attitude toward risk. You can take some comfort in the fact that the risk involved in investing in common stocks and long-term bonds is reduced the longer the time period over which you accumulate and hold your investments. But you must have the temperament to accept considerable short-term fluctuations in your portfolio's value. How did you feel when the market dropped almost 600 points when it reopened after September 11, 2001? If you panicked and became physically ill because a large proportion of your assets was invested in common stocks, then clearly you should pare down the stock portion of your investment program. Thus, subjective considerations also play a major role in the asset allocations you can accept and you may legitimately stray from those recommended here depending on your aversion to risk.

A simple questionnaire is unlikely to provide you with a completely reliable index of your tolerance for risk. Nevertheless, the following quiz is designed to help you discover your investment risk tolerance level. It was designed by the personal finance expert William E. Donoghue and the editors of *Donoghue's Money Letter* to help you determine how much risk you are likely to feel comfortable accepting.

How much risk is right? A quick quiz

Smart—and happy—investors know their risk comfort zones and make money in ways they feel at ease with. Here's a quiz to help you determine how much risk you can handle.

1. Your investment loses 15 percent of its value in a market correction a month after you buy it. Assuming that none of the fundamentals have changed, do you:

   ☐ (a) Sit tight and wait for it to journey back up.

   ☐ (b) Sell it and rid yourself of further sleepless nights if it continues to decline.

   ☐ (c) Buy more—if it looked good at the original price it looks even better now.

2. A month after you purchase it, the value of your investment suddenly skyrockets by 40 percent. Assuming you can't find any further information, what do you do?

   ☐ (a) Sell it.

   ☐ (b) Hold it on the expectation of further gain.

   ☐ (c) Buy more—it will probably go higher.

3. Which would you have rather done:

   ☐ (a) Invested in an aggressive growth fund which appreciated very little in six months.

   ☐ (b) Invested in a money-market fund only to see the aggressive growth fund you were thinking about double in value in six months.

4. Would you feel better if:

   ☐ (a) You doubled your money in an equity investment.

   ☐ (b) Your money-market fund investment saved you from losing half your money in a market slide.

5. Which situation would make you feel happiest?

   ☐ (a) You win $100,000 in a publisher's contest.

   ☐ (b) You inherit $100,000 from a rich relative.

   ☐ (c) You earn $100,000 by risking $2,000 in the options market.

   ☐ (d) Any of the above—you're happy with the $100,000, no matter how it ended up in your wallet.

6. The apartment building where you live is being converted to condominiums. You can either buy your unit for $80,000 or sell the option for $20,000. The market value of the condo is $120,000. You know that if you buy the condo, it might take six months to sell, the monthly carrying cost is $1,200, and you'd have to borrow the down payment for a mortgage. You don't want to live in the building—what do you do?

   ☐ (a) Take the $20,000.

   ☐ (b) Buy the unit and then sell it on the open market.

7. You inherit your uncle's $100,000 house, free of any mortgage. Although the house is in a fashionable neighborhood and can be expected to appreciate at a rate faster than inflation, it has deteriorated badly. It would net $1,000 monthly if rented as is; it would net $1,500 per month if renovated. The renovations could be financed by a mortgage on the property. You would:

   ☐ (a) Sell the house.

   ☐ (b) Rent it as is.

   ☐ (c) Make the necessary renovations, and then rent it.

8. You work for a small, but thriving, privately held electronics company. The company is raising money by selling stock to its employees. Management plans to take the company public, but not for four or more years. If you buy the stock, you will not be allowed to sell until shares are traded publicly. In

the meantime, the stock will pay no dividends. But when the company goes public, the shares could trade for 10 to 20 times what you paid for them. How much of an investment would you make?

☐ (a) None at all.

☐ (b) One month's salary.

☐ (c) Three months' salary.

☐ (d) Six months' salary.

9. Your longtime friend and neighbor, an experienced petroleum geologist, is assembling a group of investors (of which he is one) to fund an exploratory oil well which could pay back 50 to 100 times its investment if successful. If the well is dry, the entire investment is worthless. Your friend estimates the chance of success is only 20 percent. What would you invest?

☐ (a) Nothing at all.

☐ (b) One month's salary.

☐ (c) Three months' salary.

☐ (d) Six months' salary.

10. You learn that several commercial building developers are seriously looking at undeveloped land in a certain location. You are offered an option to buy a choice parcel of that land. The cost is about two months' salary and you calculate the gain to be ten months' salary. Do you:

☐ (a) Purchase the option.

☐ (b) Let it slide; it's not for you.

11. You are on a TV game show and can choose one of the following. Which would you take?

☐ (a) $1,000 in cash.

☐ (b) A 50 percent chance at winning $4,000.

☐ (c) A 20 percent chance at winning $10,000.

☐ (d) A 5 percent chance at winning $100,000.

12. It's 1992, and inflation is returning. Hard assets such as precious metals, collectibles, and real estate are expected to keep pace with inflation. Your assets are now all in long-term bonds. What would you do?

☐ (a) Hold the bonds.

☐ (b) Sell the bonds, and put half the proceeds into money funds and the other half into hard assets.

☐ (c) Sell the bonds and put the total proceeds into hard assets.

☐ (d) Sell the bonds, put all the money into hard assets, and borrow additional money to buy more.

13. You've lost $500 at the blackjack table in Atlantic City. How much more are you prepared to lose to win the $500 back?

☐ (a) Nothing—you quit now.

☐ (b) $100.

☐ (c) $250.

☐ (d) $500.

☐ (e) More than $500.

Your score

Now it's time to see what kind of investor you are. Total your score, using the point system listed below for each answer you gave.

1. a–3, b–1, c–4
2. a–1, b–3, c–4
3. a–1, b–3
4. a–2, b–1
5. a–2, b–1, c–4, d–1
6. a–1, b–2
7. a–1, b–2, c–3
8. a–1, b–2, c–4, d–6
9. a–1, b–3, c–6, d–9
10. a–3, b–1
11. a–1, b–3, c–5, d–9
12. a–1, b–2, c–3, d–4
13. a–1, b–2, c–4, d–6, e–8

If you scored...

Below 21: You are a conservative investor, allergic to risk. Stay with sober, conservative investments.

21 to 35: You are an active investor, willing to take calculated, prudent risks to gain financially.

36 or more: You are a venturesome, aggressive investor.

Reprinted with permission from *Moneyletter*, P.O. Box 6020, Holliston, MA, (800) 890-9670.

3. Persistent Saving in Regular Amounts, No Matter How Small, Pays Off

One final preliminary before presenting the asset-allocation guide. What do you do if right now you have no assets to allocate? So many people of limited means believe it is impossible to build up a sizable nest egg. Accumulating meaningful amounts of retirement savings such as $50,000 or $100,000 often seems completely out of reach. Don't despair. The fact is that a program of regular saving each week—persistently followed, as through a payroll savings plan—can in time produce substantial sums of money. Can you afford to put aside $23 per week? Or $11.50 per week? If you can, the possibility of eventually accumulating a large retirement fund is easily attainable, if you have many working years ahead of you.

The table below shows the results from a regular savings program of $100 per month. An interest rate of 8 percent is assumed as an investment rate. The last column of the table shows the total values that will be accumulated over various time periods.* It is clear that regular savings of even moderate amounts of money make the attainment of meaningful sums of money entirely possible, even for those who start off with no nest egg at all. If you can put a few thousand dollars into the savings fund to begin with, the final sum will be increased significantly.

How Retirement Funds Can Build:
What Happens to an Investment of $100 a Month, Earning an 8 Percent Return Compounded Monthly

Year	Cumulative Investment	Annual Income	Cumulative Income	Total Value
1	$1,200	$53	$53	$1,253
2	2,400	157	210	2,610
3	3,600	270	480	4,080
4	4,800	392	872	5,672
5	6,000	524	1,396	7,396
10	12,000	1,368	6,414	18,414
20	24,000	4,501	35,284	59,284
30	36,000	11,422	113,594	149,594

*I assume that the savings can be made in an IRA or other tax-favored savings vehicle, so income taxes on interest earnings are ignored.

If you are able to save only $50 per month—a bit more than $11.50 per week—cut the numbers in the table in half; if you are able to save $200 per month, double them. You will need to pick no-load mutual funds to accumulate your nest egg because direct investments of small sums of money would be prohibitively expensive. Also, mutual funds permit automatic reinvestment of interest, or dividends and capital gains, as is assumed in the table. Finally, make sure you check if your employer has a matched savings plan. Obviously, if by saving through a company-sponsored payroll savings plan you are able to match your savings with company contributions and gain tax deductions as well, your nest egg will grow that much faster. Moreover, a company savings/retirement program, such as a 403(b) or 401(k) plan, shelters your earnings from tax.

The Life-Cycle Investment Guide

The chart on pages 350 and 351 presents a summary of the life-cycle investment guide. In the Talmud, Rabbi Isaac said that one should always divide his wealth into three parts: a third in land, a third in merchandise (business), and a third ready at hand (in liquid form). Such an asset allocation is hardly unreasonable, but we can improve on this ancient advice because we have more refined instruments and a greater appreciation of the considerations that make different asset allocations appropriate for different people. The general ideas behind the recommendations have been spelled out in detail above. For those in their twenties, a very aggressive investment portfolio is recommended. At this age, there is lots of time to ride out the peaks and valleys of investment cycles and you have a lifetime of earnings from employment ahead of you. The portfolio is not only heavy in common stocks but also contains a substantial proportion of international stocks including the higher risk emerging markets. As mentioned in chapter 9, one important advantage of international diversification is risk reduction. Because cycles in economic activity are not perfectly correlated across countries, a portfolio that is diversified internationally will tend to pro-

Life-Cycle Investment Guide
Recommended Asset or Savings Allocations

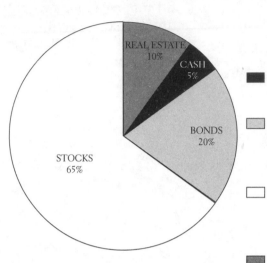

Age: Mid-Twenties

Lifestyle: Fast, aggressive. With a
steady stream of earnings, capacity for
risk is fairly high. Need discipline of
payroll savings to build nest egg.

CASH (5%): money-market fund or
short-term-bond fund (average
maturity 1 to 1½ years).

BONDS (20%): zero-coupon Treasury
bonds, no-load GNMA funds, or no-
load high-grade bond fund, some
Treasury inflation protection
securities (5% of portfolio).*

STOCKS (65%): two-thirds in U.S.
stocks with good representation of
smaller growth companies; one-third
international stocks, including
emerging markets.

REAL ESTATE (10%): portfolio of
REITs or real estate fund.

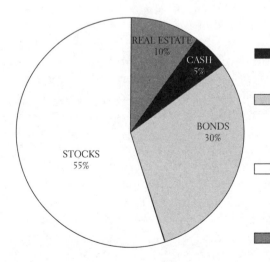

Age: Late Thirties to Early Forties

Lifestyle: Midlife crisis. For childless
career couples, capacity for risk is still
quite high. Risk options vanishing for
those with college tuitions looming.

CASH (5%): money-market fund or
short-term-bond fund (average
maturity 1 to 1½ years).

BONDS (30%): zero-coupon Treasury
bonds, no-load GNMA funds, or no-
load high-grade bond fund, some
Treasury inflation protection
securities (5% of portfolio).*

STOCKS (55%): two-thirds in U.S.
stocks with good representation of
smaller growth companies; one-third
international stocks, including
emerging markets.

REAL ESTATE (10%): portfolio of
REITs or real estate fund.

*If bonds are to be held outside of
tax-favored retirement plans, tax-
exempt bonds should be used.

Life-Cycle Investment Guide
Recommended Asset or Savings Allocations

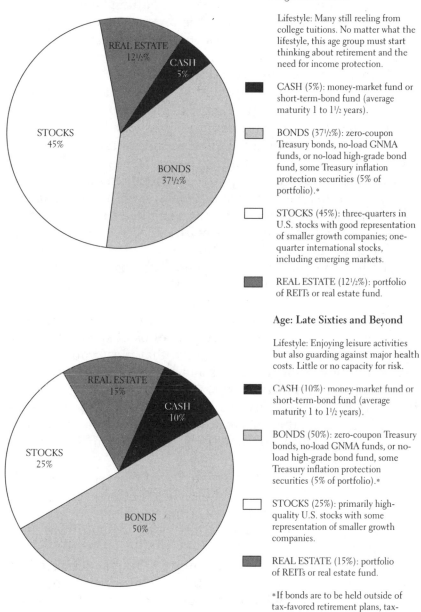

Age: Mid-Fifties

Lifestyle: Many still reeling from college tuitions. No matter what the lifestyle, this age group must start thinking about retirement and the need for income protection.

CASH (5%): money-market fund or short-term-bond fund (average maturity 1 to 1½ years).

BONDS (37½%): zero-coupon Treasury bonds, no-load GNMA funds, or no-load high-grade bond fund, some Treasury inflation protection securities (5% of portfolio).*

STOCKS (45%): three-quarters in U.S. stocks with good representation of smaller growth companies; one-quarter international stocks, including emerging markets.

REAL ESTATE (12½%): portfolio of REITs or real estate fund.

Age: Late Sixties and Beyond

Lifestyle: Enjoying leisure activities but also guarding against major health costs. Little or no capacity for risk.

CASH (10%): money-market fund or short-term-bond fund (average maturity 1 to 1½ years).

BONDS (50%): zero-coupon Treasury bonds, no-load GNMA funds, or no-load high-grade bond fund, some Treasury inflation protection securities (5% of portfolio).*

STOCKS (25%): primarily high-quality U.S. stocks with some representation of smaller growth companies.

REAL ESTATE (15%): portfolio of REITs or real estate fund.

*If bonds are to be held outside of tax-favored retirement plans, tax-exempt bonds should be used.

duce more stable returns from year to year than one invested only in domestic issues. Plus, international diversification enables an investor to gain exposure to other growth areas in the world.

As investors age, they should start cutting back on riskier investments and start increasing the proportion of the portfolio committed to bonds and stocks that pay generous dividends such as REITs. By the age of fifty-five, investors should start thinking about the transition to retirement and moving the portfolio toward income production. The proportion of bonds increases and the stock portfolio becomes more conservative and income-producing and less growth-oriented. In retirement, a portfolio heavily weighted in a variety of bonds is recommended. A general rule of thumb that will make sense for many investors is to make the proportion of bonds in one's portfolio almost equal to one's age. Nevertheless, even in one's late sixties, 25 percent of the portfolio is committed to regular stocks and 15 percent to real estate equities (REITs) to give some income growth to cope with inflation.

For most people, I recommend broad-based total stock-market index funds rather than individual stocks for portfolio formation. I do so for two reasons. First, most people do not have sufficient capital to diversify properly. Obviously, if you have enough money to buy portfolios of stocks yourself, you may do so. Second, I recognize that most younger people will not have substantial assets and will be accumulating portfolios by monthly investments. This makes mutual funds almost a necessity. You don't have to use the index funds I suggest, but do make sure that any mutual funds you buy are truly "no-load" and pick safer, income-producing funds later in life.

You will also see that I have included real estate explicitly in my recommendations. I said earlier that everyone should attempt to own his or her own home. I believe everyone should have substantial real estate holdings and, therefore, some part of one's equity holdings should be in real estate investment trust (REIT) index mutual funds described in chapter 12. With respect to your bond holdings, the guide recommends taxable bonds. If, however, you are in the highest tax bracket and live in a high-tax state such as New York and your bonds are held outside of your retirement plan, I recommend that you use tax-exempt money funds and bond funds tailored to your state so that they are exempt from both federal and state taxes.

15
Three Giant Steps Down Wall Street

Annual income twenty pounds, annual expenditure nineteen
nineteen six, result happiness. Annual income twenty pounds,
annual expenditure twenty pounds ought and six, result misery.
—Charles Dickens, *David Copperfield*

This chapter offers rules for buying stocks and
specific recommendations for the instruments you can use to
follow the asset allocation guidelines presented in chapter 14.
By now you have made sensible decisions on taxes, housing,
insurance, and how to get the most out of your cash reserves.
You have reviewed your objectives, your stage in the life cycle,
and your attitude toward risk, and decided how much of your
assets to put into the stock market. Now it is time for quick
prayer at Trinity Church and then some bold steps forward,
taking great care to avoid the graveyard on either side. My rules
can help you avoid costly mistakes and unnecessary sales
charges, as well as increase your yield a mite without undo
risk. I can't offer anything spectacular, but I do know that often
a 1 or 2 percent increase in the yield on your assets can mean
the difference between misery and happiness.

How do you go about buying stocks? Basically, there are
three ways: I call them the No-Brainer Step, the Do-It-Yourself
Step, and the Substitute-Player Step.

In the first case, you simply buy shares in various broad-
based index funds designed to track the different classes of
stocks that make up your portfolio. This method also has the

virtue of being absolutely simple. Even if you have trouble chewing gum while walking randomly, you can master it. And you are guaranteed the same yearly rate of return as the asset class as a whole. The market, in effect, pulls you along with it.

Under the second system, you jog down Wall Street, picking your own stocks and getting—in comparison with the yield obtained with index funds—much higher or much lower rates of return. This involves work, but also, in the opinion of those who wouldn't play the game any other way, a lot of fun. I don't recommend this approach for most investors. Nevertheless, if this is how you prefer to invest, I've provided a series of stock-picking rules to help tilt the odds of success a bit more in your favor.

Third, you can sit on a curb and choose a professional investment manager to do the walking down Wall Street for you. The only way investors of modest means can accomplish this is to purchase mutual funds. I don't recommend this step either, but later in the chapter I will at least present some helpful suggestions that may help you avoid the pitfalls.

Earlier editions of my book described a strategy I called the Malkiel Step: buying closed-end investment company shares at a discount from the value of the shares held by the fund. When the first edition of this book was published, discounts on U.S. stocks were as high as 40 percent. Discounts are far smaller now, as these funds are more efficiently priced. The investment world is a broader place today, however, and those extending their horizons will find that, for certain kinds of funds, attractive discounts can arise and savvy investors can sometimes take advantage. The Malkiel Step is described later in this chapter.

The No-Brainer Step: Investing in Index Funds

The Standard & Poor's 500-Stock Index, a composite that represents about three-quarters of the value of all U.S.-traded common stocks, beats most of the experts over the long pull. Buying a portfolio of all companies in this index would be an easy way to own stocks. I argued back in 1973 (in the first edition of this book) that the means to adopt this approach was sorely needed for the small investor:

What we need is a no-load, minimum-management-fee
mutual fund that simply buys the hundreds of stocks making
up the broad stock-market averages and does no trading from
security to security in an attempt to catch the winners. Whenever below-average performance on the part of any mutual
fund is noticed, fund spokesmen are quick to point out, "You
can't buy the averages." It's time the public could.

Shortly after my book was published, the "index fund" idea
caught on. At first, only large pension clients were offered this
investment opportunity. But one of the great virtues of capitalism is that when there is a need for a product, someone usually
finds the will to produce it. In 1976, a fund was created that
allowed the public to get into the act as well. The Vanguard 500
Index Trust is a mutual fund that purchases the 500 stocks of
the S&P 500 in the same proportions as their weight in the
index. Each investor shares proportionately in the net income
and in the capital gains and losses of the fund's portfolio. Management expenses (custodian fees, the costs of collecting and
distributing dividends, and preparing summary reports for
investors, etc.) run at less than $2/10$ of 1 percent of assets, far less
than the expenses incurred by most mutual funds or bank trust
departments. You can now buy the market conveniently and
inexpensively. Today, most mutual-fund complexes offer an
S&P 500 fund. You can also buy exchange-traded S&P 500
index funds offered by State Street Bank (called SPDRs or Spiders) and by Barclays Global Investors (called i shares).

The logic behind this strategy is the logic of the efficient-
market theory. The above-average long-run performance of the
S&P 500 compared with that of major institutional investors
has been confirmed by numerous studies described in previous
chapters of this book. Between 1974 and 2002, for example, the
S&P 500 outperformed more than three-quarters of the public
equity mutual funds—the average annual total return for the
S&P 500 was close to 2 percentage points better than that of the
median fund.

Similar studies done of pension funds and of bank and
insurance company-pooled equity funds confirm the same
results. The S&P beat approximately two-thirds of professionally managed portfolios in the decades of the 1980s and 1990s.
Moreover, you can count on the fingers of your hands the num-

ber of mutual funds that have beaten any index fund by any significant margin.

The Index-Fund Solution: A Summary

Let's now summarize the advantages of using index funds as the primary investment vehicle to achieve your investment goals. Index funds have regularly produced rates of return exceeding those of active managers by close to 2 percentage points. There are two fundamental reasons for this excess performance: management fees and trading costs. Public index funds are typically run at a fee of less than ²⁄₁₀ of 1 percent. Actively managed public mutual funds charge annual management and market expenses that on average are 150 basis points (1½ percentage points) per year. Moreover, index funds trade only when necessary, whereas active funds typically have a turnover rate close to 100 percent, and often even more. Using very modest estimates of trading costs, such turnover probably costs the active manager at least another ½ to 1 percent of performance a year, and probably a lot more. Even if stock markets were less than perfectly efficient, active management as a whole cannot achieve gross returns exceeding the market as a whole and therefore they must, on average, underperform the indexes by the amount of these expense and transactions costs disadvantages. Unfortunately, active managers as a group cannot be like radio personality Garrison Keillor's fictional hometown of Lake Wobegon where "all the children are above average."

Index funds are also tax-friendly. Index funds allow investors to defer the realization of capital gains or avoid them completely if the shares are later bequeathed. To the extent that the long-run uptrend in stock prices continues, switching from security to security involves realizing capital gains that are subject to tax. Taxes are a crucially important financial consideration because the earlier realization of capital gains will substantially reduce net returns. Index funds do not trade from security to security and, thus, they tend to avoid capital gains taxes.

Index funds are also relatively predictable. When you buy an actively managed fund, you can never be sure how it will do relative to its peers. When you buy an index fund, you can be

"Leaping tall buildings in a single bound is nice, but can you outperform the S&P Index?"

© 2002 by Thomas Cheney. Reprinted by permission.

reasonably certain that it will track its index and that it is likely to beat the average manager handily. Moreover, the index fund is always fully invested. You should not believe the active manager who claims that her fund will move into cash at the correct times. We have seen that market timing does not work. Finally, index funds are easier to evaluate. During 2002, there were almost 5,000 stock mutual funds out there, and there is no reliable way to predict which ones are likely to outperform in the future. With index funds, you know exactly what you are getting, and the investment process is made incredibly simple.

Despite all the evidence to the contrary, suppose an investor still believed that superior investment management really does exist. Two issues remain: First, it is clear that such skill is very rare; and second, there appears to be no effective way to find such skill *before* it has been demonstrated over time. As I indicated in chapter 8, the best performing funds in one period of time are not the best performers in the next period. For example, the top performers of the late 1990s had perfectly dreadful returns in the first three years of the 2000s. Paul Samuelson sums up the difficulty in the following parable. Suppose it was demonstrated that one out of twenty alcoholics could learn to become a moderate social drinker. The experienced clinician would answer, "Even if true, act as if it were false, for you will never identify that one in twenty, and in the attempt five in twenty will be ruined." Samuelson concludes that investors should forsake the search for such tiny needles in huge haystacks.

Stock trading among institutional investors is like an isometric exercise: lots of energy is expended, but between one investment manager and another it all balances out, and the commissions the managers pay detract from performance. Like greyhounds at the dog track, professional money managers seem destined to lose their race with the mechanical rabbit. Small wonder that many institutional investors, including Intel, Exxon, Ford, American Telephone and Telegraph, Harvard University, the College Retirement Equity Fund, and the New York State Teachers Association, have put substantial portions of their assets into index funds. In 1977, $1 billion in assets were invested in index funds. By 2002, more than $2 trillion of investment funds were "indexed."

How about you? When you buy an index fund, you give up the chance of boasting at the golf club about the fantastic gains you've made by picking stock-market winners. Broad diversification rules out extraordinary losses relative to the whole market; it also, by definition, rules out extraordinary gains. Thus, many Wall Street critics refer to index-fund investing as "guaranteed mediocrity." But experience conclusively shows that index-fund buyers are likely to obtain results exceeding those of the typical fund manager, whose large advisory fees and substantial portfolio turnover tend to reduce investment yields. Many people will find the guarantee of playing the stock-market game at par every round a very attractive one. Of course, this strategy does not rule out risk: If the market goes down, your portfolio is guaranteed to follow suit.

The index method of investment has other attractions for the small investor. It enables you to obtain very broad diversification with only a small investment. It also allows you to reduce brokerage charges. When an individual investor buys stocks, he or she pays very high brokerage fees on small trades (even if a discount broker is used). The index fund, by pooling the moneys of many investors, trades in larger blocks and can

negotiate a brokerage fee of pennies per share on its transactions. The index fund does all the work of collecting the dividends from all of the stocks it owns and sending you each
quarter one check for all of your earnings (earnings that, incidentally, can be reinvested in the fund if you desire). In short,
the index fund is a sensible, serviceable method for obtaining
the market's rate of return with absolutely no effort and mini-
mal expense.

A Broader Definition of Indexing

The indexing strategy is one that I have recommended
since the first edition in 1973—even before index funds
existed. It was clearly an idea whose time had come. By far the
most popular index used is the Standard & Poor's 500-Stock
Index, an index that well represents the major corporations in
the U.S. market. But now, as one of the earliest supporters of
the 500-Stock Index, I want to modify my advice. Although I
still recommend indexing, or so-called passive investing, there
are valid criticisms of too narrow a definition of indexing.
Many people incorrectly equate indexing with a strategy of
simply buying the S&P 500 Index. That is no longer the only
game in town. The extraordinary 1990s performance of the
large-capitalization domestic stocks that dominate the S&P 500
did not continue at the start of the new millennium and the
long-run superiority of small capitalization stocks may well
reassert itself. The S&P 500 omits the thousands of small companies that are among the most dynamic in the economy. Thus,
I now believe that if an investor is to buy only one U.S. index
fund, the best general U.S. index to emulate is the broader
Wilshire 5,000-Stock Index—not the S&P 500.

There are two reasons for my recommendation. First, the
S&P indexing strategy has become so popular that it may have
affected the pricing of the component stocks in the index. This
can clearly be seen when changes are made in the composition
of the index as unavoidably happens from time to time. During
the merger and buyout boom of the late 1980s and 1990s, many
S&P 500 companies disappeared and had to be removed from
the index. These companies were then replaced by others,
which previously had not been included in the index. It turned
out that newly included companies tended to appreciate in

price (at least temporarily) by more than 5 percent—simply because they were now a part of the S&P index. Portfolio managers who ran index funds were required to incur the transactions costs required to purchase the stocks of the new companies (in proportion to their relative size and, therefore, their weight in the index) so that their portfolio's performance would continue to conform to that of the index. Thus, the very popularity of S&P 500 indexing could make the stocks included in the index a bit pricier than comparable non–S&P index stocks, at least for some period of time. Any investment idea that becomes extremely popular can become overvalued.

There is a second reason to favor a broader, more inclusive index. Seventy-five years of market history confirm that, in the aggregate, smaller stocks have tended to outperform larger ones. For example, from 1926 to 2001 a portfolio of smaller stocks produced a rate of return of more than 12 percent annually, whereas the returns from larger stocks (such as those in the S&P 500) were about 10½ percent. Although the smaller stocks were riskier than the major blue chips, the point is that a well-diversified portfolio of small companies is likely to produce enhanced returns. For both reasons, I now favor investing in an index that contains a much broader representation of U.S. companies, including large numbers of the small dynamic companies that are likely to be in early stages of their growth cycles.

I did suggest in *Random Walk*'s fourth edition that the S&P index was far from a perfect proxy for the market. I stated then: "It would be nice to have a fund available that bought an index including the thousands of smaller companies that are among the most dynamic in the economy." Fortunately for investors, one of the mutual-fund complexes—The Vanguard Group— was listening.

Recall that the S&P 500 represents more than 75 percent of the market value of all outstanding U.S. common stocks. Literally thousands of companies represent the remaining 20 to 25 percent of the total U.S. market value. These are in many cases the emerging growth companies that offer higher investment rewards (as well as higher risks). The Wilshire 5,000 Index contains all publicly traded U.S. common stocks on the New York and American stock exchanges and in the NASDAQ market.

The Wilshire 5,000 is actually composed of about 6,000 securities and is the best representation available of the entire U.S. market. There are now a number of mutual funds based on the Wilshire index. Such index funds usually go by the name Total Stock Market Portfolio.

The chart below illustrates how the annualized returns of the S&P 500 and the Wilshire 5,000 compare with the returns of the average equity-fund manager. Although past performance can never assure future results, the evidence clearly indicates that both the S&P 500 and the Wilshire 5,000 have provided higher returns than the average equity mutual-fund manager.

Moreover, unlike charity, indexing need not begin (and end) at home. As I argued in chapter 9, investors can reduce risk by diversifying internationally; by including asset classes

Annualized Returns—Indexes vs. Average Equity Mutual Funds Manager (20 Years to December 31, 2001)

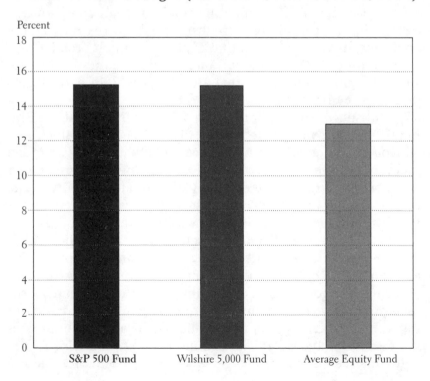

such as real estate in the portfolio; and by placing some portion of their portfolio in bonds including Treasury inflation-protection securities. This is the basic lesson of modern portfolio theory. Thus, I would never advise investors simply to buy a U.S. stock-market index fund and hold no other securities. But this is not an argument against indexing, because index funds currently exist that mimic the performance of various international indexes such as the Morgan Stanley Capital International (MSCI) index of European, Australian, and Far Eastern (EAFE) securities, and the MSCI emerging-markets index. In addition, there are index funds holding real estate trusts (REITs). Moreover, these index funds have also tended to outperform actively managed funds investing in similar securities. Finally, bond index funds are available that have also outperformed managed bond funds.

A Specific Index-Fund Portfolio

The table below presents specific index-fund selections that investors can use to build their portfolios. The table shows the recommended percentages for those in their mid-fifties— the group I call the "aging boomers." Those who are not in their mid-fifties can use exactly the same selections and simply change the weights to those appropriate for their specific age group. Remember also that you may want to alter the percentages somewhat depending on your personal capacity for and attitude toward risk. Those willing to accept somewhat more risk in the hope of greater reward could cut back on the proportion of the portfolio in bonds. Those who need a steady income for living expenses could increase their holdings of real estate equities, because they provide somewhat larger current income.

Remember also that I am assuming here that you hold most if not all of your securities in tax-advantaged retirement plans. Certainly all of your bonds should be held in such accounts. To the extent that bonds are held outside of retirement accounts, you may well prefer to purchase tax-exempt bonds rather than the taxable fixed-income securities. Moreover, if your common stocks will be held in taxable accounts, you may want to consider the tax-managed index funds discussed in the next section. Finally, note that I have given you a choice of index funds from different mutual-fund complexes. Because I am a director of The Vanguard Group, I wanted to make sure you had a number of non-Vanguard funds to choose from. All the funds listed in the table have moderate expense ratios and are no-load. More information on these funds, including telephone numbers and Web sites, are listed in the Random Walker's Address Book, which follows this chapter.

A Specific Index-Fund Portfolio for Aging Baby Boomers

Cash (5%)*

> Fidelity Spartan Money Market Fund, or TIAA-CREFF Money Market Fund, or Vanguard Prime Money Market Fund

Bonds (37½%)†

> Vanguard Total Bond Market Index Fund

Real Estate Equities (12½%)

> Vanguard REIT Index Fund

Stocks (45%)

> U.S. Stocks (34%)
>> Fidelity Spartan, T. Rowe Price, or Vanguard Total Stock Market Fund Index
>
> Developed International Markets (7½%)
>> Fidelity Spartan, Dreyfus, or Vanguard International Index Fund
>
> Emerging International Markets (3½%)
>> Vanguard Emerging Markets Index Fund

*A short-term bond fund may be substituted for one of the money-market funds listed.

†Although it doesn't fit under the rubric of an index-fund portfolio, I recommend that investors consider putting part of the bond portfolio (5% of the total portfolio) in Treasury inflation-protection securities.

NB: I am a director of the Vanguard Funds listed above.

The Tax-Managed Index Fund

One of the advantages, noted above, of passive portfolio management (that is, simply buying and holding an index fund) is that such a strategy minimizes transactions costs as well as taxes. Taxes are a crucially important financial consideration, as two Stanford University economists, Joel Dickson and John Shoven, have shown. Utilizing a sample of 62 mutual funds with long-term records, they found that, pre-tax, $1 invested in 1962 would have grown to $21.89 in 1992. After paying taxes on income dividends and capital gains distributions, however, that same $1 invested in mutual funds by a high-income investor would have grown to only $9.87.

To a considerable extent, index mutual funds help solve the tax problem. They do not trade from security to security and, thus, they tend to avoid capital gains taxes. Nevertheless, even index funds do realize some capital gains that are taxable to the holders. These gains generally arise involuntarily: either because of a buyout of one of the companies in the index, or because sales are forced on the mutual fund. The latter occurs when mutual-fund shareholders decide on balance to redeem their shares and the fund must sell securities to raise cash. Thus, even regular index funds are not a perfect solution for the problem of minimizing tax liabilities.

Exchange-traded index funds (ETFs) such as "spiders" (an S&P 500 Fund) tend to be a bit more tax-efficient than regular index funds because they are able to take advantage of "in-kind" redemptions. The in-kind redemption process proceeds by delivering low-cost shares against redemption requests. This is not a taxable transaction for the fund so there is no realization of gain that must be distributed to the fund's other shareholders. Moreover, the redeeming ETF shareholder does not acquire the fund's cost basis of the stocks it receives. The redeeming shareholder pays taxes based on his or her original cost of the shares—not the fund's basis in the basket of stocks that is delivered. And the high-cost shares that remain in the fund means that acquired companies generate smaller capital gains when they leave the index.

ETFs require the payment of transactions costs, however, including brokerage fees and bid-asked spreads. Thus, they are unsuitable for investors who will be accumulating index shares over time in small amounts. No-load mutual funds will better serve such investors. I recommend that you leave ETFs to the speculators who think it is advantageous to buy or sell ETFs at any hour of the day and to buy such funds on margin. I agree with John Bogle, founder of The Vanguard Group, who says that anything that encourages trading will hurt investors:

"Investors cut their own throats when they trade." By this argument, investors would do well to follow the practice of Little Miss Muffet and run in fright far away from the spiders and their siblings.

Enter the new mutual fund for the tax-conscious investor, the Vanguard Tax-Managed Fund: Growth and Income Portfolio. Despite the portfolio designation, which is not totally revealing, this is an S&P 500 index fund that minimizes taxes by deferring capital gains realizations. Here's an illustration of how it works. Suppose the fund earns a pre-tax 8 percent return over twenty years (the average return for the stock market over long periods of time); 2 percent comes from dividends and 6 percent from growth (i.e., capital gains). The chart on page 367 shows the results for a hypothetical initial investment of $10,000 in each of three portfolios. Portfolio A distributes taxable dividend income and capital gains each year. Portfolios B and C distribute only taxable dividend income; they realize no capital gains. In Portfolio B, the fund is sold after twenty years and gains are realized and taxed at that time. For Portfolio C, the fund is inherited and the gains are never taxed. Capital gains taxes are avoided because when a fund (or any individual stock) is inherited, the cost basis of the security is "stepped up" to current market value. It turns out that Portfolio B accumulates over $3,000 more than Portfolio A, whereas Portfolio C accumulates excess cash of more than $8,000.

The fund is able to defer capital gains by the following techniques. First, the portfolio is indexed to the S&P 500 so there is no active management that tends to realize gains. Second, when securities do have to be sold (to meet redemptions, for example), the fund sells the highest-cost securities first. Such forced sales from liquidations should be minimized, however, by the assessment of a 2 percent redemption if fund shares are held less than one year and a 1 percent redemption fee for fund shares held between one and five years. Third, the fund offsets unavoidable gains by judiciously selling other securities on which there is a loss. As a result, the fund may not perfectly track the benchmark index, but it should come very close.

Vanguard has two additional tax-managed funds. One, called the Capital Appreciation Portfolio, is identical to the

The Impact of Taxing Capital Gains After-Tax Value of $10,000 Invested for 20 Years*

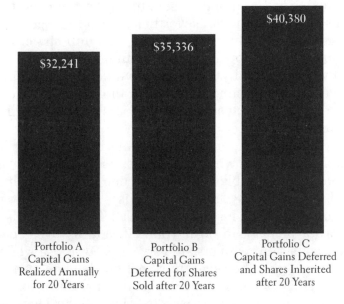

| | Portfolio A Capital Gains Realized Annually for 20 Years | Portfolio B Capital Gains Deferred for Shares Sold after 20 Years | Portfolio C Capital Gains Deferred and Shares Inherited after 20 Years |

$32,241 — Portfolio A Capital Gains Realized Annually for 20 Years

$35,336 — Portfolio B Capital Gains Deferred for Shares Sold after 20 Years

$40,380 — Portfolio C Capital Gains Deferred and Shares Inherited after 20 Years

Source: Vanguard Group of Investment Companies.

*This hypothetical example assumes a 2% return from dividend income (taxed at a marginal income tax rate of 38.6%) and a 6% return from capital gains (taxed at 20%). In Portfolio A, capital gains are realized, distributed, and taxed annually. In Portfolio B, capital gains accumulate unrealized until they are taxed in the twentieth year. Portfolio C is identical to Portfolio B except that the shares are bequeathed, and no capital gains taxes are paid.

income and growth (S&P 500) portfolio except that the index used is the Russell 1,000 Index, which includes many smaller companies with lower dividend yields. Although undoubtedly more aggressive, this portfolio is even more effective in minimizing taxes because it distributes less dividend income. A third portfolio, called the Balanced Portfolio, is composed of roughly equal parts of the capital-appreciation (Russell 1,000 Index) portfolio and a group of intermediate-term tax-exempt bonds. These low-cost index-oriented funds should prove very advantageous for people in the highest tax brackets with a long-term investment horizon and where the stocks are held outside of a tax-advantaged retirement plan. They are particularly useful for funds earmarked for inheritance.

The Do-It-Yourself Step: Potentially Useful
Stock-Picking Rules

Indexing is the strategy I most highly recommend for individuals and institutions. Nevertheless, I do recognize that it may be considered by many to be a very dull strategy. Those with speculative temperaments will undoubtedly prefer using their own steps (and wits) to pick winners, at least for some portion of their investment funds. For those who insist on playing the game themselves, the Do-It-Yourself Step may be more appealing.

Having been smitten with the gambling urge since birth, I can well understand why many investors have not only a compulsion to pick the big winners on their own but also a total lack of interest in a system that promises results merely equivalent to those in the market as a whole. The problem is that it takes a lot of work to do it yourself, and as I've repeatedly shown, consistent winners are very rare. For those who regard investing as play, however, this section demonstrates how a sensible strategy can produce substantial rewards and, at the very least, minimize the risks in playing the stock-picking game.

Before putting my strategy to work, however, you need to know the sources of investment information and how to choose an appropriate broker. Most information sources can be obtained at public libraries. You should be an avid reader of the financial pages of daily newspapers, particularly the *New York Times* and the *Wall Street Journal*. Weeklies such as *Barron's* should also be on your "must-read" list. Business magazines such as *BusinessWeek*, *Fortune*, and *Forbes* are also valuable for gaining exposure to investment ideas. The major investment advisory services are good, too. You should, for example, try to have access to Standard & Poor's *Outlook* and the *Value Line Investment Survey*. The first is a weekly publication that contains lists of recommendations; the second presents historical records, current reviews, and risk (beta) ratings of all the major securities, as well as weekly recommendations. Finally, there is a wealth of information, including security analysts' recommendations, available over the Internet.

In the first edition of *A Random Walk Down Wall Street*,

written in the early 1970s, I proposed four rules for successful stock selection. I find them just as serviceable today. In abridged form, the rules, some of which have been mentioned in earlier chapters, are as follows:

Rule 1: Confine stock purchases to companies that appear able to sustain above-average earnings growth for at least five years. As difficult as the job may be, picking stocks whose earnings grow is the name of the game. Consistent growth not only increases the earnings and dividends of the company but may also increase the multiple that the market is willing to pay for those earnings. This would further boost your gains. Thus, the purchaser of a stock whose earnings begin to grow rapidly has a potential double benefit—both the earnings and the multiple may increase.

Rule 2: Never pay more for a stock than can reasonably be justified by a firm foundation of value. Although I am convinced that you can never judge the exact intrinsic value of a stock, I do feel that you can roughly gauge when a stock seems to be reasonably priced. The market price-earnings multiple is a good place to start: You should buy stocks selling at multiples in line with, or not very much above, this ratio. My strategy, then, is to look for growth situations that the market has not already recognized by bidding the stock's multiple to a large premium. As pointed out in Rule 1, if the growth actually takes place, you will often get a double bonus—both the earnings and the price-earnings multiple can rise, producing large gains. By the same token, beware of the stock with a very high multiple and many years of growth already discounted in the price. If earnings decline rather than grow, you will usually get double trouble—the multiple will drop along with the earnings, and heavy losses will result. Following this rule would have avoided the heavy losses suffered by investors in the premier high-tech growth stocks that sold at astronomical price-earnings multiples in early 2000.

Note that, although similar, this is not simply another endorsement of the "buy low P/E stocks" strategy. Under my rule it is perfectly all right to buy a stock with a P/E multiple slightly above the market average—as long as the company's growth prospects are substantially above average. You might call this an adjusted low P/E strategy. Some people call this a GARP (growth at a reasonable price) strategy. Buy stocks whose P/E's are low relative to their growth prospects. If you can be even reasonably accurate in picking companies that do indeed enjoy above-average growth, you will be rewarded with above-average returns.

Rule 3: It helps to buy stocks with the kinds of stories of anticipated growth on which investors can build castles in the air. I stressed in chapter 2 the importance of psychological elements in stock-price determination. Individual and institutional investors are not computers that calculate warranted price-earnings multiples and then print out buy and sell decisions. They are emotional human beings—driven by greed, gambling instinct, hope, and fear in their stock-market decisions. This is why successful investing demands both intellectual and psychological acuteness. Of course, the market is not totally subjective either; if a positive growth rate appears to be established, the stock is almost certain to develop some type of following. But stocks are like people—some have more attractive personalities than others, and the improvement in a stock's multiple may be smaller and slower to be realized if its story never catches on. The key to success is being where other investors will be, several months before they get there. So my advice is to ask yourself whether the story about your stock is one that is likely to catch the fancy of the crowd. Is it a story from which contagious dreams can be generated? Is it a story on which investors can build castles in the air—but castles in the air that really rest on a firm foundation?

Rule 4: Trade as little as possible. I agree with the Wall Street maxim, "Ride the winners and sell the losers," but not because I believe in technical analysis. Frequent switching accomplishes nothing but subsidizing your broker and increasing your tax burden when you do realize gains. I do not say, "Never sell a stock on which you have a gain." The circumstances that led you to buy the stock may change, and, especially when it gets to be tulip time in the market, many of your successful growth stocks may become way overpriced and overweighted in your portfolio, as they did during the Nifty Fifty craze of the 1970s or the Internet bubble of 1999–2000. But it is very difficult to recognize the proper time to sell, and heavy tax costs may be involved. My own philosophy leads me to minimize trading as much as possible. I am merciless with the losers, however. With few exceptions, I sell before the end of each calendar year any stocks on which I have a loss. The reason for this timing is that losses are deductible (up to certain amounts) for tax purposes, or can offset gains you may already have taken. Thus, taking losses can actually reduce the amount of loss by lowering your tax bill. I don't always take all losses. If the growth I expect begins to materialize and I am convinced that my stock will work out a bit later, I may hold on for a while. But I do not recommend too much patience in losing situations, especially when prompt action can produce immediate tax benefits.

The efficient-market theory warns that following even sensible rules such as these is unlikely to lead to superior performance. And nonprofessional investors labor under many handicaps. Earnings reports cannot always be trusted, as investors sadly learned in the cases of companies such as Enron and WorldCom during the early 2000s. And once a story is out in the regular press, it's likely that the market has already taken account of the information. Picking individual stocks is like breeding thoroughbred porcupines. You study and study and make up your mind, and then proceed very carefully. In the final analysis, as much as I hope that investors have achieved successful records following my good advice, I am well aware that the winners in the stock-picking game may have benefited mainly from Lady Luck.

For all its hazards, picking individual stocks is a fascinating game. My rules do, I believe, tilt the odds in your favor while protecting you from the excessive risk involved in high-multiple stocks. But if you choose this course, remember that a large number of other investors—including the pros—are trying to play the same game. And the odds of anyone's consistently beating the market are pretty slim. Nevertheless, for many of us, trying to outguess the market is a game that is much too much fun to give up. Even if you were convinced you would not do any better than average, I'm sure that most of you with speculative temperaments would still want to keep on playing the game of selecting individual stocks with at least some portion of your investment funds. My rules permit you to do so in a way that significantly limits your exposure to risk.

You may also employ a mixed strategy: Index the core of your portfolio and try the stock-picking game for the money with which you can afford to take somewhat greater risks. If the main part of your retirement funds are broadly indexed and your stocks are diversified with bonds and real estate, you can safely take a flyer on some individual stocks knowing that your basic nest egg is reasonably secure.

The Substitute-Player Step: Hiring a Professional Wall Street Walker

There's an easier way to gamble in your investment walk: Instead of trying to pick the individual winners (stocks), pick the best coaches (investment managers). These "coaches" come in the form of mutual-fund managers, and there are close to 5,000 for you to pick from.

In addition to offering risk reduction through diversification, the mutual funds provide freedom from having to select stocks, and relief from paperwork and record-keeping for tax purposes. Most funds also offer a variety of special services, such as automatic reinvestment of dividends and regular cash-withdrawal plans. A mutual fund is particularly attractive as the investment vehicle for an Individual Retirement Account or Keogh plan.

In previous editions of this book, I provided the names of several investment managers who had enjoyed long-term records of successful portfolio management as well as brief biographies explaining their investment styles. These managers were among the very few who had shown an ability to beat the market over long periods of time. I have abandoned that practice in the current edition for two reasons.

First, with the exception of Warren Buffett, those managers have now retired from active portfolio management, and Buffett himself was at retirement age in the early 2000s. Second, I have become increasingly convinced that the past records of mutual-fund managers are essentially worthless in predicting future success. The few examples of consistently superior performance occur no more frequently than can be expected by chance.

Assuming that you prefer to invest in an actively managed equity mutual fund, is it really possible to select a fund that will be a top performer? One plausible method, favored by many financial planners and editors, is to choose funds with the best recent performance records. The financial pages of newspapers and magazines are filled with fund advertisements claiming that a particular fund is number one in terms of its performance record. There are at least two problems with this approach. First, investors should be aware that many fund advertisements are quite misleading. The number one ranking is typically for a self-selected specific time period and compared with a particular (usually small) group of common stock funds. For example, one fund advertised itself as: "Now Ranked #1 for Performance.* The Fund That's Performed Through Booms, Busts and 11 Presidential Elections." It is implied that this fund was a top performer over a period of forty-four years. The truth of the matter, revealed in a small footnote referenced by the asterisk, was that the fund was number one only during one specific three-month period and only compared with a specific category of funds with an asset value between $250 and $500 million.

The more important reason to be skeptical of past performance records is that, as I have mentioned earlier, there is no consistent long-run relationship between performance in one period and investment results in the next. I have studied the persistence of mutual-fund performance over a quarter of a century and conclude that it is simply impossible for investors to guarantee themselves above-average returns by purchasing those funds with the best recent records. Although there have been a few examples (such as Buffett's Berkshire Hathaway) of fairly consistent long-run superb performance, the general result is that there is no dependable long-term persistence. You can't assure yourself of superior performance by buying mutual funds that may have beaten the market in some past period. Once again, the past does not predict the future.

I have tested a strategy whereby at the start of each year

investors would rank all general equity funds based on the funds' records over the past twelve months. In alternative strategies, I have assumed that the investor buys the top ten funds, the top twenty funds, and so on. You can't consistently beat the market by purchasing the mutual funds that have performed best in the past.

I also tested a strategy of purchasing the "best" funds as ranked by the leading financial magazines. The clear implication of these tests in the laboratory of fund performance, as well as the academic work reported in Part Two of this book, is that you cannot depend on an excellent record of any particular manager continuing persistently in the future. Indeed, it's often the case that the hot performers of one period are the dogs of the next.

The Morningstar Mutual-Fund Information Service

If recent performance is not a reliable indicator in chasing a mutual fund, what is? I have often said that the two best things that have happened to the mutual-fund industry are the arrival of Jack Bogle (who started the low-cost consumer-friendly Vanguard Group of mutual funds during the mid-1970s) and Don Phillips (who in the early 1990s initiated the extremely useful Morningstar Service, which publishes information on mutual funds). For each mutual fund, Morningstar publishes a report crammed full of relevant data. A sample of the report data provided is presented on page 376 and 377 for the Vanguard Total Stock Market Index Fund.

Basically, Morningstar is one of the most comprehensive sources of mutual-fund information an investor can find. Its reports show past returns, risk ratings, portfolio composition, and the fund's investment style (for example, seeks established large companies or smaller growth companies; favors "value" stocks with low P/E ratios; buys foreign or domestic stocks or both; and so on). The reports indicate whether the fund has any sales charges (load fees) and shows the annual expense ratios for the fund and the percentage of the fund's asset value represented by unrealized appreciation. If you buy actively managed funds you should look for no-load, low-expense funds with little unrealized appreciation to minimize future tax liability. For bond funds, Morningstar gives data on returns, effective maturity, quality of bonds held, and information on loads and expenses.

The Morningstar Service also uses a five-star rating system. It rates past performance, taking into account broad-market returns and the costs and risks associated with getting those returns. The top funds are given five stars—two more than Michelin assigns to the top restaurants in the world. The stars are useful in categorizing past performance. Unlike the Michelin stars that virtually guarantee the diner a meal of the designated quality, however, the Morningstar ratings do not guarantee an investor continued superior performance. Five-star funds do not do better than three-star funds or even one-star funds, and the wise investor will look beyond the stars in making appropriate investment decisions.

A Primer on Mutual-Fund Costs

We've talked about the magic of compound interest—how even modest rates of interest can compound to produce extraordinary investment results after a few years. After several years, even small differences in the interest rates you earn on your money will result in vast differences in the final sum of money you can accumulate for retirement or for other savings needs. For this reason, it is critically important that every investor understand how to measure both the explicit and the less transparent elements of investment transactions and management costs. Because many investors will be using mutual funds as their primary vehicle for buying stocks and bonds, they must be able to understand the facts and implications of mutual-fund costs. It is for this reason that the following "primer" is required reading for cost-conscious investors.

The mutual-fund industry has developed a system of charging expenses to investors that is as complicated as IRS income tax regulations and equally unpleasant. There are two broad categories of mutual-fund costs: "load" fees charged when you buy or sell shares, and "expense charges" that are taken out of your investment returns each year.

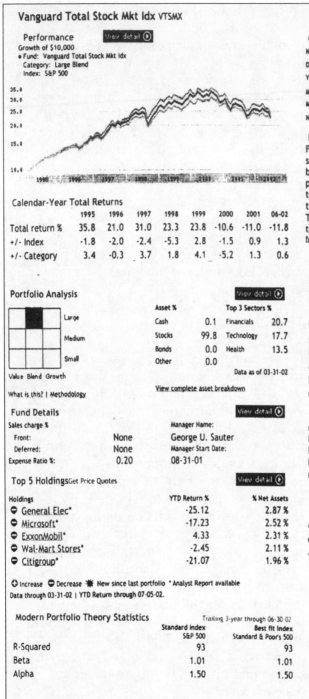

Vanguard Total Stock Mkt Idx VTSMX

Performance
Growth of $10,000
- Fund: Vanguard Total Stock Mkt Idx
- Category: Large Blend
- Index: S&P 500

Calendar-Year Total Returns

	1995	1996	1997	1998	1999	2000	2001	06-02
Total return %	35.8	21.0	31.0	23.3	23.8	-10.6	-11.0	-11.8
+/- Index	-1.8	-2.0	-2.4	-5.3	2.8	-1.5	0.9	1.3
+/- Category	3.4	-0.3	3.7	1.8	4.1	-5.2	1.3	0.6

Portfolio Analysis

Large / Medium / Small
Value Blend Growth

What is this? | Methodology

Asset %		Top 3 Sectors %	
Cash	0.1	Financials	20.7
Stocks	99.8	Technology	17.7
Bonds	0.0	Health	13.5
Other	0.0		

Data as of 03-31-02

View complete asset breakdown

Fund Details

Sales charge %		Manager Name:
Front:	None	George U. Sauter
Deferred:	None	Manager Start Date:
Expense Ratio %:	0.20	08-31-01

Top 5 Holdings Get Price Quotes

Holdings	YTD Return %	% Net Assets
⊖ General Elec*	-25.12	2.87 %
⊖ Microsoft*	-17.23	2.52 %
⊖ ExxonMobil*	4.33	2.31 %
⊖ Wal-Mart Stores*	-2.45	2.11 %
⊖ Citigroup*	-21.07	1.96 %

⊕ Increase ⊖ Decrease ✳ New since last portfolio * Analyst Report available
Data through 03-31-02 | YTD Return through 07-05-02.

Modern Portfolio Theory Statistics

Trailing 3-year through 06-30-02

	Standard index S&P 500	Best fit Index Standard & Poor's 500
R-Squared	93	93
Beta	1.01	1.01
Alpha	1.50	1.50

Quick Stats

NAV (07-05-02)	$22.41
Day Change	$0.76
YTD Return	-12.47%
Morningstar Rating™	★★★
Morningstar Category	Large Blend
Net Assets ($mil)	15,945

Inside Scoop
For low-cost exposure to the broad stock market, this fund is tough to beat. It buys and holds most publicly traded stocks in an effort to give investors returns that mirror those of the broader market. Thanks to its low costs, its long-term returns are excellent. ⊳ Read full analysis

Style Box Details
Size
Average Mkt Cap $Mil   29,663

Market Capitalization	% of Portfolio
Giant	41.06
Large	29.59
Medium	19.55
Small	6.76
Micro	3.02

Investment Valuation	Stock Portfolio	Rel to S&P 500
Price/Book	4.4	0.9
Price/Earning	28.9	1.0
Price/Cash Flow	15.4	1.0

Data as of 06-30-02

Asset Allocation

		% of Net Assets
♦	Cash	0.1
♦	Stocks	99.8
♦	Bonds	0.0
	Other	0.0
	Foreign	0.0

(as a % of Stocks)

Chicago-based Morningstar, Inc. is a global investment research firm that provides financial data, research, online advice, consulting services, and investment solutions for individuals, financial advisers, institutions, and the media worldwide. Morningstar is a trusted source of investment information and

Vanguard Total Stock Mkt Idx VTSMX

 Morningstar's Take | 06-07-2002
by William Harding

Vanguard Total Stock Market Index Fund is the prototypical core holding.

As good as older sibling Vanguard 500 Index VFINX is, this fund is a marginally superior option for investors seeking broad market exposure. To be sure, nearly 30% of the fund's assets are dedicated to stocks outside the large-cap realm, compared with about 12% for Vanguard 500 Index.

This slant has been a relative boon to the fund as smaller-cap stocks have generally outpaced their larger-cap counterparts in recent years. Consequently, the fund's 15.5% loss for the trailing 12 months ended June 5, while disappointing on an absolute basis, bests the S&P 500 index by 157 basis points. And while nonindexed large-blend funds have had the leeway to favor small-cap stocks, the fund has also fared well relative to that group.

Though large-cap stocks are often thought of as fairly safe investments, all stocks court issue-specific risk and can implode for various reasons. Enron has been the biggest collapse of late, but other big names have also been punished. Fortunately, the fund's diversified nature--a hallmark of index funds--dampened the impact of such disasters on the portfolio. The fund also benefited from avoiding Tyco TYC altogether because the company is based in Bermuda, and the benchmark Wilshire 5000 index shuns stocks based outside the U.S.

Moreover, the fund's low costs give it a mighty and lasting advantage over its peers. Indeed, most actively managed large-cap funds have failed to overcome their expense hurdles over time. In addition, Gus Sauter is arguably the best index manager around, and he has done a great job of tracking the fund's bogy.

All told, this fund can be used either for all domestic-stock exposure, or as the core of a portfolio that is complemented with other small-cap, growth, or value funds.

See Previous Analyst Reports

Year	Total Return (%)	+/- Category
YTD	-11.84	0.63
2001	-10.97	1.33

Kudos
- Low costs.
- Broad market exposure.
- Experienced management.
- High tax efficiency.

Risks
- As is the case with other index funds, one gives up the chance for market-beating returns.

Strategy
The fund shadows the Wilshire 5000 index, which tracks nearly all publicly traded stocks. It would be impractical to own each smaller company in the index, so among the tiniest firms, manager Gus Sauter selects a representative sample. In an effort to boost returns by a few basis points, Sauter uses a variety of techniques, including securities lending.

Management
Few index-fund managers are as experienced as Sauter. Moreover, no one is better than Vanguard's indexing team at beating benchmark indexes with savvy trading decisions.

Inside Scoop
For low-cost exposure to the broad stock market, this fund is tough to beat. It buys and holds most publicly traded stocks in an effort to give

Nuts and Bolts
Vanguard Total Stock Mkt Idx

Fees and Expenses
Maximum Sales Fees

Initial	0.00%
Deferred	0.00%
Redemption	0.00%

Maximum Fees

Administrative	0.00%
Management	0.18%
12b-1	0.00%

Total Cost Projections (per $10,000)

3-Year	$64
5-Year	$113
10-Year	$255

Actual Fees

12b-1	0.00%
Management	0.13%
Total Expense Ratio	0.20%

Purchase Information
Minimum Investments

Initial	$3000
Additional	$100
Initial IRA	$1000
Additional IRA	$100
Initial AIP	$3000
Additional AIP	$50

Correspondence Information
Vanguard Group
Vanguard Financial Ctr. P.O. Box 2600
Valley Forge, PA 19482
800-662-7447

Management
Fund Inception   04-27-92

Manager Name: George U. Sauter
Manager Start Date: 08-31-01
Biography:
Sauter is a managing director of The Vanguard Group, his employer since 1987. He has managed portfolio investments since 1987 and has worked in investment management since 1985.

Fund Advisor(s)
Vanguard Quantitative Equity Group

Loading Fees

1. Front-end load. The front-end load is a commission charge that is paid when you purchase fund shares. Front-end loads are often as high as 5¾ percent. That means that if you put $1,000 into a high-load mutual fund, you will have only $942.50 invested for you. You would need to earn 6.1 percent on your investment just to break even and get your investment back to $1,000. Not all fees are so excessive. So-called low-load funds charge only a 1 to 3 percent sales charge. Best of all are no-load funds, which have no front-end sales charges at all.

2. Back-end loads and exchange fees. Back-end loads are charges incurred when you redeem fund shares. The charge could be as much as 6 percent of the value of your redeemed shares if you sell out in the first year, with a declining percentage charge in subsequent years. Exchange fees are generally flat rate charges incurred when you exchange your fund shares for other funds within the same mutual-fund family.

Expense Charges

1. Operating and investment management expenses. A fund's expense ratio expresses the total operating and investment advisory fees incurred by the fund as a percentage of the fund's average net assets. These expense ratios range from a low of less than ²⁄₁₀ of 1 percent per year (for index funds) to as much as 2 percent per year. (Note that the latter is ten times higher than the former—and that can make a huge difference over time.) Beware the loss leader come-on. Some new funds (especially money funds) temporarily waive all fees to enhance the advertised current yield. Investors should be alert to the fact that they will be socked for full expenses as soon as the introductory "come-on" period ends.

2. 12b-1 charges. 12b-1 charges are fund-distribution expenses charged not as a front-end load but rather as a continuing annual charge against fund assets. The "12b-1" refers to an SEC rule that permits these charges. More than half of the publicly offered mutual funds have 12b-1 fees.

The important point to realize is that mutual-fund asset performance bears no relationship to the expenses charged. Although you may "pay for what you get" in some products, you don't buy any better investment management by paying high fees. Quite the opposite—high fees lead to inferior investment performance.

Comparing Mutual-Fund Costs

The SEC requires funds to tabulate all fees and expenses in their prospectuses. An SEC-required fee table for three representative mutual funds is shown below. This fee table must also show the cumulative expenses (expressed in dollars) paid on a $1,000 investment at the end of one-, three-, five-, and ten-year periods, assuming a 5 percent return on the fund's assets.

A Sample Prospectus Fee Table*

Shareholder Transaction Expenses	Fund A	Fund B	Fund C
Sales load imposed on purchases	None	None	4.75%
Sales load imposed on reinvested dividends	None	None	4.75%
Redemption fees	None	None	None
Exchange fees	None	None	None
Annual Fund Operating Expenses			
Management and administrative expenses	0.22%	0.60%	0.70%
Investment advisory expenses	0.02	–	–
12b-1 marketing fees	–	0.30	–
Marketing and distribution costs	0.02	–	–
Miscellaneous expenses	0.03	0.32	0.26
Total operating expenses	**0.29%**	**1.22%**	**0.96%**
Expenses on a $10,000 Investment			
1 year	$30	$124	$587
3 years	93	387	823
5 years	163	670	1,077
10 years	368	1,477	1,805

Source: The Vanguard Group of Investment Companies.

*This table illustrates all expenses and fees that a shareholder of three hypothetical mutual funds would incur. The table is intended to help investors understand the various costs and expenses that a shareholder in the funds bears, whether directly or indirectly. The example shows the expenses that investors would incur on a $10,000 investment over various time periods, assuming a 5% annual rate of return and redemptions at the end of each period. Note that this table does not imply the returns available on any particular investment made.

Note that Fund A has no loading or redemption charges and a modest operating expense ratio of 0.29 percent. Although Fund B has no sales or redemption fees, it has a high operating expense ratio and a 12b-1 fee of ³⁄₁₀ of 1 percent—bringing total fees to almost 1¼ percent annually. Fund C has a 4¾ percent load and "average" operating expenses of close to 1 percent per year. The bottom of the exhibit shows the total dollar costs per $1,000 of investment. The annual percentage and dollar-cost differentials may appear small, but their impact can be substantial over time, as is shown in the bottom panel of the table. Cost-conscious investors get the best investment results from no-load funds with low expense ratios.

The Malkiel Step

As readers of previous editions know, I like to buy, when they are available at attractive discounts, shares in a special type of mutual fund called a closed-end fund (officially, a closed-end investment company). Closed-end funds differ from open-end mutual funds (the kind discussed in the previous section) in that they neither issue nor redeem shares after the initial offering. To buy or sell shares, you have to go to the market—generally the New York Stock Exchange.

The price of the shares depends on what other investors are willing to pay for them; however, unlike shares in an open-end fund, this price is not necessarily related to net asset value. Thus, a closed-end fund can sell at a premium above or at a discount from its net asset value. During much of the 1970s and at the start of the 1980s, these funds were selling at substantial discounts from their net asset value. Closed-end funds hire professional managers, and their expenses are no higher than those of ordinary mutual funds. So for those who believe in professional investment management, here was a way to buy it at a discount, and I told my readers so.

A small proportion of the discounts on closed-end funds could be explained by rational considerations. Some funds had a substantial amount of unrealized capital gains in their portfolios that could affect the timing of an individual's tax liabilities. Other funds had substantial holdings of "letter stock," the sale of which was restricted and whose market prices might not have been accurate reflections of their true value. But these considerations could at best explain only a minor proportion of the discounts that ran as high as 40 percent during the late 1970s. My own explanation for the discounts ran in terms of an unexploited market inefficiency and I urged investors to take full advantage of the opportunity for as long as it lasted.

The beauty of buying these highly discounted closed-end funds was that, even if the discounts remained at high levels, investors would still reap extraordinary rewards from their purchase. If you could buy shares at a 25 percent discount, you would have $4 of asset value on which dividends could be earned for every $3 you invested. So even if the funds just equaled the market return, as believers in the random walk would expect, you would beat the averages.

It was like having a $100 savings account paying 5 percent interest. You deposit $100 and earn $5 interest each year. Only this savings account could be bought at a 25 percent discount—in other words, for $75. You still got $5 interest (5 percent of $100), but because you paid only $75 for the account, your rate of return was 6.67 percent (5 ÷ 75). Note that this increase in yield was in no way predicated on the discount narrowing. Even if you got only $75 back when you cashed in, you would still have received a big bonus in extra returns while holding the account. The discount on closed-end funds provided a similar bonus. You got your share of dividends from $1 worth of assets, even though you paid only 75 cents.

The strategy worked even better than expected. Discounts have narrowed significantly on U.S. closed-end funds. Although the publicity given closed-end funds in my books may have helped to close the discounts, I think the fundamental reason for the narrowing is that our capital markets are reasonably efficient. The market may misvalue assets from time to time, creating temporary inefficiencies. But if there is truly some area of pricing inefficiency that can be discovered by the market and dependably exploited, then value-seeking investors will take advantage of these opportunities and thereby eliminate them. Pricing irregularities may well exist and even persist for periods of time, but the financial laws of gravity will eventually take hold and true value will out.

I mentioned in previous editions that I gave my son, Jonathan, the royalties from the first edition of this book. Practicing what I preached, I invested them in a portfolio of closed-end funds selling at substantial discounts. The investments were made mainly at the end of 1973 (near a peak in the market and thus a terrible time to invest) and near the end of 1974 (after the market had suffered a very sharp decline). The strategy has significantly outperformed the market. The narrowing of the discounts helped to produce quite spectacular returns. The strategy required courage, however. The 1973 investments, made when the market was very high, were under a good deal of water at the end of 1974.* Fortunately, new royalty checks came in at that time, more shares were bought for Jonathan, and the overall results have been more than satisfactory.

With their discounts for the most part dried up at the time this edition goes to press, most domestic U.S. closed-end funds are no longer an especially attractive investment opportunity.† But with the highly unsettled conditions in the stock markets of emerging markets, some very attractive discounts opened up during the late 1990s and early 2000s on funds holding investments in some of the hardest hit regions. If discounts remain large in the future, diversified portfolios of emerging market closed-end funds selling at substantial discounts are a viable—and probably a preferable—alternative to an emerging market index fund. When discounts of 20 percent or more exist, it is time to open your wallet to closed-end funds. The table below lists a few closed-end emerging market funds with their discounts as of August 2002.

---

*According to my Rule 4, I might have switched to other closed-end funds to gain some tax advantages in 1974. However, Jonathan's tax situation did not warrant incurring the brokerage charges to effect such a switch.

† Indeed, when you buy a new closed-end fund at par value plus about 8 percent for underwriting commissions, not only do you get hit with the equivalent of a large loading fee but you also run the risk that the fund will sell at a discount at some time in the future. Never buy a closed-end fund at its initial offering price. It will almost invariably turn out to be a bad deal. It may be worth checking, however, to see if discounts widen in the future during unsettled market conditions.

Selected Emerging Market Closed-End Funds Selling at Discounts from Asset Values
(August 2002)

Fund Name (Ticker Symbol)	Net Asset Value (NAV)	Price	Discount	Average Discount (5 years)	Description
Templeton China (TCH)	$10.97	$9.27	−15.5%	−20.67%	Hong Kong, China, Taiwan
Scudder New Asia (SAF)	10.22	8.50	−16.8	−18.48	Asian markets (17% Japanese)
Latin American Discovery (LDF)	9.04	7.81	−18.0	−17.65	All Latin American emerging markets
India fund (IFN)	11.33	8.76	−22.5	−22.44	Equity securities of Indian companies
Korea Fund (KF)	19.37	15.42	−20.4	−10.54	Korean securities and money market instruments
Malaysia Fund (MF)	5.4	4.29	−20.6	−10.78	Equity securities of Malaysian companies
Singapore Fund (SGF)	6.74	5.26	−22.0	−11.87	Singapore securities (at least 65%) and investments in other Pacific Basin countries
Canadian General Investments (CGI)	12.05	8.85	−26.6	−23.34	Investments in Canadian companies

A Parodox

Although some emerging market closed-end funds appeared quite attractive in the early 2000s, domestic funds holding U.S. equities were no longer selling at the bargain-basement levels that existed in earlier periods. This illustrates an important paradox about investment advice, as well as the maxim that true values do eventually prevail in the market. There is a fundamental paradox about the usefulness of investment advice concerning specific securities. If the advice reaches enough people and they act on it, knowledge of the advice destroys its usefulness. If everyone knows about a "good buy" and they all rush in to buy, the price of the "good buy" will rise until it is no longer particularly attractive for investment. Indeed, there will be pressure on the price to rise as long as it is still a good buy.

This is the main logical pillar on which the efficient-market theory rests. If the spread of news is unimpeded, prices will react quickly so that they reflect all that is known about the particular situation. This led me to predict in the 1981 edition that such favorable discounts would not always be available. I wrote: "I would be very surprised to see the early-1980s levels of discounts perpetuate themselves indefinitely." For the same reason, I am skeptical that very simple currently popular rules such as "buy low P/E stocks" or "buy small company stocks" will perpetually produce unusually high risk-adjusted returns. And I am also skeptical that the unusually large discounts on some emerging market funds will persist indefinitely.

I have recounted the story of the finance professor and his students who spotted a $100 bill lying on the street. "If it was really a $100 bill," the professor reasoned out loud, "someone would have already picked it up." Fortunately, the students were skeptical, not only of Wall Street professionals but also of learned professors, and so they picked up the money.

Clearly, there is considerable logic to the finance professor's position. In markets where intelligent people are searching for value, it is unlikely that people will perpetually leave $100 bills around ready for the taking. But history tells us that unexploited opportunities do exist from time to time, as do periods of speculative excess pricing. We know of Dutchmen paying astronomical prices for tulip bulbs, of Englishmen splurging on the most improbable bubbles, and of modern institutional fund managers who convinced themselves that some Internet stocks were so unlike any other that any price was reasonable. And when investors were overcome with pessimism, real fundamental investment opportunities such as closed-end funds were passed by. Yet eventually, excessive valuations were corrected and investors did snatch up the bargain closed-end funds. Perhaps the finance professor's advice should have been, "You had better pick up that $100 bill quickly because if it's really there, someone else will surely take it." It is in this sense that I consider myself a random walker. I am convinced that true value will out, but from time to time it doesn't surprise me that anomalies do exist. There may be some $100 bills around at times and I'll certainly interrupt my random walk to purposefully stoop and pick them up.

Some Last Reflections on Our Walk

We are now at the end of our walk. Let's look back for a moment and see where we have been. It is clear that the ability to beat the average consistently is most rare. Neither fundamental analysis of a stock's firm foundation of value nor technical analysis of the market's propensity for building castles in the air can produce reliably superior results. Even the pros must hide their heads in shame when they compare their results with those obtained by the dartboard method of picking stocks.

Sensible investment policies for individuals must then be developed in two steps. First, it is crucially important to understand the risk-return trade-offs that are available and to tailor your choice of securities to your temperament and requirements. Part Four provided a careful guide for this part of the walk, including a number of warm-up exercises concerning everything from tax planning to the management of reserve funds and a life-cycle guide to portfolio allocations. This chapter has covered the major part of our walk down Wall Street— three important steps for buying common stocks. I began by suggesting sensible strategies that are consistent with the existence of reasonably efficient markets. The indexing strategy is the one I most highly recommend. I recognized, however, that telling most investors that there is no hope of beating the averages is like telling a six-year-old there is no Santa Claus. It takes the zing out of life.

For those of you incurably smitten with the speculative bug, who insist on picking individual stocks in an attempt to beat the market, I offered four rules. The odds are really stacked against you, but you may just get lucky and win big. I also am very skeptical that you can find investment managers who have some talent for finding those rare $100 bills lying around in the marketplace. Never forget that past records are far from reliable guides to future performance.

Investing is a bit like lovemaking. Ultimately, it is really an art requiring a certain talent and the presence of a mysterious force called luck. Indeed, luck may be 99 percent responsible for the success of the very few people who have beaten the averages. "Although men flatter themselves with their great actions," La Rochefoucauld wrote, "they are not so often the result of great design as of chance."

The game of investing is like lovemaking in another important respect, too. It's much too much fun to give up. If you have the talent to recognize stocks that have good value, and the art to recognize a story that will catch the fancy of others, it's a great feeling to see the market vindicate you. Even if you are not so lucky, my rules will help you limit your risks and avoid much of the pain that is sometimes involved in the playing. If you know you will either win or at least not lose too much, and if you index at least the core of your portfolio, you will be able to play the game with more satisfaction. At the very least, I hope this book makes the game all the more enjoyable.

A Random Walker's Address Book and Reference Guide to Mutual Funds

Data on Selected General Equity Index Funds (July 2002)

Fund Name	Index	Maximum Sales Charge (%)	Year Organized	Minimum Initial Purchase ($) (IRA Minimum)	Minimum Subsequent Purchase ($) (IRA Minimum)	Recent Expense Ratio	Net Assets ($ millions)	Payroll Deduction	Keogh Plan	IRA Plan
Fidelity Spartan Total Index www.fidelity.com 800-343-3548	Wilshire 5,000	None	1997	$15,000 ($15,000)	$1,000	0.25	1,010.0	Yes	Yes	Yes
Schwab 1000 Investor www.schwab.com 800-435-4000	Custom Index	None	1991	$2,500 ($1,000)	$500	0.46	3,991.6	Yes	Yes	Yes
SSgA S&P 500 Index www.ssga.com 800-647-7327	S&P 500	0.25	1992	$10,000 ($250)	$100	0.17	1,996.0	Yes	Yes	Yes
USAA S&P 500 Index www.usaa.com 800-531-8181	S&P 500	None	1996	$3,000 ($2,000)	$50	0.18	1,716.8	Yes	Yes	Yes
Vanguard 500 Index* www.vanguard.com 800-662-7447	S&P 500	None	1976	$3,000 ($1,000)	$100	0.18	69,084.9	Yes	Yes	Yes
Vanguard Tax-Managed Growth&Income www.vanguard.com 800-662-7447	S&P 500	None	1994	$10,000 ($0)	$100	0.18	1,419.6	Yes	Yes	Yes
Vanguard Total Stock Market Index www.vanguard.com 800-662-7447	Wilshire 5,000	None	1992	$3,000 ($1,000)	$100	0.20	15,944.5	Yes	Yes	Yes

*Vanguard 500 Index has an "Admiral" class with an expense ratio of only 0.12% when the investor makes a very large initial purchase.

Data on Selected International Index Stock Funds (July 2002)

Fund Name	Index	Maximum Sales Charge (%)	Year Organized	Minimum Initial Purchase ($) (IRA Minimum)	Minimum Subsequent Purchase ($) (IRA Minimum)	Recent Expense Ratio	Net Assets ($ millions)	Payroll or Bank Plan	Keogh Plan	IRA Plan
Dreyfus International Stock Index www.dreyfus.com 800-373-9387	MSCI-EAFE	None	1997	$2,500 ($750)	$100	0.60	90.3	Yes	Yes	Yes
Fidelity Spartan International Index www.fidelity.com 800-343-3548	MSCI-EAFE	None	1997	$15,000 ($15,000)	$1,000	0.35	332.6	Yes	Yes	Yes
Merrill Lynch International Index A www.ml.com 800-995-6526	MSCI-EAFE	None	1997	$1,000 ($100)	$50	0.64	27.2	Yes	Yes	Yes
Schwab International Index www.schwab.com 800-266-5623	Custom Index	None	1997	$2,500 ($1,000)	$500	0.58	577.0	Yes	Yes	Yes
Vanguard Emerging Markets Stock Index www.vanguard.com 800-662-7447	Custom Index	None	1994	$3,000 ($1,000)	$100	0.60	1,007.0	Yes	Yes	Yes
Vanguard Intl. Stock Market Index www.vanguard.com 800-662-7447	MSCI-EAFE, Pacific, Emerging Markets	None	1996	$3,000 ($1,000)	$100	0.35	3,306.8	Yes	Yes	Yes

Some Information on Real Estate Mutual Funds (July 2002)

Fund	Sales Charge	Year Organized	Expense Ratio (%)	Assets 2002 (millions)	1-Year Total Return to 12/31/2001	3-Year Total Return to 12/31/2001	Risk Measure (Beta)
Cohen&Steers Realty 800-437-9912	No	1991	1.09	1510	12.08	13.89	0.18
Fidelity Real Estate 800-544-8888	No*	1986	0.84	1,801.65	7.93	14.95	0.18
Stratton Monthly Dividend REIT 800-634-5726	No	1972	1.09	133.87	20.88	15.15	0.15
Vanguard REIT Index Fund 800-662-7447	No	1996	0.28	1790	14.87	13.93	0.11

* 0.75% redemption fee on shares sold within 90 days of purchase.

390

Data on Selected Taxable Money-Market Funds (July 2002)

Fund Name	Year Organized	Minimum Initial Purchase ($) (IRA Minimum)	Minimum Subsequent Purchase ($) (IRA Minimum)	Minimum Amount for Check Withdrawal	Net Assets ($ millions)	7-day Average Yield (%)	Average Maturity in Days	Recent Expense Ratio
Fidelity Spartan Money Market Fund www.fidelity.com 800-343-3548	1989	$20,000 ($10,000)	$1,000	$1,000	7,979.7	1.56	67	0.43
Schwab Value Advantage Money Market Fund www.schwab.com 800-435-4000	1992	$25,000 ($15,000)	$5,000 ($2,000)	No minimum	41,178.1	1.58	59	0.45
Scudder Money Market Fund www.scudder.com 800-225-2470	1974	$1,000 ($500)	$50	$500	5,020.7	1.50	63	0.44
TIAA-CREF Money Market Fund www.tiaa-cref.com 800-223-1200	1997	$1,500 ($500)	$50	$250	706.8	1.65	63	0.29
USAA Money Market Fund www.usaa.com 800-531-8181	1961	$3,000 ($250)	$50	$250	3,563.0	1.51	64	0.38
Vanguard Prime Money Market Fund www.vanguard.com 800-662-7447	1975	$3,000 ($1,000)	$100	$250	50,478.0	1.58	63	0.33

Data on Selected Tax-Exempt Money-Market Funds (July 2002)

Fund Name	Year Organized	Minimum Initial Purchase ($)	Minimum Subsequent Purchase ($) (IRA Minimum)	Minimum Amount for Check Withdrawal	Net Assets ($ millions)	7-day Average Yield (%)	Maturity in Days	Recent Expense Ratio
Fidelity Municipal Money Market Fund www.fidelity.com 800-343-3548	1980	$5,000	$500	$500	11,409.4	1.04	29	0.43
Prudential Tax-Free Money Fund www.prudential.com 800-225-1852	1979	$1,000	None	$500	220.3	0.70	53	0.67
Strong Municipal Money Market Fund www.strongfunds.com 800-368-1030	1986	$2,500	$100	$500	2,512.0	1.21	35	0.56
USAA Tax-Exempt Money Market Fund www.usaa.com 800-531-8181	1984	$3,000	$50	$250	1,902.8	1.06	39	0.48
Vanguard Tax-Exempt Money Market Fund www.vanguard.com 800-662-7447	1980	$3,000	$100	$250	9,950.3	1.22	40	0.18

Data on Selected Bond Funds (July 2002)

Fund Name	Maximum Sales Charge (%)	Year Organized	Minimum Initial Purchase ($) (IRA Minimum)	Minimum Subsequent Purchase ($) (IRA Minimum)	Recent Expense Ratio	Net Assets ($ millions)	5-year Annualized Return (%)	Payroll Deduction	Keogh Plan	IRA Plan
Dodge & Cox Income Fund www.dodgeandcox.com 800-621-3979	None	1989	$2,500 ($1,000)	$100	0.45	2,042.2	7.83	Yes	Yes	Yes
Dreyfus Bond Market Index—Basic www.dreyfus.com 800-373-9387	None	1993	$10,000 ($5,000)	$1,000	0.40	78.0	7.11	Yes	Yes	Yes
Fidelity Intermediate Fund www.fidelity.com 800-544-8888	None	1975	$2,500 ($500)	$250	0.64	5,112.3	6.95	No	Yes	Yes
Galaxy II: US Treasury Index www.galaxyfunds.com 800-628-0414	None	1991	$2,500 ($500)	$100	0.42	158.3	7.17	Yes	Yes	Yes
USAA Income Fund www.usaa.com 800-531-8181	None	1974	$3,000 ($250)	$50	0.41	1,641.5	7.23	Yes	Yes	Yes
Vanguard Long-Term Bond Index Fund www.vanguard.com 800-662-7447	None	1994	$3,000 ($1,000)	$100	0.21	611.1	8.35	Yes	Yes	Yes
Vanguard Total Bond Market Index Fund www.vanguard.com 800-662-7447	None	1986	$3,000 ($1,000)	$100	0.22	15,092.8	7.32	Yes	Yes	Yes

Data on Selected GNMA Bond Funds (July 2002)

Fund Name	Maximum Sales Charge (%)	Year Organized	Minimum Initial Purchase ($) (IRA Minimum)	Minimum Subsequent Purchase ($) (IRA Minimum)	Recent Expense Ratio	Net Assets ($ millions)	5-year Annualized Return (%)
American Century GNMA Investors Fund www.americancentury.com 800-345-2021	None	1985	$2,500 ($1,000)	$50	0.59	1,778.2	6.91
Fidelity GNMA Fund www.fidelity.com 800-343-3548	None	1985	$2,500 ($250)	$250	0.62	4,425.3	6.96
T-Rowe Price GNMA Fund www.troweprice.com 800-225-5132	None	1985	$2,500 ($1,000)	$100	0.70	1,222.9	7.11
USAA GNMA Trust Fund www.usaa.com 800-531-8181	None	1991	$3,000 ($250)	$50	0.32	586.7	6.70
Vanguard GNMA Fund www.vanguard.com 800-662-7447	None	1980	$3,000 ($1,000)	$100	0.27	17,772.5	7.43

Data on Selected High-Yield Bond Funds (July 2002)

Fund Name	Maximum Sales Charge (%)	Year Organized	Minimum Initial Purchase ($) (IRA Minimum)	Minimum Subsequent Purchase ($) (IRA Minimum)	Recent Expense Ratio	Net Assets ($ millions)	5-year Annualized Return (%)	Payroll Deduction	Keogh Plan	IRA Plan
Columbia High-Yield Fund www.columbiafunds.com 800-547-1707	None	1993	$1,000 ($1,000)	$100	0.85	420.7	4.89	No	Yes	Yes
Strong Short-Term High-Yield Bond Fund www.strongfunds.com 800-368-1030	None	1997	$2,500 ($250)	$50	0.80	326.1	4.53	Yes	Yes	Yes
T-Rowe Price High-Yield Bond Fund www.troweprice.com 877-804-2315	None	1984	$2,500 ($1,000)	$100	0.85	420.7	4.89	Yes	Yes	Yes
Vanguard High-Yield Corporate www.vanguard.com 800-662-7447	None	1978	$3,000 ($1,000)	$100	0.27	5,396.5	3.16	Yes	Yes	Yes

Data on Selected Tax-Exempt Bond Funds [July 2002]

Fund Name	Maximum Sales Charge (%)	Year Organized	Minimum Initial Purchase ($)	Minimum Subsequent Purchase ($)	Recent Expense Ratio	Net Assets ($ millions)	5-year Annualized Return (%) through 6/30/02	Payroll Deduction
American Century Tax-Free Bond Fund www.americancentury.com 800-345-2021	None	1987	$5,000	$50	0.51	$535.02	5.81	Yes
Dreyfus Municipal Bond Fund www.dreyfus.com 800-379-9387	None	1976	$2,500	$100	0.72	2,429.3	4.79	Yes
Fidelity Spartan Municipal Income Fund www.fidelity.com 800-544-8888	None	1977	$10,000	$1,000	0.47	4,668.6	6.26	Yes
T.Rowe Price Tax-Free Income Fund www.troweprice.com 800-683-5660	None	1976	$2,500	$100	0.54	1,437.6	5.74	Yes
USAA Tax-Exempt Long-Term Fund www.usaa.com 800-382-8722	None	1982	$3,000	$50	0.45	2,135.8	5.53	Yes
Vanguard Municipal Insured Long-Term Fund www.vanguard.com 800-662-7447	None	1984	$3,000	$100	0.19	1,219.9	6.14	Yes

Index